Third Edition

Developing Readers and Writers in the Content Areas K–12

David W. Moore
Arizona State University West

Susan Arthur Moore
Arizona State University West

Patricia M. Cunningham
Wake Forest University

James W. Cunningham
University of North Carolina, Chapel Hill

LONGMAN

An imprint of Addison Wesley Longman, Inc.

New York • Menlo Park, California • Reading, Massachusetts • Harlow, England
Don Mills, Ontario • Sydney • Mexico City • Madrid • Amsterdam

Acquisitions Editor: Ginny Blanford
Associate Editor: Arianne Weber
Project Editor: Ellen MacElree
Senior Designer: Betty Sokol
Text and Cover Designer: Betty Sokol
Art Studio: Fine Line Inc.
Electronic Production Manager: Su Levine
Desktop Project Administrator: Laura Leever
Senior Manufacturing Manager: Willie Lane
Electronic Page Makeup: ComCom
Printer and Binder: Maple-Vail Book Manufacturing Group
Cover Printer: Coral Graphic Services, Inc.

Library of Congress Cataloging-in-Publication Data

Developing readers and writers in the content areas K-12 / David W.
    Moore . . . [et al.]. — 3rd ed.
        p.   cm.
    Includes bibliographical references and index.
    ISBN 0-8013-1856-4
    1. Language arts—Correlation with content subjects.   2. Content
area reading.   I. Moore, David W.
LB1576.D455   1998
42B.4'3—DC21   97-15087
                                                                                    CIP

ISBN 0-8013-1856-4
1 2 3 4 5 6 7 8 9 10-MA-00999897

Contents

chapter 5 **Meaning Vocabulary 151**

chapter **6**   ## Writing   194

chapter 7   **Studying   239**

PART II

. . . In the Content Areas: K–12   307

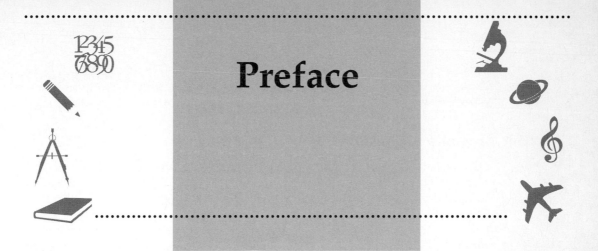

Preface

*O*f the many responsibilities that teachers assume, helping students use reading and writing as tools for learning certainly ranks near the top. *Developing Readers and Writers in the Content Areas, K–12* introduces prospective and practicing teachers to this compelling aspect of education. Elementary- and secondary-school teachers alike will find this book to be a practical guide. Its engaging prose and numerous examples describe the theory underlying specific teaching practices, which are explained fully. The chapters devoted solely to teachers' journal entries about their content area literacy instruction bring the descriptions to life and show how they fit into the everyday world of the classroom.

Developing Readers and Writers in the Content Areas, K–12 can be used in courses with titles such as *Literacy Across the Curriculum* and *Content Area Reading.* Its attention to elementary and secondary teaching concerns makes it appropriate for courses aimed at either audience as well as for courses with a mixture of upper-grade and lower-grade teachers. It is intended for use in undergraduate or postbaccalaureate teacher preparation programs, during staff development activities, and in introductory graduate teacher education courses.

SHARED FEATURES OF EARLIER EDITIONS AND THE THIRD EDITION

This third edition of *Developing Readers and Writers in the Content Areas, K–12* retains features of the earlier editions that our students and colleagues found especially noteworthy. These features include the following.

Narrative Accounts of Teaching

Like the first two editions, this third edition is divided into two parts. Part I contains eight chapters written in expository form; the information is explained in a straightforward, objective fashion. The final four chapters, which make up Part II, follow a nontraditional form for textbooks, being written in narrative style. Each is a fictional account of how one teacher spends a school year developing readers and writers in the content areas. These narratives are meant to portray everyday classroom life when teachers are implementing the instructional methods presented in Part I.

Instructors opt to use the narrative chapters differently. Some have students read selected narratives before reading any of Part I, thinking that the stories contextualize the specifics of Part I. Some have students get together in book study groups and react to successive portions of selected chapters. Some instructors culminate their course by having students evaluate selected teachers' actions. Comparisons can be made between Part I suggestions and Part II teachers' actions or between one teacher and another.

Focus on Basic Learning Processes

Chapter 1 describes nine thinking processes that contribute substantially to learning. The remaining chapters then demonstrate how these processes play out in teachers' instructional methods and students' learning strategies. Our concentration on these processes provides coherence to the numerous suggestions presented in this book.

Thorough Explanations of Key Concepts

We assumed that our audience did not already know what we were presenting, so we sought to develop our concepts clearly and completely. Our goal was to allow ready implementation and adaptation of the teaching practices we presented.

Integration of Elementary and Secondary Instruction

We chose to address K–12 instruction in this book because learning and teaching processes across the grades are fundamentally similar. We also believed it important to show how literacy and subject matter instruction can be combined even as subject matter becomes more complex and specialized across the grades.

Integration of Reading and Writing

We believe that treating written language as a whole preserves the benefits that reading and writing have for each other and for the exploration of subject matter. For this reason, even though separate chapters highlight comprehension and writing, each chapter addresses literacy, the combination of reading and writing.

Pedagogical Features

The learning aids in Part I of the text are meant to enhance understanding and retention. The following aids are found either at the beginning or at the end of each chapter to help you anticipate, review, and elaborate chapter contents:

Looking Ahead, which appears at the beginning of each chapter, presents an overview of that chapter's contents.

Key Ideas are listed at the opening of each chapter, following the Looking Ahead section. They form the main headings for the chapters, indicating the major points within each chapter.

Looking Back summaries occur at the end of each chapter.

Add to Your Journal also appears at the end of each chapter. This learning aid suggests topics to consider and questions to answer when responding to this book in journal form.

Additional Readings, the final section of each chapter, suggests books and articles that amplify the material presented in the chapter.

Along with the learning aids at the beginning and end of the Part I chapters, we interspersed the following pedagogical features throughout these chapters to promote interaction with the ideas presented:

Do It Together suggests group activities. Small-group collaborative effort can promote learning.

Listen/Look and Learn contains suggestions for checking out chapter contents with students and practicing teachers. It is a reality check for ideas and an opportunity to develop them.

Try It Out encourages application. Learning occurs best when you do something with the ideas you encounter.

NEW FEATURES IN THE THIRD EDITION

The scholarship related to content area literacy continues to change over the years, and some portions of the earlier editions have seemed to communicate better than others. To keep pace with the field of content area literacy instruction and to improve communication, we revised every chapter. In some instances we clarified the presentation, modified the emphasis, and updated the examples; in other instances we made substantial changes. Four especially noteworthy changes in this third edition are as follows.

General to Specific Progression

We revised the first three chapters to show how moving from the general to the specific enhances instructional planning. Chapter 1 continues to present a rationale for content literacy instruction and describe essential thinking processes, then it presents new material on classroom settings for effective content literacy instruction (e.g., meaningfulness, active participation, social support) and cycles of instruction (e.g., introduce, guide, culminate). It portrays assessment as an ongoing process with an emphasis on self-reflection. Chapter 2 presents integrated and interdisciplinary units along with classroom grouping practices, and Chapter 3 describes possible print resources teachers and students could access during subject matter explorations. The remaining chapters in Part I present ways to plan specific daily lessons.

Specific Content Area Applications

Although the teaching suggestions contained in the comprehension, vocabulary, writing, and studying chapters apply to all subject areas, the applications are not always readily apparent to newcomers. For instance, comprehension has many common properties, but comprehending poetry in English class differs somewhat from comprehending pioneers' journal entries in history, and both differ somewhat from comprehending directions in a technological work environment. Consequently, we described specific content area applications at the end of certain chapters. The content areas we addressed are English/language arts, mathematics, science, second language, social studies, and "activity," a term for hands-on courses.

New Chapter on Studying

The topic of studying is set off in a separate chapter in this edition. It concentrates on learning strategies and principles of instruction leading to independent students and lifelong learners. This chapter contains information from previous editions as well as some new ideas.

New Narrative Chapter on Middle School

Hugh Mann, who teaches English and social studies, now teaches in a middle school. We changed his position to show how literacy instruction plays out in distinctive middle-school instructional arrangements such as interdisciplinary teaming.

ACKNOWLEDGMENTS

We thank our students and colleagues who have commented on earlier editions of this text and on the manuscript of this third edition. They have sharpened our thinking. We thank the schoolchildren with whom we have worked, especially those in Arizona and North Carolina. They are excellent informants about which literacy tools and teaching methods help them learn about the world. We also thank the following reviewers whose comments have helped guide this particular revision:

Robert Burroughs, University of Cincinnati

Mary L. Dunton, Boise State University

Patricia A. Edwards, Michigan State University

Wanda B. Hedrick, University of Texas at San Antonio

Cathleen D. Rafferty, Indiana State University

Mary F. Roe, University of Delaware

Eldon L. Storer, Northeastern State University

Katherine M. Stroup, Southeastern Oklahoma State University

David W. Moore
Susan Arthur Moore
Patricia M. Cunningham
James W. Cunningham

PART

1

Developing Readers and Writers . . .

chapter 1

Content Area Reading and Writing

Looking Ahead

Content areas are bodies of thought that present ideas about the world in a systematic fashion. Some of the content areas are science, mathematics, and fine arts. Elementary-, middle-, and high-school students acquire an incredible amount of knowledge from studying the content areas. They learn that Confucius was a Chinese philosopher, lizards are reptiles, yeast causes dough to rise, an isosceles triangle has two sides of equal length, and countless other facts. They also discover that facts are tied together by subject matter principles. These principles include interdependence in social studies, supply and demand in economics, diffusion in biology and chemistry, and exponential growth in mathematics. Such concepts are gained in part from the numerous interactions that reading and writing provide.

Effective elementary teachers extend their literacy instruction beyond the times set aside specifically for reading and language arts. Effective middle-grade and high-school teachers support their students' literacy efforts when teaching academic specialties such as science, mathematics, social studies, and vocational education. During subject matter study these teachers improve their students' learning of both subject matter and subject-specific literacy strategies. One of the best ways to promote literacy across the curriculum is to capitalize on the thinking processes that underlie reading, writing, and learning. Teachers can plan learning activities that elicit one or more thinking processes when students read and write about subject matter. They can shape general classroom situations and specific instructional events that foster reading and writing.

At this point, you might be wondering about focusing on literacy in the content areas. "After all," you might think, "shouldn't reading and writing be taught during classes devoted exclusively to those subjects?" If you are a middle- or secondary-school teacher, you might think literacy skills should be taught only by elementary teachers: "Shouldn't lower-grade teachers emphasize students' reading and writing so that upper-grade teachers can present their content?" These reactions are common when people first consider reading and writing in the content areas.

This book applies to teachers of all subjects at all grade levels because it emphasizes the mutual relations between literacy and subject matter study. It calls attention to the ways reading and writing enhance subject matter learning; it also calls attention to the ways subject matter learning enhances literacy. It explains learning opportunities that capitalize on and improve reading, writing, and subject matter study. This book concentrates on helping students learn with texts.

The value of all teachers attending to literacy during subject matter instruction is well recognized by the many educational standards produced from the late 1980s to the mid-1990s. Numerous school-governing agencies, educational associations, and government task forces produced standards, or criteria, to initiate reform in teaching and learning. Practically every document on educational standards has spoken to the issue of literacy. Here are some samples:

> Every adult American will be literate and will possess knowledge and skills necessary to compete in a global economy and exercise the rights and responsibilities of citizenship. (The Goals 2000: Educate America Act)

> In grades K–4 the study of mathematics should include numerous opportunities for communication so that students can realize that representing, discussing, reading, writing, and listening to mathematics are a vital part of using and learning mathematics. (National Council of Teachers of Mathematics, 1989, p. 26)

> In grades 9–12, the mathematics curriculum should include the continued development of language and symbolism to communicate mathematics ideas so that all students can read written presentations of mathematics with understanding. (National Council of Teachers of Mathematics, 1989, p. 140)

> Students read a wide range of print and nonprint texts to build an understanding of texts, of themselves, and of the cultures of the United States and the world; to acquire new information; to respond to the needs and demands of society and the workplace; and for personal fullfillment. (International Reading Association/National Council of Teachers of English, 1996, p. 25)

> Without the ability to read a diverse set of materials, workers cannot locate the descriptive and quantitative information needed to make decisions or to recommend courses of action. . . . Most jobs will call for writing skills to prepare correspondence, instructions, charts, graphs, and proposals, in order to make requests, explain, illustrate, and convince. (Secretary's Commission on Achieving Necessary Skills, U.S. Department of Labor, 1991, pp. 6–7)

Another indicator of the increasing national attention to literacy across the curriculum involves reading coursework requirements for secondary-school teachers. As of 1996, 47 states require either specific coursework or demonstrated competencies in reading methods for some teachers (e.g., English, social studies) or all teachers (Romine, McKenna, & Robinson, 1996). This number has increased slightly since the 1980s.

This chapter addresses reasons for stressing literacy across the curriculum and some general approaches for accomplishing it. Four key ideas are presented here.

1. Compelling reasons support content area literacy instruction.
2. Thinking underlies reading, writing, and learning.
3. Classroom settings influence literacy development.
4. Instruction occurs in cycles.

COMPELLING REASONS SUPPORT CONTENT AREA LITERACY INSTRUCTION

Many educators have presented reasons for instruction that links literacy with subject matter (Moore, Readence, & Rickelman, 1983; McKenna & Robinson, 1990). Three of the most compelling reasons for linking students' reading and writing proficiencies with subject matter study are (a) reading and writing are tools for learning; (b) literacy requirements continually increase in school and society; and (c) content area teachers can teach content area reading and writing best.

Reading and Writing Are Tools for Learning

Because content areas consist of language, the study of content entails the study of language. Years ago Postman (1979) presented the case this way:

> Biology is not plants and animals. It is language about plants and animals. History is not events. It is language describing and interpreting events. Astronomy is not planets and stars. It is a way of talking about planets and stars. (p. 165)

Biologists, historians, and astronomers do not work wordlessly; they use language to construct and convey knowledge. Consequently, reading newspapers, magazine articles, textbooks, brochures, library books, and other printed materials is an important avenue for meeting, thinking about, and learning subject matter. Writing observational notes, character sketches, reactions to experiences, reports, and other forms of expression is another important way to think and learn about the world. When you help students read and write, you multiply their opportunities for thinking and learning about their worlds in general and your academic specialization in particular. Individuals who lack proficiency with literacy rely on listening, viewing, and speaking for communication; their opportunities expand tremendously when they gain proficiency with print.

Now that lifelong learning is an accepted requirement for staying abreast of our ever-changing worlds, access to print has become especially crucial. What happens when students leave their teachers? What will students do when they have no one to assist them with the print encountered in their personal and occupational lives? The role of literacy as a tool for learning is neatly encapsulated by the popular aphorism, "Give me a fish, and I eat for a day. Teach me to fish, and I eat for a lifetime." Teachers are responsible for helping individuals become independent students and lifelong learners, and developing literacy is a powerful way to accomplish this.

Literacy Requirements Continually Increase in School and Society

Literacy requirements increase sharply as students move from elementary to secondary school and as our society moves from an industrial base to a technical/informational one (Cole, 1990; Resnick, 1987). You have the responsibility to help students handle their increasing literacy demands.

School literacy requirements increase from grade to grade. As students progress through school, they are expected to read more and more expository material. For instance, students read about neighborhood helpers in the primary grades, world geography in the middle grades, and comparative governments in the upper grades. The materials students encounter as they read about these topics become increasingly difficult. Figure 1.1 shows excerpts from materials that represent what students might face at successive levels of difficulty. The concepts move from the familiar to the unfamiliar, from the simple to the complex, and from the concrete to the abstract. Upper-grade students require help learning from their unfamiliar, complex, and abstract passage contents just as lower-grade students do with their familiar, simple, and concrete passage contents.

Due to the technical/informational changes of our time, people require reading and writing abilities that are more sophisticated than those needed decades before. To illustrate, practically all occupations have been affected by revolutionary changes in technology. Office workers a generation ago relied on manual typewriters, filing cabinets, and single-line telephones; office workers today use word processing programs, computerized databases, computerized multiline telephone systems, fax machines, and electronic mail. Future office workers will need to master technology unheard of today as well as respond to the new demands it will bring. Jobs that call for predictable, simple, stable routines are giving way to work that requires complex problem solving and decision making.

In brief, students require reading and writing instruction across the curriculum and throughout their school careers because literacy instruction provided during only one part of the day for the first few years of school no longer suffices. Extended subject-specific instruction in reading and writing is needed so that individuals can handle the dramatic changes they will experience in school, in their future workplaces, in society, and in their personal lives.

Basic

Quicksand can swallow a pig, or a human, or even an elephant.

Quicksand often looks like plain wet sand. But it is really a soupy sand with so much water between the grains that you can't stand on it.

If you step into quicksand, you will slowly sink up to your knees. (Mullis & Jenkins, 1990, p. 26)

Intermediate

Have you heard of the National Boxball Association, the Los Angeles boxball team, or Kareem Abdul-Jabbar, the famous boxball player? Or have you ever heard of boxball at all? Well, it is the game that almost was.

Today we call the game basketball, of course, but it almost became known as boxball. (Mullis & Jenkins, 1990, p. 28)

Adept

One of the greatest victories of the Progressive movement has not yet been mentioned. This victory came when women won the right to vote.

The battle for women's suffrage was a long one. Ever since the 1840's, some women had demanded the right to vote. They had hoped to get the vote after the Civil War, but the Fifteenth Amendment gave voting rights only to Black men. A few women ran for President, but they got very few votes. (Mullis & Jenkins, 1990, p. 31)

Advanced

In the years between 1940 and 1960, literature, the arts, and culture in general became increasingly oriented to the many. In an economy of high productivity, deluging millions of people daily with movies, magazines, books, and television programs, American culture achieved a degree of homogeneity never dreamed of before. However, if such cultural homogeneity spelled loss of individuality—which it undoubtedly did—and if mass culture was often produced primarily for profit and only secondarily for aesthetic reasons, nevertheless mass productions of "art" made available to millions of people what in previous times had been the privilege only for the aristocratic few. (Mullis & Jenkins, 1990, p. 33)

Figure 1.1   Excerpts from Reading Materials at Successive Levels of Difficulty

Content Teachers Can Teach Content Area Reading and Writing Best

Primary-grade teachers directing the study of topics such as neighborhoods and animals' habitats can best present ways to read and write about these topics. Senior-high physics teachers presenting a unit on quantum mechanics can best teach strategies for exploring and learning about this topic and others. Those who regularly guide learners through subject matter are in optimum positions to improve students' content area reading and writing competencies.

One reason subject matter specialists can best teach reading and writing is because different subjects' different perspectives on the world require different literacies. Think how various subject matter specialists might perceive a large

Students integrate reading and writing in order to learn content area information.

boulder they encounter during a walk in a meadow: a paleontologist might look for fossils in order to learn about the prehistoric plant and animal life of the area; an anthropologist might look for pictographs to obtain greater insight about ancient cultures; a sculptor might search for the inspiration to compose an original piece; and a metallurgist might analyze the rock to determine what it revealed about the metallic elements in the surrounding area.

To further appreciate the different perspectives among content areas, consider the following brief samples of subject matter text:

> Cells enclose protoplasm, the substance of life. Protoplasm consists of two parts. The nucleus is the more solid central part, and the cytoplasm is the softer, more liquid part. The bulk of protoplasm is made up of carbon, hydrogen, oxygen, and nitrogen.

> In 1215, a group of barons forced King John of England to sign the Magna Carta. The barons wanted to restore their privileges; however, the Magna Carta grounded constitutional government in political institutions for all English-speaking people.

> An angle is the union of two rays that do not lie on the same line. When the sum of the measure of two angles is 90°, the angles are complementary; when the sum of the measure is 180°, the angles are supplementary.

The technical terms in these passages such as *protoplasm, constitutional government,* and *sum* refer to somewhat challenging concepts found in various disciplines. Other terms—such as *cell, grounded, angle,* and *ray*—not only can be challenging by themselves, but they have different meanings in different content areas. Cell can refer to a unit of protoplasm, a holding space in prison, or a receptacle for chemical reactions to generate electricity. In addition, these passages, like the analyses of the boulder in the meadow described previously, present diverse perspectives on the world. The science passage describes the structure of a substance, the social studies piece explains the outcome of a human action, and the math text presents measurements. The first piece explores the world of nature, the second discusses human actions, and the third concerns spatial relations. Those with deep understandings of a discipline can best explain the reading and writing strategies required by that discipline. To illustrate, people who want help interpreting tax forms typically go to tax preparers rather than reading teachers. Tax preparers are the logical choice because these individuals know the special vocabulary of taxation, the structure of the materials, and generally what it takes to make sense of the forms.

Finally, students need help learning to manage the distinct literacy demands of the numerous content areas, and students seem most receptive to receiving such help when they need it to accomplish specific assignments. Teaching students to take notes about social studies concepts seems most appropriate when they need to understand and remember these concepts. Teaching students how to solve mathematics word problems is done best in math class when they are expected to solve such problems. Students who are taught how to take social studies notes or solve math word problems in a reading or an English class frequently lack motivation and have difficulty transferring what they were taught. Literacy learning occurs best when students have the need to know.

Do It Together

The preceding section presented three reasons for promoting reading and writing during subject matter study. As a pair or a group, list these reasons and produce personal examples to illustrate each. For instance, how have you used reading and writing as a tool for learning? What experiences have you had with increased literacy requirements? After producing your list, compare it with that of another pair or group. Do you understand each of these reasons for content area literacy instruction? Did your pair or group think of other reasons for content area literacy instruction?

THINKING UNDERLIES READING, WRITING, AND LEARNING

Since antiquity, philosophers and learning theorists have attempted to identify the processes of thinking that underlie reading, writing, and learning. Countless books and articles have been written on this subject, with countless thinking processes suggested. The nine processes listed below account for a large share of the cognitive activity involved in most reading, writing, and learning. Our selection of these nine was shaped by many influences; sources that we believe to be especially valuable presentations of thinking processes are listed in the additional readings at the end of this chapter.

Nine Thinking Processes
1. Call up
2. Connect
3. Predict
4. Organize
5. Generalize
6. Image
7. Self-monitor
8. Evaluate
9. Apply

Before you read further about the thinking processes that will help your students read and write about your subject matter, think back to your mid-teens when you were preparing for your driver's license test. You probably obtained a copy of your state's driving manual and sat down to learn the driving rules, regulations, and suggested operating techniques. As the nine thinking processes are described in this section, think about the processes you went through back then to learn the information in the manual.

Call Up

Most likely, you began learning the rules of the road when you were a child, sitting buckled into your seat belt in the backseat of the family car during trips and outings. You absorbed a lot of information about driving a car in this country. You noticed, subconsciously perhaps, that the driver of the car sits in a particular seat and performs a sequence of activities to make the car start and keep it moving along the road safely and at a desirable speed. You also noticed that certain signs cause a driver to respond in certain ways. You came to know that red means "stop" and green means "go" before you entered kindergarten.

As a teenager studying the driver's manual, you began to *call up* all those insights and bits and pieces of information about driving that you had absorbed over the years. Without that background knowledge and experience to build upon, learning how to drive would have been nearly impossible to accomplish in the relatively short time you took. Calling up what you already knew about road signs, for example, would have allowed you to skim through that section because the information was so familiar. You probably needed to concentrate on just the few unusual signs that you had not yet learned.

The point of reminding you of this aspect of your experience with the driving manual is that when confronting any new topic, readers and writers call up what is already known. Calling up what you already know allows you to interact with the topic as efficiently as possible.

Connect

Learning also involves having to *connect* information. When you encounter a presentation of ideas organized around a topic with which you already have some experience, you connect the new input with what you already know. You call up previous knowledge and experience and either add to the information there or change the information to accommodate the new data. Connecting information is a matter of relating what is being presented to what is already known. As such, connecting requires calling up but goes beyond it.

Think again about your state driver's manual. You may never have considered that the road signs you had seen over the years were color-coded. You did know, however, that whenever drivers see a stop sign they are required to come to a complete stop at the designated location. What you learned upon reading your manual was that whenever you saw a red sign, no matter what shape it was or what message it contained, your basic thought should be to stop. DO NOT ENTER, WRONG WAY, and NO LEFT TURN signs are all red. While studying your manual, you might have called up your prior knowledge that a red light signals a stop and related that knowledge to the new fact that any red sign means movement is prohibited. Retrieving old information from your mind is calling up; bridging old information with new information is connecting.

Predict

When you first obtained your copy of the manual and began to thumb through it, you were trying to *predict* what it had to teach you as well as what it contained that you already knew. You engaged in this process automatically, without necessarily being aware of it. For instance, you might have thought there would be sections on starting the car and economizing on gas. In reality, however, you probably found practically no information on those topics. Upon seeing in the manual headings about road signs, on the other hand, you probably expected to find information about their shapes and messages, and your examination of the manual no doubt verified that prediction.

Like connecting, the predicting process requires that you call up information you already possess. If you had no information to call up, making predictions would be impossible. Again, you can call up without predicting anything; you cannot predict without calling up what you already know. You almost never simply call up information; generally you call up information so that you can do something with it. In the case of predicting, as you opened the driver's manual you anticipated what you might find there. You based those predictions upon any prior knowledge that you could call up about driving and learning to drive.

Predicting involves thinking about what is to come, thus giving you a head start on learning. Predicting also tends to motivate you to get involved with the material. Why do movie theaters show previews of coming attractions? This motivates customers to come back to the theater.

Organize

To have made sense of the driver's manual, you needed to *organize* the information presented there. You probably arranged the information according to some type of framework, perhaps according to the headings you found in the manual. Most manuals are divided into chapters with such headings as Parking, Turns, and Licenses. Within each chapter are headings that group the information into related subsets. A chapter on hazardous driving conditions might include topics such as driving at night, driving in adverse weather, and driving under the influence of alcohol and other drugs. Readers and writers who analyze information, grouping it into meaningful categories, go far in making sense of the world.

Generalize

Readers and writers *generalize* when they draw conclusions about information. They form a generalization by noting trends, commonalities, or patterns among specifics; they discover the rule or principle that unites various phenomena. For instance, when you read the Right of Way section in the driver's manual, you probably found much information about yielding to oncoming vehicles when turning left, yielding to pedestrians whether or not they are in crosswalks, and yielding to emergency vehicles. After reading these laws, you might have concluded this: "The pattern in all this information about yielding right of way is 'Safety first.' Preventing accidents is the thread common to these laws." Coming to this conclusion helped you tie together all the right-of-way laws, which otherwise might have been a meaningless assortment of details to be memorized by rote.

When you read a passage, you might need to infer generalizations on your own or might note the generalizations that the author provides. When you write, you may explicitly state or merely imply your generalizations. Generalizing and organizing are related thinking processes since the ability to organize ideas into similar groupings underlies most generalizing. Generalizing often consists of labeling or describing what you or someone else has organized into a cluster. Organizing sometimes means placing ideas under headings or descriptions that you or someone else has generalized.

Image

Engaging your senses internally and cognitively as you read and write adds to the learning experience and makes it more memorable. This process often consists of having to *image.* Visual images are used most frequently, although other sense images certainly come into play. Vicariously seeing, feeling, hearing, smelling, or tasting what is described in print can all help you think deeply and richly about the ideas you are reading or writing about.

Imagery may have helped you with your driver's manual. Think about the part of the manual that discussed the appropriate distances to maintain between two vehicles in motion. Safe following distances vary according to how fast you are traveling. For instance, at 50 miles per hour a safe following distance is 84 yards. You could easily have forgotten these figures if there had been no way to transform them. Thus, you might have imagined a 100-yard football field and then mentally placed a car at one goal line and your car 84 yards down the field. This visual image would have helped you remember the appropriate distance to keep between two vehicles traveling at 50 miles per hour.

Imagery also may have helped you deal with the information about turning at intersections. You probably studied the abstract diagrams and discussions about turning and visualized particular instances of those procedures. In your mind's eye you might have run a little motion picture of pulling up to a multiple-lane intersection and then executing the appropriate turn.

Self-Monitor

Throughout your study of the driver's manual, you needed to *monitor* how well you were doing with the information. Internally, and probably subconsciously, you asked yourself, "Am I understanding this? Am I getting what I need? Does this make sense?" Part of self-monitoring is checking internally to determine how well your learning or thinking is progressing.

The other part of self-monitoring involves repair work. If you sense a problem with what you are trying to learn, then you need to do something about it. If their understanding breaks down, good thinkers stop, identify the source of the difficulty, and try to get over it. For instance, when you got to the part in your driver's manual about different kinds of licenses, you might have plunged into information about chauffeur's license expirations, the minimum age for driving mopeds, and the cost of instruction permits. Eventually you realized that you were being overwhelmed, so you stopped and thought, "Now, what do I need from this section?" You might have determined that the renewal period and minimum age for a regular operator's license was all that was important, so you selected that particular information for careful study before moving on to the next section. Self-monitoring your learning by assessing its status and repairing breakdowns is a crucial thinking process.

Evaluate

The difference between self-monitoring and evaluating concerns processes, or strategies, and contents, or ideas. Whenever you assess the quality of your reading or writing process while you are actively engaged in it, you are self-monitoring. Whenever you assess the contents of what you are reading or writing, you are *evaluating.*

One of the hallmarks of proficient readers is deciding whether or not passages are believable, accurate, and appropriate. When you evaluate, you judge the content being presented. The root word of *evaluate* is *value.* Readers and writers who decide the value of information strengthen their grasp of it; those who simply accept information without examining it critically are at a disadvantage. As you read your driver's manual, you might have encountered a section on driving in unsafe conditions that caught your eye. "Does steering in the direction that a car is sliding on ice really help? It sure seems counterintuitive!" you might think. "Are there viable alternatives to what this passage says?"

Critical literacy theorists such as Shor (1987) have expanded notions of evaluation by concentrating on the links between print and power relations in society. Critical literacy educators have readers and writers examine the ways print maintains or transforms social privilege. For instance, they might question state authorities' linking of a driver's license with performance on a pencil-and-paper multiple-choice test. Why must potential drivers succeed in a traditional school-like task? Does this practice support or impede marginalized groups' access to full participation in society? Critical theorists want to know whose interests are served relative to reading materials that are selected and communications patterns that are enacted. They have called attention to materials and classroom discourse that predominantly portray scientists as male rather than female. They have shown how printed messages shape and are shaped by the power structures of society.

Apply

The ninth thinking process is *apply.* The reasons you plowed through the driver's manual were so that you could pass the driver's test, obtain a license, and get behind the wheel of a car. When you finally got behind the wheel, you were required to remember all the rules and regulations: how fast to go on various streets under various conditions, who has the right of way in different situations, and what the road signs mean. Applying is adapting what you have learned to anticipated or actual situations.

When you apply knowledge, you select the most appropriate response from all the ones you have acquired. As was noted at the beginning of this chapter, this book is meant to help you teach students to read and write in the content areas. Our goal is to help you plan and actually use (i.e., apply) the thinking processes described here in classroom situations.

Thinking Is Complex

Because thinking is a complex phenomenon, you should keep in mind several points about the nine processes presented above. One point is that our labels and descriptions overlap those presented by many other authors. Fostering thinking is a time-honored common goal among educators, and many types of thinking have been discussed. The professional literature about thinking contains such terms as hypothesizing, speculating, inferring, extrapolating, elaborating, problem solving, synthesizing, analyzing, creating, and categorizing. Metacognition frequently is used to denote a special constellation of thinking processes considered to be above the others. Indeed, our list contains many of the cognitive behaviors presented in Bloom's classic *Taxonomy of Educational Objectives* (1956). The essential thinking processes presented in this chapter are listed in the table below alongside the ones presented by Bloom and his colleagues. We believe that the nine terms and descriptions of mechanisms presented in this chapter cover the most important types of thinking. Our terms are often synonymous with several others available, and ours share most of the characteristics of the others. Our list provides a solid basis for fostering thinking through content area reading and writing instruction.

Essential Thinking Processes	*Bloom's Taxonomy of Educational Objectives*
Call up	Knowledge
Connect	Comprehension
Predict	Application
Organize	Analysis
Generalize	Synthesis
Image	Evaluation
Self-monitor	
Evaluate	
Apply	

A second point about our essential thinking processes is that presenting them separately implies that each is isolated from the others. And listing them from call up to apply suggests that thinkers do first one, then another, then a third, and so on, in a prescribed sequence. But these thinking processes do not stand alone and are not used in a rigid order. Instead, each thinker integrates the processes differently according to the demands of each situation. Students might form images and predict upcoming information simultaneously; they might evaluate the first few sentences of what they read or write, organize their thoughts, and continue processing the information. Our point is that students combine thinking processes and emphasize certain ones at different times in order to conceptualize what they are reading or writing about.

Third, students at all grade levels can benefit from assistance with the thinking processes outlined above. To paraphrase Bruner's famous quotation from *The Process of Education* (1977): We begin with the hypothesis that any thinking process can be taught effectively in some intellectually honest form to any child at any stage of development. This principle means that organizing, for example, can be presented in the primary- as well as the high-school grades. Primary-school children might categorize pictures of animals according to those that fly, those that walk, and those that swim; high-school students might classify one-celled life forms according to their kingdom, phylum, class, order, family, genus, and species. Similarly, very young children can learn to evaluate by thinking about questions like "Did a real boy named Jack climb a beanstalk and meet a giant?" "Should Jack have climbed the beanstalk?" Older students can ponder how well *Lord of the Flies* portrays basic human nature. In brief, schoolchildren seem to share the same mental processes. Students from kindergarten through twelfth grade call up, connect, predict, organize, generalize, image, monitor, evaluate, and apply with varying degrees of sophistication. This book addresses K–12 reading and writing because of the fundamental similarity of these processes across the various grades.

Fourth, motivation shapes thinking and learning (Corno & Kanfer, 1993; Pintrich, Marx, & Boyle, 1993). Students who become engaged with ideas and independently seek knowledge have a distinct advantage over unmotivated students. Think about how well your education proceeded when you had an intense desire to know something as opposed to when you were not interested in the subject. Many adolescents who perform poorly in school do amazingly well with the relevant, compelling demands of their driver's manual. Teachers should remember that promoting students' motivation to learn and think is at least as important as developing their thinking processes.

Finally, our list of thinking processes helps enable you to plan productive learning experiences. You can continually ask yourself how you can provide opportunities for students to call up, connect, predict, and so on. The remainder of this chapter and the remaining chapters in this book explain how to generate learning activities that engage students in these thinking processes.

Listen/Look and Learn

Visit a class during a subject matter lesson or tape-record a lesson that you present. Pretend that you are a student during this activity and list the chief thinking processes you would use. Which were used most frequently? Which were used least frequently? What could be done to elicit the thinking processes that were not tapped?

CLASSROOM SETTINGS INFLUENCE LITERACY DEVELOPMENT

Two classes with the identical title might be taught at the same time of day, have the same course outline and assignments, and employ the same materials for teaching and testing. Despite these identical circumstances, the teachers and students in the two class probably would experience them differently, and students' literacies would be affected differently. For instance, two teachers might plan and conduct discussions about a passage using identical questions during the same hour, yet one discussion might consist of individuals debating the flaws perceived in each others' assertions, and the other might consist of classmates mutually constructing statements of the passage's central message. When students read in these two classes, they would look for ideas to help with the type of discussion they typically experience. The differences in the classes would be due to their settings.

Settings, or environments, embed teachers' and students' actions. They define classroom learning opportunities that influence reading and writing development (Moore, 1996). In this section we present five general aspects of classroom settings that foster content area reading, writing, and learning. These aspects characterize effective teaching-learning circumstances (Applebee, 1996; Moje, 1996; National Council for Social Studies, 1994; Newmann & Wehlage, 1993).

Like the essential thinking processes just presented, the aspects of classroom settings presented here provide a solid basis for productive content area reading and writing instruction. You can use these characteristics as reminders when planning instruction and as criteria for evaluating instruction. Five aspects of classroom settings that deserve attention are literacy engagement, meaningfulness, active participation, academic challenge and support, and social support.

Literacy Engagement

Literacy engagement refers to students' frequency and depth of involvement with reading and writing. Students who are engaged readers and writers actively use print for sustained periods of time. They frequently refer to print while interacting with their classmates and teachers. Students who are engaged in literacy read and write for diverse utilitarian and pleasurable purposes; they learn new ideas, perform tasks, and escape into imaginary literary worlds. They read and write because they expect personal satisfaction from the experience.

Teachers who demonstrate a deep-seated commitment to engaging students with literacy offer print-rich classrooms with multiple reading materials, numerous displays of students' work, and regular attention to literacy. Classroom interactions often center about print; classroom success depends on reading and writing. These teachers believe that formal education should result in highly literate graduates. They see the role of schools, the purpose of the subjects they teach, and the way students should be treated naturally leading to a concentration on literacy. They actively promote classroom settings conducive to frequent involvement with reading and writing.

Meaningfulness

When students answer a series of rapid-fire, low-level questions about the facts of a passage they have read, they are involved with what we call popcorn questions. Popcorn questions tend to be lightweight and go out to students randomly. A steady diet of these questions leads to the belief that school is simply a place to memorize facts and give them back on demand. Students come to view reading as a means of locating isolated bits of inconsequential information. Many students tire of this situation and disrupt or retreat from it.

Meaningful classroom settings avoid popcorn questions and involve students in activities that call for the range of thinking processes presented in the previous section. Learners in meaningful situations transform information and make it their own. By predicting, connecting, organizing, generalizing, imaging, evaluating, and applying information they use their minds fully to solve problems and construct significant ideas. They are involved in higher-order thinking about worthwhile ideas. Rather than participate in rote recitations about the contents of a driver's manual, students in meaningful classroom settings would explain situations that exemplify driver's manual guidelines, participate in decision-making simulations, and demonstrate their knowledge while actually driving a car.

Meaningful activities call for authentic products. In the case of meaningful letter writing, this means students would produce all the components of a letter in a situation that calls for the complete act of genuine letter writing. Students would work on an entire letter that they have good reason to mail rather than on isolated worksheets stressing salutations, opening paragraphs, and so forth. When students have a sense that what they are producing has integrity in its own right, they are on their way toward participating in meaningful activities.

An important feature of meaningful teaching-learning situations is a sense of *connectedness*. This sense comes when there are clear relations among the ideas learners encounter. Connectedness allows learners to assimilate and explore content through coherent frameworks. Connections are made among ideas from outside and inside the classroom.

Connected classroom settings are relevant to students' lives, engaging them at personal rather than abstract academic levels. Students learn information and strategies because they are seen as being useful now rather than only in some unforeseen future. Students address important timely goals like making sense of a chaotic world, affecting change, and expressing a sense of self. Isolated letter writing occurs when students practice the forms of friendly and business letters only to receive a grade. Meaningful, connected letter writing occurs when students expect a response from authentic audiences such as pen pals, sports figures, and newspaper editors. It moves students from relying on lifeless textbook assignments to seeking out flesh-and-blood individuals and experiences.

Linking learning activities to the world beyond the classroom is another way to promote meaningful connections. When students' personal, societal, and occupational worlds are connected to the academic world, schooling can be seen as a meaningful enterprise. For instance, smoking is an issue that upper grade students face daily, so it has an intrinsic appeal that more academic topics such as propaganda techniques and government controls lack. Deciding whether or not to smoke is a personal value-based decison that individuals make. Moreover, a study of smoking can lead to critical examinations of governmental and societal issues such as, "Why does the U.S. government subsidize an industry that presents health risks?" and "Why do people subject themselves to health risks?" Job-related issues worth exploring involve workplace restrictions and incentives related to smoking. As these smoking activities demonstrate, beyond-the-classroom connections situate ideas so they come together as part of a mosaic, a tapestry, a clear pattern with personal relevance; they are not seen as meaningless and fragmented entities.

Active Participation

Active participation is another aspect of classroom contexts associated with effective literacy learning. Learners who are active participants do more than just passively receive information through lectures, assigned readings, and audiovisuals. They energetically respond to situations, interacting with teachers and each other while manipulating print and nonprint resources. They are animated in class, taking part in lively activities.

Students often tire of attending to teachers' directions for every move they make, so they become apathetic or antagonistic. Because of this, early in the year successful teachers explicitly present ways to work independently so students can participate on their own later on. If you visit such classrooms late in the year, you will see motivated independent learners controlling most of their own learning activities. Many beginning teachers wonder when they will get classes full of such independent students. The truth, of course, is that the classrooms were created by explicit teaching and much persistence early in the year.

Classrooms with active participation also exhibit flexible grouping practices. Students sometimes meet as a whole class for teachers to introduce something new, build common experiences, and review what has been presented. But for especially active participation, students also meet in small groups to collaborate on projects and share ideas, and they work on their own to pursue individual goals, apply strategies, and assess their learning. If a class were producing possible solutions to a community problem, then the teacher's initial explanation and demonstration might occur before the whole class, the students might meet in small groups to brainstorm potential problems and solutions, and individuals might draft their own letters to community leaders.

Another way to enhance participation is to provide students with choices. As much as possible, have students decide their learning activities. Learners are advantaged when they generate their own learning goals and experiences. When you decide on the activities for students, offer them choices regarding which ones to perform and the order in which to complete them. Given two possible writing assignments, students could pick the one they are most interested in completing. Given certain vocabulary words, students could select their own ways of presenting the words' meanings. Given a set of short stories, students could decide the sequence in which to read them.

Active participation also means involving everyone every chance you have. Imagine that you are teaching a group of first-graders a lesson on living

Students can actively participate in collaborative learning groups.

and nonliving things. You have presented the differences, and now you want to help students apply their understandings. You might show some pictures so students can decide whether each picture represents a living or nonliving thing. You could simply call on volunteers, but only one child at a time would be responding, with many children uninvolved and not attending. To make this an activity in which all are involved, have each draw a picture of himself or herself on one side of a piece of drawing paper and a picture of a book on the other side. Then as you display each of your pictures, say "Ready, set, show," and have the children show the picture of themselves if they believe the object is living (like them) and the picture of their book if they believe the object is nonliving (like the book).

Quick writes are another way to elicit active participation. Imagine that you want to review the major aspects of communicable diseases. You could ask, "Who remembers something we learned about communicable diseases?" You probably would elicit some comments, but you might notice that they come from the same few individuals. Do those who remain silent not know or simply not care to participate? A review activity that gets everyone involved would be to have everyone take out a sheet of scrap paper and quickly write three things they remember about communicable diseases. Then you might ask students to nominate themselves to speak.

Academic Challenge and Support

One of us, David Moore, has played racquetball regularly. David marks his greatest gain in racquetball enjoyment and skill during a two-year time span when he had a weekly game with Dean, a one-time state-level doubles champion in Iowa. Dean loved the game; he would play anyone just so he could be on the court. The first time they played, David scored only a few points, but Dean commented on his potential and suggested ways he could improve his backhand strategy. David remembers walking away from that game believing he could do better.

Sometimes Dean would give David an advantage by hitting only straight drives to his backhand or serving only at half speed, and Dean continued demonstrating stroke and court positioning techniques. Over time David's racquetball improved so much that Dean actually worked up a sweat when they played—and David even won a few of their matches just before moving from the state.

As with racquetball, literacy improves in situations with appropriate challenges, ones that stretch students' abilities. Appropriate challenges call for special effort, but they are not defeating. They strengthen students' wills to succeed. They are at the cutting edge of students' abilities, neither too easy nor too demanding. Appropriate challenges are tasks that students are unable to accomplish at first but are able to accomplish with the help of others or with reasonable individual effort. Such levels of challenge allow students the pleasure of exerting themselves and experiencing success. Dean's racquetball challenge was such that David always believed he was within sight of a higher level of play.

For challenging learning environments to be most effective, however, students require support. David's racquetball would have improved little if Dean had left him in a sink-or-swim situation. Fortunately, they entered into something like a master-apprentice relationship. Before, during, and after the games, Dean supported David's development by offering encouragement—along with an occasional criticism—and demonstrating and explaining pertinent techniques to get to the next level. Dean supported David's development.

Academic supports, which often are termed *scaffolds* (Graves & Graves, 1994; Langer & Applebee, 1986; Rosenshine & Meister, 1992), bridge gaps between learners' current abilities and their successful completion of complex activities. In racquetball, Dean scaffolded the early racquetball games by not exploiting a weak backhand, by slowing his serve, and by explaining what to do in certain situations. In school, teachers scaffold complex writing activities by displaying model papers previous students completed; explaining how to complete such papers; providing checklists, cue sheets, and rubrics; orchestrating whole class, small group, and individual activities; and regulating the level of sophistication expected for the papers. Much of the remainder of this book presents ways to scaffold challenging learning opportunities.

Social Support

The final aspect of effective instructional contexts considered here, *social support*, calls attention to interpersonal relations. It focuses on the emotional and attitudinal climate of a class. Social supports are as necessary as the academic supports presented above in promoting literacy learning.

Positive expectations are an important type of social support. Teachers' expectations for students are especially important because they often result in self-fulfilling prophecies: teachers who believe students will (or will not!) succeed with challenging activities communicate this to students, and students follow suit. Learners do best when they and their teachers expect their efforts to result in high-quality accomplishments. To return to the racquetball story, Dean seemed convinced that David's racquetball game would improve, and David came to believe it, too.

Projecting enthusiasm is another way to support learners. You project enthusiasm when you convey an intense eagerness to explore class contents. Being perky and theatrical or being low-key is not crucial as long as you are passionate and sincere about the value of the topic under consideration. As with positive expectations, enthusiasm is contagious. Students learn to value what their teachers value.

Perhaps the key social support is respect. Among other things, respect is apparent when teachers and students treat each other like long-time members of a club. Rapport is evident during face-to-face interactions. Each member is an insider; there is a sense of community. Social divisions such as achievement level, ethnicity, gender, and peer affiliation do not affect concerns for individuals' well-being. Efforts are made to enfranchise those who feel alienated.

Teachers establish respect in classrooms by modeling it and expecting students to act the same. They show respect by taking individuals' statements seriously and responding to them thoughtfully. They solicit and welcome contributions from all students, not just the vocal high-achieving ones. They advocate students' contributions to class, restricting efforts to belittle what has been presented. Teachers who show respect offer true praise for students' legitimate efforts and accomplishments, not false praise in misdirected attempts to build self-esteem no matter what students do.

Listen/Look and Learn

Talk with a student about the classroom settings he or she prefers. Ask the student to describe the best teacher he or she has had. What did the teacher do that he or she liked? What was so good about that teacher's class? Compare your findings with the characterisitics of effective settings presented in this section.

INSTRUCTION OCCURS IN CYCLES

This concluding section of Chapter 1 describes how to sequence content area literacy learning opportunities. It points to a general plan, or framework, for teaching that should occur within the classroom settings just described. The pattern of instruction described here is based on the idea of cycles, regularly recurring events.

Cycles of Instruction

Cycles consist of regularly recurring events in some action. As Figure 1.2 shows, four events, or phases, are in cycles of instruction. Teachers repeatedly plan, introduce, guide, and culminate subject matter literacy study.

Planning   In the planning phase you determine what you wish to accomplish and how you will approach it. Planning can be for different blocks of time (e.g., hour, day, week, grading period, semester, year) and for different blocks of content. If you are studying the solar system for three weeks, you decide what you want to accomplish relative to descriptions and distances of the planets; the sun, moon, comets, and asteroids; space exploration; and so on. You consider issues about linking subject matter such as the solar system with learning processes such as image and apply. You devise teaching-learning situations that are meaningful and connected. You gather print and nonprint resources for your class. You decide on reading and writing options. Planning is especially compelling when you first start teaching. You will be struck with the awesome responsibility of determining objectives and scheduling appropriate learning opportunities for the students entrusted to you. When this happens, consult the most productive references you have available. Curriculum guides, colleagues, and textbooks are good sources of information; indeed, many schools have quite specific plans already established. Once you get rolling, planning tends to become more manageable.

Introducing   As with planning, introducing applies to different blocks of time and subject matter. You might devise introductions that apply to general procedures for the entire year (e.g., how to gain the floor during class discussions,

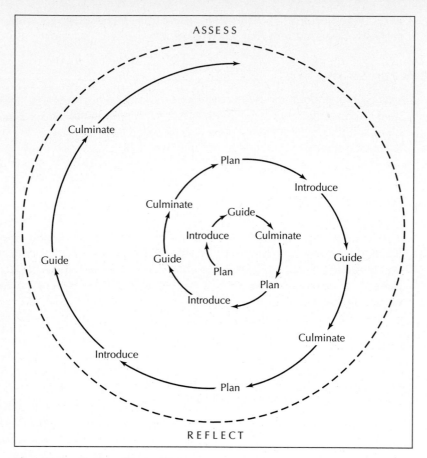

Figure 1.2 Cycles of Instruction

how to take notes) or to specific content being explored during the next hour (e.g., distances between planets).

While the bulk of planning is done away from learners, introducing occurs in their presence. During this stage of instruction, you prepare learners for upcoming ideas and procedures. You share your plans with students, arousing their curiosity and interest and acquainting them with your expectations and available resources. You orient learners to the topics being addressed, the reasons for exploring them, and the procedures for accomplishing the learning activities. You show students—through modeling—how to do what they are expected to do. Introducing lessons and units of instruction is when you set the stage for subject matter literacy learnings.

Guiding After planning and introducing learning activities, you continue your interactions with learners by offering guidance. After setting the stage, you oversee the production. Learners get in on the act during this phase, exploring ideas on their own or practicing what has been modeled. This phase of the instructional cycle typically consumes the most time. Guiding learners takes innumerable forms. If class members are discussing what they have read, you might facilitate the discussion. If everyone is writing, you might consult with individuals. If small groups are brainstorming generalizations about a passage, you might move from group to group with probing questions. If students are solving problems, you could contribute to their efforts. During this phase, you monitor learners' progress, offering feedback, encouragement, and praise where appropriate.

Culminating   Culminating activities bring events to a close. Effective culminations help learners reflect on their experiences, clarify what they have learned, review what is unclear, and celebrate accomplishments.

Culminating activities can last only a few minutes, such as when you review and summarize an hour's lesson, or they can last a week or more, such as when students exhibit projects they have completed. Assessing what students have learned through a quiz, test, or exam is a traditional way to culminate instruction, although many teachers now are relying on ongoing assessments that check students' performance throughout learning activities. No matter what type of assessment you use, follow up the results and reteach what is needed either in the culmination or in the next cycle of instruction.

Cycles of Instruction Are Complex   It is important to realize that effective literacy instruction moves through four phases of a cycle. But there is more to it than just moving through phases. Two points about cycles of instruction should be considered.

First, the cycles are connected across time. As Figure 1.2 shows, the instructional cycle moves in a continuous spiral. One series of events merges into and builds on another. Although the culminating phase of the instructional cycle involves closure, it simultaneously is a springboard for the next round of instruction. What was learned today about Jupiter leads into tomorrow's consideration of Saturn. In the earlier section we stressed meaningful connections among ideas related to topics and to the world beyond the classroom. However, the relations among ideas on the vertical spiral plane considered here refer to connections among ideas encountered in the classroom.

Ideas and insights obtained in one setting become the ground for assimilating and refining ideas and insights in a later setting (Dewey, 1938). Procedures for solving two-step math word problems can become the basis for solving three-, four-, and five-step problems later. Understanding characterization in a Brothers Grimm story leads to better understandings of Shakespeare's writings. Segmenting *triangle* into its meaningful word parts (*tri* plus *angle*) to determine its meaning can become the ground for segmenting *antibacterial* later. Expert teachers routinely help students connect what they already know with what they are learning (Good & McCaslin, 1992). Especially when planning instruction, think of a spiral and look for ways that students can build on earlier classroom experiences.

The second point about instructional cycle decisions centers on the terms *assess* and *reflect* contained in Figure 1.2. Arrows do not connect these terms because they refer to actions that occur during all phases of the cycle. The line separating assess and reflect from the others is broken to indicate fluidity; there is continual flow among these actions and the others. This means that teachers constantly gather data about instructional events to make informed decisions. Assessment occurs throughout instruction, not just during culminating activities (Darling-Hammond, Ancess, & Falk, 1995; Stiggins, 1994; Wiggins, 1993). Reflection also happens continually. Thinking about one's practices informs decisions about future plans as well as daily on-the-spot actions (Schön, 1983). Finally, students who regularly reflect on their academic performance enhance their opportunities to become independent students and lifelong learners (Corno, 1992)

Fading

A long-term teaching approach devoted to developing independent lifelong learners that is consistent with instructional cycles is termed *fading.* Fading calls for teachers to support students through complex learning activities and then to diminish their support gradually until the students can perform the activities by themselves. Fading is an essential part of reading and writing instruction.

Fading is used extensively when teaching sports. Imagine that you are an accomplished tennis player and have a friend who would like to learn to play. What would you do? You probably first would involve your friend in actual tennis, hitting the ball back and forth and perhaps playing a match. At some point, you would focus on a particular aspect of the game in which your friend

Teachers demonstrate what students are to practice and apply.

obviously needed help—gripping the racquet, perhaps. You would take some time to demonstrate, or model, the correct grip and talk about it at the same time. You might say, "Watch how I grip my racquet. I am holding the leather like a firm handshake." The instruction at this introductory phase involves a teacher performing the task while describing what he or she is doing.

After demonstrating the grip, you would move rapidly to the guiding, or guided practice, phase of instruction by having your friend try it. Not expecting immediate success, you might say, "Now it's your turn. Give it a try, and I'll be here to help you get it right. Believe me, it takes a while to get the hang of this." You would provide feedback right away about the grip your friend produces, pointing out specific things that were right or needed to be improved. You would have him or her apply the grip to hit some balls. You might have your friend grip the racquet and hit a ball up, down, or against a backboard. You two would go back to hitting some balls back and forth so your friend uses the grip in actual situations. You also would encourage your friend to keep trying. During this phase, you oversee learners' attempts to perform what you have just demonstrated.

Finally, after your friend grips the tennis racquet reasonably well, you might play a set and keep score. Your purpose would be to help your friend apply the grip in actual tennis situations. This would be the culmination phase. You provide realistic opportunities for learners to use what has been demonstrated and practiced, assess their proficiencies, celebrate their successes, and revisit their shortcomings.

You might never teach anyone how to play tennis, but you might teach students how to determine the meanings of unfamiliar words or take notes from a passage in your content area. To teach note taking through fading, first select a passage related to the topic you are teaching that seems within the grasp of your students. Then demonstrate how you would take notes from the passage by actually producing notes and explaining how you decided to write what you did. Next, guide students as they practice note taking. Direct them to a portion of the passage, telling them to write notes about it like you just did. Compare your notes with some of the students' notes and have students compare their notes with one another's. Provide feedback about how they are doing. Eventually, in order to promote application, direct students to record their notes in a notebook and check them occasionally.

Instructional fading moves from introducing to guiding to culminating as teachers fade out and students fade in. Teachers support students through subject-related literacy activities and then gradually move back so the students can do it on their own. Scaffolds are in place when they are needed and removed when the construction can stand alone.

Looking Back

Developing students' reading, writing, and thinking abilities in the content areas is one of the schools' major responsibilities, and content area teachers are the most effective agents in accomplishing this goal. Focusing on thinking processes enables teachers to plan and deliver learning activities that enhance content area literacy and content acquisition. Students who call up, connect, organize, and apply, among other processes, go far in bringing active thought to their schooling. Academic experiences that build these processes can be planned within a context of literacy engagement, meaningfulness, active participation, academic challenge and support, and social support as well as an instructional cycle of planning, introducing, guiding, and culminating. These are the key ideas presented in this chapter: (1) Compelling reasons support content area literacy instruction; (2) thinking underlies reading, writing, and learning; (3) classroom contexts influence literacy development; and (4) instruction occurs in cycles.

Add to Your Journal

Think about the four key ideas of this chapter, and use the nine thinking processes to compose a response. You might organize the chapter by summarizing or outlining it. You might connect the chapter's information with past experiences and report events that are associated with what is presented. You also might evaluate the chapter and pass judgment on its contents. What is your opinion of the ideas so far? Why do you think this way? Finally, you could begin to apply what you have read. How do you plan to use what you have learned so far? What applications do you foresee between what has been presented in this chapter and your future teaching?

REFERENCES

APPLEBEE, A. N. (1996). *Curriculum as conversation.* Chicago: The University of Chicago Press.

BLOOM, B. S. (Ed.). (1956). *Taxonomy of educational objectives. Handbook I: Cognitive domain.* New York: McKay.

BRUNER, J. (1977). *The process of education.* Cambridge, MA: Harvard University Press.

COLE, N. S. (1990). Conceptions of educational achievement. *Educational Researcher, 19*(3), 2–7.

CORNO, L. (1992). Encouraging students to take responsibility for learning and performance. *Elementary School Journal, 93,* 69–83.

CORNO, L., & KANFER, R. (1993). The role of volition in learning and performance. In L. Darling-Hammond (Ed.), *Review of research in education* (Vol. 19, pp. 301–341). Washington, DC: American Educational Research Association.

DARLING-HAMMOND, L., ANCESS, J., & FALK, B. (1995). *Authentic assessment in action.* New York: Teachers College Press.

DEWEY, J. (1938). *Experience and education.* New York: Macmillan.

GOOD, T. L., & McCASLIN, M. M. (1992). Teaching effectiveness. In M. C. Alkin (Ed.), *Encyclopedia of educational research* (6th ed.) (pp. 1373–1388). New York: Macmillan.

GRAVES, M., & GRAVES, B. (1994). *Scaffolding reading experiences: Designs for student success.* Norwood, MA: Christopher-Gordon.

INTERNATIONAL READING ASSOCIATION/NATIONAL COUNCIL OF TEACHERS OF ENGLISH (1996). *Standards for the English language arts.* Newark, DE: Author.

LANGER, J. A., & APPLEBEE, A. N. (1986). Reading and writing instruction: Toward a theory of teaching and learning. In E. Z. Rothkopf (Ed.), *Review of research in education* (Vol. 13, pp. 171–194). Washington, DC: American Educational Research Association.

McKENNA, M. C., & ROBINSON, R. D. (1990). Content literacy: A definition and implications. *Journal of Reading, 34,* 184–186.

MOJE, E. B. (1996). "I teach students, not subjects": Teacher-student relationships as contexts for secondary literacy. *Reading Research Quarterly, 31,* 172–195.

MOORE, D. W. (1996). Contexts for literacy in secondary schools. In D. J. Leu, C. K. Kinzer, K. A. Hinchman (Eds.), *Literacies for the 21st century: Research and practice.* Forty-fifth Yearbook of the National Reading Conference (pp. 15–46). Chicago: National Reading Conference.

MOORE, D. W., READENCE, J. E., & RICKELMAN, R. (1983). An historical exploration of content area reading instruction. *Reading Research Quarterly, 18,* 419–438

MULLIS, I. V. S., & JENKINS, L. B. (1990). *The reading report card, 1971–88.* Princeton, NJ: National Assessment of Educational Progress, Educational Testing Service.

NATIONAL COUNCIL FOR THE SOCIAL STUDIES (1994). *Expectations of excellence.* Washington, DC: Author.

NATIONAL COUNCIL OF TEACHERS OF MATHEMATICS (1989). *Curriculum and evaluation standards for school mathematics.* Reston, VA: Author.

NEWMANN, F. M., & WEHLAGE, G. G. (1993). Five standards of authentic instruction. *Educational Leadership, 50*(7), 8–12.

PINTRICH, P. R., MARX, R. W., & BOYLE, R. A. (1993). Beyond cold conceptual change: The role of motivational beliefs and classroom contextual factors in the process of conceptual change. *Review of Educational Research, 63,* 167–199.

POSTMAN, N. (1979). *Teaching as a conserving activity.* New York: Delacorte.

RESNICK, L. (1987). *Education and learning to think.* Washington, DC: National Academy Press.

ROMINE, B. G. C., McKENNA, M. C., & ROBINSON, R. D. (1996). Reading coursework requirements for middle and high school content area teachers: A U.S. survey. *Journal of Adolescent and Adult Literacy, 40,* 194–198.

ROSENSHINE, B., & MEISTER, C. (1992). The use of scaffolds for teaching higher-level cognitive strategies. *Educational Leadership, 49*(7), 26–33.

SCHÖN, D. (1983). *The reflective practitioner: How professionals think in action.* New York: Basic Books.

SHOR, I. (Ed.) (1987). *Freire for the classroom.* Portsmouth, NH: Boynton/Cook.

STIGGINS, R. J. (1994). *Student-centered classroom assessment.* New York: Merrill.

WIGGINS, G. (1993). *Assessing student performance: Exploring the purpose and limits of testing.* San Francisco: Jossey-Bass.

ADDITIONAL READINGS

The following surveys have described educators' and students' preferred content area reading and writing interventions:

GEE, T. C., & RAKOW, S. J. (1991). Content reading education: What methods do teachers prefer? *NASSP Bulletin, 75,* 104–110.

SCHUMM, J. S., VAUGHN, S., & SAUMELL, L. (1992). What teachers do when the textbook is tough: Students speak out. *Journal of Reading Behavior, 24,* 481–503.

These are some classic and some modern references that are helpful in specifying the thought processes essential for learning content area information:

AUSUBEL, D. P. (1968). *Educational psychology: A cognitive view.* New York: Holt, Rinehart & Winston.

COLLINS, C, & MANGIERI, J. N. (Eds.). (1992). *Teaching thinking: An agenda for the twenty-first century.* Hillsdale, NJ: Erlbaum.

DEWEY, J. (1910). *How we think.* Boston: D. C. Heath.

JAMES, W. (1925). *Talks to teachers on psychology, and to students on some of life's ideals.* London: Longman.

MARZANO, R. J. (1991). Language, the language arts, and thinking. In J. Flood, J. M. Jensen, D. Lapp, & J. R. Squire (Eds.), *Handbook of research and teaching the English language arts* (pp. 559–586). New York: Macmillan.

SEGAL, J. W., CHIPMAN, S. F., & GLASER, R. (Eds.). (1985). *Thinking and learning skills* (Vol. 1). Hillsdale, NJ: Erlbaum.

SMITH, F. (1990). *To think.* New York: Teachers College Press.

STROUD, J. B. (1956). *Psychology in education.* New York: Longman, Green.

SWARTZ, R. J., & PERKINS, D. N. (1989). *Teaching thinking: Issues and approaches.* Pacific Grove, CA: Midwest Publications.

WEINSTEIN, C. E., & MAYER, R. E. (1985). The teaching of learning strategies. In M. C. Wittrock (Ed.), *Handbook of research on teaching* (3rd ed.) (pp. 315–327). New York: Macmillan.

chapter 2

Instructional Units and Classroom Organization

Looking Ahead _____

The ability to name the seven continents and five oceans is a traditional school expectation. But expectations have been changing. While today's students still name the continents and oceans, they also are expected to predict the effects changes in the oceans might have on the land.

Many educators are responding to the changing expectations of schools by integrating instruction. Teachers are linking language arts with subject matter. They are connecting learnings from inside the classroom with those from outside. Rather than presenting topics such as oceans one week and continents the next, teachers are presenting them together. Traditional individualized recitations over bits of information are giving way to learning activities in which students explore connected domains of knowledge in meaningful ways.

Teachers also are organizing their students into various combinations. To maximize active participation during units of study, students enter into whole-class, small-group, and individual arrangements.

From an extremely broad perspective, instructional decision making can be seen as ranging from your first daydreams about teaching to the minute-to-minute decisions you make when actually interacting with students. To manage our presentation here, we present only three frames within which teachers make decisions: year, unit, and lesson. By moving from general to specific—by first planning the year, then units, then lessons—teachers present a series of connected experiences (Clark & Peterson, 1986).

Yearly plans are at the long-term end of instructional decision making. (Secondary teachers who might not be with particular groups for an entire academic year might think of this level as course, or semester, planning.) Yearly planning is the time to think about grand outcomes. It calls for you to decide on the major understandings, strategies, and values you want for students. At this level of planning, you think about all the content to be covered (or uncovered!) and about helping students become critical thinkers, attentive listeners, autonomous learners, respectful citizens, and so on. Establishing year-long outcomes before meeting students the first day of class is important because, as the old saying goes, "When you're up to your neck in alligators, it's hard to remember that you came to drain the swamp!" Having a focus for the year helps you aim at the important substantive aspects of teaching while managing its immediate everyday aspects.

Units are at the middle level of teachers' planning. Units indicate how the year's curriculum will be divided among blocks of time lasting from a few days to a few weeks. Space, weather, and plants are units of study commonly addressed in the early grades. Science teachers in middle school often divide their courses among topics such as astronomy, meteorology, and geology. Senior-high English literature teachers might address survival, change, and defining oneself. This chapter addresses unit planning.

Lessons are at the short-term end of instructional decision making. Lessons specify the learning activities of a unit; they detail the actions teachers and students will perform. Beginning teachers' written lesson plans often are detailed enough so that a knowledgeable outsider—like a substitute teacher—could step into a classroom, read the lesson plans, and lead a class through the day's learning activities. Chapters 4 through 8 of this text emphasize lesson planning.

Classroom organization, a second major dimension of decision making addressed in this chapter, involves grouping practices. Teachers decide when to situate students in whole class, small group, or individual settings. Each of these grouping arrangements offers different opportunities for literacy and subject matter learning.

This chapter addresses unit planning and classroom organization as they relate to literacy and subject matter learning. It presents four key ideas:

1. Integrated units combine numerous aspects of instruction.
2. Planning integrated units involves many decisions.
3. Interdisciplinarity is a special feature of integrated units.
4. Literacy activities are linked to classroom grouping practices.

INTEGRATED UNITS COMBINE NUMEROUS ASPECTS OF INSTRUCTION

Integrated units are excellent ways to bring about the meaningful aspects of classroom settings presented in Chapter 1. Integrated units are designed to maximize higher-order thinking, personal engagement, authentic products, connections among subject matter, and links to the world beyond the classroom.

Integrated units' emphases on meaningfulness differ from ordinary units. A unit on the Civil War would be ordinary if it consisted only of a presentation of details about the causes of the war, the battles, the generals, and the outcomes. During an integrated unit on the Civil War, students might compare their living conditions with those of plantation owners and slaves, assert confederations' rights to secede from a nation, talk in small groups about novels set during the war, and compose a diary from the perspective of a soldier or citizen from the North or South. Multiple modes of learning prevail.

Integrated units grew out of a dissatisfaction with schooling that emphasized rote memorization of facts transmitted through lectures and textbooks (Vars, 1991). Proponents of integrated instruction share an aversion to fragmented isolated instruction. They prefer unified systems of instruction, seeing integrated units as a powerful way to help individuals learn about the world. They believe schooling should be meaningful and connected because life is meaningful and connected.

In order to promote meaningful integrated learning and literary engagement, educators regularly combine all the language arts with subject matter study. Reading, writing, listening, and speaking are emphasized in integrated units. For instance, an integrated unit on tobacco smoking might call for students to read about the physical effects of smoking, listen while interviewing people about smoking's effects, write their observations of smoking-related experiments, and talk about what they are learning. Capitalizing on all the language arts this way provides deep and multifaceted views of a topic; it allows learners to follow many routes when exploring an area. Listening to a lecture sheds some light on a topic, but too many aspects of it are left in the dark. Reading multiple resources, talking, and writing about a topic illuminate it substantially.

If you have students read, write, listen, and talk about what they are investigating, then you have many opportunities to enhance their language competencies. For instance, students who prepare for and actually conduct an interview with an authority on the effects of smoking can be expected to increase their insights into effective speaking-listening strategies. If students are expected to read about smoking's physical effects, then you can spend time teaching and talking about reading strategies that will help students accomplish the task. If students are expected to record their observations of smoking-related experiments, then you can provide explicit instruction and promote peer discussions on writing appropriate notes. Students tend to develop reading and writing strategies best when they have a clear need and desire to use them. Integrated units go far in promoting this need and desire.

Literature is an important component of language arts and subject matter integration (Silva & Delgado-Larocco, 1993). Students who vicariously experience subject matter events can obtain a more meaningful grasp than what is available from a textbook. Historical fiction, biography, and narrative nonfiction allow readers to share others' experiences. For instance, Gary Paulsen's *The Crossing,* the story of a homeless boy living in Juarez, Mexico, provides a compelling account of someone who wants to enter the United States. Students who read this book have access to ideas that personalize the Mexico-United States immigration situation.

Along with the language arts, you can also incorporate various classroom grouping patterns into integrated units of instruction. This is typically done by conducting whole-class presentations throughout units when you introduce new concepts and strategies, promote materials, read aloud, and culminate activities. During small-group collaborative learning activities, students support one another while responding to books, collaborating on activities, and participating in minilessons. For example, during a unit on smoking, students could form collaborative groups to brainstorm what they already knew, share the new information they discovered, and help one another produce finished products. Individual work allows students to read self-selected materials, accomplish projects and assignments, and participate in evaluations. Whole-class, small-group, and individual patterns of classroom organization are mixed during integrated units.

Finally, integrated units merge students' personal experiences with schooling. Students' worlds often are separated from the academic world, resulting in the perception that school is irrelevant. Integrated units counteract this situation by combining students' personal experiences with the unit. Topics, resources, and learning activities build on students' interests and abilities. As noted in Chapter 1, smoking is an issue that upper-grade students face daily, so it has an intrinsic appeal. Moreover, a study of smoking can lead to fundamental issues that students find interesting, such as, "Why does the U.S. government subsidize an industry that presents health risks?" and "Why do people subject themselves to health risks?" Activities such as interviewing and conducting surveys and experiments are other ways to integrate students' experiences with school. They move students from relying on a lifeless textbook to seeking out flesh-and-blood individuals and experiences.

To be sure, there are many versions of what it takes for a unit to be integrated. Authorities have described instruction that incorporates multiple intelligences (Gardner, 1991; Lazear, 1992), brain-based adaptations (Sylwester, 1995), and thinking skills (Costa, 1991; Perkins, 1992), to name a few. Because this text is not meant to survey general instructional methods, here we purposely emphasize some productive overarching features of integration. In brief, integrated units promote meaningful learning by bringing together subject matter, language arts, grouping patterns, and personal experiences. Combining these elements is meant to produce a complete and compelling view of the world, enhancing students' concepts, strategies, and attitudes. It is meant to promote learning by helping students see the relationships and uses of ideas.

Listen/Look and Learn _____

Observe a class at least three times and note the students' learning activities. Describe instances where language arts, classroom grouping patterns, and personal experiences were integrated with subject matter. Also describe instances where these instructional features were not integrated but could have been.

PLANNING INTEGRATED UNITS INVOLVES MANY DECISIONS

There are many decisions to be made when planning integrated instructional units. The following lists several points at which decisions need to be made and actions need to be taken. Like most dimensions of teaching, these decision points occur neither in isolation nor in a rigid step-by-step manner. However, a general approach to unit planning involves working backwards. You first think about what you want to accomplish, then work backwards when planning ways to bring about the accomplishments. What follows are some major decisions to be made—in the approximate order in which they are first encountered—when planning integrated units.

Establishing the Focus of the Unit

Integrated units have a focus that connects ideas and activities. A unit's focus—like the hub of a wheel, the core of an apple, or the central node of a network—connects and holds together related items. The focus of an integrated unit is expressed through its organizing center, central question, and culmination.

Organizing Center   Organizing centers often consist of topics that are general enough to allow multiple perspectives and avenues of investigation. To illustrate, tobacco smoking could be an effective topic for upper-grade students because many language arts, grouping patterns, and personal experiences can be utilized when investigating it. The study of dinosaurs is an organizing center that occurs in countless primary-grade units of study. Pioneers, weather, and adventure are good candidates for integrated units in the middle grades; radiation, toxic waste, and substance abuse fit upper-grade students' interests. Topics such as patterns, flight, and bridges, which deliberately and ambiguously refer to physical, emotional, and social phenomena, also have proven effective as organizing centers.

Along with topics, the organizing center of a unit can be presented as an event. Historical occurrences and contemporary happenings are events that make good candidates for integrated study. For instance, common events that occur in students' daily lives, such as walking home from school, performing daily chores, and finding a job, lead to multiple avenues of investigation. Local and national elections, sports team activities, and current news features are events that can also be organizing centers for integrated units.

Literary novels or works of nonfiction also serve well as organizing centers (Smith & Johnson, 1993, 1994). For example, as students read *Roll of Thunder, Hear My Cry,* the historical fictional story of an African-American family's Depression-era experiences in the rural South, they could explore issues such as injustice, rural life, friendship, post-Civil War social patterns, and responsibility. Or a teacher might select *A Wind in the Door,* a science ficiton sequel to *A Wrinkle in Time.* In this story Charles Wallace is seriously ill and others must miniaturize themselves and enter his body in order to combat his disorder. Students could combine this book with their study of human anatomy, cell structure, medical breakthroughs, good versus evil, or character traits and motivations. Students could interact with others in different grouping patterns and through all the language arts while reacting to these books. Finally, language arts or English teachers often select a genre (e.g., poetry, science fiction, adventure) or an author (e.g., Jean George, Gary Paulsen, Jean Fritz) as the organizing center for an integrated unit.

Central Question   Along with identifying a unit's organizing center in terms of a topic, event, book, genre, or author, form a central question to focus integrated units. Central questions, which place students as problem solvers, provide an overarching purpose to units. Potentially inert ideas and facts students encounter in relation to organizing centers become ideas-in-action and facts-in-action when applied to central questions (Onosko, 1992). Central questions increase the productivity of the organizing center as a stimulus to learning.

Central questions share certain characteristics. They tap worthwhile meaningful issues. They are provocative and emotionally engaging. They highlight issues that connect with students' worlds. Central questions position students as investigators rather than passive recipients of content. They allow multiple responses because they have no single correct answer. They allow all students to form an answer, although the sophistication of the reactions might vary. With regard to smoking, a productive central question could be, "Why do people smoke?" If 1900 to 1970 were the topic of a history unit, then you might turn it into a central question such as, "In which decade of the 1900s were people better off?"

When addressing central questions, you still help students understand the numerous ideas and facts associated with the organizing center, but this information is considered the building blocks of thinking. After all, students have to think about something. Students would shuttle among the various thinking processes, sometimes organizing information, sometimes forming generalizations, and sometimes evaluating what they are learning. At the end of each session when students explored the organizing center, you might direct their attention to the central question with an inquiry such as, "How can what you learned today lead to answering the central question?" Students would use their minds fully to solve the problem, bringing ideas together and constructing significant ideas.

Examples and nonexamples (crossed out) of central questions include the following:

Is the United States today more like ancient Athens or Sparta?
What are appropriate limits to freedom of speech?
~~What are mammals?~~
What makes a work of art outstanding?
What factors most influence healthy development?
Who am I?
~~What are spiders' lives like?~~
How can our community be better prepared for natural disasters that
   probably will occur?
~~What do living things need for survival?~~
What does it take to be a hero?
What career is best for me?
What new invention might be most beneficial?
How can we handle our garbage problem?
~~Who are the major characters in this story?~~
Why is the weather difficult to predict?

Culminating Activity   Unit culminations allow students to tie together and celebrate what they have learned. They provide opportunities for students to achieve closure for what they have learned and to share their resolutions of the central question. End-of-unit culminating activities can take numerous forms (Stevenson & Carr, 1993):

Performance—a reenactment, panel discussion, conference, persuasive presentation, advertising campaign, one-act play, debate, or documentary;
Presentation—to parents, community groups, political bodies, school
   administrators, schoolmates, or younger or older children;
Product—museum, videotape, slide presentation, editorial, scientific
   demonstration or experiment, art display, class book, newspaper photo-
   graphic display, multimedia production, poster talk, or book; or
Outing—field trip to the outdoors, a museum, an historical site, an arbore-
   tum, a zoo.

As the above list suggests, units can culminate with more than one event. They can finish with a somewhat open-ended activity such as a field day and with a more convergent activity such as a report. Culminating activities can capitalize on creative outlets such as dramatic productions and visual displays as well as on traditional pencil-and-paper outlets.

Culminating activities typically involve some public sharing of what has been accomplished. Students can share what they learned with you, with their age-mates inside and outside the classroom, and with adults such as parents, teachers, administrators, and community members. The public nature of such sharings serves to motivate students, help them crystallize what has been accomplished, provide focus to the unit, recognize what has been done, offer students a chance to refine their presentation abilities, and provide others access to the thinking processes used in the project. The sharing may also reveal additional questions for investigation.

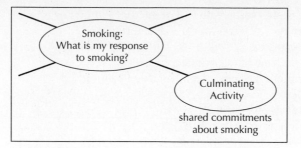

Figure 2.1   The Focus of a Curriculum Web

Many educators have students exhibit what they have learned so there is a product for evaluation. While your assessments should include ongoing daily indicators of students' accomplishments, you can decide whether or not to evaluate the culminating activity, too.

In the culmination for an integrated unit on smoking, students might share what they plan to do about it. These sharings could be in the form of posters, videos, interviews, and essays. They might range from reasons for students' personal decisions about whether or not to smoke when they reach legal age, to ways they can inform themselves about the effects of smoking, to avenues for social action relative to smoking.

Once an organizing center, central question, and culminating activity for your integrated unit are identified, place them in a graphic device called a *curriculum web*, as depicted in Figure 2.1. Establishing a focus for your unit this way is like deciding where to go on a journey. It specifies the destination. Once you know where you are headed, you can work backwards to decide how to get there and how to evaluate the experience. You now are ready to establish general unit objectives.

Do It Together

Discuss characteristics of organizing centers, central questions, and culminations. Practice generating possibilities for these three items. First generate several potential topics, events, or books that could serve as the organizing centers of integrated units. Construct possible central questions associated with each organizing center. Then produce possible culminating activities. Share these in class.

Establishing General Unit Objectives

General unit objectives, or learning targets, describe the major concepts, strategies, and attitudes students should acquire from participating in the unit. Unit objectives are the outcomes you expect students to demonstrate eventually as a result of the instructional journey you are leading. They are the learnings that you intend for students—realizing that students will pick up unintentional learnings during the course of study. Remember that objectives can be added when your students express opinions about the direction in which they would like the unit to move. The freedom you have in deciding objectives will be determined by the curriculum policies of your teaching team, school, and school district.

To begin forming general unit objectives, work backwards from the unit's focus. First, list key words or phrases associated with the focus. As the web of general unit topics shown in Figure 2.2 demonstrates, smoking covers diverse areas. Examine this list with the purpose of identifying what will help students satisfy the central question. Perhaps you and your students decide that physical effects, advertising techniques, and government assistance and controls could be what students need to understand in order to make an informed decision about their response to smoking.

The brainstormed key words and phrases then can be developed into more complete statements of general unit objectives. General objectives for a three-week unit on smoking might be stated as follows:

- To establish a personal commitment about smoking
- To describe the health risks and physical-performance effects of smoking
- To identify and evaluate predominant cigarette advertising techniques
- To explain reasons for government assistance and control of the tobacco industry

Unit objectives typically are stated in general terms, although their forms may vary. Many educators like to call unit objectives *goals* and state them in phrase form describing observable actions such as the ones above. No matter what form is used, unit objectives are needed to direct teachers' and students' efforts.

Unit objectives might be considered the stops you intend to make en route to the unit's culmination as well as the final stop at the culmination. They define the sections of terrain you will learn about when traveling. As shown in Figure 2.3, general objectives indicate the scope of a unit; they show what is to be accomplished.

Brainstorming Resources and Procedures

Resources are the teaching materials you use, and procedures are the activities you and your students perform. Brainstorming is a productive way to call up potential resources and procedures. Working backwards from the unit's focus and general objectives, imagine possibilities in an open-ended, freewheeling manner so that innovative ideas emerge. This stage of unit planning, which need not take much time, is intended to stimulate thinking about how you might accomplish general unit objectives in creative engaging ways.

What information sources can you think of that might contribute to students accomplishing the unit objectives? To generate a list of instructional

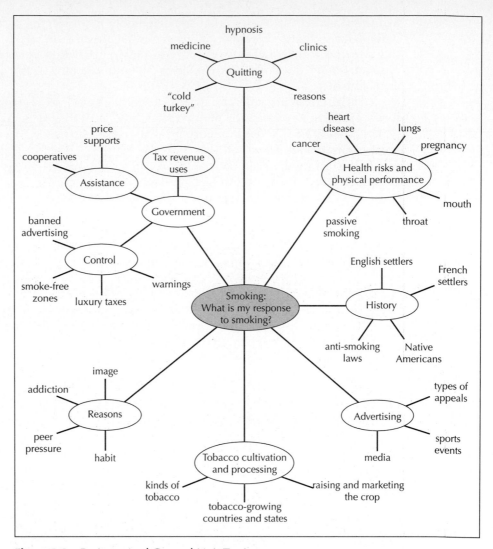

Figure 2.2 Brainstormed General Unit Topics

resources that contain print, brainstorm what you have relative to reference books, magazine articles, computer software, Internet access, CD-ROMs, trade books, and textbooks. Printed resources, on which we elaborate in Chapter 3, typically consist of sets of reading materials for the entire class, sets for small groups, and enough individual titles for each student. You should also identify nonprint resources such as videos, filmstrips, field trips, television shows, and guest speakers.

While thinking about resources, brainstorm instructional procedures, too. What are some activities you and your students might perform that lead to the

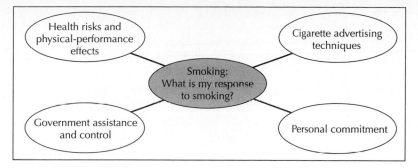

Figure 2.3   Revised General Unit Topics

unit objectives? For example, you might decide that creating advertisements for a particular segment of smokers not already targeted by cigarette manufacturers (e.g., senior citizens or urban dwellers) would be a good way to culminate the study of cigarette advertising techniques. After listing instructional procedures under your unit objectives, identify the grouping pattern(s) associated with each procedure and indicate which ones tap personal experiences. Coding the procedures this way reveals features that are overrepresented or underrepresented.

Gathering Resources

Once you have decided a unit's focus and objectives and have thought about possible resources and procedures, sharpen your planning. The brainstorming stage of unit planning provides the basis for identifying resources and procedures, but now you intensify the search, making definite decisions and listing them on a revised curriculum web.

During this stage seek help from department heads, team leaders, media specialists, experienced teachers, friends, and acquaintances. Post notes in conspicuous places and personally contact potential helpers. Notify your colleagues about units you are planning and you may be amazed at what assistance you receive.

Experienced teachers collect resources over time. When a classroom magazine contains a good article about a topic, teachers save that issue. They might maintain picture files for what they teach. They locate and request library books and audiovisual materials each year when the appropriate unit of study comes up because they have kept a list with their unit materials, and they update that list to include new resources and eliminate ones less useful.

There are many ways to obtain print resources for your students without spending money. You can check materials out of the school or the public library to use in your classroom. Many public libraries will compile a "Book Box" for teachers with 50 to 100 books on a topic. While searching is a bit time-consuming, the number of books and magazines available makes it worthwhile. You can also have students produce reading materials for their peers. In only a few years, you will have collected a veritable cornucopia of resources. Talk with your public librarian as well as your school librarian. Ask them to contact you when they are ready to discard content area books. Typically, books are discarded when they have become too worn for continued use by the public. Sometimes they have even gone through one rebinding process, but that won't matter to you. Look through the books. Is the content useful to you? Are the passages you would like to use in good condition? If so, collect the books, find a razor blade, and slice the passages you want from each book. Create a series of brochures, one for each selection you want to use.

Students may be willing to bring their copies of magazines or books to school to share, though they are rarely willing to donate them. Two or three weeks before you begin a unit, request that students who are willing to share related materials bring them to school a full week before the unit will begin. This gives you some time to go through the available materials and organize them for the students. Remind them to mark their materials with a name before bringing them to school. Also tell them that you cannot guarantee the safety of anything, so if a particular issue of a magazine is a prized one that they could not bear to lose, they ought not to bring it to school.

Two other sources of materials require the expenditure of money, though not yours! Request from your school's parent-teacher organization a specific amount of money for a list of books and magazines that you have compiled. It is often wise to ask for a lot more than you think you will be able to get. If you show that you have a really great need for a large number of special materials, then you are more likely to get at least some of those materials. Submit the list as soon as you can. Such organizations plan their budget early.

Another source of supplies is the paperback book clubs that continually send order forms to teachers. Distribute the forms to your students. When they return their order forms and money for books they want, you will discover that your class has earned a number of bonus points you can apply toward the purchase of free books or other content area materials such as maps or filmstrips.

Designing Instructional Procedures

At this point you are ready to specify the instructional procedures you and your students will perform. Once you know what you wish to accomplish and what you have to work with, you can plan a range of specific teaching-learning procedures. Plan for students to participate in whole-class, small-group, and individual efforts that involve reading, writing, listening, and speaking. Ensure that students can relate personal experiences to the objectives and procedures. Consider a balance of instructional experiences as the means to accomplish your learning objectives.

As noted in Chapter 1, cycles of instruction include planning introducing, guiding, and culminating. Instructional units follow this cycle. The overall unit you conduct should have a clear beginning, middle, and end during which you respectively introduce, guide, and culminate student learnings. Further, each exploration of the unit objectives needs to be introduced, guided, and culminated.

By working backwards from the focus of the unit—as well as from the general objectives—your planning stays on track. Use your organizing center, essential question, general objectives, and culminating activity to guide your selection of activities throughout the unit. Do not decide to dissect a cow's heart just because your brother-in-law is a butcher and you can get them free. Each activity should move students toward a clear destination. Knowing the destination enables you to plan effective introductory and guidance procedures.

Introducing   Once the end points, resources, and procedures of your unit are clear, plan how to draw students in. While the culminating activity is crucial for effectively planning a unit, the introduction is equally essential when first presenting it to a class. The time and energy spent engaging students at the beginning of a unit saves time and energy trying to salvage it toward the end. The opening days of a unit are critical for its success.

A unit's introduction should grab students' attention and arouse their curiosity. To accomplish this, plan to kick off your units of study with concrete sensory phenomena. Providing firsthand experiences with objects and events and providing vicarious experiences through simulations and other media arouse interest and quickly lead to questions such as "Why does this happen?" "What can we do about it?," and "What do you think would happen if . . . .?" Emphasizing real-world, relevant experiences is another way to engage students. Situate the organizing center, essential question, and culmination in students' worlds; connect what will be occuring inside the classroom with what occurs outside.

Schedule at least the first day of units for introductory activities, knowing that additional time can be spent on them if needed. It takes some time to motivate students and call up and connect their previous experiences and prior knowledge. In a unit on smoking, for example, you might display empty cigarette packages and other paraphernalia, visuals of smoking's effects, and a few magazine advertisements. By displaying coins to symbolize what it takes to buy tobacco, you could set the stage for your essential question, "What is your response to smoking?" Such props and activities can go far in promoting interest and thinking about the topic.

Guiding   Guidance, which occurs during the middle of the unit, takes the most time. You can guide students to and through resources that provide rich detail about unit contents. Guidance often is provided through a balance of teacher-directed and student-directed activities. A good organizational plan is to present (a) required activities for everyone to accomplish, (b) suggested activities from which students select a specified number, and (c) opportunities for students to design their own activities. Such a balance recognizes the need for common learnings, classroom cohesion, and student decision making.

Just as units are presented according to the instructional cycle, the teaching associated with general unit objectives also is cyclical. Given an objective, you plan how to introduce, guide, and culminate students' learning. Just like the unit introduction, introduce objectives in a motivating, interest-grabbing manner. Then guide students through the tasks. Monitor students' progress, and reteach when needed. Close the activities roughly the same way as you culminate the unit.

Guiding students to various learning objectives is complex. To illustrate, examine the tasks in the middle of the procedures listed in Figure 2.4. "Portray effects of smoking on life-size diagram of human body," "Create original ad," and "Compose a letter to a young child explaining why the U.S. government simultaneously assists and controls the tobacco industry" signal complicated teaching-learning activities. Students would need access to subject matter (effects of smoking, advertising contents, government policies) as well as to techniques for learning and sharing subject matter (how to produce a diagram, ad, and letter). You would need more specific plans—lesson plans—to accomplish this.

Most of the remaining chapters in this book are devoted to the specifics of lesson planning. Later chapters on comprehension, vocabulary, writing, study, and inquiry address lessons that guide students toward course content through literacy. To repeat the statement from the opening of this chapter, here we emphasize middle, unit-level planning; information on more specific, lesson-level planning comes later.

Planning Evaluation

Another step in planning integrated units is deciding on evaluation techniques. Determinations are needed about how well students are fulfilling the unit's learning objectives in order to guide their learning and your teaching. These determinations are made through ongoing observations of classroom actions, evaluations of daily products and special projects, and test performance.

Some of the assessment and evaluation decisions that need to be made are as follows:

1. Who will evaluate (the teacher, the teacher in conjunction with the student, students themselves, teachers from outside the classroom, parents, community members)? How will students be involved in evaluation; how will they engage in self-reflection?
2. How will special-needs children be evaluated? What are the consequences of not meeting a criterion? May students continue working until they achieve a satisfactory evaluation? Will deadlines exist?
3. Will evaluation standards be specified beforehand and distributed to students? How will the standards be written? Will work samples at various levels of accomplishment be available as models? May students appeal an evaluation?

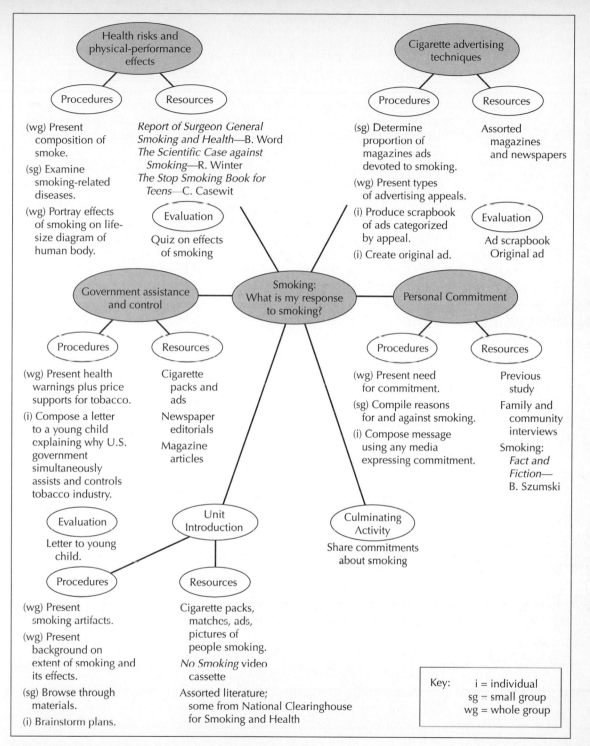

Figure 2.4 Instructional Procedures and Resources

4. What is the balance among daily work, projects, tests, and effort as means of assessment? How will individual accountability be determined during group interactions?

5. How many formal assessments will be recorded? What types of tests will be used (curriculum or norm referenced; multiple choice, fill in the blank, true false, short answer, or essay; performance of tasks)?

6. How will the evaluation be reported (written comments, letter grades, percentages of possible points)? How will it be communicated to students, parents, the school, and the community?

Because evaluating the outcomes of instruction is as complex as guiding instruction, we also address it in more depth in the remaining chapters. Moreover, you might consult resources relative to performance assessment (e.g., Maeroff, 1991; Stiggins, 1994; Wiggins, 1993) and grading (e.g., Brookhart, 1994; O'Connor, 1995) if you have not already studied these issues in depth during your professional development efforts.

Scheduling Unit Events

By the time you reach this point in planning an integrated unit, you should have a good idea about students' learning outcomes, resources, instructional procedures, and evaluation procedures. The final step is to design a timetable of events. You need to decide the sequence of instruction, the order in which instructional procedures will occur.

Figure 2.5 shows a three-week calendar for an integrated unit on smoking. Seeing what is to be done each day helps you determine the feasibility of your plans. If your unit turns out to need three months, then you probably need to reduce it. Schedules also help determine how to overlap activities. For instance, you can plan to have students work in groups in one aspect of the unit while you confer with individuals about another aspect. Finally, a schedule of unit events helps organize your efforts, informing you about what lessons to plan and helping you monitor the pace of instruction. To be sure, your schedule might change once you begin a unit: a school assembly, fire drill, or power outage might disrupt a day's planned procedures; particular resources such as a video or guest speaker might not show up as scheduled; and students might accomplish tasks faster or slower than expected. Nevertheless, a schedule allows you to plan ahead and to accommodate unforeseen events.

Try It Out

Figures 2.6 through 2.9 present curriculum webs and schedules for two integrated units: *Space* for the primary grades and *Native Americans of the Southwest* for the middle grades. These plans, along with Figure 2.4 on *Smoking*, represent one way to depict integrated unit plans. They show finished products rather than what is produced at each step of the planning process.

Form small groups and plan an integrated unit by following the steps described in this section. Share your completed plan with other groups.

Monday	Tuesday	Wednesday	Thursday	Friday
Introduce unit. Brainstorm understandings, beliefs, and questions.	Continue general introduction. Introduce written commitment task. Demonstrate how to interview.	Introduce health risks. Produce life-size diagrams of human body.	Gather information about diseases. Begin small-group collaboration.	Present guest speaker. Continue gathering information about diseases.
Begin portraying smoking effects on diagram. Introduce government assistance and control.	Gather information about government and smoking. Continue working on diagram.	Finalize portrayals of smoking effects. Give quiz on smoking effects.	Continue gathering information about government and smoking.	Finalize letter explaining government's role in tobacco industry.
Introduce cigarette advertising.	Prepare ad scrapbook.	Produce written commitments. Finalize ad scrapbook.	Finalize written commitments. Finalize original ad.	Culminate unit. Share commitments.

Figure 2.5   Schedule for Unit on Smoking

INTERDISCIPLINARITY IS A SPECIAL FEATURE OF INTEGRATED UNITS

A feature worth adding to integrated units is *interdisciplinarity*. Interdisciplinary study brings together disciplines, or school subjects, such as science, social studies, mathematics, language arts, fine arts, and vocational arts. Interdisciplinarity adds subject matter to the mix of instructional features worth integrating. As the preceding section demonstrated, integrated units can occur within the confines of a single discipline. Interdisciplinary units go beyond subject matter confines.

Like integrated units, interdisciplinary units connect instruction. They link the various disciplines while exploring a particular topic, event, or novel. For instance, language arts, social studies, science, mathematics, and fine arts could

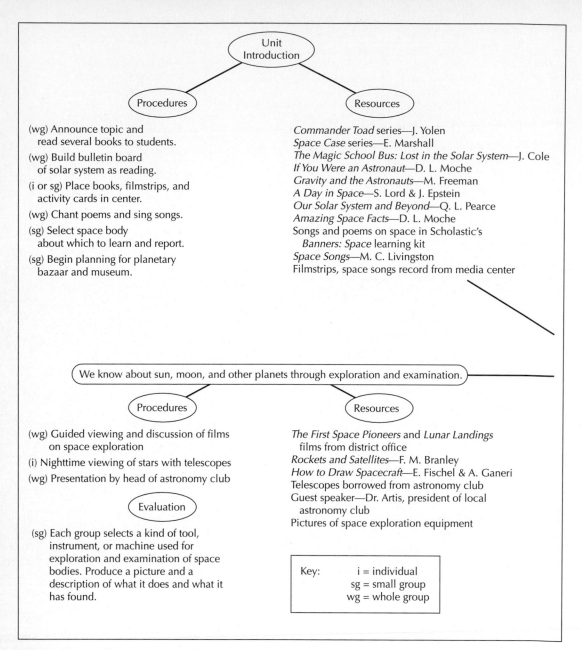

Figure 2.6 Primary-Grade Integrated Unit on Space

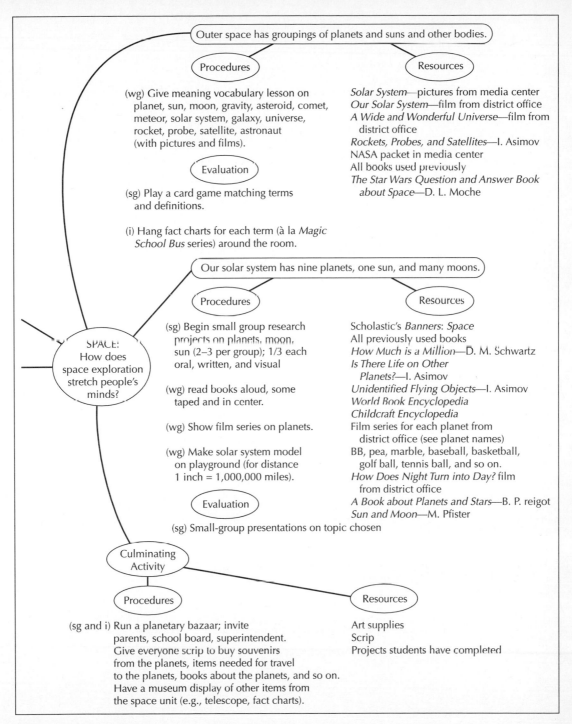

Outer space has groupings of planets and suns and other bodies.

Procedures

(wg) Give meaning vocabulary lesson on planet, sun, moon, gravity, asteroid, comet, meteor, solar system, galaxy, universe, rocket, probe, satellite, astronaut (with pictures and films).

Evaluation

(sg) Play a card game matching terms and definitions.

(i) Hang fact charts for each term (à la *Magic School Bus* series) around the room.

Resources

Solar System—pictures from media center
Our Solar System—film from district office
A Wide and Wonderful Universe—film from district office
Rockets, Probes, and Satellites—I. Asimov
NASA packet in media center
All books used previously
The Star Wars Question and Answer Book about Space—D. L. Moche

Our solar system has nine planets, one sun, and many moons.

SPACE: How does space exploration stretch people's minds?

Procedures

(sg) Begin small group research projects on planets, moon, sun (2–3 per group); 1/3 each oral, written, and visual

(wg) read books aloud, some taped and in center.

(wg) Show film series on planets.

(wg) Make solar system model on playground (for distance 1 inch = 1,000,000 miles).

Evaluation

(sg) Small-group presentations on topic chosen

Resources

Scholastic's *Banners: Space*
All previously used books
How Much is a Million—D. M. Schwartz
Is There Life on Other Planets?—I. Asimov
Unidentified Flying Objects—I. Asimov
World Book Encyclopedia
Childcraft Encyclopedia
Film series for each planet from district office (see planet names)
BB, pea, marble, baseball, basketball, golf ball, tennis ball, and so on.
How Does Night Turn into Day? film from district office
A Book about Planets and Stars—B. P. reigot
Sun and Moon—M. Pfister

Culminating Activity

Procedures

(sg and i) Run a planetary bazaar; invite parents, school board, superintendent. Give everyone scrip to buy souvenirs from the planets, items needed for travel to the planets, books about the planets, and so on. Have a museum display of other items from the space unit (e.g., telescope, fact charts).

Resources

Art supplies
Scrip
Projects students have completed

Figure 2.6 *Continued*

Monday	Tuesday	Wednesday	Thursday	Friday
Introduce Space unit. Read books throughout day. Sing songs. Read poems. Introduce science center. Explain planetary bazaar.	Introduce Space unit. Read throughout day. Sing songs. Read poems. Start bulletin board (add to as can).	Introduce Space unit. Read throughout day. Sing songs. Read poems. Choose space body for report.	Meaning vocabulary lesson. Show *Solar System* pictures. Show *Our Solar System* film. Continue reading.	Meaning vocabulary lesson. Show *Solar System* pictures. Show *Wide/ Wonderful Universe* film. Continue reading. Play card game to practice terms.
Meaning vocabulary lesson. Show *Solar System* pictures. Use pictures and information in NASA space packet. Continue reading. Construct and hang fact charts.	Show *Sun* film. Read books and parts of encyclopedias. Visual display by small group.	Continue to read. Oral report by small group.	Continue to read. Written report by small group.	Show *Earth* film. Visual display by small group. Make solar system model on playground with balls to show distances and proportional sizes.
Show *Moon* film. Oral report by small group. Show *How Does Night Turn into Day?* film.	Written report by small group. Plan for bazaar and museum.	Visual display by small group. Prepare materials for planetary bazaar and museum.	Oral report by small group. Prepare materials for planetary bazaar and museum.	Show *Jupiter* film. Written report by small group. Prepare materials for planetary bazaar and museum.
Visual display by small group. Prepare materials for bazaar and museum.	Oral report by small group. Prepare materials for bazaar and museum.	Show *1st Space Pioneers* film. Evening: View stars with telescopes.	Show *Lunar Landings* film. Select tool and so on for research. Make pictures and one-paragraph report of tool.	Culminate unit. Hold planetary bazaar and museum. Guest speaker. Display pictures, reports, and so on.

Figure 2.7   Schedule for Unit on Space

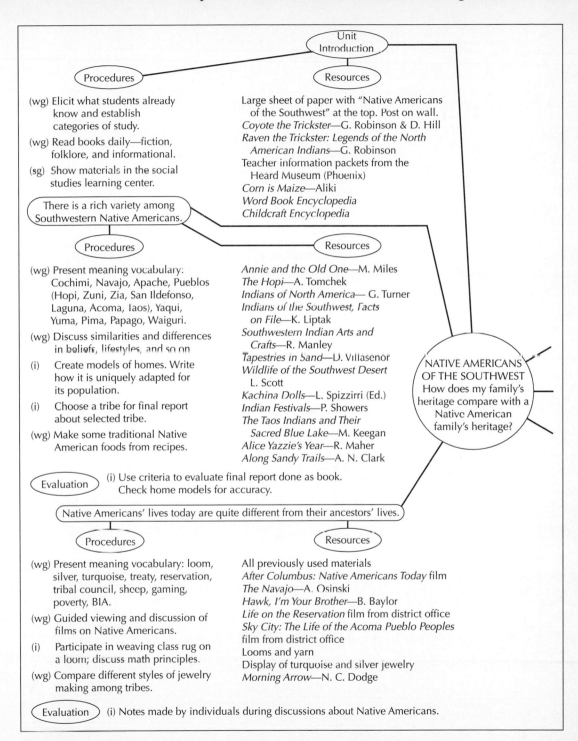

Unit Introduction

Procedures

(wg) Elicit what students already know and establish categories of study.

(wg) Read books daily—fiction, folklore, and informational.

(sg) Show materials in the social studies learning center.

Resources

Large sheet of paper with "Native Americans of the Southwest" at the top. Post on wall.
Coyote the Trickster—G. Robinson & D. Hill
Raven the Trickster: Legends of the North American Indians—G. Robinson
Teacher information packets from the Heard Museum (Phoenix)
Corn is Maize—Aliki
Word Book Encyclopedia
Childcraft Encyclopedia

There is a rich variety among Southwestern Native Americans.

Procedures

(wg) Present meaning vocabulary: Cochimi, Navajo, Apache, Pueblos (Hopi, Zuni, Zia, San Ildefonso, Laguna, Acoma, Taos), Yaqui, Yuma, Pima, Papago, Waiguri.

(wg) Discuss similarities and differences in beliefs, lifestyles, and so on.

(i)   Create models of homes. Write how it is uniquely adapted for its population.

(i)   Choose a tribe for final report about selected tribe.

(wg) Make some traditional Native American foods from recipes.

Resources

Annie and the Old One—M. Miles
The Hopi—A. Tomchek
Indians of North America— G. Turner
Indians of the Southwest, Facts on File—K. Liptak
Southwestern Indian Arts and Crafts—R. Manley
Tapestries in Sand—D. Villasenor
Wildlife of the Southwest Desert L. Scott
Kachina Dolls—L. Spizzirri (Ed.)
Indian Festivals—P. Showers
The Taos Indians and Their Sacred Blue Lake—M. Keegan
Alice Yazzie's Year—R. Maher
Along Sandy Trails—A. N. Clark

NATIVE AMERICANS OF THE SOUTHWEST How does my family's heritage compare with a Native American family's heritage?

Evaluation   (i) Use criteria to evaluate final report done as book. Check home models for accuracy.

Native Americans' lives today are quite different from their ancestors' lives.

Procedures

(wg) Present meaning vocabulary: loom, silver, turquoise, treaty, reservation, tribal council, sheep, gaming, poverty, BIA.

(wg) Guided viewing and discussion of films on Native Americans.

(i)   Participate in weaving class rug on a loom; discuss math principles.

(wg) Compare different styles of jewelry making among tribes.

Resources

All previously used materials
After Columbus: Native Americans Today film
The Navajo—A. Osinski
Hawk, I'm Your Brother—B. Baylor
Life on the Reservation film from district office
Sky City: The Life of the Acoma Pueblo Peoples film from district office
Looms and yarn
Display of turquoise and silver jewelry
Morning Arrow—N. C. Dodge

Evaluation   (i) Notes made by individuals during discussions about Native Americans.

Figure 2.8   Intermediate-Grade Integrated Unit on Native Americans of the Southwest

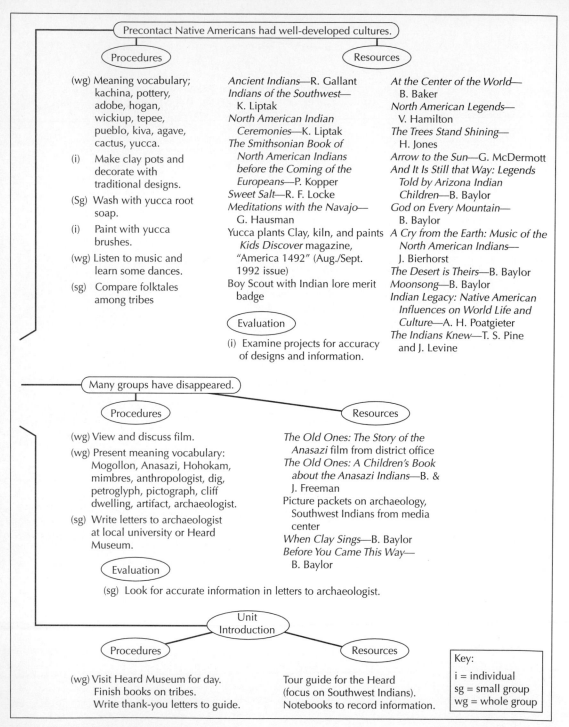

Precontact Native Americans had well-developed cultures.

Procedures

(wg) Meaning vocabulary; kachina, pottery, adobe, hogan, wickiup, tepee, pueblo, kiva, agave, cactus, yucca.

(i) Make clay pots and decorate with traditional designs.

(Sg) Wash with yucca root soap.

(i) Paint with yucca brushes.

(wg) Listen to music and learn some dances.

(sg) Compare folktales among tribes

Resources

Ancient Indians—R. Gallant
Indians of the Southwest— K. Liptak
North American Indian Ceremonies—K. Liptak
The Smithsonian Book of North American Indians before the Coming of the Europeans—P. Kopper
Sweet Salt—R. F. Locke
Meditations with the Navajo— G. Hausman
Yucca plants Clay, kiln, and paints
Kids Discover magazine, "America 1492" (Aug./Sept. 1992 issue)
Boy Scout with Indian lore merit badge

At the Center of the World— B. Baker
North American Legends— V. Hamilton
The Trees Stand Shining— H. Jones
Arrow to the Sun—G. McDermott
And It Is Still that Way: Legends Told by Arizona Indian Children—B. Baylor
God on Every Mountain— B. Baylor
A Cry from the Earth: Music of the North American Indians— J. Bierhorst
The Desert is Theirs—B. Baylor
Moonsong—B. Baylor
Indian Legacy: Native American Influences on World Life and Culture—A. H. Poatgieter
The Indians Knew—T. S. Pine and J. Levine

Evaluation

(i) Examine projects for accuracy of designs and information.

Many groups have disappeared.

Procedures

(wg) View and discuss film.

(wg) Present meaning vocabulary: Mogollon, Anasazi, Hohokam, mimbres, anthropologist, dig, petroglyph, pictograph, cliff dwelling, artifact, archaeologist.

(sg) Write letters to archaeologist at local university or Heard Museum.

Resources

The Old Ones: The Story of the Anasazi film from district office
The Old Ones: A Children's Book about the Anasazi Indians—B. & J. Freeman
Picture packets on archaeology, Southwest Indians from media center
When Clay Sings—B. Baylor
Before You Came This Way— B. Baylor

Evaluation

(sg) Look for accurate information in letters to archaeologist.

Unit Introduction

Procedures

(wg) Visit Heard Museum for day.
Finish books on tribes.
Write thank-you letters to guide.

Resources

Tour guide for the Heard (focus on Southwest Indians).
Notebooks to record information.

Key:
i = individual
sg = small group
wg = whole group

Figure 2.8   *Continued*

Monday	Tuesday	Wednesday	Thursday	Friday
Introduce unit. Show pictures. Show map. Read passage from informational packet.	Introduce unit. Brainstorm knowledge. Browse and free read.	Introduce unit. Brainstorm knowledge. Share learning objectives. Browse and free read.	Meaning vocabulary: Southwest tribes. Emphasize similarities and differences among groups as shown in movie.	Choose a tribe/ group to study and report in book form. Begin collecting information from classroom resources.
Meaning vocabulary: Precontact cultures and artifacts. Illustrate and plan construction of models of homes and cultural artifacts.	Read folktales aloud. Construct models of homes and cultural artifacts.	Monitor tribe/ group reports. Perform traditional dances.	Read folktales aloud. Construct models of homes and cultural artifacts.	Display models of homes. Cook traditional recipes.
Meaning vocabulary: Extinct groups. Read folktales aloud.	Compare folktales. Construct cultural artifacts.	Meaning vocabulary: modern and ancient lives. Monitor tribe-group reports.	Watch movie and orally compare differences in modern and ancient lives. Plan letter to archaeologist.	Display artifacts (pots, rugs). Cook traditional foods from recipes.
Submit letter to archaeologist.	Plan questions and observations for museum visit.	Monitor tribe-group reports.	Culminate unit. Visit museum.	Culminate unit. Write thank-you letters to museum guide. Share books on tribes

Figure 2.9 Schedule for Unit on Native Americans of the Southwest

be readily connected about the topic of tobacco smoking. Students could critique and produce cigarette advertisements for language arts, research legislation for smoke-free areas for social studies, study the physical effects of smoking for science, determine the percentage of full-page magazine ads devoted to cigarettes for mathematics, and produce a musical or visual statement related to smoking for fine arts.

Planning wheels are useful graphic aids for producing an overview of interdisciplinary units (Palmer, 1991). Teachers of self-contained classes can use them to ensure balanced treatment of all the disciplines they cover. Teachers who are part of interdisciplinary teams, such as those found in most middle schools and in many high schools, can use these wheels to initiate joint planning.

As Figure 2.10 shows, a unit's organizing center is written in the hub of the wheel, and general unit objectives are placed in the pie-shaped, discipline-designated sections connected to the hub. The number of sections about the hub can change as organizing centers change. By providing a good overview of instructional experiences planned for a group of students, this graphic planning tool allows you to identify appropriate connections. Planning wheels help organize discipline-specific objectives for interdisciplinary units. Once you have these objectives, you work backwards generating resources, procedures, evaluations, and a schedule just as you would for an integrated unit.

The decisions involved in planning integrated interdisciplinary units might seem intimidating, but your concerns will lessen when you actually begin preparations. One way to reduce any anxiety is to remember that planning is an ongoing repetitive process. It does not occur overnight. Addi-

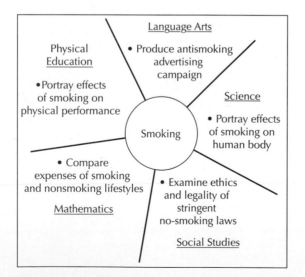

Figure 2.10   Planning Wheel for Interdisciplinary Unit on Smoking

tionally, you often have access to plans produced by others. Previously designed units, district curriculum guides, commercial teaching materials, and plans available on the Internet are good beginnings for your own instruction. And as noted before, students can and should participate in the planning process. You might identify an organizing center, then enlist your class in producing central questions, culminating activities, unit objectives, resources, and procedures. One teacher we know asks her primary-grade students what they want to learn during the year. The web they construct guides her interdisciplinary instruction in science and social studies throughout the year.

Additionally, teachers employ integrated interdisciplinary units to various degrees. Some integrate all features of instruction all year long, whereas others present traditional as well as integrated instruction. Elementary teachers sometimes offer traditional instructional routines in spelling while integrating language arts, social studies, science, and fine arts. Some units might include all the major disciplines; others might not. Secondary teachers often integrate their instruction in certain classes but not in others. A social studies teacher might collaborate with an English teacher to offer two American studies classes per day yet teach drama in a more traditional manner. And some might combine instruction for one month and not another.

Try It Out

Produce an overview of an interdisciplinary integrated unit using a planning wheel. Include at least three content areas in the plan.

LITERACY ACTIVITIES ARE LINKED TO CLASSROOM GROUPING PRACTICES

When planning instructional units, effective teachers use assorted grouping practices to bring students together with content reading materials. Common groupings consist of whole-class, small-group, and individual situations (Pardo & Raphael, 1991). As noted in Chapter 1, students who move among such groupings participate actively in their learning because they have multiple approaches to unit objectives. Understanding the distinctive opportunities provided by each practice contributes to effective decision making. This section describes opportunities for literacy learning that each grouping practice emphasizes.

Whole Class

Most of the administrative procedures associated with schooling (e.g., taking attendance) and instruction (e.g., informing students of your plans and expectations) occur with the whole class. Disseminating ideas for common knowledge through lectures, video presentations, guest speaker presentations, and so on also typically occurs in this setting. Whole-class instruction allows you to expose everyone to information in the shortest possible time.

When students meet as a whole class, they share common experiences. For instance, teachers typically introduce units of study as well as lessons to the whole class. They engage students in the upcoming materials. The following describes whole-class activities best suited for promoting students' literacy.

Introducing New Concepts and Strategies   You generally assemble the whole class when presenting concepts and strategies for the first time. If unit plans call for producing brochures on particular locations, then you would present introductory information about the places to the entire class. If the plans stipulate that students obtain information from the Internet and from interviews with adults to produce their brochures, then you probably would demonstrate and explain to the entire class how to accomplish these activities. Next, students would carry out these activities individually and possibly in small groups.

Promoting Materials   Promoting materials so students will want to read is an important part of instruction done with whole classes. You can display posters, book jackets, and other enticements to attract students to materials in the classroom. These displays change as the unit of study changes.

In order to inform students about the contents of selected materials and hook them on the idea of reading, you can present book talks. These are sales pitches where you describe the books, connecting their contents with the unit of study, and point out their noteworthy parts. Present information about the author and describe similarities between other books. You might summarize the beginning of a passage or read a portion of it aloud in a manner similar to priming a pump: The passage gets students started so the reading flows easily.

Reading Aloud   Listening to well-crafted English read well orally allows class members to be carried away by the magic of the spoken word (Trelease, 1990). Listening also presents content for units of instruction. For instance, as someone reads *The Witch of Blackbird Pond*, students can vicariously experience Hannah's and Kit's adventures while learning about the Puritans' disdain for outsiders. Students can concentrate on the ideas of the passage, forming especially vivid images and encountering new vocabulary. Students thereby come in contact with materials they might otherwise miss due to a passage's difficulty.

Reading aloud can occur in many forms. You can initially select materials and read them to the class. The material can be a short story, a poem, a novel, or a compelling piece of nonfiction. Students might then perform the reading as part of an exercise in dramatization or oral interpretation. Sitting in an author's chair, a designated seat for student writers, individuals might read aloud what they have produced (Graves, 1983). To close the day's read aloud session, students might share what they liked best about the portion they heard, ask questions, and predict what will happen next.

Culminating Activities   Whole-class configurations also are the norm for culminating activities. Student presentations such as sharings of group and individual projects often occur with the whole class as the audience. Closing a unit, a lesson, and a day typically occur when all students are facing the teacher. This allows opportunities for everyone to reflect on what they have learned, fill in gaps, crystallize new understandings, and gain a sense of closure and accomplishment.

Whole-class activities have many uses, but overusing any one grouping practice precludes active classroom settings. As already noted, whole-class activities should be balanced with small-group and individual ones.

Small Group

Small groups promote peer interaction and support. The low numbers of students (from 2 to 8) in small groups offer settings that favor interpersonal relations more than whole-class settings. Cooperative learning principles contribute substantially to small-group interactions and the formation of communities of learners (Johnson, Johnson, & Holubec, 1994; Slavin, 1995). Small-group activities also enhance students' opportunities to assume greater control of their learning. The following describes three literacy-related activities well suited for small groups.

Responding to Books   Small-group activities where students talk about what they read go by names such as *book clubs* (McMahon & Raphael, 1994), *literature study groups* (Gilles, 1989; Keegan & Shrake, 1991), and *literature circles* (Simpson, 1995). Here we refer to this concept as *book study groups* because we want to open the door to nonfiction as well as fiction.

The photo on page 58 shows students in a book study group. One child begins a conversation about a book and others join in. This group has formed a community of readers. The children know how to talk about the book partly because their teacher has demonstrated such conversations several times and has specified guidelines for them. Those who have not read the book question the reader and react to ideas in order to develop their subject matter knowledge.

The books selected for study groups relate to the unit of study. All participants can select the same book to read and talk about, or individuals can select their own titles. Group members can share their reactions two days a week, a chapter at a time, or at other designated points. Additionally, the group members might evaluate themselves according to how well their group interacted and how well they learned new knowledge.

Collaborating on Activities   Along with book study groups, individuals collaborate in small groups to accomplish projects. To illustrate, they work together dramatizing what they read, gathering timeline information for a particular era, and completing activity packets or study guides. They brainstorm what individuals might say in a writing activity, then react to the person's rough draft.

Children in a book study group.

Small-group members also concentrate on reading strategies. They might participate in reciprocal teaching (Palincsar, 1994) by conversing about their predictions, summaries, clarifications, and questions of passage contents. Sometimes individuals form pairs, or study buddies, and take turns orally reading and interpreting difficult passages. Again, these activities probably would be introduced and culminated during whole-class meetings. The literacy-related activities are performed in small groups due to the opportunities for active participation and support.

Participating in Minilessons   Teachers often join small groups to conduct brief lessons, called minilessons. Minilessons help group members accomplish something that requires special help. For instance, individuals in the group might need help planning what to write, maintaining focus while writing, or using descriptive language. If the need fit a group more than the whole class, then that is where the instruction would occur. Moreover, if a group takes on a complex exercise that no others do (e.g, presenting a readers' theater production), then a minilesson on that exercise is presented only to the group.

Individual

Individual learning activities offer students opportunities to follow personal interests and goals. Enabling students to work alone—in the company of others—also allows them to reflect on new concepts and strategies and provide information on learning progress. Some literacy-oriented activities appropriate for individuals are as follows.

Reading Self-Selected Materials   When students participate in units of instruction, they can locate and read materials by themselves that address organizing centers. Once students know how to access materials available through reference lists such as card catalogs, online catalogs, and Internet search engines, they can obtain their own materials for specific information about academic topics. They also can select topic-related books for sustained reading and response. In this situation, teachers frequently offer a list of suitable possibilities or require approval of what students locate independently. Students then might share responses to their books with adults in one-to-one conferences, with classmates in small-group settings, or with the whole class.

Teachers often provide class time for students to read self-selected materials. One way to accomplish this in an era of crowded curriculums is to have students read on their own when they finish assigned tasks. However, many teachers provide reading opportunities by setting aside a certain time on certain days for reading. Students may not work on assignments, and teachers may not grade papers. A substantial value of teachers reading silently is the model it presents. Rather than telling students about the value of reading, teachers who silently read to themselves demonstrate the value. Teachers who show themselves to be readers walk the walk.

Reading time frequently is scheduled immediately after breaks in the day, such as before or after lunch or when classes change, because reading tends to

Younger students enjoy time to read a good book.

calm young people. Students might remain in their seats during this time; however, they also might go to an attractive designated free-reading area. A specific time is set, from 5 to 20 minutes, and students are held to it. If some form of accountability is required beyond what the shared responses or numbers of books completed offer, teachers can record the amount of time spent reading.

Accomplishing Projects and Assignments   Individuals can interact with learning materials on their own terms when they work alone. Most individual activities involve composing a product through writing or art, although other outcomes certainly could be appropriate. Students might complete think sheets, or study guides, as well as numerous composition forms such as letters, diaries, posters, and brochures.

Maintaining journals about what has been read is a powerful way for individuals to interact with materials. The reading materials could be selected for the whole class, small group, or the individual, but the journal entries would be produced only by individuals. Recording personal responses to what has been read allows learners to express their ideas in a nonthreatening manner, explore what is unclear, and control examinations of what they read.

Participating in Evaluations   Perhaps the most promising literacy evaluations come from individuals' ongoing reading and writing in the context of daily interactions. Many opportunities exist during the school day to observe and document individual students' literacy strategies and subject learnings. For instance, teachers who confer with individuals about what they are reading record impressions of the students' competencies. Samples of individuals' writing plans, rough drafts, and polished work are gathered. Students reflect on their own literacy performances and preferences. The amount of reading accomplished in a certain time period is recorded. Completed study guides and worksheets are saved. All this information can be stored in individuals' portfolios to chart progress and final attainments.

Listen/Look and Learn

Vist a class and observe approximately three content area lessons. Describe the grouping practices that were used and the literacy activities that occurred during each grouping. Which grouping practices and literacy activities were most frequent? Which were least frequent? What could be done to utilize the practices and activities that were not utilized?

Looking Back

Teachers plan integrated and interdisciplinary units and various grouping patterns to offer effective classroom settings. They plan integrated units that incorporate subject matter with language arts, grouping patterns, and personal experiences. They also add several disciplines to the mix during integrated interdisciplinary units. They use whole-class, small-group, and individual grouping patterns to encourage active participation. You encountered four key ideas in this chapter: (1) Integrated units combine numerous aspects of instruction; (2) planning integrated units involves many decisions; (3) interdisciplinarity is a special feature of integrated units; and (4) literacy activities are linked to classroom grouping practices.

Add to Your Journal

Record in your class journal your reactions to this chapter. What integrated units have you experienced? What were their strengths and limitations? What were their similarities and differences? What experiences have you had with interdisciplinary units? How do you plan on implementing them in your teaching and why? What do you think of varying classroom grouping practices?

REFERENCES

BROOKHART, S. M. (1994). Teachers' grading: Practice and theory. *Applied Measurement in Education, 7*, 279–301.

CLARK, C. M., & PETERSON, P. L. (1986). Teachers' thought processes. In M. C. Wittrock (Ed.), *Handbook of research on teaching* (3rd ed.) (pp. 255–296). New York: Macmillan.

COSTA, A. L. (1991). *Developing minds* (rev. ed.). Alexandria, VA: Association for Supervision and Curriculum Development.

GARDNER, H. (1991). *The unschooled mind: How children think and how schools should teach.* New York: Basic Books.

GILLES, C. (1989). Reading, writing, and talking: Using literature study groups. *English Journal, 78*, 38–41.

GRAVES, D. (1983). *Writing: Teachers and children at work.* Exeter, NH: Heinemann.

JOHNSON, D. W., JOHNSON, R. T., & HOLUBEC, E. J. (1994). *The new circles of literacy: Cooperation in the classroom and school.* Alexandria, VA: Association for Supervision and Curriculum Development.

KEEGAN, S., & SHRAKE, K. (1991). Literature study groups: An alternative to ability grouping. *The Reading Teacher, 44*, 542–547.

LAZEAR, D. G. (1992). *Teaching for multiple intelligences* (Phi Delta Kappa Fastback #342). Bloominton, IN: Phi Delta Kappa Educational Foundation.

MAEROFF, G. I. (1991). Assessing alternative assessment. *Phi Delta Kappan, 73*, 272–281.

MCMAHON, S. I., & RAPHAEL, T. E. (1994). Book club: An alternative framework for reading instruction. *The Reading Teacher, 48*, 102–117.

O'CONNOR, K. (1995). Guidelines for grading that support learning and student success. *NASSP Bulletin, 79*, 91–101.

ONOSKO, J. J. (1992). An approach to designing thoughtful units. *The Social Studies, 83*, 193–196.

PALINCSAR, A. (1994). Reciprocal teaching. In A. C. Purves (Ed.), *Encyclopedia of English studies and language arts*, Vol. 2 (pp. 1020–1021). New York: Scholastic.

PALMER, J. M. (1991). Planning wheels turn curriculum around. *Educational Leadership, 49,* 57–60.

PARDO, L. S., & RAPHAEL, T. E. (1991). Classroom organization for instruction in content areas. *The Reading Teacher, 44,* 556–565.

PERKINS, D. (1992). *Smart schools: From training memories to educating minds.* New York: The Free Press.

SILVA, C., & DELGADO-LAROCCO, E. L. (1993). Facilitating learning through interconnection: A concept approach to core literature units. *Language Arts, 70,* 469–474.

SIMPSON, A. (1995). Not the class novel: A different reading program. *Journal of Reading, 38,* 290–294.

SLAVIN, R. E. (1995). *Cooperative learning: Theory, research, and practice* (2nd ed.). Boston: Allyn & Bacon.

SMITH, J. L., & JOHNSON, H. (1993). Bringing it together: Literature in an integrative curriculum. *Middle School Journal, 25*(1), 3–7.

SMITH, J. L., & JOHNSON, H. (1994). Models for implementing literature in content studies. *The Reading Teacher, 48,* 198–209.

STEVENSON, C., & CARR, J. F. (1993). Integrated studies planning framework. In C. Stevenson & J. F. Carr (Eds.), *Integrated studies in the middle grades: "Dancing through walls"* (pp. 26–39). New York: Teachers College Press.

STIGGINS, R. J. (1994). *Student-centered classroom assessment.* New York: Merrill.

SYLWESTER, R. (1995). *A celebration of neurons: An educator's guide to the human brain.* Alexandria, VA: Association for Supervision and Curriculum Development.

TRELEASE, J. (1990). *The new read aloud handbook.* New York: Penguin.

VARS, G. F. (1991). Integrated curriculum in historical perspective. *Educational Leadership, 49,* 14–15.

WIGGINS, G. (1993). *Assessing student performance: Exploring the purpose and limits of testing.* San Francisco: Jossey-Bass.

ADDITIONAL READINGS

The following present convincing rationales for integrating subject matter and language arts instruction.

ANDERS, P. L., & PRITCHARD, T. G. (1993). Integrated language curriculum and instruction in the middle grades. *Elementary School Journal, 93,* 611–624.

LIPSON, M. Y., VALENCIA, S. W., WIXSON, K. K., & PETERS, C. W. (1993). Integration and thematic teaching: Integration to improve teaching and learning. *Language Arts, 70,* 252–263.

McCARTHEY, S. J., CORMAN, L., & NORDIN, A. (1996). Building a community of learners: Team-teaching interdisciplinary units in multiage classrooms. *Language Arts, 73,* 395–401.

SHUELL, T. J. (1993). Toward an integrated theory of teaching and learning. *Educational Psychologist, 28,* 291–312.

Descriptions of integrated units that include—but do not emphasize—reading and writing are found in the following:

ARNOLD, J. (1990). *Visions of teaching and learning: Eighty exemplary middle level projects.* Columbus, OH: National Middle Level Association. [Note: this reference outlines units; it does not offer fully developed descriptions.]

FOGARTY, R. (1991). *The mindful school: How to integrate the curriculum.* Palatine, IL: Skylight.

JACOBS, H. H. (Ed.). (1989). *Interdisciplinary curriculum: Design and implementation.* Alexandria, VA: Association for Supervision and Curriculum Development.

KATZ, L. G., & CHARD, S. C. (1990). *Engaging children's minds: The project approach.* Norwood, NJ: Ablex.

MITCHELL, R., WILLIS, M., & THE CHICAGO TEACHERS UNION QUEST CENTER (1995). *Learning in overdrive: Designing curriculum, instruction, and standards, A manual for teachers.* Golden, CO: North American Press.

PATE, E., HOMESTEAD, E., & McGINNIS, K. (1997). *Making integrated curriculum work.* New York: Teachers College Press.

STEVENSON, C., & CARR, J. F. (Eds.) (1993). *Integrated studies in the middle grades: "Dancing through walls."* New York: Teachers College Press.

VARS, G. F. (1993). *Interdisciplinary teaching in the middle grades: Why and how.* Columbus, OH: National Middle School Association.

WIGGINTON, E. (1985). *Sometimes a shining moment: The Foxfire experience.* Garden City, NY: Anchor Press/Doubleday.

WIGGINTON, E., AND HIS STUDENTS (1991). *Foxfire: 25 years.* New York: Doubleday.

Descriptions of integrated units that emphasize reading and writing are found in the following publications listed below according to general grade levels.

Lower Grades

GAMBERG, R., AND OTHERS, WITH GAIL EDWARDS. (1988). *Learning and loving it: Theme studies in the classroom.* Portsmouth, NH: Heinemann.

THAISS, C. (1986). *Language across the curriculum in the elementary grades.* Urbana, IL: Clearinghouse on Reading and Communication Skills and the National Council of Teachers of English.

WALMSLEY, S. (1994). *Children exploring their world: Theme teaching in elementary school.* Portsmouth, NH: Heinemann.

Upper Grades

ATWELL, N. (1987). *In the middle: Writing, reading, and learning with adolescents.* Portsmouth, NH: Boynton/Cook.

RIEF, L. (1992). *Seeking diversity: Language arts with adolescents.* Portsmouth, NH: Heinemann.

Most read-aloud sessions consist of fiction. This article presents a compelling case for balancing reading aloud with nonfiction and presents a starter set of appropriate books:

DOIRON, R. (1994). Using nonfiction in a read-aloud program: Letting the facts speak for themselves. *The Reading Teacher, 47,* 616–624.

The first two articles listed below present students' thoughts on curricular integration; the third report presents upper-grade students' thoughts on whole-class and small-group discussions:

MANSFIELD, B. (1989). Students' perceptions of an integrated unit. *The Social Studies, 80*(4), 135–141.

PATE, P. E., HOMESTEAD, E., & MCGINNIS, K. (1994). Middle school students' perceptions of integrated curriculum. *Middle School Journal, 26*(2), 21–23.

ALVERMANN, D. E., YOUNG, J. P., WEAVER, D., HINCHMAN, K. A., MOORE, D. W., PHELPS, S. F., THRASH, E. C., & ZALEWSKI, P. (1996). Middle- and high-school students' perceptions of how they experience text-based discussions: A multicase study. *Reading Research Quarterly, 31,* 244–267.

Concept-oriented reading instruction (CORI) is a promising framework for integrating language arts and subject matter instruction. John T. Guthrie, who originated this approach, has reported descriptions and outcomes of CORI in the following publications:

GUTHRIE, J. T. (1996). Educational contexts for engagement in literacy. *The Reading Teacher, 49,* 432–445.

GUTHRIE, J. T., MCGOUGH, K. BENNETT, L., & RICE, M. E. (1996). Concept-oriented reading instruction: An integrated curriculum to develop motivations and strategies for reading. In L. Baker, P. Afflerbach, & D. Reinking (Eds.), *Developing engaged readers in school and home communities* (pp. 165–190). Mahwah, NJ: Erlbaum.

GUTHRIE, J. T., VAN METER, P., MCCANN, A. D., WIGFIELD, A., BENNETT, L., POUNDSTONE, C. C., RICE, M. E., FAIBISCH, F. M., HUNT, B., & MITCHELL, A. N. (1996). Growth of literacy engagement: Changes in motivations and strategies during concept-oriented reading instruction. *Reading Research Quarterly, 31,* 306–332.

The following are good presentations of central questions, called essential questions by those affiliated with Theodore Sizer's Coalition of Essential Schools.

Asking the essential questions. (1993, June). *Horace, 5*(5). (Available from the Coalition of Essential Schools, Box 1938, Brown University, Providence, RI 02912).

JORGENSEN, C. M. (1994–1995). Essential questions—inclusive answers. *Educational Leadership, 52*(4), 52–55.

chapter 3

Reading Materials, Reports, and Responses

Looking Ahead

Students deserve access to diverse print and nonprint materials in order to promote the subject matter and literacy learning expected today. Students who regularly use brochures, encyclopedias, periodicals, telecommunications, informational library books, and textbooks have an advantage over those who rely on a single source of information. These materials can foster advanced thinking as well as positive values in our multicultural society. Having access to various reading materials should be complemented by receiving opportunities to report on and respond to these materials in various ways. Students who produce collages, bring to class representative objects, dramatize scenes, and write and talk about what they are reading have an advantage over those who react only one way.

As Chapter 2 noted, planning and implementing instructional units can be compared to a journey. You and your students traverse new terrain. When you are on tour, you might travel by car using different types of roads. You might use freeways, divided and undivided highways, residential streets, and unpaved trails. These roads serve different functions while allowing you to explore and learn about the area. Similarly, you and your students have access to many paths during subject matter study. For example, when you use print, you might employ library books, magazines, newspapers, computer technology, and textbooks.

Think of traveling through your state via different types of roads. Freeways get you through the territory quickly and efficiently. Freeway planners did not design routes to show off the surroundings or develop people's thinking but to move people through the area with maximum speed. Freeways traverse only a small part of the territory within your state; if you want to get to a special area of interest—such as a small town, a lake, a state park, or a historical site—you most likely would use a freeway for only part of your trip. A freeway might speed your journey to a certain point, but it will rarely take you directly to where you want to go. Even when you arrive at a major city, freeways whisk you around on a perimeter belt loop or shoot you through the city (unless it is rush hour!), revealing only a few outstanding landmarks.

Traditional content area textbooks are like freeways. They may get you through a lot of territory, but they move you so quickly that you are unable to obtain close, personal insights about the area. In order to genuinely know an area, you need to get off the freeway and travel the connecting roads. The connecting roads of subject matter study are such print forms as library books, magazines, newspapers, and computer software. These avenues allow you and your students to explore an area more thoroughly, make decisions about the side routes you want to take, and obtain personal meanings from your journey. They provide multiple avenues to learning.

This chapter, which introduces content area reading materials and ways to react to them, contains three key ideas:

1. Students deserve a variety of content area reading materials.
2. A variety of content area reading materials is available.
3. Report and response projects take many forms.

STUDENTS DESERVE A VARIETY OF CONTENT AREA READING MATERIALS

Students ought to have the opportunity to exit subject matter freeways and travel the connecting roads. Students deserve a variety of content area reading materials for at least seven reasons: (a) depth of information, (b) motivation to read, (c) distinctive points of view, (d) recency of information, (e) materials that fit reading competencies, (f) sense of ownership, and (g) opportunities for a range of thinking.

Depth of Information

A major reason for providing students access to many reading materials during subject matter study is to deepen understandings. Reliance on a single source of information can lead to superficial knowledge. Think of how a typical middle-school social studies textbook presents the ancient Greeks. The textbook probably devotes ten to twenty pages to such topics as Greek mythology, government, social order, culture, art, architecture, warfare, and overall influ-ence on modern life. The text most likely gives passing mention to landmarks such as Zeus, Aesop, Homer, Plato, and Alexander; to Athens, Sparta, and Macedonia; and to city-states, democracies, and republics. This is quite a lot of ground to cover in only ten pages, but the Roman Empire comes next, and it, too, has several noteworthy features that must be covered.

But now think of library books and magazine articles on ancient Greece. For instance, *Gods, Men, and Monsters from the Greek Myths* (Gibson, 1982) takes 152 pages to describe only one aspect of ancient Greek life: mythology. This book con-tains a full account of the exploits of the mythical characters, memorable graphics depicting scenes from the various myths, a chart depicting the relationships and roles of the gods, and an index. Prometheus, Apollo, Jason, Helios, and others come alive in this book. Such a carefully detailed, well-crafted treatment of a topic is not possible in a textbook because textbooks must cover too many topics.

To further appreciate the differences between the depth available in tradi-tional textbooks and well-written library books, think back to what you learned in this text about the organize and connect thinking processes. Remem-ber that good readers arrange information into categories and good readers form associations between what they already know and what a passage con-tains. Likewise, good writers enable readers to apprehend the organization of a passage and make connections (Graves et al., 1991); good writers do not pro-duce baskets of facts. Successful authors are well aware of the pitfalls of typical textbook writing, so they make organizing and connecting seem effortless. Returning to ancient Greek mythology, consider how good writers might orga-nize and connect this information for their readers.

Organizing Information   A typical middle-school social studies textbook might mention Greek myths in a paragraph on festivals in ancient Greece. The text might point out that Herodotus, the first historian, shared his knowledge through public speaking; that many theaters were dedicated to Dionysius, the god of festivals; and that in these theaters myths were occasionally acted out. The next paragraph might shift to a discussion of the early Greek thinkers: Socrates, Plato, and Aristotle. Such a treatment of mythology is not well-orga-nized. The fact that the ancient Greeks retold myths could just as easily have been inserted into the presentation of the Acropolis and the Parthenon. Stu-dents thus face an assortment of isolated facts that need to be organized into some type of system that the author did not provide.

On the other hand, the writer of a book that might be found in a school library has many opportunities to point out the relationships among ideas. Two books of myths, *Wings* (Yolen, 1991) and *Persephone and the Pomegranate: A Myth from Greece* (Waldherr, 1993), exemplify solid organization. These books include only the myths that center on each main character, Daedalus and Persephone. One personality ties together the numerous stories in each book. Mythology can appear fragmented and disconnected, but order is imposed by using single main characters as unifying elements. The information is arranged in such a way that readers do not need to impose an organizational scheme of their own.

Connecting Information   Learners who connect information tie together already learned information with the new information being presented. Learners link what they already know to what they are trying to learn. Writers help readers make connections by reminding their audience of what they already know, then comparing that knowledge with new facts and generalizations.

Textbook writers rarely are able to suggest connections for readers, whereas writers of content area trade books usually have enough space for this. They can call up direct experiences for readers: science writers might connect untied balloons flying through a room to jet propulsion; social studies authors might link families voting on where to go out for dinner to democracy; and math writers might relate dividing a snack among friends to fractions.

Michael Gibson, the writer of *Gods, Men, and Monsters from the Greek Myths* (1982), presented a connection for his readers that was quite effective. In one chapter of this book he compares Hades, the ancient Greek concept of the underworld, to modern notions of hell. The author points out that Hades, like hell, was a place for the dead where sinners suffer eternal damnation. However, Gibson explains, Hades differed from hell because all the dead—good and bad—first traveled to Hades to have their fates decided. Those who had led commendable lives then continued on to an afterlife of great happiness. Young readers who encounter this concept of Hades for the first time probably will have little difficulty understanding and remembering it, thanks to the author's connecting it to a familiar concept.

Motivation to Read

Textbook authors rarely devote much page space to motivating readers because they realize that they have a captive audience once their book is adopted. Textbook writers know that adults, not students, select the books. Thus, the composition of textbooks is designed to impress adults who look for extensive coverage of information.

Writers not involved with textbooks, on the other hand, realize that their readers will be working mostly on their own. Writers and publishers know that teachers tend to explain what is presented in textbooks but will not have time to explain the material in most library books. Writers and publishers also know that young readers select and stay only with books that are interesting to read. Therefore, they know that they must present their information in as interesting a way as possible. Such a presentation might include introductory comments, questions, and scenarios that arouse curiosity; vivid images and analogies; explanations of how the information might be used in real-life situations; humor and personalized anecdotes; and print size, graphics, and layout that appeal to the intended audience.

Distinctive Points of View

Students also deserve a variety of content area reading materials because such literature can present distinctive points of view on a topic, whereas textbooks tend to present no specific viewpoint or only a traditional perspective. For instance, *The Roots of Crime* (LeShan, 1981), an adolescent-level book, argues that children who learn to hate themselves frequently grow into lawbreakers. The roots of criminal behavior are said to be found in such problems as child abuse, uncaring families, and unemployment. This argument offers a clear contrast to neutral presentations of crime-related facts and to fervid appeals for strong-armed law and order. Such a contrasting view might interest an otherwise apathetic student.

In *The Accident* (Strasser, 1988), another book for adolescents, teenagers confront their own mortality while reading about the drunk-driving deaths of the book's characters. They deal with concerns such as jumping to conclusions and placing blame without evidence. Norma Klein's *No More Saturday Nights* (1988) helps students understand the implications of becoming an unwed parent and trying to continue an education. An interesting wrinkle on this one is that the parent is a teenage boy who has custody of his child. Readers will empathize as this boy makes the transition to adulthood. Content area materials also can present alternative, interesting points of view on issues such as the environment, genetic engineering, UFOs, war and conflict, and the mentally or physically handicapped.

Recency of Information

Textbooks, like dictionaries, offer a rearview mirror image of the world. No matter how comprehensive and well-researched textbooks are, they describe only what happened in the past. They might speculate about the future, but they are unable to specify future events. It takes an ongoing stream of information best available through media such as newspapers, magazines, and the Internet to remain up-to-date.

The rapidly changing state of knowledge in the social studies is an especially good example of the need for a variety of content area reading materials. Current events, by definition, change regularly, so regular updates are needed to keep abreast of the times. Multiple sources are needed to cover ongoing political and social events. The rate of change in science also is staggering. Again, students and teachers require access to responsive media to keep up with scientific and technological advances. And teachers of English, mathematics, vocational arts, and other subjects do well by updating their course offerings with the best current thinking and by tying in their course contents with ongoing local, national, and global happenings.

Materials That Fit Reading Competencies

If you took students out on a football field and had them run 100 yards, individuals would finish at different times, and some would enjoy the exercise

Students enjoy opportunities to browse through a variety of reading materials.

more than others no matter which place they came in. In fact, the differences among students' running times and feelings about running probably would increase as students got older. The same holds true for literacy. When you give your class a reading and writing assignment, you can count on students finishing at different times, with different amounts of understanding and degrees of interest. Thus, a variety of materials is needed to match the variety of students you meet. Incorporating many library books, periodicals, encyclopedias, newspapers, brochures, and other reading materials into the study of subject matter allows students to work with what they can best handle.

One finding that has consistently emerged from classroom research is that students who spend time on tasks they can do well learn the most (Cunningham, 1985). Students do best when reading and writing tasks are well within their limits. In addition, students' behavior on a task is related to the task's level of difficulty. Understandably, students tend to avoid frustrating assignments and search for something else to do. Making available a variety of reading materials allows more students to succeed.

Sense of Ownership

Let's face it, students do not always appreciate teachers telling them what to learn. Sometimes students like to figure things out for themselves. Substituting varied materials for the single all-powerful textbook allows students to read for the purposes that they find satisfying, seeking the answers to their own questions. Instead of reading a chapter because it was assigned, students read a book or an article because it captures their attention. In this way, students may spend even more time actively engaged in reading and learning. Students who have a choice in what they will read and write about develop a sense of ownership in the assignment. They are willing to go the extra mile because it means something to them.

Opportunities for a Range of Thinking

A final reason why students deserve a variety of content area materials involves opportunities to employ the various thinking processes. Teaching practices centered about a textbook tend to emphasize only information recall. This situation seems due partly to the authoritative tone of textbooks. Textbook language has an all-knowing stance, dispensing information in domineering fashion. Textbooks give an impression of objectivity and validity and appear comprehensive.

Teachers who follow textbook-based instruction typically end up having students read the passage and then providing corrective feedback as students recall the contents. Such instruction inhibits opportunities for students to employ such thinking processes as evaluate, apply, and generalize. On the other hand, multiple materials are more conducive to problem solving and decision making than a single textbook. For instance, teachers who use a variety of materials can have students compare different versions of the same Greek myth or, with *Realms of Gold: Myths and Legends from Around the World* (Pilling, 1993), compare Greek myths with those from other cultures. A useful book for teachers to identify other themes and related resources is *From Hinton to Hamlet: Building Bridges Between Young Adult Literature and the Classics* (Herz & Gallo, 1996). Such activities, which elicit thinking that goes beyond a rote level, help demystify print. They allow students to control what they read by showing that some authors disagree with one another, some present a topic more clearly and completely than others, and some provide inaccurate or biased accounts.

Listen/Look and Learn

Informally interview a teacher who uses multiple reading materials during subject matter study. Ask why he or she uses multiple materials rather than a single text. Compare the reasons you obtain from the interview with the six listed in this section.

A VARIETY OF CONTENT AREA READING MATERIALS ARE AVAILABLE

We hope that by now you are convinced to provide your students with a variety of reading materials. You should realize the advantages of allowing students to interact with multiple sources of information. To repeat, multiple materials give students a chance at getting something meaningful from their reading; they meet students halfway. Some of the time you might spend helping students understand their textbooks would be better spent getting other materials into their hands.

This section presents general types of materials students should access. It describes major types of content area reading materials that are available: reference materials, periodicals, computer technology, trade books, textbooks, and multicultural literature.

Reference Materials

Students consult reference materials for facts or general background information. These materials typically display information in a straightforward, concise manner. Two types of reference materials are available: compendiums and special-interest publications.

Compendiums, handy collections of fields of information, include encyclopedias, dictionaries, atlases, almanacs, and yearbooks. Students frequently are intimidated by compendiums because the information in them is presented differently than the information in other books. Compendiums usually have extremely dense text summarizing a great deal of information in very little space. Nonetheless, some materials are better than others. Some publications contain striking visuals, accurate information, and accessible writing. In one book's presentation of the layers of the atmosphere, an illustration shows the sea, the world's tallest building, an eagle flying, Mt. Everest, and an airborne jumbo jet in order to provide concrete examples of height.

Computer-based compendiums have several features lacking in traditional print. General encyclopedias such as *Compton's Multimedia Encyclopedia*, *Encarta*, and *The New 1993 Grolier Electronic Encyclopedia* come in CD-ROM format containing sound and film clips. Seeing and hearing portions of President Kennedy's inaugural address through multimedia differs from reading about it. Computerized encyclopedias also allow searches using combinations of terms (e.g., mammals and North American), and they offer immediate links from one topic to another. Finally, computer-based encyclopedias allow students to copy information from the reference and paste it in a word-processing application. Although this might raise concerns about plagiarism, it offers opportunities to explain how reports are to be constructed in the information age.

Brochures, pamphlets, and fliers exemplify special-interest references. When studying cities or states, students often obtain colorful promotional literature from chambers of commerce; when investigating occupations, students examine brief publications produced by trade unions, professional organizations, and government agencies. Classrooms stocked with special-interest references have filing cabinets and shelves full of such real-life reading materials as maps, application forms, menus, food labels, legal documents, and telephone books.

While the majority of reference materials is aimed at good readers in the intermediate grades and above, there are some excellent materials for primary-grade students. When searching for reference materials, keep student reading abilities in mind and examine the composition of the materials. Are they well organized? Are examples provided? If the material is too sparse, students will not be informed and may even go away from the material confused because information was missing.

Periodicals

A wide range of published material is available by subscription. Periodicals are excellent content area materials because they are timely and include short, lively, well-illustrated articles on interesting topics. Periodicals can provide students with an introduction to a new subject, pique student interest in a subject not considered interesting, and summarize information after students have done other research. Periodicals from *Ranger Rick's Nature Magazine* to *Popular Mechanics* to *Zillions* to the community newspaper are available for class or individual subscriptions. Practically every subject area has at least one periodical appropriate for upper-grade students, and general periodicals that report the weekly news and special features exist for all grades. S. Richardson (1991) and D. Stoll (1994) provide extensive lists of magazines for children.

Computer Technology

Fundamental shifts in education occurred in antiquity when printed materials became the primary storehouses of information and in the late Middle Ages when printing presses resulted in affordable books. Learners depended less on other individuals and more on themselves to become educated. Today's computer technology might affect teaching and learning as much as these past innovations.

Advocates of computer technology have moved beyond extolling its uses as a tutor and a word processor. Now they note the computer's incredible potential in making information accessible. With appropriate resources and training plus a few keystrokes, students can locate and record information from World Wide Web sites and Internet domains. Students can experience phenomena through multimedia presentations that include print but go beyond the capacity of books. They can participate in real-time video conferencing and long-distance collaborations. They can digitally record what they produce. Virtually every school district today is attempting to capitalize on what computers have to offer.

Although separating the hype from the reality can be difficult, educational possibilities and occupational realities make computer technology an important part of content area materials. Computer technology is a tool for learning that includes many components. The ones most applicable as content reading materials include telecommunications, simulations, gamelike simulations, and multimedia.

Telecommunications The Internet and World Wide Web provide access to vast amounts of information (Ryder & Graves, 1996–1997). Students using web

Computer technology offers many literacy resources.

search engines such as *Yahoo* (http://www.yahoo.com) and *AltaVista* (http://altavista.digital.com) can access countless sources on countless topics. Many students' inquiries now are are based largely on information obtained through telecommunications. In fact, so much is available that the information superhighway now is at risk of becoming the information flea market. Students need to negotiate their way through countless commercial offerings and individuals' home pages to find worthwhile information. One director of technology and media claims that only about 10 percent of *Yahoo's* lists of curriculum-related sites contains rich content (McKenzie, 1996). Separating the wheat from the chaff is essential for effective use of telecommunications.

A good way to locate useful information is to rely on publications and home pages of individuals and school-based teams who serve as selection guides. Selection guides list only recommended sites, sometimes annotating web site contents and offering links that bypass introductory menus and go directly to the heart of the information. Teachers who use these guides have access to instructional tips, lesson plans, event updates, and subject matter information which they, in turn, can make available to their students. A useful general publication about the Internet is by Barron and Ivers (1996). *Internet Adventures Newsletter* (http://www.primenet.com/~xplora) has taken on the mission of providing services for schools and teachers to fully utilize the Internet as a tool for teaching and learning. It is commited to integration, addressing one topic per issue (e.g., rain forests) and describing sites teachers and students might visit for information.

A sample of web sites with links to many content literacy information sources (which are available as we write this book) are as follows:

Bellingham (WA) Public Schools (http://www.bham.wednet.edu)

Classroom Connect (http://www.classroom.net/)

Content Area Literacy (http://miavx1.muohio.edu/~andrewcs/conlit. htmlx)

Content Literacy Information Consortium (CLIC) (http://www.ced. appstate.edu/clic)

Kathy Schrock's Guide for Educators (http://www.capecod.net/Wixon/ wixon.htm)

Ron Mackinnon's Educational Bookmarks (http://juliet.stfx.ca/people/ stu/x94emj/bookmark.html)

Teacher Resource Homepage (http://www.aps.edu/aps/teach_resources/ page.e.html)

Internet access also allows students to communicate with others across time and space. Students enjoy communicating with other individuals through e-mail to gain and share information on topics being studied and life in another location. Motivation is built into such projects. Students seem to be motivated to access information electronically and write for long-distance readers.

Simulations   Students who cannot participate in scientific or historical events firsthand can take part in them vicariously through computer simulations. Simulations allow students to investigate phenomena through virtual reality. *Operation Frog* is a well-known science simulation that allows students to explore beneath the skin of this amphibian without the expense and invasiveness of an actual dissection. *Lunar Greenhouse* is another science-oriented simulation that has students control variables affecting the growth of vegetables. They set levels of temperature, light, water, and plant food for different types of crops. Information that is acquired from initial experiments is used to inform decisions about subsequent experiments at increased levels of difficulty.

Gamelike Simulations   Many simulations have gamelike features, with points scored for desirable decisions, that only hint at actual firsthand experiences. For instance, the popular *Oregon Trail II* has students reenact part of the westward expansion saga. Players decide what provisions they should set out with; what food rations and travel pace they should follow; and how they should acquire food, cross rivers, and handle adversity. Successful players reach Oregon's Willamette Valley; unsuccessful ones are said to die on the trail. On the *Amazon Trail* students learn about rain forest plants and animals as they try to get medicine to a village downriver. They must solve problems as they go, and they can take "snapshots" of plants and animals encountered for future reference.

Other popular gamelike simulations include *SimCity 2000,* which uses natural disasters to test students' plans for developing a city, and *Gold Rush,* which calls for decisions about how to get from New York to the 1849 California gold fields. The *Magic School Bus* series allows 6- to 10-year-old children to accompany Ms. Frizzle and her class as they explore the ocean, solar system, human body, inside of the earth, and the age of dinosaurs.

Multimedia Courseware   Like the electronic encyclopedias noted above, multimedia contains incredible amounts of information in the form of print, still images, graphics, sound, animation, and video. Students can view it individually on a monitor or as a group by having the visuals projected onto a screen. The presentation of multimedia can be controlled by moving from one link to another in a desired order. For instance, science teachers might talk through the human heart's system of blood circulation by presenting pictures one-at-a-time, then showing a video of an actual heart beating, then displaying a diagram of the human body's arteries and veins. Deciding whether or not to show blood passing through the lungs can be made relative to how the class is responding.

The PBS award–winning documentary *Eyes on the Prize,* which is available on videodisc, presents America's Civil Rights movement from the mid-1950s to 1980s. It contains videotaped speeches by equal-rights activists, texts from pertinent documents, anthems and theme songs, maps, and profiles of key people and organizations. In this case students have access to the sights, sounds, and printed words of a social movement. National Geographic offers the *Wonders of Learning CD-ROM Library* with titles such as *The Human Body, Our Earth,* and *People Behind the Holidays.* These collections include stunning pictures and drawings, narration accompanied by music and sound effects, and interactive picture buttons that invite exploration.

Multimedia projects are possible as students gather, organize, and report on information contained in multimedia courseware. *Time Shift Radio* transports students to scientific and mathematic breakthroughs such as the discovery of germs, DNA, and pi. Students use journals to gather information, and they engage in follow-up experiments and activities. *Cultural Reporter* is an interdisciplinary kit that involves students as writers, photographers, and filmmakers as they examine the diversity of cultures in their communities.

Trade Books

Trade books are intended for sale in general bookstores; they make up a bookseller's trade. Some educators use the terms *trade book* and *library book* as synonyms. Trade books differ from textbooks, technical manuals, reference materials, and the like.

Content area trade books, which frequently excel at providing organizational patterns and connections along with other features of fine writing, come in a wide range of types for preschool children through adults. The following are the major categories of trade books likely to be found in elementary- and secondary-school libraries: concept books, poetry, fiction, nonfiction narrative, how-to, and biography.

Concept Books   We use the term *concept books* somewhat more broadly than those who typically write about literature for schoolchildren. We use two related definitions. The first is the traditional definition of books appropriate primarily for very young children. These books introduce such concepts as size, shape, color, spatial relations, the alphabet, numeral recognition, and number sets. For instance, T. Hoban's *Exactly the Opposite* (1990) depicts various opposites. This wordless book of photographs allows preschoolers and early readers to identify more than one correct response. In *Animalia* (Base, 1987) each page contains dozens of lavish pictures of items that begin with that page's letter of the alphabet. *The Handmade Alphabet* (Rankin, 1991) uses sign language to illustrate each letter. Such alphabet books not only help children understand the sound-symbol code of English but also help build concepts and children's meaning vocabulary.

The other type of concept books we refer to are those that deal with a single topic or specific subject in expository fashion. These books are written for very young children through adults. Some authorities call these nonfiction informational books. *What Lives in a Shell?* (Zoehfeld, 1994), *Shadows of the Night: The Hidden World of the Little Brown Bat* (Bash, 1993), *To the Top of the World: Adventures with Arctic Wolves* (Brandenburg, 1993), *Is a Blue Whale the Biggest Thing There Is?* (Wells, 1993), and *The Story of Money* (Maestro, 1993) are examples of nonfiction informational concept books.

Poetry   While the use of rhyme and rhythm to teach concepts has much appeal, poetry books are not as readily available as are ones in the other categories. In general, there are fewer poetry books published than those in other genres, and of those published there are a limited number that can be used to teach content information. However, poetry can be used as supplements to develop mood, a sense of fun, or lighten the content presentation. Use maps to locate homes of various endangered species with Heard's (1992) *Creatures of Earth, Sea, and Sky*. A unit on weather would be enhanced with haiku poetry from Hopkins's (1994) *Weather*. Insect study would be more fun with *Flit, Flutter, Fly! Poems About Bugs and Other Crawly Creatures* (Hopkins, 1992). *Tyrannosaurus Was a Beast* (Prelutsky, 1988) is a wonderful way to begin or conclude a unit on those prehistoric beasts.

When teaching a unit on the late nineteenth and early twentieth centuries, let students better understand what life was like with Lewis's two books, *Long Ago in Oregon* (1987) and *Up in the Mountains and Other Poems of Long Ago* (1991). Hopkins's (1995) *Hand in Hand: American History in Poetry* also supports social studies instruction.

Fiction   There is a whole realm of materials that presents facts in the context of a story. For instance, books that follow a story line while presenting extremely valuable information include *Warm as Wool* (Sanders, 1992), *Tchaikovsky*

Discovers America (Kalman, 1995), *Voices of the Wild* (London, 1993), *The Cuckoo Child* (King-Smith, 1993), and *The Star Fisher* (Yep, 1991). We would say that a great deal of your knowledge about the climate, language, flora, fauna, and ethnic groups in certain parts of the world came from reading fiction by such authors as James A. Michener.

There are two basic types of fiction suitable for content area classrooms: realistic fiction and historical fiction. *Realistic fiction* portrays events and people who seem to be involved in the recognizable trials and uncertainties of life. Books such as *I'll Get There, It Better Be Worth the Trip* (Donovan, 1969) and *A Day No Pigs Would Die* (Peck, 1972) are classic statements of young adults' changes from dependent children to independent adults. Many books now are available that deal with such issues as divorce, developing sexuality, mental and physical handicaps, and death and dying. For instance, *Johnny Got His Gun* (Trumbo, 1939) is a compelling piece of antiwar fiction that has a place in an English or a social studies class. Homelessness becomes more than a word when students read engaging literature like *Fly Away Home* (Bunting, 1991), *Monkey Island* (Fox, 1991), *Uncle Willie and the Soup Kitchen* (DiSalvo-Ryan, 1991), and *Sophie and the Sidewalk Man* (Tolan, 1992). Students trying to make sense out of death might read and discuss books like *I'll See You in My Dreams* (Jukes, 1993).

Historical fiction attempts to re-create a believable past. Authors of such works often create fictional characters who interact with people who actually shaped events in history. Through these imagined and real characters, the past can be interpreted. After reading *Across Five Aprils* (Hunt, 1964), *Pink and Say* (Polacco, 1994), or *Behind the Lines* (Holland, 1994), students begin to understand much better why the Civil War was so devastating on a personal as well as a national scale. Issues of race, class, and injustice are easily accessed.

Nonfiction Narrative   A category of content area trade books that deserves attention is narrative accounts of actual happenings. These nonfiction narratives contain events and dialogue as it is remembered or recorded by the participants. Authors typically maintain a journal of the events if they were participants, or they interview those who actually participated and present a story that documents the events. Classic examples of nonfiction narratives appropriate for secondary students include *Black Like Me* (Griffin, 1977), *The Double Helix* (Watson, 1968), *Hiroshima* (Hersey, 1946), *Never Cry Wolf* (Mowat, 1963), and *The Right Stuff* (Wolfe, 1979). Elementary students would learn much about the horror of the first atomic bomb through the account of a real-life child in *Sadako* (Coerr, 1993).

Other nonfiction narratives are exemplified by *The Go-Around Dollar* (Adams, 1992) and the "Magic School Bus" series by Joanna Cole. In these books, conveying accurate information is the prime consideration, but the information is interwoven with a story. "The Magic School Bus" books tell a humorous tale of school children learning about some topic their teacher, Ms. Frizzle, wants them to know. In various books they have explored the water cycle, human anatomy, space, earth's interior, dinosaurs, and the ocean. *The Magic School Bus Inside a Beehive* (Cole, 1996) helps students understand the intricacies of hive life and how honey is made. These books describe the ultimate field trip!

How-to   How-to books describe a process and explain how to perform such activities as playing chess, conducting science experiments, folding paper artistically, cooking, repairing cars, and making music. This category has somewhat limited usefulness because it applies to only a few content areas. Numerous how-to books exist to support the sciences, mathematics, and vocational skills; however, such books are rare in the social sciences and the humanities.

Biography   Books about people who have made contributions to the content areas are numerous. Biographies are available about people prominent in reform movements, politics, sports, medicine, war, and entertainment, to name only a few fields. Abraham Lincoln, Jim Thorpe, Marie Curie, James Audubon, Anne Frank, Elizabeth Blackwell, and Bill Cosby are only a small sampling of those whose life histories have been written. Young readers often appreciate biographies as they search for heroes and heroines to emulate. Unfortunately, some biographers let their own infatuation with the subject interfere with the honest depiction of a multifaceted human being. Students need to be on the alert for folklore that passes for truth from one book to another. For instance, the story about George Washington and the cherry tree is not substantiated. Some myths are easily spotted; others pass into the general culture as truths. Though more biographies exist for people in the content areas of the arts, humanities, and social sciences, biographies have been written about important figures associated with all major curricular areas.

Textbooks

By now you might be convinced that we are totally opposed to the use of textbooks. This is not so! After all, we wrote the textbook that you currently are reading. Textbooks play a needed role in education: They systematically introduce readers to a body of knowledge; they save teachers time by outlining learning sequences for students; and they specify content beforehand so that teachers know how to plan. Textbooks provide the glue that holds together a wide assortment of facts and generalizations.

Although textbooks are found in practically every classroom, the way teachers use them varies substantially (Alvermann & Moore, 1991; Stodolsky, 1989). At one extreme, some teachers slavishly cover their texts' contents from front to back, following suggestions from the teacher's manual and piloting students through as many of the activities as possible. Those who teach by the book daily might have students take turns reading orally and answering end-of-chapter questions. At the other extreme, some teachers leave textbooks on the classroom shelves or in the closet. These individuals might have students rely only on lectures, audiovisual presentations, and hands-on manipulatives.

Teachers in the middle of these extremes use textbooks selectively. They guide students through parts of the book that present content appropriately, point out textbook portions that reinforce what was introduced in class, and consult the text as a reference source. They selectively use the resources that often accompany textbooks. Such resources consist of supplemental readings, workbooks, and tests; simulations and gamelike simulations; overhead transparencies, videotapes, and computer software; cassettes and CDs; bulletin board materials; and manipulatives such as flash cards, geometric shapes, and puzzles.

Assessing the match among instructional materials, students, and curriculum is an important aspect of teaching. Deciding if one book—or one section of a book—is more effective than another contributes to instructional decision making. Two ways to make such assessments involve textbook rating scales and tryouts.

Textbook Rating Scales   Rating scales are a good way to assess the potential effectiveness of texts. Rating scales focus on aspects such as the clarity of introductions and the depth of explanations offered for a topic. Scales can go into these complex aspects of a text because they rely on individuals' judgments; they call for you to examine material and assign a subjective, but informed, rating. Rating scales pinpoint aspects of a text, and you judge whether these are strengths or limitations.

Figure 3.1 contains a textbook rating scale that we have found to be useful. It is one tool to help you select appropriate materials and identify appropriate parts of a text for use with your students. As you use a rating scale such as this one, continually ask yourself how much support your students would probably require to read and learn from that text well. As you study this scale, ask yourself what you might add, modify, or delete. Indeed, the most effective textbook rating scales seem to be ones that reflect individual or small-group judgments about what makes materials appropriate for students. Locally produced scales can be tied to individual or group preferences as well as specific subject matter. Among other things, one group of social studies educators might consider primary sources to be essential in a textbook; a group of math teachers might emphasize vivid and feasible application activities; and a group of English instructors might be quite interested in authors from a particular region.

Tryouts   Another way to assess materials is to conduct a tryout. As the name implies, you try out the material with your students. Think of it as a pretest. You see how well your students can do with a particular passage with no supporting instruction.

To conduct a tryout, first select a portion of a text that contains some of the most important information, one that students should be able to complete in a single class session. Then decide what you would want your students to learn from their reading and what you can have students do to demonstrate their understanding and learning (e.g., answer questions, discuss the passage, write

Title _____

Author(s) _____

Publisher _____ Copyright date _____

School district's intended audience _____

Directions: Rate the text according to each item below using a five-point scale, with 5 being high and 1 being low. Compare the text to an ideal instead of known materials.

After rating each item, decide how much you would need to guide students through the material in order to compensate for its shortcomings. Finally, form a holistic rating of the overall value of the text.

Very Desirable—"I would love to teach with this text!"
Desirable—"With a little support on my part, this text could be quite useful."
Fair—"I could get by with this text, but I would keep hoping for a better one."
Undesirable—"I would have to spend a great deal of time and energy making up for the shortcomings of the few parts of this text I might use."
Very Undesirable—"I would not even hand out this text to my students!"

Adjunct Aids

____ 1. The text contains a detailed table of contents, index, and glossary.

____ 2. Objectives, introductions, graphic overviews, and summaries occur at appropriate intervals and indicate major ideas.

____ 3. Headings, subheadings, and italic and boldfaced words occur at appropriate intervals and indicate major ideas.

____ 4. Graphic aids such as illustrations, maps, and tables occur on the same page as the discussion or at least the facing page. These graphics clarify major ideas presented in the text; they do not introduce new ideas or simply decorate the page.

____ 5. Review, extension, and application activities such as questions, suggested readings, and projects occur at appropriate intervals. They relate directly to the major ideas and elicit a wide range of thinking.

Conceptual Development

____ 6. The chapters emphasize fundamental concepts or principles; they are more than encyclopedic collections of related information. Facts are presented to develop the explicitly stated concepts or principles.

____ 7. Explanations of new ideas include memorable analogies, clear references to previously presented information, and concrete examples. The explanations consist of more than dull dictionary-type wording.

____ 8. The amount of technical vocabulary on each page is appropriate for the intended audience.

Motivation Arousal

____ 9. The text includes introductory comments, questions, and scenarios to arouse curiosity about the upcoming contents.

____ 10. The text explains how learners might use the information in real-life situations.

____ 11. The text cover, print size, graphics, and layout are appealing to the intended audience.

Organization

____ 12. The chapters could be outlined easily. The paragraphs and sections move forward in a logical manner.

____ 13. The text explicitly signals how information is arranged. Topic paragraphs and sentences include such statements as, "There are three reasons for this outcome" and "The following presents the key events."

Special Concerns

____ 14. The text fits the course objectives.

____ 15. Groups of people are presented authentically. There is no bias.

____ 16. A teacher's manual provides helpful suggestions for presenting the textual information.

Figure 3.1 Textbook Evaluation Rating Scale

a summary). You simply present the task and see how well students perform on their own.

Students' performance during a tryout provides you with insight about the match among their reading abilities, the materials, and the reading task. A rough rule of thumb for assessing performance is that a score of around 90 percent means the students can work independently with the material; it is so familiar and comfortable that students can easily understand and remember it on their own. Students do not need your help with these materials; they can learn the important information independently. A score of around 75 percent indicates instructional level. With support, students at this level can readily learn the information and think about the important ideas. The materials are teachable. Students who score around 50 percent or less probably are on frustration level with these materials; simply put, these materials quite likely are beyond their grasp, regardless of how much help and support you offer. Frustration level materials typically require more prior knowledge and reading ability than you can provide your students in a reasonable time.

A word of caution: When determining whether textbooks are appropriate for students, remember that one book is rarely at the same level of difficulty for all students. The reading competence and prior knowledge of individuals vary considerably. A text that is independent for one student will be frustrating for another. Given this situation, teachers usually seek materials that are teachable for the majority of their students. Accommodations for students at the extremes then are achieved through techniques such as providing alternative reading materials, research projects, peer tutoring, and collaborative group work.

You probably will inherit from your school a class set of textbooks and accompanying materials for the subjects you will teach. The way you use these resources is something for you to decide. In this section we hope to have informed your decision by describing other forms of print for use during daily classroom instruction as well as ways to assess what you will have available.

Multicultural Literature

Multicultural literature is a category that differs from the others in this section because it refers to the content of materials rather than to their form. Multicultural literature is printed matter that reflects the cultural diversity of American society; it recognizes features such as ethnicity, race, religion, age, gender, socioeconomic class, and exceptionality. Reference materials, periodicals, computer technology, trade books, and instructional materials and textbooks might or might not demonstrate multicultural awareness.

Multicultural awareness during subject matter study is part of educators' responses to a pluralist vision of the ideal society (Greene, 1993). This vision prizes diversity, viewing group membership as an integral and a beneficial part of individuals' identities. The pluralist position holds that various groups in a society should retain their cultural ways so long as all the groups can coex-

Secondary students find a range of reading materials engaging.

ist in peace. Pluralists often present a metaphor of the ideal society as a salad, a vegetable soup, or a mosaic, each of which contains identifiable elements contributing to a first-rate collective.

To create and sustain multicultural awareness, educators need to address factors such as community participation, testing procedures, and school staff attitudes (Banks & Banks, 1993). Culturally sensitive instruction honors and builds on styles of responding to print that students bring to classrooms from their communities (e.g., retelling passages as a group or individually; interpreting characters' actions playfully or seriously) (Ladson-Billings, 1994). Including multicultural reading materials during subject matter study is another important aspect of this instruction. Students should have access to reading materials whose contents, illustrations, and language accurately and fairly represent diverse groups.

One way to ensure accurate and fair treatment of groups is to check materials for stereotyping, omissions, distortions, and language bias (Hernandez, 1989). Stereotyping occurs when all individuals in a particular group are depicted as having the same attribute: Are Native Americans characterized as warlike? Are women presented as dependent? Omissions occur when the contributions of particular groups are underrepresented: Are women's roles in westward expansion described? Are scientific discoveries by physically disabled individuals noted? Texts present distortions when they systematically misrepresent certain groups. For instance, referring to Asian Americans rather than to Japanese or Chinese Americans gives a false impression of uniformity between these two groups. And depicting Native Americans in only historical or ceremonial settings ignores their contemporary status. Finally, language bias happens when subtle, frequently subconscious choices about words affect the message about certain groups. Are revolutionaries working to overthrow an established government called terrorists or freedom fighters? Did Americans in the 1860s fight a Civil War or a War Between the States? Were African Americans given the right to vote, or did they win it? Do you receive letters from a mailman or a mailcarrier?

A good way to integrate multicultural literature into your curriculum is through a transformation approach (Banks & Banks, 1993). Those who follow this approach enable students to view the world from the perspective of diverse groups. This approach goes beyond merely displaying posters, having a one-day multicultural fair with ethnic foods for lunch, and adding a list of diverse heroes and holidays to be memorized. For example, rather than have students simply remember what happened to Crispus Attucks during the colonial revolution, have them study this event from the points of view of Anglo revolutionaries, Anglo loyalists, African Americans, Native Americans, the French, and the British. Compare the sympathetic view of the revolution presented in *Johnny Tremain* (Forbes, 1946) with the one presented in *My Brother Sam Is Dead* (Collier & Collier, 1974). When studying the age of discovery, provide *The First Voyage of Christopher Columbus* (Smith, 1992), which maps out the voyage in exceptional detail, along with *The Encounter* (Yolen, 1992), an account of the arrival of Columbus as seen through the eyes of the Tianos people who met him.

Myriad books with multicultural perspectives fit the myriad topics covered in school. Young children studying shelter will see the different types of houses built throughout the United States in *The House I Live In: At Home in America* (Seltzer, 1992) and gain perspective on the children who live in them. *Rosa Parks: Mother to a Movement* (Parks, 1992) offers older children a personal account of the events that led this woman in 1955 to refuse to give her bus seat to a white man in Alabama, turning the civil rights movement into a national issue.

Transforming your curriculum with multicultural literature allows you to help students understand how diverse groups of people have participated in the formation of U.S. culture and society. It can sensitize members of one group to the heritages of others, resulting in the appreciation of their contributions. And it can affirm individuals' particular cultural identities.

Do It Together

Form small groups of three or four students each according to academic specialization (e.g., social studies, mathematics, English). If you teach all subjects, select a particular one for this activity. Go on a scavenger hunt to locate and bring to class on a certain date published materials that fit your specialization in each of the categories below. On the day that everything is brought in, share the materials you found. Indicate what is special about their contents, writing style, and potential classroom uses.

Reading Materials Scavenger Hunt List

Reference materials
Periodical
Computer technology
   Simulation
   Multimedia
   Telecommunication
Trade books
   Concept book
   Poetry
   Fiction
   Nonfiction narrative
   How-to
   Biography
Textbooks
Multicultural literature

REPORT AND RESPONSE PROJECTS TAKE MANY FORMS

As noted in Chapter 2, "Instructional Units and Classroom Organization," teachers provide access to reading materials during units conducted in whole-class, small-group, and individual situations. Teachers make some materials available and enable students to acquire others, they relate what is being read to unit objectives, they present reading and writing strategy lessons, they provide time for reading and accomplishing projects, and they assess literacy competencies.

This section details one component of the literacy-related events conducted during units. It describes projects for students while reporting on and responding to what they read. Most of the following projects are appropriate as culminations to entire units, to specific unit objectives, or to lessons.

Projects consist of factual reports as well as literary responses. Factual reports consist of objective accounts of a phenomenon; literary responses refer to one's subjective experiences associated with a phenomenon. After reading *Behind the Lines,* students might report the facts of the Civil War in a detached distant manner, or they might tell how they felt while vicariously living the story. Notwithstanding the distinction between reporting facts and sharing feelings, many projects blend the two. Dramatizing key events in famous historical figures' lives conveys information as well as feelings; it merges factual reporting and literary responding. This section presents projects that tap reporting as well as responding.

Projects are meant to elicit from students a wide range and depth of thought and feeling about what they are reading. Projects lead students to insights about what they have read. Students activate essential thinking processes while participating in projects. In fact, meaningful projects can lead students to all nine of the thought processes we have described. When left alone, students can slip into passive reading habits, barely attending to the print. Books become a sort of mental chewing gum; they feel good for a while but have no long-lasting benefit. Students require opportunities to read freely and experience well-written prose, but they also benefit from sharpening and extending their understanding of what they read by expressing their reactions through various projects.

Perhaps the greatest contribution of response projects is the criteria they provide for students to self-monitor their comprehension independently. In order to produce some tangible reaction to print, students need to step back mentally and collect their thoughts. If students find portions of their under-standing to be unclear, they can reread and rethink the passage that contains the confusing information. Without projects, students can remain at superficial levels of understanding.

A common reason for having students react overtly to print is to have them demonstrate that they actually read what they claim to have read. That is, projects are for purposes of assessment. We would emphasize instructional pur-poses rather than assessments. Projects should lead students to increased under-standing; they should not just allow teachers to assess what was understood.

Projects take many forms. Students can make visuals, locate or create con-crete objects related to passage contents, dramatize events, produce somewhat lengthy written or spoken reactions, maintain a journal of their reactions, and discuss what they read with others. These projects can be done as part of out-of-school or in-school reading, be in response to any single material or set of materials, and be assigned by the teacher or selected by the student. The point is that students' report and response projects can and should take many forms. Some effective forms include visuals, concrete objects, dramatizations, and written and oral reactions.

Visuals

A picture is worth a thousand words. Students benefit from viewing visuals in order to learn information, and they also benefit from producing visuals in reaction to what they read. If the purpose of a response project is, "Identify three pieces of new information that you learned," the best way to represent the new learning may be visually.

Illustrations   Illustrations and photographs are good substitutes for the real thing. Students often draw pictures, collect photographs, or take their own photographs in order to depict what they encountered in a passage. They may also make posters or bulletin boards. Such visuals graphically depict what words can only suggest. For example, the Grand Canyon, cell division, parts of the body, and geometric figures are natural candidates for illustrated projects.

Time Lines and Murals   The key events of a phenomenon are frequently displayed on a time line. Any number of illustrations, or none at all, may be on a time line. The essential feature is that events are labeled and represented in sequence on a linear chart. Murals are similar to time lines in that they represent a sequence of events; the difference, of course, is that murals consist solely of pictures.

Maps   Representing an area graphically requires careful reading and composing. Students need to decide what locations to represent and then produce that representation. Illustrations can be added to maps for greater detail. Maps can depict locations on many scales. For instance, locations within a building, a neighborhood, a community, a state, a nation, the world, or the universe can be mapped.

Collages   Collages are groups of pictures and various other materials glued to a surface. These artistic compositions generally symbolize a topic. Making a collage of an area of study such as ethnic and racial groups, geographic locations, inventions, or animal groups is a good project for students of all ages.

Homemade Transparencies   Older students can make their own overhead transparencies. Have your students take thin-line, permanent-ink felt-tip markers and either draw or trace pictures on a sheet of acetate. Give the pictures a few minutes to dry and cover them with clear adhesive plastic. If appropriate, cut the pictures apart so they can be reassembled when the report is presented. Homemade transparencies made up of separate parts are especially useful when presenting development, such as the growth of the United States; components, such as the parts of a plant or animal; and processes, such as photosynthesis and weather changes.

Concrete Objects

Concrete objects either represent or actually are the phenomenon being studied. Models are concrete representations of objects (such as buildings) and processes (such as radiation). Actual objects, models, and simulations can be displayed in the classroom in order to approximate direct, firsthand experiences. A table of books and concrete objects that students prepared for a unit of study in American history is shown in the photograph on page 88.

Students can buy, borrow, or make concrete objects as part of their projects. For instance, young students reacting to frontier living might collect objects that represent life on the western frontier in the 1800s. Farm tools, kitchen implements, clothing, and assorted household items can be brought into class to depict aspects of a bygone way of life. Students who read about the formation of islands could fashion a clay-and-water representation of geologic actions. Older students who read about cooking could bring in representative pots, implements, and other devices that are used. Students who read about scientific processes such as evaporation, covalent bonding, and friction

Assembling a display of objects and related reading materials is an effective book project.

cannot bring in the actual "thing," but they can demonstrate the outcomes that result from those intangible forces. Indeed, science fairs, which are traditional parts of many schools' curriculums, are excellent examples of students producing concrete objects.

Dramatizations

Many students like to stage short skits in reaction to what they have read, simulating certain phenomena through action and dialogue. For example, older students might read Elisabeth Kubler-Ross's *On Death and Dying* (1974) and then present different skits that portray the stages people exhibit when facing their own imminent deaths. Other students might take Studs Terkel's *Working* (1981) and present selected scenes wherein people talk about the emotional side of their jobs and how their jobs affect their whole lives. Young students who read about collecting rocks could go through a series of scenes that illustrate the recommendations for gathering a personal collection.

Another option is for students to break into pairs or small groups and simulate an interview with the author of or a character from the reading. Television talk shows provide a model for the interviewing format. Along this same line, students can form pairs to review what they have read, with one student emphasizing the positive features and the other stressing the negative. Finally, students dramatically reading selected portions of a text to their classmates or younger students is another form of dramatization.

Readers' theater is a way for students to dramatize narratives they have read. It is a method of oral interpretation that provides a relevant purpose for reading orally. You do not need to prepare special scripts for readers' theater; have students read right from the passage. Most children who have basic reading proficiencies enjoy reading plays; readers' theater allows playlike reading with regular prose.

When you first introduce readers' theater, have a small group demonstrate the process. Show how each speaking part is indicated in the text with quotation marks and how the speaker is revealed by the flow of the conversation. The narrator's role of reading all the material outside the quotation marks should be made clear. When first presenting this activity, the narrator might read all the "he said" and "she said" phrases, but this practice should be stopped when the students become adept. Explain that only the key parts of a book and the parts that contain extensive dialogue should be selected for readers' theater.

When readers' theater groups are formed, have the students first react to the entire passage so they have a good understanding of what they are staging. Then have them identify and practice their parts before reading. Some groups tape-record themselves and submit the recording as their response project, and others perform for the class. Simple props and sound effects frequently are included. Readers' theater is quite popular among students, so you might consider setting aside a certain time of the week for these presentations.

Try It Out

Produce a visual, a concrete object collection, or a dramatization in response to this chapter. Share your project with your class or a small group of classmates.

Prompting Oral and Written Reactions

To stimulate and help structure students' oral and written reactions, teachers provide prompts. Prompts can be questions ("What was the most important message of what you read?") or directives ("Describe the most important message of what you read"). Prompts also can be content specific. Content-specific prompts refer to specific information in a passage ("How does sunlight help produce oxygen?"); they contain terms from the passage so they are appropriate for only the specific contents of that passage. Students who preview a passage then ask questions about it typically produce content-specific language. For instance, in response to the first sentence of *Sounder*, "The tall man stood at the edge of the porch," one group of students asked the following content-specific questions:

How old is the man?
Why standing on the *edge* of the porch?
What is the man's race?
Whose porch is it?
What is he looking at? (Ash, 1992, p. 62)

Unlike content-specific prompts, generic ones fit any passage. They contain general language ("What did you learn from this passage?") that is appropriate for anything students have read. An advantage of generic prompts is their applicability to more than one piece of text. For instance, students can learn to ask, "What have I learned?" after each reading, thereby refining their thinking. Such self-questioning is a powerful learning strategy. In addition, teachers can demonstrate how they answer a question such as, "What have I learned?", thereby providing a pattern for students to follow. Generic prompts also allow divergent thinking within a clear structure. Students have a clear focus in mind yet substantial latitude for forming their responses. Finally, applying a few questions to many materials produces a routine for teachers and students. Routines help ensure that students receive the necessary continual exposure to become proficient.

Figure 3.2 contains numerous generic prompts for written and oral compositions. These prompts are meant to elicit students' thinking about the contents of what they read; they can be the core of many reading-response projects. Upcoming chapters on comprehension and writing go further in describing how such prompts can be used during subject matter study. What follows are four specific reading-response formats that structure classroom interactions to capitalize on these prompts: discussions and recitations, reading journals, conferences, and reaction guides.

Discussions and Recitations   Discussions and recitations specify two types of classroom communication. Discussions are give-and-take dialogues in which teachers are not necessarily committed to a single correct answer. Recitations are classroom interactions in which teachers expect students to produce specific information. Discussions are suited more for problem solving and applying and evaluating concepts; recitations are more conducive to factual learning. Recitations typically contain content-specific prompts that allow students to recall the contents of a text and receive feedback about their performance. Discussions seem to work best with prompts containing generic language. Recitations currently predominate in most U.S. classrooms (Goodlad, 1984), although authorities recommend holding more discussions in order to promote the higher-order thinking that our society requires.

Discussions are open explorations of ideas among teachers and students and among students themselves. Discussants seek to arrive at an answer to a question or a solution to a problem; they do not recite an answer or a solution that has been determined beforehand. Discussions involve students in reacting to what they read and supporting their reactions with facts and ideas from the materials, with the teacher initiating and sustaining students' thoughts and

Universal Reading-Response Prompts

What will I/you remember about this material?

What ideas did I/you gain from my/your reading?

How did this material help me/you better understand the world?

What is the most important word, sentence, or section?

What materials have I/you read that are similar?

What does this material remind me/you of?

What was I thinking while reading?

What did I/you notice while reading?

What was the author trying to share?

What is the most important message of this material?

How will I/you think differently after reading this material?

What questions did the material leave unanswered?

Why did I/you choose to read this material?

Information for a Best Friend

How could I convince my best friend to read this material?

What would my/your best friend like to know about this material?

Should I/you tell a friend to read this? Why?

Image

What pictures, sounds, and other sensory feelings did I/you experience while reading this material?

Evaluation

What did I/you like best about this material?

What was my/your favorite part of this material?

Should the material receive a literary award? Why?

Is anything missing that should be included? What?

What caused me/you to keep reading?

How far did I/you go before wanting to finish the material?

If I/you rewrote this, what would I/you change?

Is the material unique? Why?

What part of the material was realistic or unrealistic?

Will I/you choose other materials by this author?

Literary Structure

What event begins the story?

What situation in the story reminded me/you of a situation from my/your own life?

What did I/you think was going to happen when _____?

How would I/you have reacted to the situations in the story?

If I/you were _____, what would I/you have done when _____?

If I/you could become a part of the story, at what point would I/you like to enter? What would I/you do?

Characterization

Why did the main character behave as he or she did?

Which characters, if any, did I/you especially like or dislike? Why?

Did any characters change? If so, how?

What did the characters learn?

What advice would I/you give the characters?

Figure 3.2 Generic Prompts for Written and Oral Compositions

Emotions

How did _____ feel when _____ happened?

How did I/you feel when reading this material?

What parts made me/you feel the strongest?

Did any part of the material surprise me/you? Why?

Author's Craft

How did the author hold my/your attention?

How did the author signal important information?

How did the author reveal the meanings of difficult or unfamiliar terms?

How did the author organize the material?

How did the author balance illustrations and print?

How did the author develop his or her ideas?

Figure 3.2   *Continued*

feelings. Ideal patterns of talk move from student to student rather than from teacher to student in ping-pong fashion.

To begin a discussion, use an open-ended prompt such as the ones listed in Figure 3.2. Prompts such as these start students talking about what they have read (Morgan & Saxton, 1991). An important rule is to ask only those questions that you consider to have more than one possibly acceptable answer. If you are committed to a single correct answer, then the students' task becomes one of determining what is in your mind rather than of thinking through the contents of a passage on their own terms.

To keep a discussion going after a student has finished speaking, consider the four moves presented by J. T. Dillon (1988): statements, student questions, signals, and silence. Statements are someone's selected thoughts to what has just been said. You might state your understanding ("As I understand it, you're saying . . ."), describe what you would like to have expanded ("I'm interested in hearing more about . . ."), indicate your state of mind ("I'm confused about . . ."), or relate what has just been said with what has been previously stated ("So you're saying . . . , while _____ is saying . . ."). Interestingly, students respond to statements.

Students' questions often seem to invigorate discussions more than teachers' questions. Your role, then, is to encourage and facilitate such questions. You might state, "This seems to be a good time to know what else we should be asking about," then wait for someone to initiate a new direction in the exchange. Discussion signals are somewhat neutral gestures that indicate you heard what a student said and are ready for someone else to talk. Signals might consist of a comment such as, "All right," "Well said," or "Okay." You can nod your head in agreement or lift your hands and eyeballs in wonder. Finally, deliberate teacher silence can go far in encouraging students to speak. Keeping silent for at least five seconds after a prompt by you or after a comment by a student might not seem like much, but it is a clear indication that someone should speak.

Reading Journals   Many teachers have students maintain journals about what they are reading (Berger, 1996; Hancock, 1993). Reading journals allows students to express their feelings freely about any aspect of what they are reading, explore new ideas, and ask questions. One teacher who used reading journals with literary materials found that many of her students' comments fell into five broad categories:

1. Opinions about plot episodes and characters
2. Direct expressions of personal engagement ranging from enthusiastic appreciation to placing the book within the framework of the child's life and concerns
3. Discussion of the author's style, language, and techniques
4. Reflections on the reading process and on expectations for narrative texts
5. Questions about vocabulary, language, or plot. (Wollman-Bonilla, 1989, p. 118)

A good way to promote students' thinking about what they read is to rely on generic questions such as the ones in Figure 3.2. They also can use several of the essential thinking processes described in Chapter 1. Connecting, generalizing, forming an image, evaluating, and applying are powerful processes. Responses to these prompts are entered into the journals.

Teachers often introduce reading journals by presenting an entry or two and describing important features such as their informality and personal involvement. Students typically write in their journals several times a week. They might read selected journal responses to their book study group as a way to initiate conversation. Some teachers have students produce their entries in the form of an informal letter to the teacher. Replying to the students as an aunt or uncle instead of as teacher-as-examiner goes far in allowing you to express interest in students' insights and strategies and prevents the journals from becoming an exercise no different from assigned writing.

Growth in motivation to read and in confidence are two of the most noticeable outcomes of having students maintain reading journals. Students who write on their own terms about what they are reading and who receive sincere reactions to their entries tend to respond more than they would to assigned factual prompts. At the same time, teachers are able to monitor students' progress in reading and writing when they read the journals. A special feature of journals is that they allow teachers to stay in touch with each individual in class, not just the vocal ones; teachers can maintain a dialogue with the shyest student through reading journals.

Conferences   Teachers often schedule individual conferences with students to talk about what they are reading. While other students are reading silently or accomplishing projects, the teacher and a student hold a conversation either about a passage or about a journal entry. The subject to talk about can be selected by the student, the teacher, or jointly.

The somewhat private settings of book conferences enable teachers and students to forge a relationship that is rarely possible in whole-class or small-group situations. The situation enhances opportunities for students and teachers to reflect on their personal connections with texts. It also allows teachers to ascertain how readers are handling text difficulties.

Reaction Guides   Teachers frequently distribute reaction guides to help structure students' reactions to what they read (Wood, 1993). Although similar to study guides, reaction guides are designed more for trade books than textbooks (see Chapter 4, "Comprehension," pages 108–109 for information about study guides).

Reaction guides for narratives might contain prompts grouped according to literary elements such as character, plot, setting, and theme. Figure 3.3 displays a sample guide for older readers that contains two prompts under each literary element; other prompts certainly might be included. Figure 3.4 shows a sample literary reaction guide for young readers. Teachers often have students choose the prompts they wish to complete or create ones for themselves.

Directions: Complete one task that is listed under each literary element.

Character

1. Write to a friend, a member of your family, or an actor or actress a letter that describes how he or she is like a character in your book.
2. Pretend that you are one of the characters in your book. Write a letter to Ann Landers to get her advice on coping with the main problem you faced. Write her response.

Plot

1. Produce a calendar of events that reflects the story line. (The calendar can be divided among hours, days, weeks, months, or years.)
2. Produce a diary that one of the characters might have kept in order to chronicle the events of his or her life.

Setting

1. Pretend that the book is being turned into a one-hour special or a miniseries for television. Describe at least five locations where five different scenes should be filmed.
2. You are responsible for obtaining the props for a stage production of your book. List five props that are essential for the production and justify their use.

Theme

1. Describe at least one insight that the main character gained by the end of the book.
2. Describe how another book that you know makes the same point as the one you read.

Figure 3.3   Sample Literary Response Guide for Older Readers

---

1. Tell how far you read before you knew for sure that you wanted to finish the book.
2. Describe your favorite part of a chapter or of the entire book.
3. Think of a book that is like the one you just read and explain how the two are alike.
4. Identify the main problem and its solution in the book.
5. Explain why you would or would not choose someone in the book for a friend.

Figure 3.4   Sample Literary Response Guide for Younger Readers

1. Tell what you learned from this book.
2. Explain why you would or would not choose to read other books by this author.
3. Describe what information in this book you would like to know more about.
4. Describe what made this book interesting.
5. Explain how you might use what you learned from this book.

Figure 3.5   Sample Expository Response Guide

Directions: Complete items 1 and 2 listed below.
1. Describe what became clear to you while reading this material.
2. Describe one question you had after reading.

Directions: Mark one item from the list below and complete it.
_____ Poster advertising the book
_____ Display of at least five items representing the book
_____ Skit depicting an event from the book
_____ Conference on selected parts of the book

Directions: Create one additional way to react to your book. Describe below what you will do.

_____

_____

Figure 3.6   Sample Reaction Guide Offering Choices

Expository reaction guides differ from guides for narrative materials because expository guides do not refer to story characters or the main problem and solution of the plot. However, many of the items in expository guides could be applied to literary materials. Figure 3.5 shows an expository guide that fits younger as well as older readers.

Generic expository guides are helpful, but guides containing content-specific language also can be produced. For instance, if a student chooses to produce a written or an oral composition in response to *Megatrends* (Naisbitt, 1982), then the teacher might help him or her decide which questions about the book need to be addressed: Should the student explain the ten new forces transforming modern lives? Should the most important new trend be selected and reasons for the selections described? Should the actual, foreseeable impact of one trend on the student producing the composition be predicted?

Many teachers produce reaction guides that fit certain types of materials. For instance, a prompt for a biography might be to describe how the individual was influenced by others as well as how he or she exerted an influence on others. If a passage is associated with a movie, you might ask students to describe at least three differences. After reading a mystery, students might list the clues that led to its solution.

Finally, reaction guides can offer choices. Teachers might require one or two activities, provide options (e.g., "Select two of the following four choices"), and encourage students to create their own way to react. Figure 3.6 displays a reaction guide that offers choices.

Looking Back

When you use multiple reading materials in your classroom, you and your students will benefit greatly. Your teaching and your students' learning is energized. Reading materials vary from computer technology to trade books to periodicals. Students can respond to these materials in many ways, too. In this chapter you encountered three key ideas: (1) Students deserve a variety of content area reading materials; (2) a variety of content area reading materials are available; and (3) reports and response projects take many forms.

Add to Your Journal

Think about the role of multiple reading materials in the classes that you will be teaching. How far beyond the text do you intend to go? What types of materials will you use? How do you intend to have students react to what they read?

REFERENCES

Professional Publications

ALVERMANN, D. E., & MOORE, D. W. (1991). Secondary school reading. In R. Barr, M. L. Kamil, & P. D. Pearson (Eds.), *Handbook of reading research* (Vol. 2, pp. 951–983). White Plains, NY: Longman.

ASH, B. H. (1992). Student-made questions: One way into a literary text. *English Journal, 81*(5), 61–64.

BANKS, J. A., & MCGEE BANKS, C. A. (Eds.) (1993). *Multicultural education: Issues and perspectives* (2nd ed.). Boston: Allyn & Bacon.

BARRON, A. E., & IVERS, K. S. (1996). *The Internet and instruction: Activities and ideas.* Englewood, CO: Libraries Unlimited.

BERGER, L. R. (1996). Reader response journals: You make the meaning . . . and how. *Journal of Adolescent and Adult Literacy, 39,* 380–385.

CUNNINGHAM, J. (1985). Three recommendations to improve comprehension teaching. In J. Osborn, P. T. Wilson, & R. C. Anderson (Eds.), *Reading education: Foundations for a literate America* (pp. 255–274). Lexington, MA: Lexington Books.

DILLON, J. T. (1988). *Questioning and teaching: A manual of practice.* New York: Teachers College Press.

GOODLAD, J. I. (1984). *A place called school.* New York: McGraw-Hill.

GRAVES, M. F., PRENN, M. C., EARLE, J., THOMPSON, M., JOHNSON, V., & SLATER, W. H. (1991). Improving instructional text: Some lessons learned. *Reading Research Quarterly, 26,* 110–122.

GREENE, M. (1993). The passions of pluralism: Multiculturalism and the expanding community. *Educational Researcher, 22*(1), 13–18.

HANCOCK, M. R. (1993). Exploring and extending personal response through literature journals. *The Reading Teacher, 46,* 466–474.

HERNANDEZ, H. (1989). *Multicultural education: A teacher's guide to content and process.* Columbus, OH: Merrill.

HERZ, S. K., & GALLO, D. R. (1996). *From Hinton to Hamlet: Building bridges between young adult literature and the classics.* Westport, CT: Greenwood Press.

HUCK, C. S., HEPLER, S., & HICKMAN, J. (1993). *Children's literature in the elementary school* (5th ed.). Fort Worth, TX: Harcourt Brace.

LADSON-BILLINGS, G. (1994). *The dreamkeepers: Successful teachers of African American children.* San Francisco, CA: Jossey-Bass.

MCKENZIE, J. (1996). Making WEB meaning. *Educational Leadership, 54*(3), 30–32.

MORGAN, N., & SAXTON, J. (1991). *Teaching, questioning, and learning.* London: Routledge.

RICHARDSON, S. K. (1991). *Magazines for children.* Chicago: American Library Association.

RYDER, R. J., & GRAVES, M. F. (1996–1997). Using the Internet to enhance students' reading, writing, and information-gathering skills. *Journal of Adolescent and Adult Reading, 40,* 244–254.

STODOLSKY, S. S. (1989). Is teaching really by the book? In P. W. Jackson & S. Haroutunian-Gordon (Eds.), *From Socrates to software: The teacher as text and the text as teacher* (Eighty-eighth Yearbook of the National Society for the Study of Education, Pt. 1) (pp. 159–184). Chicago: University of Chicago Press.

STOLL, D. R. (Ed.) (1994). *Magazines for kids and teens: A resource for parents, teachers, librarians, and kids.* Newark, DE: International Reading Association.

WOLLMAN-BONILLA, J. E. (1989). Reading journals: Invitations to participate in literature. *The Reading Teacher, 43,* 112–120.

WOOD, K. D. (1993). Promoting lifelong readers across the curriculum. *Middle School Journal, 24*(5), 63–66.

Children's and Young Adults' Trade Books

ADAMS, B. J. (1992). *The Go-Around Dollar.* New York: Four Winds.

BASE, G. (1987). *Animalia.* New York: Abrams.

BASH, B. (1993). *Shadows of the night: The hidden world of the little brown bat.* San Francisco: Sierra Club.

BRANDENBURG, J. (1993). *To the top of the world: Adventures with arctic wolves.* New York: Walker.

BUNTING, E. (1991). *Fly away home.* New York: Clarion.

COERR, E. (1993). *Sadako.* New York: Putnam.

COLE, J. (1996). *The magic school bus inside a beehive.* New York: Scholastic.

COLLIER, J. L., & COLLIER, C. (1974). *My brother Sam is dead.* New York: Four Winds Press.

DISALVO-RYAN, C. (1991). *Uncle Willie and the soup kitchen.* New York: Morrow.

DONOVAN, J. (1969). *I'll get there, it better be worth the trip.* New York: Harper & Row.

FORBES, E. (1946). *Johnny Tremain.* New York: Houghton Mifflin.

FOX, P. (1991). *Monkey island.* New York: Orchard.

GIBSON, M. (1982). *Gods, men, and monsters from the Greek myths.* New York: Schocken.

GRIFFIN, J. H. (1977). *Black like me.* Boston: Houghton Mifflin.

HEARD, G. (1992). *Creatures of earth, sea, and sky.* Honesdale, PA: Wordsong/Boyds Mill Press.

HERSEY, J. (1946). *Hiroshima.* New York: Knopf.

HOBAN, T. (1990). *Exactly opposite.* Westport, CT: Greenwillow.

HOLLAND, I. (1994). *Behind the lines.* New York: Scholastic.

HOPKINS, L. B. (1992). *Flit, flutter, fly! Poems about bugs and other crawly creatures.* New York: Doubleday.

HOPKINS, L. B. (1994). *Weather.* New York: HarperCollins.

HOPKINS, L. B. (1995). *Hand in hand: American history in poetry.* New York: Simon & Schuster.

HUNT, I. (1964). *Across five Aprils.* Chicago: Follett.

JUKES, M. (1993). *I'll see you in my dreams.* New York: Knopf.

KALMAN, E. (1995). *Tchaikovsky discovers America.* New York: Orchard.

KING-SMITH, D. (1993). *The cuckoo child.* New York: Little, Brown.

KLEIN, N. (1988). *No more Saturday nights.* New York: Knopf.

KUBLER-ROSS, E. (1974). *On death and dying.* New York: Macmillan.

LESHAN, E. (1981). *The roots of crime.* New York: Scholastic.

LEWIS, C. (1987). *Long ago in Oregon.* New York: HarperCollins.

LEWIS, C. (1991). *Up in the mountains and other poems of long ago.* New York: HarperCollins.

LONDON, J. (1993). *Voices of the wild.* New York: Crown.

MAESTRO, B. (1993). *The story of money.* New York: Clarion.

MOWAT, F. (1963). *Never cry wolf.* Boston: Little, Brown.

NAISBITT, J. (1982). *Megatrends.* New York: Warner Books.

PARKS, R. (1992). *Rosa Parks: Mother to a movement.* New York: Dial.

PECK, R. N. (1972). *A day no pigs would die.* New York: Dell.

PILLING, A. (1993). *Realms of gold: Myths and legends from around the world.* New York: Kingfisher.

POLACCO, P. (1994). *Pink and Say.* New York: Philomel.

PRELUTSKY, J. (1988). *Tyrannosaurus was a beast.* New York: Greenwillow.

RANKIN, L. (1991). *The handmade alphabet.* New York: Dial.

SANDERS, S. R. (1992). *Warm as wool.* New York: Bradbury.

SELTZER, I. (1992). *The house I live in: At home in America.* New York: Macmillan.

SMITH, B. (1992). *The first voyage of Columbus.* New York: Viking.

SMITH, D. E. (1972). *Report from Engine Co. 82.* New York: McCall Books.

STRASSER, T. (1988). *The accident.* New York: Delacorte.

TERKEL, S. (1981). *Working.* New York: Simon & Schuster.

TOLAN, S. S. (1992). *Sophie and the sidewalk man.* New York: Four Winds.

TRUMBO, D. (1939). *Johnny got his gun.* Philadelphia: Lippincott.

WALDHERR, K. (1993). *Persephone and the pomegranate: A myth from Greece.* New York: Dial.

WATSON, J. D. (1968). *The double helix.* New York: Atheneum.

WELLS, R. E. (1993). *Is a blue whale the biggest thing there is?* Morton Grove, IL: Whitman.

WOLFE, T. (1979). *The right stuff.* New York: Farrar, Straus & Giroux.

YEP, L. (1991). *The star fisher.* New York: Morrow.

YOLEN, J. (1991). *Wings.* New York: Harcourt.

YOLEN, J. (1992). *The encounter.* San Diego: Harcourt Brace Jovanovich.

ZOEHFELD, K. W. (1994). *What lives in a shell?* New York: HarperCollins.

Computer Software

AMAZON TRAIL; GOLD RUSH! SIERRA ON-LINE, INC., P.O. BOX 485, COARSEGOLD, CA 93614; (800) 344-7448.

COMPTON'S MULTIMEDIA ENCYCLOPEDIA. COMPTON'S NEW MEDIA, 2320 CAMINO VIDA ROBLE, CARLSBAD, CA 92009; (800) 862-2206.

ENCARTA; MAGIC SCHOOL BUS SERIES. MICROSOFT CORPORATION, ONE MICROSOFT WAY, REDMOND, WA 98052; (800) 426-9400.

EYES ON THE PRIZE. PBS VIDEO, 1320 BRADDOCK PLACE, ALEXANDRIA, VA 22314; (800) 424-7963.

LUNAR GREENHOUSE; OREGON TRAIL II. MINNESOTA EDUCATIONAL COMPUTING CORPORATION, 6160 SUMMIT DRIVE NORTH, MINNEAPOLIS, MN 55430-4003; (800) 685-MECC.

THE NEW 1993 GROLIER ELECTRONIC ENCYCLOPEDIA. GROLIER ELECTRONIC PUBLISHING, SHERMAN TURNPIKE, DANBURY, CT 06816; (800) 365-5590.

OPERATION FROG; SIMCITY 2000. BRODERBUND SOFTWARE, 500 REDWOOD BOULEVARD, P.O. BOX 6121, NOVATO, CA 94948 (415) 382-4400.

CULTURAL REPORTER; TIMESHIFT RADIO. TOM SNYDER PRODUCTIONS, 80 COOLIDGE HILL ROAD, WATERTOWN, MA 02172-2817; (800) 342-0236.

WONDERS OF LEARNING CD-ROM LIBRARY. NATIONAL GEOGRAPHIC EDUCATIONAL SERVICES, P.O. BOX 98019, WASHINGTON, DC 20090-8019; (800) 368-2728.

ADDITIONAL READINGS

These publications extend reasons and practices for using multiple reading materials with elementary students.

CULLINAN, B. E. (1993). *Fact and fiction: Literature across the curriculum.* Newark DE: International Reading Association.

FREEMAN, E. B., & PERSON, D. G. (Eds.) (1992). *Using nonfiction tradebooks in the elementary classroom: From ants to zeppelins.* Urbana, IL: National Council of Teachers of English.

MOSS, B. (1991). Children's nonfiction trade books: A complement to content area texts. *The Reading Teacher, 45,* 26–32.

As computer technology becomes a common tool for subject matter study, more and more references suggest ways to use it wisely.

GRABE, M., & GRABE, C. (1996). *Integrating technology for meaningful learning.* Boston: Houghton Mifflin.

ROBLYER, M. D., EDWARDS, J., & HAVRILUK, M. A. (1997). *Integrating educational technology into teaching.* Upper Saddle River, NJ: Merrill.

Several professional references focus on trade books for the young. The following are first rate. The first addresses literature for children, and the second addresses literature for young adults.

HUCK, C. S., HEPLER, S., & HICKMAN, J. (1993). *Children's literature in the elementary school* (5th ed.). Fort Worth, TX: Harcourt Brace.

REED, A. J. S. (1994). *Reaching adolescents: The young adult book and the school.* New York: Merrill.

Scholars are beginning to examine the contents and roles of textbooks; three good collections of this research are as follows:

ALTBACH, P. G., KELLY, G. P., PETRIE, H. G., & WEIS, L. (Eds.) (1991). *Textbooks in American society.* Albany: State University of New York Press.

DECASTELL, S., LUKE, A., & LUKE, C. (1989). *Language, authority and criticism: Readings on the school textbook.* London: Falmer.

VENEZKY, R. L. (1992). Textbooks in school and society. In P. W. Jackson (Ed.), *Handbook of research on curriculum* (pp. 436–461). New York: Macmillan.

Many book selection guides are available partly because they constantly need updating to stay abreast of current publications. Some sample guides worth examining are listed on the next page.

Mathematics

THIESSEN, D., & MATTHIAS, M. (1992). *The wonderful world of mathematics: A critically anno-tated list of children's books in mathematics.* Reston, VA: National Council of Teachers of Mathematics.

Science

TCHUDI, S. (Ed.) (1993). *The astonishing curriculum: Integrating science and humanities through language.* Urbana, IL: National Council of Teachers of English.

Social studies

TUNNELL, M., & AMMON, R. (1993). *The story of ourselves: Teaching history through children's literature.* Portsmouth, NH: Heniemann.

ZARNOWSKI, M., & GALLAGHER, A. F. (1993). *Children's literature and social studies: Selecting and using notable books in the classroom.* Dubuque, IA: Kendall/Hunt.

The following emphasize the role of reading materials in promoting multicultural learning:

BISHOP, R. S. (Ed.) (1994). *Kaleidoscope: A multicultural booklist for grades K–8.* Urbana, IL: National Council of Teachers of English.

HARRIS, V. J. (1993). *Teaching multicultural literature.* Norwood, MA: Christopher-Gordon

OLSON, C. B. (Ed.) (1996). *Reading, writing, and thinking about multicultural literature.* Glenview, IL: Scott Foresman.

SMALLWOOD, B. A. (1991). *The literature connection: A read-aloud guide for multicultural classrooms.* Reading, MA: Addison-Wesley.

Two publications that suggest ways to promote students' second-language literacy learning in multicultural settings are as follows:

HUDELSON, S. (Ed.) (1993). *English as a second language curriculum resource handbook: A practical guide for K–12 ESL programs.* Millwood, NY: Kraus International Publishers.

SPANGENBERG-URBSCHAT, K., & PRITCHARD, R. (Eds.) (1994). *Kids come in all languages: Reading instruction for ESL students.* Newark, DE: International Reading Association.

The following reports convey what researchers have learned about students' responses to literature:

BEACH, R., & HYNDS, S. (1991). Research on response to literature. In R. Barr, M. L. Kamil, P. Mosenthal, & P. D. Pearson (Eds.), *Handbook of reading research* (Vol. II, pp. 453–489). White Plains, NY: Longman.

MARTINEZ, M. G., & ROSER, N. L. (1991). Children's responses to literature. In J. Flood, J. M. Jensen, D. Lapp, & J. R. Squire (Eds.), *Handbook of research on teaching the English language arts* (pp. 643–654). New York: Macmillan.

These two articles present valuable suggestions for eliciting students' responses to what they read:

SAUL, E. W. (1989). "What did Leo feed the turtle?" and other nonliterary questions. *Language Arts, 66,* 295–303.

SIMPSON, M. K. (1986). A teacher's gift: Oral reading and the reading response journal. *Journal of Reading, 30,* 45–50.

The following two books offer response guides for children's and young adults' literature; although the guides contain more content-specific questions than we recommend, their lists of related readings and writing activities are good examples of possible reading-response projects:

PARSONS, L. (1990). *Response journals.* Portsmouth, NH: Heinemann.

SOMERS, A. B., & WORTHINGTON, J. E. (1984). *Candles and mirrors.* Littleton, CO: Libraries Unlimited.

Conducting discussions of what students have read is not as easy as it might seem; the following suggest ways to conduct productive discussions:

ALVERMANN, D. E. (1991). The Discussion Web: A graphic aid for learning across the curriculum. *The Reading Teacher, 45,* 92–99.

ALVERMANN, D. E., DILLON, D. R., & O'BRIEN, D. G. (1987). *Using discussion to promote reading comprehension.* Newark, DE: International Reading Association.

GAMBRELL, L. B., & ALMASI, J. F. (Eds.) (1996). *Lively discussions! Fostering engaged reading.* Newark, DE: International Reading Association.

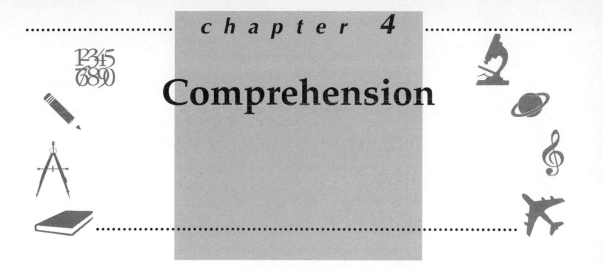

chapter 4

Comprehension

Looking Ahead

Comprehension is thinking while you read, listen, or view. Teachers can help students think more and better about what they are reading, listening to, or viewing by scaffolding their comprehension. They can build background knowledge so that students have more information to call up and connect to new information they will encounter when they attempt to comprehend. Teachers also help students to think by having them predict, organize, image, or self-monitor as they read or listen for specific purposes. During and after reading or listening, teachers can help students generalize about, evaluate, and apply information they learned. There are three increasing levels of scaffolding, depending on how difficult the text is for the students: comprehension follow-up, study guides, and content comprehension lessons. Teachers support students' comprehension of challenging, but teachable, texts by planning and carrying out content comprehension lessons in which the purposes are made clear and their fulfillment is ensured by group tasks and feedback.

Think back to your years as an elementary- and secondary-school student. What do you remember about reading your science, social studies, and other content area books? Perhaps you remember a scene like this:

The teacher has everyone open the book to the beginning of the chapter. Each student takes a turn reading part of the chapter aloud while everyone else follows along. Some students read well and fluently. Others stumble and miss words, and you think they will never get through. You look ahead instead of following along to figure out what part you might have to read so you can rehearse it before being called on. After the students take turns reading orally, the teacher spends some time firing questions at different students. The questions almost always have short answers, and if a student does not answer a question right away, the teacher calls on another student to answer it. For each question, the teacher continues to call on students until getting the desired answer. Finally, the students are assigned to finish reading the chapter and write answers to the questions at the end of the chapter.

The scene just described exemplifies an ineffective way to use content area books that you may have experienced as a student. This chapter will present you with much more effective ways to use content area materials.

Most of the time, we take reading comprehension for granted. We read words and automatically understand what we are reading. But comprehension does not always occur automatically. The following passage from a statistics book (Kirk, 1972) shows that comprehension is more than a matter of being able to read each word:

> Fractional factorial designs have much in common with confounded factorial designs. The latter designs, through the technique of confounding, achieve a reduction in the number of treatment combinations that must be included within a block. A fractional factorial design uses confounding to reduce the number of treatment combinations in the experiment. As is always the case when confounding is used, the reduction is obtained at a price. There is considerable ambiguity in interpreting the outcome of a fractional factorial experiment, since treatments are confounded with interactions. For example, a significant mean square might be attributed to the effects of treatment A or to a BCDE interaction. (p. 256)

Did you understand what you read? Could you retell it to someone in your own words without looking back at the text? Most people who are not knowledgeable about statistics could not comprehend that paragraph, although to statisticians, the paragraph makes perfect sense. As a teacher, you are knowledgeable in all the content subjects you will teach. Elementary- and secondary-school textbooks almost always make perfect sense to you because you already know a lot about what you are reading. You may feel as if you are learning a whole new set of facts by reading the text, but, in fact, you already know much of the information presented and are simply adding a little new information to the vast amount you already understand. Comprehension is indeed automatic when you are reading about topics for which you have adequate background, know most of the appropriate vocabulary, and know enough higher concepts to sort out important from trivial information. Students are seldom in that position when reading in the content areas.

These are the key ideas in this chapter:

1. Materials require different levels of scaffolding to support student comprehension.
2. Planning a content comprehension lesson includes deciding on clear learning purposes, background knowledge, and motivation.
3. Content comprehension lessons support students through the before, during, and after phases of reading.
4. There are many variations within the content comprehension lesson framework.
5. Students become independent comprehenders when teachers gradually fade their scaffolding and turn over responsibility to students.

MATERIALS REQUIRE DIFFERENT LEVELS OF SCAFFOLDING TO SUPPORT STUDENT COMPREHENSION

Think back to some of the books you have read. Do you remember any that read like the fractional factorial designs passage? Hopefully, you don't; realistically, you probably do. When text is this hard for you, you cannot possibly comprehend it, and your only choices are to skip it or—if there is a test—try to memorize it. We call this type of text "too challenging" for you. Most likely, the books you have available will not be this foreign to any of your students.

Most of what you read and listen to is very easy. Recall the scene we described at the beginning of this chapter. Because you have probably experienced the kind of instruction in that scene, your comprehension of our written description of it was probably immediate, instantaneous, and effortless. You called up classrooms in which this kind of instruction was the modus operandi. Perhaps you even imaged the voice, face, and scent of a particular teacher. You probably predicted that there might be a pop quiz on the day after the chapter was assigned. You may have generalized that "this was the way things were in social studies." Perhaps you evaluated: "I hated it. It was so boring." You may even have applied: "I'm not going to teach like that!"

When you read something that is so familiar and well-known to you that comprehension seems effortless and automatic, you are probably reading text we would describe as "easy" or "comfortable." The write-up in the sports page of last night's basketball game, which your favorite team won, is probably easy for you to read with good comprehension. Even if you did not see the game, you know all the players, their positions, and the likely moves they would make. The escape novel you read last summer was probably comfortable for you to read with understanding. You did not know exactly what would happen to the characters, but you have read many novels with similar characters and plots. If you devoured a series of books as an early adolescent (about Nancy Drew, Star Trek, or Dr. Who), you were increasing your reading speed and fluency by reading lots of easy materials.

Text that is too challenging for us is so unfamiliar and difficult that we never read it unless we are forced to. Text that is easy for us is so familiar and comfortable that we read it whenever we have the time, freedom, and interest in the topic or type of writing. Most books that we use in classrooms, however, are neither too challenging nor too easy for the majority of students; rather, most books are in that range of difficulty we describe as "teachable." *Teachable text* is text that students will understand and learn from better if teachers scaffold their comprehension than if they approach it independently. Teachable text is not so difficult that nothing the teacher says or does can help the majority of students understand and learn from it. It is not so easy and well written that most students can read it and think along with it just as well independently as with the teacher guiding them. In other words, teachable texts are those for which it helps to have a teacher.

When reading teachable text, students often need support. This support takes many different forms but involves the teacher in doing some activities with the students before, during, and/or after they read, view, or listen. For example, before reading, teachers can help students access background knowledge they may have but cannot automatically call up or build prior knowledge they may lack. Background knowledge is accessed or built when students watch videos, brainstorm ideas, or engage in discussion and interaction, sharing what they collectively know. Students also may need support in setting purposes, which require them to connect, predict, organize, image, generalize, evaluate, or apply. Purpose setting includes helping students use pictures and other visuals as clues to the important information, predict what they will learn, or form an opinion prior to reading and then reading to find support for that opinion. After reading, teachers can help students self-monitor whether their reading purposes were met or help them connect the new information to what they already knew.

Activities in which teachers support students before, during, and/or after reading, viewing, or listening are called *scaffolding.* Numerous research studies have investigated the effects of a variety of scaffolding on student learning. The almost unanimous conclusion from this research is that when students are reading something that is not easy for them, their learning is significantly increased when the teacher engages them before, during, or after activities that scaffold their comprehension.

Do It Together

From a book used in a course in your major or area of expertise and interest, choose a four- or five-page section. Read it once, close the book, and quickly write everything you remember from your reading. Have a friend who has a different major or area of expertise and interest do the same thing with a book section he or she selects.

Once you have separately read and recalled as much as possible from the books you chose, swap books, read the same sections the other read, close the book, and write everything you recall.

Compare the results. Did you recall more from the book you chose than from the one your friend chose? Can you see from the amount recalled that your chosen book was probably easy for you and your friend's book was probably teachable text for you?

The content area you choose to teach is usually one in which you are very interested and about which you have much accumulated knowledge; thus the books you read in that area always seem "remarkably simple." Looking at a book through the eyes of a novice will help convince you that most students require instruction to help them think and learn from reading in various content areas.

Materials that are easy for almost all your students do not require you to provide scaffolding. However, a lack of materials that are teachable for your students may indicate that the materials you have are inappropriate for your class. Certainly, it is expected throughout K–12 schooling that students in general are asked to read, view, and listen to materials sufficiently challenging to them that a teacher's scaffolding helps them increase their comprehension and learning. Anything less can indicate that the materials have been "dumbed down" and that more appropriate materials should be obtained.

It is hoped that the materials you have to use with your students contain a mixture of easy and teachable selections, with little or nothing that is too challenging. If so, it is helpful to remember that providing scaffolding helps your students in general to get more from the teachable materials but that the amount of scaffolding that is best in particular cases still varies. In other words, teachable materials exist across a range from teachable-but-quite-challenging to teachable-but-quite-comfortable. It is within this range of teachable materials that you will find it beneficial to consider which of three levels of comprehension scaffolding to provide: comprehension follow-up, study guides, or content comprehension lessons.

Just remember that evaluating how difficult your materials are or predicting how well your students will be able to read and comprehend them is not an exact science. If students have difficulty comprehending what you ask them to read, increase the level of comprehension scaffolding you provide. If students breeze through what you ask them to read, decrease the level of scaffolding. All classes have a range of students, so provide as much scaffolding as you can for those who need it but vary how you provide scaffolding to keep it from being boring for those who do not need it.

Comprehension Follow-Up

When content area materials are teachable in difficulty for most of your students, but on the comfortable end of that range, the scaffolding you provide should come *after* they have read, viewed, or listened to the material. Comprehension follow-up is the lowest level of scaffolding and consists of discussions, comprehension tasks (such as webbing or summarizing), and response activities (such as dramatizing or evaluating) that teachers have students engage in to follow up their independent comprehension of the material.

Comprehension follow-up helps students understand and remember. The disadvantage of comprehension follow-up is that it does not help students read (or view or listen to) material better than they would without scaffolding. When material is on the challenging end of the teachable range for most students, they may get little or nothing from their independent comprehension of the material or even give up trying. That is why comprehension follow-up provides sufficient scaffolding only to students who find the material on the comfortable end of the teachable range.

The advantage of comprehension follow-up is that it does not diminish incidental learning. *Incidental learning* is the learning of concepts in the material other than that on which the teacher focuses the students' attention by scaffolding. As you will see, higher levels of scaffolding gain advantages by preparing students to comprehend and learn targeted concepts. Research is clear, however, that such targeting increases students' *intentional learning* at the expense of their incidental learning. In other words, students focus on what is targeted (what they "intend" to learn) and pay less attention to everything else (what is "incidental"). Sacrificing incidental learning for students who would have understood little of what they were reading independently is not much of a sacrifice. However, sacrificing incidental learning for students who would have understood much of what they were reading should be avoided.

Study Guides

Study guides are generally lists of questions that guide students' reading. Because they directly influence how students read, they represent a higher level of scaffolding than comprehension follow-up. Study guides have been used for years and, while well-intentioned, can easily become monotonous busywork that many students do not find very helpful. On the other hand, study guides can also help teachers clarify reading purposes when the materials that students read for the study guide are teachable.

The most useful and "nonboring" study guides we have come across are the point-of-view reading guide and the interactive reading guide. The point-of-view reading guide (see Figure 4.1) engages the reader by making that reader and his or her reactions the central focus of the questions. The guide invites students to become one of the participants in what is being described and asks for readers' thoughts about and reactions to the events. Notice the liberal use of the words *you* and *your*. No doubt, you can see that many of the questions on a point-of-view study guide require students to evaluate.

The distinctive feature of the interactive reading guide (see Figure 4.2) is the interaction it ensures among students. The circle symbols at the top indi-

---

America After 1941

America's Huge War Needs

1. As a worker in a U.S. defense plant, tell what effect the War Production Board has had on you, your coworkers, and the soldiers overseas.

Americans Go Back to Work

2. As one of the leaders in a national labor union, what is your reaction to the need for war supplies?
3. As a farmer, tell how your life has changed from the Depression days to the present days of wartime.

Opportunities for Blacks

As a black person from the South:

4. Tell why you and others moved to the northeast and midwest sections of the U.S.
5. Describe the effect of Hitler's racist doctrine on your situation at home.
6. Tell why Executive Order 8802 was important to you.

Figure 4.1   Point-of-View Guide (U.S. History—Secondary Level). *Source:* Wood, K. D., Lapp, D., & Flood, J. (1992). *Guiding Readers Through Text: A Review of Study Guides.* International Reading Association. Reprinted with permission of Karen Wood and the International Reading Association.

cate which activities are to be done by individuals, pairs, small groups, and the whole class. As you look through the guide, notice that students have clear purposes for reading and that the actual reading is often done alone or with partners taking turns "whisper reading." Small groups often provide the during-reading task completion and feedback. The whole class gets together at certain points to brainstorm and discuss what is being learned.

While giving students a lot of questions to answer individually in writing while they read is probably too boring to help the students who really need that level of scaffolding, high-quality study guides of the two types discussed can help students comprehend moderately challenging texts better.

Listen/Look and Learn

Interview two teachers who use study guides and two students who have used study guides. If possible, look at the study guides and compare them with the two samples here. How do the teachers feel about the study guides? Is this different from how the students feel? What kinds of activities are included on the study guides? Do questions require a variety of thinking processes? Do the study guides provide some activities that can be done with a partner or small group? Summarize what you learned, including the benefits and pitfalls of using study guides. Then apply this to your own teaching: What will be the place of study guides in your instruction? What kinds of study guides will you use?

Interaction codes:

◯ = Individual

◯◯ = Pairs

◯◯◯ = Group

◯ = Whole class

◯◯◯ 1. In your group, write down everything you can think of relative to the topics listed below on Japan. Your group's association will then be shared with the class.

```
                          Japan
          location ──────  /│\  ────── major cities
                land      / │ \      industry
                   seasons  │  products
                          food
```

◯
◯◯ 2. Read page 156 and jot down five things about the topography of Japan. Share this information with your partner.

◯ 3. Read to remember all you can about the "Seasons of Japan." The associations of the class will then be written on the board for discussion.

◯◯ 4. a. Take turns "whisper reading" the three sections under "Feeding the People of Japan." After each section, retell, with the aid of your partner, the information in your own words.
   b. What have you learned about the following?
      terraces, paddies, thresh, other crops, fisheries

◯◯◯ 5. Put two pencils together and allow each person in the group to try eating with chopsticks. Discuss your experiences with the group.

◯◯ 6. With your partner, use prior knowledge to predict whether the following statements are true or false *before* reading the section on "Industrialized Japan." Return to these statements *after* reading to see if you've changed your view. In all cases, be sure to explain your answers. You do not have to agree with your partner.
   a. Japan does not produce its own raw materials but instead gets them from other countries.
   b. Japan is one of the top 10 shipbuilding countries.
   c. Japan makes more cars than the U.S.
   d. Silk used to be produced by silkworms but now it is a manmade fiber.
   e. Silkworms eat mulberry leaves.
   f. The thread from a single cocoon is 600 feet long.

◯
◯◯◯ 7. After reading, write down three new things you learned about the following topics. Compare these responses with those of your group.
      Other industries of Japan
      Old and new ways of living

◯
◯◯◯ 8. Read the section on "Cities of Japan." Each group member is to choose a city, show its location on the map in the textbook, and report on some facts about it.

◯
◯◯ 9. Return to the major topics introduced in the first activity. Skim over your chapter reading guide responses with these topics in mind. Next, be ready to contribute, along with the class, anything you have learned about these topics.

Figure 4.2 Interactive Reading Guide (Social Studies—Intermediate Level). *Source:* Wood, K. D., Lapp, D., & Flood J. (1992). *Guiding Readers Through Text: A Review of Study Guides.* International Reading Association. Reprinted with permission of Karen Wood and the International Reading Association.

Content Comprehension Lessons

The highest level of comprehension scaffolding that a teacher can provide to students is a content comprehension lesson. Because scaffolding is most beneficial and most necessary when the material is on the challenging end of the teachable range for the students, the remainder of this chapter helps you learn to plan and teach content comprehension lessons.

PLANNING A CONTENT COMPREHENSION LESSON INCLUDES DECIDING ON CLEAR LEARNING PURPOSES, BACKGROUND KNOWLEDGE, AND MOTIVATION

To increase your students' comprehension and learning, you must make sure that they have enough prerequisite knowledge to make sense of what they are reading, are motivated to try to make sense of it, and know what they should learn. Imagine now that it is the first week of school. You have met your students and have a general idea of their varied abilities. You also have one or more books, a curriculum guide, and other resources that provide you with some teachable text for most of your students. You are looking through the available reading, listening, and viewing materials and have several critical decisions to make. How you make these decisions will affect how much thinking and learning your students do.

Choosing What to Use as Material for Content Comprehension Lessons

Time is a teacher's most precious commodity. Using your time well is one of the keys to successful teaching. Books, curriculum guides, and other resources are filled with information, some of which is critical to understanding in your subject area, some of which your students already know, and some of which is trivial, highly technical, or boring. Good teachers are more interested in "uncovering the mysteries and joys of their subject" than in "covering the text." Good teachers know that you cannot teach it all and that if you try, many students will retain very little.

As we discussed in Chapter 3, one of the advantages of having a variety of materials is that the best treatment of a subject for your students can be chosen from several possibilities. Alternative sources of content information can often add clarity and depth to lackluster or even erroneous textbook sections.

As you look through your available resources, rate the various sections, chapters, parts, and so forth, on a three-star scale. The selections to which you give one star are parts or resources that may not be used at all or be used by individual students as they pursue their own interests. Selections that you decide are "interesting, important, but not critical" should be given two stars,

This teacher is planning a content comprehension lesson.

and you should have students work with these selections individually or in small groups as time and student needs permit. Those resources and selections that you determine to contain critical content area information and concepts should be given three stars. Whatever class time you can devote to helping your students think as they read, listen, and view should be devoted to teaching content comprehension lessons on these three-star selections.

Determining What You Want Everyone to Learn

Once you have determined which part of your books and other resources get the three-star rating and deserve your attention, you are ready to decide what critical concepts you want students to learn from these selections. Try to read or view various selections from the naive learner's standpoint. Imagine yourself once again as a novice in your subject area. What are the critical, exciting, stimulating, generative ideas that you want your students to take away from their interaction with this selection?

Because you are an expert in this topic, it may all seem simple and important, but some concepts, generalizations, and ideas are surely more critical than others. Many teachers find it helpful to view or read the selection first and then (with the book closed or the video stopped) list the most important ideas and information. Listing what is critical does not limit students to learning or thinking about only these critical ideas, but it does mean that your students' attention will be focused on the critical concepts, thus greatly increasing the chances that most students will learn them.

Motivating Students to Read

Once you know what you want students to learn from their reading, you must think about why they would want to learn it. The most common problems cited by content area teachers are the inability of students to read well and the "who cares?" attitude many students bring to reading. You can take care of the first problem by not asking students to read text that is clearly too challenging and by providing content comprehension lessons so they can focus their efforts on a doable task rather than the frustrating one of "reading to remember everything and to be able to answer any question the teacher might think to ask you." You also must consider what to do about the second problem.

While many factors affect motivation, the two greatest factors are the expectation of success and interest. Students must feel that they can successfully do what is being asked of them or they won't even try. Many students have experienced failure with reading to learn. When reading is assigned with little background building or purpose setting, students do not know what they are "supposed to get out of it," so they just read and hope they will know whatever it is the teacher asks or they give up because their past experience tells them they won't know it. Content comprehension lessons in which you provide scaffolding by building background, giving clear purposes, and following these purposes up with group tasks will convince students that they can successfully read in your subject area and, over time, change their expectation of failure.

The interest factor, however, must still be considered. How do you engage students' interest and make them want to read? Mathison (1989) cites five research-based strategies for piquing student interest: using analogies, relating personal anecdotes, disrupting readers' expectations, challenging students to resolve a paradox, and introducing novel or conflicting information. For simplicity's sake, we will combine the last three into one.

Using Analogies   In real life, we use analogies to explain new phenomena all the time. We describe a new friend to someone who has never met him by saying something like this: "He looks a little like John Lennon, but taller, and he is always upbeat and fun just like Hank was." We describe a new restaurant by comparing it to a familiar restaurant: "The food is wonderful, a little spicier than Chico's. It has big comfortable chairs and great, leisurely service just like Armando's."

According to Mathison, analogies make "the strange familiar and the familiar strange" (p. 171). When students are presented with analogies, their interest is aroused initially because the first part of the analogy is something with which they are familiar; thus they feel secure that they will be successful. The new information appears more interesting because they become intrigued with how the new, unfamiliar information is similar to and different from what they are familiar and comfortable with.

A social studies teacher might create an analogy between parliamentary and congressional forms of government when the class is studying England,

Canada, or Israel. A science teacher might create an analogy between airplane and bird wings when the class is studying birds. An algebra teacher might compare solving an equation with two or more unknowns to how Sherlock Holmes solves mysteries.

Relating Personal Anecdotes   Aren't you always curious about the personal lives of your teachers? Have you ever been surprised to come across one of your teachers competing in a local marathon or coaching the local soccer team? Don't you enjoy meeting your teachers' spouses and/or children and imagining your teachers as "real people"?

Students are naturally curious about the lives of their teachers. When teachers tell personal stories or anecdotes as lead-ins to reading, student interest is increased because they have a personal context in which to place the new information.

A math teacher might relate a personal anecdote about his or her experience learning how to solve quadratic equations in high school during that unit of Algebra I. While teaching about famous painters, an art teacher might relate a personal anecdote about his or her first visit to an art museum as a child.

Arousing Curiosity by Disrupting Readers' Expectations or Challenging Them with a Paradox or Conflict   Our past experience with any situation colors what we expect out of similar situations. When our expectations are not met, our attention is caught. When we go to see a movie by a favorite director or read a book by a favorite author, we have expectations about the kind of work we enjoy. If the director or author has done something significantly different, we immediately take notice. We may end up concluding that the change was marvelous and "mind-boggling," or we may hope that this was a temporary aberration and that the person will soon go back to the things we know and love. We do notice when our expectations are not met.

Students bring certain expectations to each content area. Sometimes these expectations are wrong. By noting these expectations before they read and alerting them that the text will not agree with their expectations, we utilize surprise and confusion to heighten student curiosity.

A paradox is an apparent contradiction in which two situations seem like they could not both be true and yet are. Good teachers challenge students to resolve paradoxes by "leading them down the primrose path," then presenting them with some conflicting but equally convincing information. Students then are challenged to read to see how this paradox might be resolved.

A conflict is a disagreement or struggle between two persons or groups. It can also be a struggle of a person or group against some inanimate condition or foe. Readers' curiosity may be aroused by informing them of the conflict so that they want to find out how it gets resolved.

A health teacher might arouse readers' curiosity by explaining that the "no cholesterol" printed on packages of cookies or potato chips will not protect them from increasing their cholesterol level as a result of eating those foods. A French teacher might arouse readers' curiosity by stating that they will be reading a conversation in French between an advocate and an opponent of nuclear power plants.

Designing a Group Task That Clearly Communicates a Purpose

Once you know what you want students to learn and how you will motivate them to want to read, you must decide on a group task that students will complete together after reading. This task must meet two criteria: Completing the task must result in the students learning what you decided was important; and the task must be clear to the students before they read.

Imagine, for example, that you decided that from a particular science resource, students should be able to list the nine planets, know their relative positions and sizes, and explain their orbits. How would you communicate this clearly? What joint task could the class complete after reading to show that everyone had learned the important information?

There are many possibilities for this. The most traditional is to make up questions. For our example, these are some questions:

What are the nine planets?
Which planet is the largest?
Which planet is about the same size as Earth?
Which planet is closest to the sun?

Of course, there would have to be at least twenty questions to cover all the important information. Students would be told to either answer the questions or prepare to discuss them, which is not a very motivating or intriguing purpose.

What else could you do to communicate your purpose clearly? Imagine that you drew the chart in Figure 4.3 on the chalkboard. Notice that you partially fill in the chart for students, talking as you write about what is needed in each column: "Earth is the sixth-largest planet. Its mean distance from the sun

Planet Name	Size (1 = biggest)	Distance from Sun (miles)	Earth Days in Year
Earth	6	92,960,000	365
Mars			
	1		
		3,660,000,000	
			60,188

Figure 4.3 Planets in Our Solar System

is 92,960,000 miles. The year is the number of days it takes a planet to orbit the sun, and the Earth year is 365 days." Now, you point to the second row and have students explain what they will try to figure out about Mars to put in each column. For the third row, you help them to notice that, since you put a "1" in the size column, this has to be the biggest planet. The fourth row must be completed for the planet that is 3,660,000,000 miles from the sun. The planet that takes 60,188 Earth days to orbit the sun goes in the fifth row. The last four rows are filled in with the remaining four planets.

This partially filled-in chart is one example of a group task that makes the purpose for reading clear and gets at the important information. Depending on what you want students to learn, there is an endless variety of group tasks that will clearly communicate a purpose for reading. You will see many more examples of groups tasks in the section about the different forms content comprehension lessons can take.

Building Background Knowledge

Students vary in the background knowledge they are able to call up about a particular topic. Students who live in Florida or California may know about oceans and oranges; midwestern students may be more familiar with wheat and blizzards. The author of a textbook may have assumed that students can call up certain information that you know your students lack. For instance, a passage on volcanoes may assume that students are aware of the "bubbling" action of heated liquids. Thus, the passage may deal primarily with a volcano's effect on the earth's crust, while failing to explain what forces magma up through it. If students are confused about the initial thrust of the magma, they may not be able to follow the rest of the description of volcanic action. We suspect that you had difficulty understanding the paragraph on statistics at the beginning of this chapter because of your own limited background in fractional factorial designs.

If certain information seems prerequisite to students learning from a text, then you should teach this information directly, before having the students read or listen to the text. If students already know the prerequisite information, this instruction will help them call the information up. Because the initial learning or calling up of relevant information is essential for comprehension, every content comprehension lesson should include attention to it.

Wait to choose the background concepts to teach in a particular content comprehension lesson until you have chosen the purpose for comprehending. For any selection, there will probably be several background concepts you would want your students to know, but teaching concepts well takes time. In a single lesson you can teach only one or two concepts that are new to your students. By waiting until the purpose is established, you can identify what background students need to fulfill that purpose and thereby make a better choice about which new concepts are most important to preteach.

CONTENT COMPREHENSION LESSONS SUPPORT STUDENTS THROUGH THE BEFORE, DURING, AND AFTER PHASES OF READING

Once planned, a content comprehension lesson is fairly easy to teach. Before students read, you help build motivation and prior knowledge and clarify the group task they will complete after reading. After students read, you lead them to complete the task and help them self-monitor how well they did. You may also want to be sure they have connected the new information learned from reading with prior knowledge. While it is impossible to set firm guidelines about how much time to spend in each phase, many teachers find that dividing the time available roughly into thirds is a reasonable guideline. With this distribution of time, the before-, during-, and after-reading phases are seen as more or less equally important in determining what students will learn from their scaffolded reading. Younger and less-able readers usually do the during-reading phase in class and require more time for all three phases; older and more able readers usually do the during-reading phase outside of class and require less time for all three phases.

Before Reading (Or Listening or Viewing)

There are three major goals that you want to accomplish before students read, listen, or view: (1) establish the motivation that will make them eager learners; (2) provide the prerequisite knowledge that will enable them to accomplish their purposes; and (3) help them clarify and understand what they are trying to learn. Sometimes these three goals are accomplished through separate activities. Other times, one activity can accomplish all three. In the preceding example about the planets, the teacher was building background knowledge while creating the chart on the board and filling in the entire row related to Earth as well as parts of the other rows. The background concepts included these:

There are nine planets.
They are all different sizes.
They are various distances away from the sun.
They all orbit the sun, and it takes different numbers of Earth days for them to orbit. This orbit is called a year.

Partially completing the chart for students makes the task clear, so their success-driven motivation should be high. Some interest is also piqued by the students' guesses before they read. Many students might say (or think), "That must be Jupiter," when the teacher makes clear that the planet for the third row is the largest one. Students are also apt to be intrigued by the idea that a planet could be more than three and a half billion miles from the sun and that a year on some planet would take 60,188 Earth days.

A teacher recording the responses of students during a group task.

Since most students have some prior knowledge and considerable interest in the solar system, the talk engaged in as the teacher sets up the partially completed chart might be sufficient for developing both background knowledge and motivation. In this fortunate case, one activity accomplishes all three pre-reading goals.

Sometimes one lesson provides the background and motivation for another lesson later on. Students might watch a video on oceans that would build prior knowledge and pique their interest. This video could set the stage for the following day's lesson, in which they read to find out the main sources of ocean pollution and evaluate the feasibility of some proposed solutions.

How much background building and motivation are required? Generally, the less familiar a topic is to students, the more time and effort you have to expend to build background and motivation.

Perhaps the most important part of the before-reading phase of a content comprehension lesson is making clear the students' purpose for reading. What is clear to you as the teacher is often a mystery to your students. Has an English teacher ever told you to read so that you can discuss how the setting of a story or novel affects the plot development? In order to accomplish this purpose you must understand clearly what setting and plot entail, then clearly perceive the setting, follow the plot, and finally get to the task of thinking about how setting and plot interact. This complex task is further complicated by the jargon—setting and plot. Many students are confused by such terminology as setting, plot,

	Setting (Time and Place)	Plot (What Happened)
Beginning of story		
Middle of story		
End of story		
How did the setting at different points in the story affect what happened?		

Figure 4.4   Plot/Setting Diagram

main idea, and summary. When alerting students to the purposes for which you would like them to read, try to avoid unnecessary jargon or make the jargon clear by including examples.

In a situation where the interaction between setting and plot was important, students would be more apt to understand what you wanted them to read for if you drew on the board a diagram such as Figure 4.4.

After displaying the diagram, you could explain to students that the setting changes three times during the story and that certain things happen in the different settings. Students should read so they can fill in the three settings and the major events that happened in each setting. They should also think about how the different times and places affected what did and did not happen.

In this example, you have clarified the purpose by making a little chart on the board and explained what is meant by the jargon *setting* and *plot.* You have also written the chart and the question on the board so that as students read, they can look up and think about what they can contribute to the group task of filling in the chart and discussing the question.

Purposes for reading, listening, or viewing vary tremendously: Some are very specific and target particular learning; others give the students an opportunity to determine what they want to know or how they will respond to the content they are attempting to comprehend. To whatever extent you are limiting or focusing what they are to gain from their reading, listening, or viewing, you must clearly communicate that sense of purpose to them before they begin.

When students have the necessary motivation and prior knowledge and know their purpose for reading, they are ready to move into the next phase.

Reading (Or Listening or Viewing)

Now the students go to work and read, listen, or view to fulfill their purposes. Often students read silently, but the reading can take other forms. Students can be paired and read the passage together, with each one taking a page or a paragraph. As they read, you may notice their eyes going up to the board as they come upon some piece of information they want to include. During the first few content comprehension lessons, you may need to interrupt the reading after a few minutes and point to the purpose on the board to remind students of it.

Sometimes the reading phase finds the teacher reading and the students listening. If you have only one copy of a newspaper or magazine article containing information that you want to share with students, this is a perfect opportunity to do a listening content comprehension lesson. For young children and some older remedial readers, their comprehension ability is greater than their ability to figure out the words. In this case, you may want to read something to them so that their limited word identification ability does not hinder their ability to learn and think about important content area information.

Some lessons may find the teacher and the students watching and listening to a video or speaker. Because thinking underlies reading, listening, and viewing comprehension, the same plan is appropriate for all three information-gathering avenues.

After Reading (Or Listening or Viewing)

If you have set a clear purpose, what happens after comprehending is obvious: Students contribute their ideas and as a group complete the task you set for them.

As students contribute to completing the task, the teacher should try as much as possible to be nonjudgmental and record what students suggest. If there is disagreement, the teacher should resist the temptation to "be the expert" and write both responses with question marks next to them. When teachers resist the temptation to make corrections during the group comprehension task, it helps students become more responsible for their own learning.

During the initial task completion, it is generally best not to let students have their books open or look back but rather to record all the relevant ideas they have and mark with blanks or question marks what they are unsure of or have conflicting opinions about.

Once students have done as much as they can, give them a chance to reopen their books and check or seek support for those parts of the class response that are in question. (If this were a listening or viewing activity, you would reread or reshow the parts needed to clear up the confusion; fill in the gaps; or provide clues to the inferences, generalizations, or conclusions required by the task.) As students tell you what to revise or add, have them read part of the text aloud and explain how this information or statement helps to resolve the disagreement. Again, the teacher should remain a guide and not assume the expert role. If there is some misinformation or misunderstanding that students cannot resolve, help them clarify what needs fixing and why. Guide them to see what they have read as the source and you as their guide to understanding rather than you as the expert with the "right answer." Students will work harder if they know they are really responsible for finding information and thinking about what it means.

Finally, ask the group if what they have come up with represents what most of the members believe to be their best thinking. Spend a few minutes talking about what they did and how they did it. For the setting-plot purpose discussed above, you might say something like this:

> Today you did a great job of charting the time and place and the major events. You could then see the relationship between the setting and the plot. Often in books and movies, the setting affects the plot. If we think about the time and place in which things happen, we can see how this occurs.

In the planet example, your purpose is for students to learn some basic facts about the planets. Once you establish that the planet chart the group completed is as accurate and complete as possible, you might point out how much more they knew and how efficiently they had recorded it on the chart. If this information is information you want everyone to learn, you might have them copy the chart into a science notebook so that they have clear, concise notes to study.

The after-reading phase is critical to both the development of students' content knowledge and their reading strategies. As the students complete the task, they connect new knowledge to old. As they are guided to revisit parts of the texts to resolve disagreement or fill in gaps, they learn not only how to self-monitor their comprehension but also how to use some fix-up strategies when comprehension fails.

THERE ARE MANY VARIATIONS WITHIN THE CONTENT COMPREHENSION LESSON FRAMEWORK

Now that you understand the general events comprising the before-, during-, and after-reading phases of a content comprehension lesson, we want to expand your vision by presenting a variety of possibilities. This variety in the specific ways a content comprehension lesson can proceed allows you to teach lessons that provide variety and are appropriate for a wide range of reading passages, instructional goals, and types of students.

Lessons Using Graphic Organizers

You already have two examples of lessons using graphic organizers. Both the planet chart and the setting-and-plot chart are graphic organizers. *Graphic organizers* are visual diagrams that help us see the relationships among concepts. There are many kinds, and you can create your own variations. Figures 4.5 to 4.11 show popular graphic organizers in various stages of completion by students.

Famous Americans in Four Poems				
Qualities (+ / -)	Abraham Lincoln	Georgia O'Keeffe	Martin Luther King, Jr.	Betsy Ross
proud				
controversial				
artistic				
political				
_____				
_____				
_____				
_____				

Figure 4.5   Semantic Feature Matrix

If the relationships depicted by the graphic organizers in these figures are obvious, you can see how clearly graphic organizers communicate purposes to students and how well they help students see important relationships in the information they are reading. On the semantic feature matrix, students indicate with a plus or minus which qualities are possessed by various Americans depicted in poetry. On the Venn diagram, students compare and contrast how animals and humans communicate. These graphic organizers are helpful in comparing and contrasting members of a particular group.

The time line is an excellent device to use when sequence is important. Here, students fill in the important event that occurred on each date. A varia-

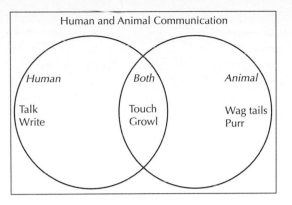

Figure 4.6 Venn Diagram

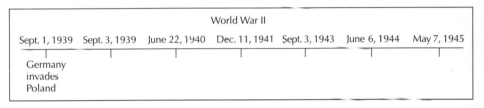

Figure 4.7 Time Line

Students construct time lines in order to display information they have gathered.

tion is to give students a time line of events and have them fill in the dates. If you want more details, draw two lines under each event line and have students fill in two details about each event.

Both the whale web (Figure 4.8) and the Yukon outline (Figure 4.9) help students organize information when they are to learn a variety of information about one big topic. Most students find it easier to web ideas than to outline them because when they outline, they often get lost in the trivia of upper- and lowercase letters and indentation. The partially completed outline allows students to concentrate on the information and the relationships because the skeleton and a few pieces of information are included.

Notice in the cause-and-effect chain that some causes have multiple effects, some effects have multiple causes, and an effect often becomes a cause of another effect. These diagrams help students sort through the complex relationships that comprise much of the information they need to understand in the real world.

These figures are a sampling of graphic organizers to spur your thinking about how to help students see important relationships by considering how you would depict those relationships graphically. When you determine that students need to learn some facts and their compare-contrast relationships, time/order relationships, topic/subtopic relationships, or causal relationships, a graphic organizer is often your most efficient group task.

Try It Out

Find a book that you might use in your teaching. Select a five- to ten-page section that you would consider important enough to teach a content comprehension lesson on. Consider the important facts and relationships. Construct a graphic organizer that your students could complete as a group task. Include enough of the pieces so that students would clearly understand what information goes where.

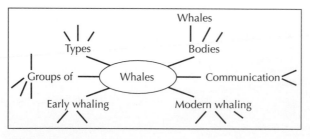

Figure 4.8   Web

THE YUKON
A. Geography
   1.
   2.
   3.
   4.
B. Economy
   1. Fishing
      a.
      b.
   2. _____
      a. lynx
      b.
      c.
   3. Manufacturing
      a.
      b.
      c.
   4. _____
      a. gold
      b.
      c.
      d.
      e.
C. Government
   1. Canadian
      a.
      b.
      c.
   2. Territorial
      a.
      b.

Figure 4.9   Outline

Lessons Using Prediction

Organizing information is one of the thinking processes we utilize to learn information; predicting is another. We are predicting whether a particular book will interest us when we peruse the title, author name(s), and cover illustration. We are predicting when we thumb through a magazine, looking at the pictures before we start to read. We are predicting when we read a heading such as "Are We Once Again Headed into Recession?" and assume that the author will give us reasons to believe we are or are not. Across the years of reading instruction, various ways of having students make predictions have been devised. We will discuss three with some unique practical features: an anticipation guide (referred to as a prediction guide in Herber, 1978), KWL, and DRTA.

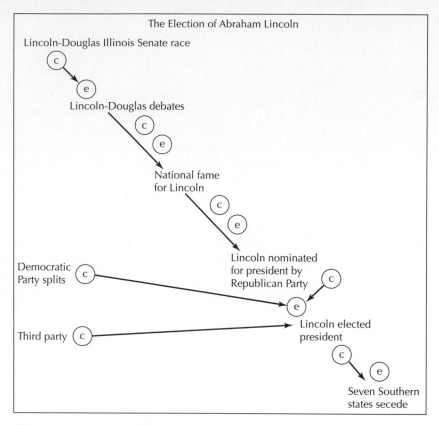

Figure 4.10 Cause-and-Effect Chain

An *anticipation guide* is a list of statements or key words, some of which are true and some of which are false. The students are presented with the statements or key words and they guess which are true and which are false. They then read to check their predictions. Below is an anticipation guide used before students read about the life of Babe Ruth. What are your guesses?

Babe Ruth
1. Orphan
2. Good kid
3. Only child
4. Irish
5. German
6. Over six feet tall

7. Right-handed
8. Pitcher
9. Catcher
10. New York Yankee
11. Still living

How did you do? Do you have some guesses about which you are quite sure and others for which you do not have a clue? Do you want to know the answers? Of course you do, and you therefore see the power of prediction as a motivating device. Students who have made some guesses want to read to "see if they were right." Students who guess about some statements before reading are nearly always motivated to read and be clear about their purposes for reading.

One of the most flexible and popular ways of organizing a content comprehension lesson based on student predictions is a KWL (Carr & Ogle, 1987; Ogle, 1986). The letters stand for what we know, what we want to find out, and what we have learned. Imagine that the class is about to read about Washington, D.C. The teacher might begin by finding Washington, D.C. on a map and asking which students have been there. A chart such as the following would then be started:

WASHINGTON, D.C.

What We Know	What We Want to Find Out	What We Learned

The teacher then has the students brainstorm what they know about Washington, D.C. and writes the facts in the first column. When the students have brainstormed all their prior knowledge, the chart might look like this:

WASHINGTON, D.C.

What We Know	What We Want to Find Out	What We Learned
Capital		
White House		
President lives there		
Lots of drugs		
Azaleas in spring		
Cold in winter		
Near Virginia		
Near Maryland		

Next, the teacher would direct the students' attention to the second column and ask them what they would like to find out about Washington, D.C. Their questions would be listed in the second column:

WASHINGTON, D.C.

What We Know	What We Want to Find Out	What We Learned
Capital	How old is it?	
White House	How big is the White House?	
President lives there	What else is in D.C.?	
Lots of drugs	Where is the FBI?	
Azaleas in spring	What kind of government does D.C. have?	
Cold in winter	Why is it not a state?	
Near Virginia	How many people live there?	
Near Maryland	What do the people do who aren't in the government?	

Once the questions are listed, students read to see which of their questions were answered and find other interesting tidbits they think are important.

After reading, the teacher begins by seeing which of the questions were answered, then leads students to add other interesting facts. This information is recorded in the third column. All class members are encouraged to contribute, and no one looks back at the book until all initial responses are shared. Disputed or unclear information is noted with question marks.

When all the initial recalls are recorded, students go back to the text to clarify, prove, or fill in gaps. The teacher leads the students to read the relevant part aloud and explain their thinking. When the information on the chart is complete and accurate, the teacher points out how much was learned and how efficiently the chart helped to record it. Inevitably, there will be questions that were not answered in the reading, and a natural follow-up is to help the students use additional resources to locate the answers.

A Directed Reading Thinking Activity—DRTA (Stauffer, 1969)—is a way of getting students to predict what they will learn. In a DRTA, the teacher usually leads the students to make predictions, read portions of the text, stop and make more predictions, read some more, and so on until the text is finished. Predictions are written on the board, checked when confirmed, and erased when not confirmed. How many times the students stop and make predictions depends on the length of what they are reading and their maturity. Here is an imaginary script for a modified DRTA on a science section about sound:

Teacher: Today we are going to begin learning about sound. What do you think we might learn?

The teacher waits for students to respond, then writes these responses on the board:

What sound is.
How you hear.

What different kinds of sounds there are.
Where sounds come from.

Teacher: Let's open our books now and see if we can predict anything else
we might learn just by looking at the visuals.

The teacher directs students' attention to several pictures, a chart, and a
diagram. Students add predictions, which the teacher writes on the board:

Sound travels in waves.
You make sounds with guitars.
Your ears let you hear sounds.
Sounds are measured in decibels.
Bats can hear sounds.

The teacher reads all the predictions aloud and ask students to read the
first three pages to see which predictions are true. Students do so. They
read a part of the text to prove each prediction, then the teacher puts a
checkmark next to that prediction. The teacher asks if there are more predictions students would like to add before finishing the sections. After students make suggestions, the teacher writes this:

Soft sounds have decibels.
Loud sounds have really big decibels.
Pitch is how high or low the sound is.

Students finish reading the section on sound, then tell which predictions
should be checked because they are true and which should be erased
because they either are not true or were not mentioned.

This section has presented three formats for lessons in which students
make predictions about what they will read. Anticipation guides, KWLs, and
DRTAs differ in how much input the teacher and students have into the predictions. All three, however, motivate students to think about what they know
and might find out and then to read with clear purposes.

Lessons That Lead Students to Generalize, Evaluate, Image, and Apply

This book began by describing the nine thinking processes most directly
involved in reading and writing. This chapter began with the idea that comprehension is thinking and can be greatly increased. The thinking processes calling up, connecting, and self-monitoring are constant players in the comprehension process. Calling up occurs as background knowledge is accessed and built
prior to comprehending as well as during comprehending when cued by
meaning vocabulary. Connecting occurs whenever new knowledge is connected to old, whether before, during, or after comprehending. Self-monitoring

occurs during comprehending as well as after, whenever students regulate their own learning.

Other thinking processes are used depending on the particular lesson. It is obvious that content comprehension lessons in which students complete a graphic organizer involve organizing and lessons that use prediction involve predicting. What may not be so obvious is that other thinking processes—generalizing, evaluating, imaging, and applying—are often included.

After completing the Venn diagram on human and animal communication Figure 4.6, the teacher may lead the students to conclude that "there are many similarities between humans and animals," a generalization based on the data students have put into the graphic organizer.

After students complete the World War II time line (Figure 4.7), teachers may lead them to talk about the events and imagine what it would have been like fighting those battles on either side. This discussion would involve the students in forming images of the events they had just organized.

Students who learned about whales and organized the information into a web (Figure 4.8) might take a stand on whether whales should be hunted. This discussion would involve the thinking process of evaluating.

Applying what you have learned to your current and future life can also occur in some of the content comprehension lessons described. After learning about the Yukon or Washington, D.C., students could be asked if they would like to live there.

In addition to eliciting discussions that extend to generalizing, evaluating, imaging, and applying, you can conduct lessons in which these thinking processes are the primary ones. Here are some group tasks, the completion of which requires students to generalize, evaluate, image, or apply.

Generalizing   Generalizing occurs whenever we take some specific pieces of information and conclude something about them. We generalize when we look at a chart showing London's average monthly rainfall and conclude: "It must rain almost every day!" Often a generalization is a main idea or summary statement. We read about the economies of various Latin American countries and conclude:. "The vast majority of the people there live below the U.S. poverty level."

When you decide that the major thing you want students to do is draw some conclusions or form some big ideas about what they are reading, you will want your group task to lead them to generalize as they read. There are many tasks that accomplish the purpose. We will describe two: GIST and Sustained Summary Writing.

In GIST, the group task is to write a summary in 20 words or less. The teacher explains that the *gist* of something is the main idea and that sometimes we do not need to remember all the details but read just to get the gist of the material. The teacher draws 20 word-size blanks on the chalkboard or on a transparency and explains to the students that, after reading, they will try to write a sentence or two of no more than 20 words that captures the gist of what they have read.

The students read a short section—no more than three paragraphs—then work with the teacher to record the gist of what they have read. Students take turns telling the teacher part of what to write. In no case will the teacher write a twenty-first word. Students must revise what they want the teacher to write so that it will fit into the 20 blanks. The discussion challenges students to distill what is really important. This is an example of a GIST statement a class might produce:

Tropical	rain	forests	are	lush
forests	near	the	equator	that
are	hot	and	get	a
lot	of	rain.		

Next, the teacher tells them to read the following section and says that they must now incorporate the information from both the first section and the second in just 20 words. Students groan but usually rise to the challenge of trying to compact twice the amount of information into the same limited set of words. This is an example of the revised GIST statement, including information from both sections:

Tropical	rain	forests	are	hot,
rainy,	and	important	because	of
the	many	species	of	plants
and	animals	that	live	there.

It is possible that the teacher might then have the students read a third short section and attempt to incorporate its information into the GIST statement. (No more than three sections should be used with this challenging task.) This is an example:

Tropical	rain	forests	lower	the
carbon	dioxide	in	the	air
and	provide	new	medicines	and
products	They	must	be	protected.

During this process, students learn how to ignore the details and just get down to the core of what they are reading. Of course, you can expect your average students to be less able to contribute as more sections are read. As a result, it is a good idea to delay calling on the ablest students until the going gets difficult. That way most students will be able to make a contribution at some point during the GIST process.

Sustained Summary Writing is similar to GIST, but students read a longer passage and are given a limited time (three to five minutes) to write the most important information they remember. When the time is up, students share their summaries as the teacher records on the board the major ideas. These ideas are then included in a group summary dictated by the class and written by the teacher.

Evaluating   You will remember from Chapter 1 that the thinking processes are not separate and distinct. Often generalizing is quickly followed by evaluating. After generalizing that it rains almost every day in London, you might decide: "I wouldn't want to live in a place like that!" After generalizing that most people in South America live below the U.S. poverty line, you might decide: "That's awful!" When we want students to decide how they feel about something, we must come up with a group task that requires them to make judgments and form opinions. Figure 4.11 is a graphic organizer that has students not only organize but also evaluate.

Here is another group task that involves evaluating:

Decide if you think our country's involvement in Bosnia was the right thing to do or did more harm than good. Come up with defensible reasons for your position.

There are many other purposes you can use: Students can prepare to debate. They can draft letters to officials. They can hold mock elections and referendums. The critical words in a group task that require evaluating are *you* and *decide*. Students must understand that they are to weigh the evidence and consider the ideas but that what you ultimately want is their opinion.

Imaging   Imaging is using the senses to learn. It involves imagining something, seeing it, and putting yourself there. When we want students to image, we must move away from the two-dimensional world of the chalkboard into the real world. Here are some suitable tasks:

Draw, paint, or sculpt a pioneer.
Create a diorama of a scene from pioneer days.
Pick or create a piece of music that evokes Switzerland.
Create a skit or play in which you act out a confrontation between the President and Congress.
Imagine that two pioneers were transported to the twentieth century. Decide what kind of food each would most prefer. What kind of car would each drive? Which baseball team would each root for?

Applying   Finally, we want students to apply what they read to their own lives. Here the key words are *use* and *do*. Students apply when they read to fig-

Advantages	Disadvantages

Which way would you vote if you were a senator?

Figure 4.11   Raising Taxes to Reduce the Deficit

ure out how to do an experiment or make a kite or fix a faucet. When the group task for a lesson is something students are actually going to do, you usually do not have to worry about motivation.

It is not always possible to actually have the students apply. Since we are all dreamers, however, you can use tasks that call for applying to help students think about how they might realize some of their dreams. Students apply when they read about certain countries to plan an ideal trip, or read a *Consumer Reports* article to choose which CD player is the best buy.

This section has contained numerous examples of comprehension tasks you can use to clarify students' purpose for reading. If you pick and choose from these kinds of tasks to match what you determine is most important in a text or video, you will not only help students learn more from their comprehending, but also ensure variety in your lessons and provide students many ways to think about what they read, listen to, or view.

Do It Together

Work with three or four others to plan a content comprehension lesson, but do not share what you come up with until everyone is finished. All group members should have the same piece of text. Working separately, list what you would like students to learn from reading this selection. Then come up with a group task that will make clear students' purpose for reading. Finally, decide what prerequisite knowledge you must build and how you will motivate students to want to read the text. Get back together and share your content comprehension lessons. Did you find some variety? Did people differ in what they thought students should learn, and thus were the group tasks different? All content comprehension lessons require students to call up, connect, and self-monitor. Decide as a group which of your lessons also required organizing, predicting, imaging, generalizing, applying, or evaluating.

STUDENTS BECOME INDEPENDENT COMPREHENDERS WHEN TEACHERS GRADUALLY FADE THEIR SCAFFOLDING AND TURN OVER RESPONSIBILITY TO STUDENTS

The major goal of all teachers is for students to become independent learners. So far in this chapter, we have stressed teacher support and scaffolding, because in content classrooms in which students are left to "sink or swim," many sink. In other classrooms, teachers keep students afloat by teaching the content without ever having students read, and, while students do learn some information, they never learn how to read content area materials. They do not sink, but they still do not swim. As far as reading content area materials is concerned, they remain on shore.

We hope that as we near the end of this chapter, you are looking at your books and other learning resources, as well as your students, and seeing the potential for a happier marriage between the two. We hope you will provide a variety of levels of comprehension scaffolding that will help all your students succeed in comprehending what they read, listen to, and view. When you arrive at this point, however, we want you to think once again about the sink-or-swim mentality. If your students can swim but only with you alongside, coaching them on, telling them what strokes to use and when they have arrived at their destination, now is the time to begin to decrease your scaffolding and move them toward independence. This chapter ends with a discussion of two ways you can move your students toward independence in comprehension: teacher fading and student self-assessment.

Fading

As Chapter 1 noted, fading is a process of gradually decreasing the scaffolds you give and letting students take on more responsibility. You will know when to fade your scaffolding as you observe the success your students experience. One of the ways you fade within the content comprehension lesson framework is to move from the specific purposes that are usable with only one piece of text to more generic purposes that can be used with many pieces of text.

Imagine, for example, that you have used many webs in class. Your students have gotten good at reading to find information for the various spokes of the web. Suddenly you remember that partially completed webs will not mysteriously appear when students need them; if they leave your classroom forever dependent on you to create the web, they will not be able to use this valuable strategy independently. Consequently, it is now time to fade your scaffolding. In fact, the next time you think a web will make a good group task, have the students create it.

Tell students that webbing is a wonderfully efficient way to organize topic/subtopic information and that they can create their own webs. On the board or an overhead transparency, write the topic in a circle and draw several lines pointing out from it. Have the students do the same on their own paper. Give students a few minutes to preview the text section you have selected and have them use the headings and visuals to create spokes of the web. Let several students come to the board and draw their web skeleton. Lead the students to understand that there is no magical number of spokes to include and that different labels for the spokes are equally good. Help them see that as long as the spokes contain main topics, the web helps them organize what they read.

Have students read and write details on the spokes of their own webs. After their reading, put students in groups of four or five to compare webs. Encourage them to accept diverse webs but also to add to their own webs information that the group sharing convinces them they need. Help students view webbing as a note-taking strategy that they can use independently.

Once students complete webs independently, discuss the other graphic organizers and move students toward independence in these. Use the same procedure to help them choose the categories for a chart or semantic feature matrix, the main topics for an outline, the important dates for a time line, or the entries for a cause-and-effect chain. Then have them read and independently complete their own organizers, which they can compare with others' in a small group.

When you have your students independently webbing, charting, outlining, and so on, your task is nearly complete. One more little piece of teacher fading is needed. Your students will not always have you there to decide how to organize the text information graphically, so let them decide. Have them preview the text and decide how best to organize the information. Let different students or groups organize the data as they think best, then share their work with the class. When students can preview something they are about to read, decide what kind of graphic organizer would most efficiently and clearly depict the important relationships, and create the graphic organizer, they are becoming independent learners.

This same kind of fading of teacher guidance and content-specific purposes can be applied to the other comprehension formats. Students who have been engaged in KWLs and DRTAs can learn that before they read they call up what they already know and try to predict what questions the text might answer or what they might learn. They can preview the text and use the headings and visuals to make these predictions. After reading, they should ask, "What do I know now that I didn't know before I read?" and "Have I learned what I wanted to learn?" Students who have been involved in creating GIST statements and summary paragraphs learn to do this for themselves. Students learn that it helps you understand, enjoy, and remember if you imagine yourself transported into the book. They learn to ask themselves the evaluate question, "What do I think about this?" and the apply question, "What can I do with this information?"

Fading is not difficult to do, but it is sometimes difficult to remember to do. Just when your lessons are going well and your students are succeeding with your support, you must remember that some day they will have to do these tasks on their own.

Self-Assessment

During fading, the emphasis is on teachers gradually providing less scaffolding while holding students to the same standards with respect to their comprehension. However, if students are to become truly independent comprehenders, they must also learn to assess their own comprehension.

The first kind of self-assessment that you should probably help your students do in comprehension is integrated with your fading process. This kind of self-assessment mirrors the thinking you do as a teacher when you attempt to determine the level of comprehension scaffolding a class needs to comprehend a particular piece of material. As you move the students through your course, the time will probably come when you have provided all three levels of comprehension scaffolding with different materials: comprehension follow-up, study guides, and content comprehension lessons. At that point, rather than making the judgment yourself, ask your students to preview the material you want them to comprehend and help you decide which level of scaffolding to provide with that material. The class should gradually improve in their ability to predict how much help they need from you.

The second kind of self-assessment that you should probably help your students do in comprehension occurs within a single level of comprehension scaffolding: comprehension follow-up. After students are very familiar with the kinds of discussions, comprehension tasks, and response activities you use to follow up their independent comprehension of material, they can be asked to help you construct the follow-up they will then engage in for something they have just read. As they work with you to create these follow-up activities, many students improve in their ability to assess what is important for them to understand and remember from the material.

The third kind of self-assessment that you should probably help your students do in comprehension occurs within a study guide or content comprehension lesson. After students are very familiar with the kinds of study guides and content comprehension lessons you prepare for them, have them accompany each comprehension response they give orally or write a 1 ("probably not right") or 2 ("probably right"). Simply predicting whether you are right or not and then later finding out helps you develop self-assessment as both a habit and an ability.

Specific Content Area Applications

● COMPREHENSION IN THE ENGLISH/LANGUAGE ARTS CLASSROOM

Attention to reading comprehension in English and language arts generally centers about novels, short stories, plays, and poetry. English teachers have countless options for promoting students' understanding of these literary forms. Given this situation, the following focuses on one specific piece of children's literature. What you gain from examining this example in depth can be used to guide decisions about other materials and other situations.

Shabanu, Daughter of the Wind is a novel about a 12-year-old nomadic Islamic girl in Pakistan. This 240-page narrative tends to hold the interest of middle-school students. There are numerous ways to scaffold understanding of it (Benedicty, 1995).

Introducing the Novel/Before Reading

A good way to begin supporting students would be to enrich their understandings of the book's setting, desert life in Pakistan. You could accomplish this by displaying photographs and slides of rural Middle Eastern life and showing videos. You might elicit students' images and the information they have about this topic. If you are fortunate, you might have someone from your class or community share firsthand experiences they had in this region of the world. List housing, transportation, and clothing features mentioned in the book, and portray them as vividly as possible. Students might benefit from imagining themselves living in tents, riding camels, and wearing turbans. You could burn incense and play Middle Eastern music, having students close their eyes and visualize life in this setting.

While helping students experience the setting of a novel or short story before reading serves to develop background knowledge, it often arouses curiosity, too. After viewing scenes from a Middle Eastern desert, students might begin to wonder what life there would be like. You might pique their interest by asking what differences they would expect if they moved to rural living in Pakistan. By focusing on one feature—transportation, for instance—you could have students imagine all the ways life with camels would differ from life with cars.

Supporting readers' comprehension also can be accomplished by focusing attention on a central question. There are many possibilities for *Shabanu;* your choices depend on how this novel fits the unit you are presenting and the school curriculum guide you are following. One productive central question might be "What is the same and what is different about my life and Shabanu's?" This question is promising because the novel touches on universal coming-of-age themes such as clashing with parental expectations and meeting a first love. It portrays events common to all cultures such as wedding rituals and religious worship, yet it offers insights into distinctive customs such as arranged marriages and informal schooling. Other questions might be "How does Shabanu change during the course of the novel?" "What is different about the qualities and concerns of the men and women in this novel?" and "How do the characters' attitudes toward obedience affect their actions in this novel?" Of course, students might produce their own central question(s) once they get into the novel, or they might choose from several offerings.

Reading aloud the first few chapters is a good way to support students' initial efforts with the novel. If you intend to read orally to the class, practice your presentation so you can effectively convey the information and tone of the story while enjoying it with your class. Demonstrate your interest in *Shabanu* by commenting on what you find fascinating and what you hope to learn in the future. To help students with self-monitoring, focus their attention on a central question: "So far, what similarities and differences have you found between your lives and Shabanu's?"

Guiding the Reading

Once students are underway with *Shabanu,* provide enough guidance to support their comprehension while you fade in and out of center stage. Many teachers use reponse journals for this purpose. Having students maintain a folder, perhaps a spiral-bound notebook or a stapled collection of papers, helps in recording thoughts about what they are reading. Be sure to produce a schedule so everyone knows when certain chapters—and the whole book—are to be completed. Also include a set of prompts to accompany the central question(s) and elicit thinking about what has been read. The prompts can be generic (e.g., "What will I remember about this section?") or content specific (e.g., "Should Shabanu marry her cousin?"). They can address essential thinking processes such as organization (e.g., "Sumarize the events of this chapter"), prediction (e.g., "What do you think will happen in the next chapter?"), and generalization (e.g., "What have you learned about Muslim life?").

Along with prompts that focus attention on the contents of the novel, you can list prompts that encourage student responsibility, reflection, and self-assessment. Students might respond to questions such as "What part of this chapter was the most difficult to understand?" and "What did I do when I encountered the difficult parts of this chapter?" Questions such as these enhance students' thinking about and control of their reading processes.

Arranging a weekly schedule for moving through *Shabanu* allows you to structure your plans. You might establish outside-of-class expectations for students to read silently and record responses in their journals, realizing that time for these activities can be offered during class, too. Designate inside-of-class time for whole-class or small-group discussions and for conferring with individuals.

Setting aside time during the week for addressing key incidents in the novel is a good way to provide needed guidance. For instance, powerful events occur when Shabanu's father sells their prize camel and when her grandfather dies in a storm. Sharing these passages orally through a teacher or student read-aloud session or through readers' theater could be time well spent. When talking about these episodes, you can refer to the central question(s), and you can explain how you employed essential thinking processes such as image, connect, and evaluate while making sense of these parts of the novel.

Culminating the Novel/After Reading

Culminating students' experiences with *Shabanu* can be accomplished many ways. If a central question is followed throughout the novel, then students' answers to it are shared. Using ideas recorded in their journals, students express differences between their lives and Shabanu's through visuals such as illustrated and captioned time lines, collections of concrete objects, skits, or essays. These forms of expression can be combined. Writing about Shabanu as a multiday project or as a one-day in-class exam are options. Displaying individuals' reactions to *Shabanu* through a class book, bulletin board, or presentations to an audience also build on the activities conducted while reading the novel.

● COMPREHENSION IN SECOND-LANGUAGE CLASSROOMS

Comprehension processes are quite similar when students read in their first and second languages because in both instances readers tap essential thinking processes such as call up, connect, image, and organize. The main difference between comprehending passages written in one's primary and one's secondary language centers on the support that is required. Second language learners require comprehensible input, exposure to language that they can and are motivated to make sense of.

Reading Materials

To ensure that reading materials provide comprehensible input—that they are challenging but not defeating—effective teachers provide a range of commercial and student-produced materials for students to read. They offer abridged, simplified versions of core reading materials so all students can access basic story lines or expository structures. They provide access to print written at various levels of difficulty so students can learn from and experience materials within their range of competence. For instance, they encourage students to read novels written for children, young adults, and adults, allowing students to select what they can handle.

Effective teachers also provide high-quality culturally relevant literature for students to read. They incorporate novels into their instructional units that center on settings and events their students recognize and characters with which their students identify. For instance, authors such as Rodolfo Anaya, Nicholasa Mohr, Gary Soto, and Gloria Velasquez have produced many young adult novels with Hispanic characters. Providing access to such literature honors the cultural backgrounds of many Hispanic students while linking home and school endeavors. It goes far in helping Spanish-speaking adolescents gain proficiency and comfort in English.

Read-aloud Sessions

Reading aloud to students who are somewhat proficient in their second language provides many opportunities to develop comprehension strategies. When reading aloud, take special care to select passages that are within students' capabilities. In fact, you might read vivid and interesting passages more than once so students are able to grasp them at different levels. As students listen, they should concentrate on understanding the passage's ideas and experiencing the characters' worlds. Teachers and students then might share what images they formed while listening, what connections they made between the passage and their lives, how they organized the information, and so on.

Response Sketches

Second-language students often benefit from responding to literature verbally and through sketches rather than through writing. After reading, have students sketch an illustration that represents their understanding of the passage. They might react to prompts such as "What did the passage mean to you?" "What is the author's message?" or "What do you see after reading the passage?" You might display some sketches you or your students drew for previously read texts to demonstrate the possibilities (in our case, we rely on minimal stick figures and geometry as art forms!). After displaying a sketch to the class or small group, the illustrator remains silent and the audience interprets its message about the passage. The sketcher then explains what he or she meant the drawing to express. Following these sharings, you might explore the variety of alternative interpretations the sketches represent.

Fluency

Teachers also support second-language comprehension by enhancing readers' fluency or their ability to decode a passage's words automatically so they can attend to the passage's ideas. To promote fluency, teachers often have students first read silently and then orally. They occasionally have students prepare to read orally just as they would for an oral interpretation event. They encourage groups of students to read selected portions of passages chorally.

Having students read a passage repeatedly until fluency is achieved is a powerful teaching practice. Students might tape-record themselves, repeating a passage several times until they are satisfied with their performance. Teachers often provide audiotaped recordings of passages with which students repeatedly follow along while looking at the text. Students also carry books home so they can have daily access to repeated reading in their home environment. These fluency practices always are conducted with meaningful passages connected to units of study, and students always respond to the meanings of what they have read fluently.

Social Support

Another way effective teachers support second-language comprehension involves social support during classroom interactions. Effective teachers recognize cultural sources of students' behaviors and adjust their instruction accordingly. For instance, students' culturally patterned ways of taking turns and gaining the conversational floor during text-based discussions might differ from their teacher's. If students are used to interrupting others and the teacher is not, then the situation should be addressed. Get the issue out in the open and talk about it. The case could be that students view interruption as a way for group members to express community and solidarity and jointly produce a message, whereas teachers view an interruption as a takeover attempt by an outspoken individual. If this is the case, teachers might promote discussions that follow students' expectations, or they might promote students' self-monitoring so they can behave differently in different situations.

Effective teachers also accommodate the uncertainties and pressures second-language learners typically experience. Realizing how vulnerable language users can feel when practicing a nonnative language, teachers promote risk-free nonthreatening learning climates. They make it clear to students that linguistic miscues are expected and are considered learning opportunities rather than mistakes. They allow second-language learners ample time to reply to questions, and they repeat and rephrase questions that appear unclear. They encourage students to initiate questions about what has been read. They elicit comments from all students in whole-class and small-group settings so that more than just a few vocal individuals participate.

● COMPREHENSION IN THE MATHEMATICS CLASSROOM

Because math teachers generally received no comprehension scaffolding when they were K–12 math students and did not observe other math teachers providing it when they were in teacher education, they often feel it has no place in the mathematics classroom. Yet, math word problems are perennially difficult for most students. Math is among the most homework-intensive subjects; students need to be able to understand the explanations and directions in their math textbooks when they have trouble figuring out their homework problems. As in the example from a statistics book presented early in this chapter, one must not assume that students can comprehend math word problems or text explanations and directions simply because they can read them aloud, pronouncing most of the words correctly. Fortunately, the current standards for teaching mathematics recognize the failure of traditional mathematics instruction to address the literacy demands of mathematics. Here are some specific ways math teachers use the ideas in this chapter to help students learn how to comprehend the written language of mathematics.

Comprehending Word Problems

Students for whom word problems are highly challenging benefit from being taught short content comprehension lessons with a single word problem as the text. Before they read the problem, they are given the task they will complete after reading the problem or part of it. For example, when students have difficulty interpreting word problems, they can be given a set of solutions for that problem, all computed correctly, which they examine before looking at the problem. Only one of that set of solutions performs the correct operations in the correct order. The task is to circle the correct solution. The students then read the problem and circle the solution. The beauty of this lesson is that students cannot become distracted by whatever computation difficulties they have. They must focus entirely on figuring out how to go about solving the problem. Discussion during the group task is essential. Fading from whole-class to small-group to individual tasks with this particular task gradually helps students learn how to interpret word problems significantly better.

As another example, when students fail to read word problems slowly and carefully before trying to solve them, you can use GIST with them. In GIST, when the text is a word problem, the group task is to write a summary of the problem in 12 words or less. Draw 12 word-size blanks on the chalkboard or on a transparency and explain to the students that they will try to write a sentence of no more than 12 words that captures the gist of the word problem. The students read the first sentence in the problem and then work with you to record the gist of that sentence. Students take turns telling you part of what to write. In no case do you write a thirteenth word. Students must revise what they want you to write so that it will fit into the 12 blanks. Next, tell them to read the following sentence and say that they must now incorporate the information from both the first sentence and the second in just 12 words. Continue in the same way through all the sentences of the problem. During this process, students learn how to distill the essence of the word problem. At the end, the resulting GIST statement is solved and then compared with the solution to the full problem to see if the GIST statement is correct and complete.

Students who have some but not serious difficulty with word problems are often helped by having comprehension follow-up before they actually try to work the problem. For example, give them a copy of a word problem and ask them to read it. Then, have them mark through every word in the problem that will not actually be part of the computation they do to solve it. This follow-up is particularly helpful to students who are confused by extraneous numbers in a problem.

Comprehension of Text Explanations and Directions

On occasion, students should be taught a content comprehension lesson where the material to be read is the explanation in the math textbook of how to solve a certain kind of computational problem. A problem of the type being introduced that day, and different from any in the book, is written on the board. However, instead of working that problem while students watch and listen, students read the explanation in the textbook for how to solve that kind of problem and then take turns telling you how to solve the problem on the board. Over time, these content comprehension lessons can be faded from whole-class to small-group to individual tasks.

Students who cannot use the written explanations in their math textbooks to help them when they have trouble doing their homework are totally dependent on the math abilities of their parents. When the parents are unable to help, students experience frustration and failure.

● COMPREHENSION IN THE SCIENCE CLASSROOM

Science is a subject in which there is always a great deal of new information to be learned. Students (and teachers!) are often overwhelmed by the sheer volume of what needs to be taught and learned. When there is so much to cover, helping children develop comprehension strategies is particularly critical. Here are some specific ways science teachers use the ideas in this chapter to help students understand critical science concepts.

Graphic Organizers

Earlier in this chapter, you learned that graphic organizers help students see the relationships between various facts and pieces of information. Learning to create graphic organizers also help students become aware of text structure. Text structure is the way ideas are tied together in written language. Some common text structures include sequence, compare and contrast, cause and effect, problem and solution, and description/listing of important characteristics. While all of these idea structures appear in science texts, two commonly used structures are description and compare and contrast. Students can learn to construct webs when the information they are reading describes one main topic, Venn diagrams when the information is organized to compare and contrast two or three topics, and data charts when the information includes many different members of the same category.

Most teachers begin with the web because it is the easiest graphic organizer to teach and the most valuable for helping students organize and remember descriptive information presented hierarchically (i.e., topic, subtopics, sub-subtopics, and so on). Working together you and the students write the main topic in the center of the web and then put the other information going out from the center using subtopics as needed. Generally, you and the class work together to create the first several webs and then students work together in small groups to create several more; finally ask students to create individual webs. (Figure 4.8 shows the beginning of a science web on whales.)

Once students have become proficient at making their own webs, you can teach a second graphic organizer format. Direct students' attention to a part of the text that describes two things, telling characteristics they share and differences between the two. Using the same class, small-group, individual progression, students can learn to create a Venn diagram like that shown in Figure 4.6. Some teachers call this Venn diagram a "double bubble."

When students are good at creating webs, double bubbles, and triple bubbles, direct their attention to a text passage in which many different members of a category are described/compared and contrasted. Interlocking circles would get cumbersome and indeed impossible to construct when there are more than three things being contrasted, and students can learn to make data charts such as that shown in Figure 4.3.

Once students have learned to create these separate graphic organizers, help them see that, depending on the structure of the text they are reading, one or the other of these would help them better organize the material. Deciding which one to use is the final step, which allows students to use this valuable comprehension strategy independently when reading on their own.

If the students already know how to create these graphic organizers or if the text you want them to read and understand has many passages in which sequence or cause-effect is the dominant structure, use the same procedures to teach them to create time lines (Figure 4.7) or cause-effect chains (Figure 4.10).

Anticipation Guides

In science class, prior knowledge, which is generally helpful in comprehension, can sometimes actually impede comprehension. Based on observation and prior experience, some students have misconceptions about the way things work. Students may have seen objects falling and assumed that objects always fall in a straight line. Some students may have been told that warts are caused by frogs or that getting one's feet wet would cause a cold. To help students access their prior knowledge before reading, some teachers create anticipation guides in which some of the statements directly confront the possible misconceptions. Students indicate whether they agree or disagree with the statements before reading and then read to see which of the statements are actually true. Research on misconceptions has shown that students must have their misconception directly refuted either by the text, the teacher, or peers. Otherwise they may learn the new information but fail to discard the old misconception. Many students who learn that colds are caused by viruses still believe that they are also caused by getting your feet wet!

An anticipation guide, which directs students to think about and predict what they will learn, can directly confront common misconceptions. Going back to the statements after reading (or listening or viewing), students discuss what their misconceptions were and how they now understand the phenomenon under consideration.

Critical Thinking

We always want our students to think critically but it is crucial that they get in the habit of thinking that way in science classrooms. As they confront their misconceptions, we want them to realize that some of these misconceptions were based on the "best scientific evidence" that was available a generation ago. They also need to realize that some ideas that many think science has "proven" are really only our current best theory or one—but not the only—theory. When we say that we want students to think critically, we usually mean the thinking processes we have called image, generalize, evaluate, and apply. As we go through our activities and lessons and help them predict and organize information, we must never lose sight of the reason students are required to take science courses. We want students who can imagine how things were and how things might be different. We want students who can generalize and draw conclusions from the facts they have organized. We want students who evaluate and form well-founded opinions and students who apply what they learn in science to their own lives. As science teachers help students improve their comprehension, they must always strive to remember that comprehension is thinking and that thinking includes by definition the higher-order critical thinking processes.

● COMPREHENSION IN THE SOCIAL STUDIES CLASSROOM

Graphic Organizers

Earlier in this chapter, you learned that graphic organizers help students see the relationships between various facts and pieces of information. Learning to create graphic organizers can also help students become aware of text structure. Text structure is the way ideas are tied together in written language. Some common text structures include sequence, compare and contrast, cause and effect, problem-solution, and description/listing of important characteristics. While all of these idea structures appear in social studies texts, sequence, cause-effect, and problem-solution structures are omnipresent. Students can learn to construct time lines when sequence or dates are important, cause-effect chains which causal relationships are what matters, and problem-solution maps when that is the dominant theme.

Time lines are fairly easy to construct and are often the first graphic organizer taught in history classes. Working together you and students draw the line and put in a starting date and an ending date. Next, go through the text and add other dates and important events. In the space under the event, add one or two key facts to each event. Generally, you and the class work together to create the first several time lines and then students work together in small groups to create several more; finally students are asked to create individual time lines.

Once students become proficient at making their own time lines, you can teach a second graphic organizer format. Direct students' attention to a part of the text in which a certain "chain of events" unfolds, with each event resulting in another event. Using the same class, small-group, individual progression, students learn to create a cause-effect chain like that shown in Figure 4.10.

Another common text-structure seen in social studies texts is one in which there is a problem and various attempts at solution. Sometimes, the solution creates an unforeseen new problem, which then needs some kind of solution. Students can learn to create a problem-solution map.

Once students have learned to create these separate graphic organizers, you can help them see that depending on the structure of the text they are reading, one or the other of these would help them better organize the material. Deciding which one to use is the final step which allows students to use this valuable comprehension strategy independently when reading on their own.

KWLs

Social studies tends to be a subject in which the pooled prior knowledge and interest of the whole class about any topic is substantial. When most students already know a little and a few students know a lot, a KWL is a wonderful way to activate everyone's prior knowledge and interest. When you place a large sheet of roll paper across the board, label a column *K* for what we know and say, "We're going to be learning about the civil rights struggle in this country, but I know that you already know a lot about this so I want to list here everything that we jointly know." Student interest is piqued. As you list everything they brainstorm (even if it is not correct and will need to be edited or deleted later in the unit), students enlarge their prior knowledge stores by listening to their most important experts—their peers. Perhaps you spend most of one period creating a gigantic list. For homework, you assign them to discuss this issue with someone they know who lived through or participated in the struggle and see if they can come to class tomorrow with something to add. After adding what they learned from their "informed sources," you begin the second column, the *W*—what we want to know! Again, list all their questions even if you know some of the answers can probably not be found or agreed upon. As you begin your class study of this unit, return each day to the scroll and add to the *L* column—what we have learned. You may want to also let them add to the *W* column because as students learn more, they generate more questions.

Prediction is the major thinking process used to launch and sustain the KWL activity. Prediction is when that little voice inside all our minds whispers, "I wonder if . . ." "I think that . . ." or "I wish I knew. . . ." Prediction helps keep our brains and sometimes our hearts actively engaged in learning.

Critical Thinking

We always want our students to think critically, but it is crucial that they get in the habit of thinking that way in social studies classrooms. In spite of the fact that there are a lot of facts, dates, terms, and so forth to learn, we all know that these are only means to the end of having students think about what they are learning. When we say that we want students to think, we usually mean the thinking processes we have called image, generalize, evaluate, and apply. As we go through our activities and lessons and help them predict and organize information, we must never lose sight of the reason students are required to take history, economics, politics, and other social studies courses. We want students who can imagine how things were and how things might be different. We want students who can generalize and draw conclusions from the facts they have organized. We want students who evaluate and form well-founded opinions and students who apply what they learn in social studies to their individual and community responsibilities. As social studies teachers help students improve their comprehension, they must always strive to remember that comprehension is thinking and that thinking includes by definition the higher-order critical thinking processes.

● COMPREHENSION IN THE "ACTIVITY" CLASSROOM

Have you been to a large newsstand lately? Isn't it amazing how many different kinds of magazines there are? Think about classifying all those magazines into the different content areas in school. There are a few titles that would fit best under English, a few more that would fit best under social studies, and several more that would fit best under science. There are almost none that would fit best under foreign language or mathematics. A very large number, however, would fit best under our "activity" category. In other words, they are magazines for people who engage in a particular pursuit, say gardening, golf, or gun collecting. And many of the articles in these magazines actually outline procedures for doing some aspect of the pursuit to which the magazine is devoted. Likewise, time spent in a major bookstore reveals that this is an era of "self-help" books and manuals for doing, using, or repairing almost anything.

In your course, you are attempting to teach your students to do a number of varied procedures. Wouldn't it be helpful to them to learn how to *read to do* in your subject? Granted, nothing beats the coaching or apprenticeship model for learning how to do something. Reading is a useful and practical substitute or source for review, however, for those who need to or prefer to learn independently.

You may well have a textbook for your course. If not, you may have access to brochures, manuals, or even trade books and magazines that exist to help people perform better in your field. That is the material, diagrams and all, that you can teach your students how to comprehend as a part of your course. If so, your students will be more able to take advantage of the books, magazines, and other reading materials available to them after they no longer have you for their teacher.

Comprehension follow-up is automatic in your course when you have students read to do something. Also, the materials you have are often study guides of a sort in that they lead students through the procedure, step-by-step. Content comprehension lessons can readily be planned and taught by previewing and describing the procedure students are to be able to perform during or after reading.

What is crucial is that students have opportunities to read what to do under your guidance and supervision. Most people are unable to follow directions to program their VCR or learn how to use their personal computer because no one ever taught them how to comprehend such material. Certainly, such materials are never included in reading or English courses.

Most students are totally dependent on their teachers in activity courses because they are unable to use reading to add to their skills. Reading should never become a major part of any activity course, but reading what to do is one aspect of what it means today to be educated in any field, from playing the guitar to playing the stock market, and from painting with watercolors to accomplishing weight loss.

Looking Back

Most of what we choose to read is on topics for which we have a great deal of background knowledge, thus motivation is usually quite high. When we read this easy (for us) material, comprehension seems to occur effortlessly and automatically as we process the words. In content area classrooms, however, students often read materials for which they have little prior knowledge and motivation. It is when students are reading this teachable text that content comprehension lessons are needed. In this chapter, you learned the why and how of supporting students' comprehension and some strategies for weaning them off this support. These are the five key ideas: (1) Materials require different levels of scaffolding to support student comprehension; (2) planning a content comprehension lesson includes deciding on clear learning purposes, background knowledge, and motivation; (3) content comprehension lessons support students through the before, during, and after phases of reading; (4) there are many variations within the content comprehension lesson framework; and (5) students become independent comprehenders when teachers gradually fade their scaffolding and turn over responsibility to students.

Add to Your Journal _____

Reflect on this chapter's key ideas: Do you see why students need support as they read unfamiliar text? Does the procedure for planning content comprehension lessons make sense? Can you imagine yourself guiding students through the before, during, and after phases of reading, listening, or viewing? Do you see that within the basic framework there are almost endless variations? Do some of these variations seem more applicable to your content area and your purposes for reading? Finally, what do you think about fading and self-assessment as ways to make students more independent learners? Describe your reactions to each of the five key ideas and generalize about the role of content comprehension lessons and independence in your classroom. What do you believe will be most useful to you?

REFERENCES

BENEDICTY, A. (1995). Reading *Shabanu:* Creating multiple entry points for diverse readers. *Voices from the Middle,* 2 (1), 12–17.

CARR, E., & OGLE, D. (1987). KWL plus: A strategy for comprehension and summarization. *Journal of Reading, 30,* 626–631.

HERBER, H. L. (1978). *Teaching reading in content areas* (2nd. ed.). Englewood Cliffs, NJ: Prentice-Hall.

KIRK, R. E. (1972). Classification of ANOVA designs. In R. E. Kirk (Ed.), *Statistical issues: A reader for the behavioral sciences.* Belmont, CA: Wadsworth.

MATHISON, C. (1989). Activating student interest in content area reading. *Journal of Reading, 33,* 170–176.

OGLE, D. (1986). K-W-L: A teaching model that develops active reading of expository text. *The Reading Teacher, 39,* 564–570.

STAUFFER, R. G. (1969). *Directing reading maturity as a cognitive process.* New York: Harper & Row.

WOOD, K. D., LAPP, D., & FLOOD, J. (1992). *Guiding readers through text: A review of study guides.* Newark, DE: International Reading Association.

ADDITIONAL READINGS

More examples of graphic organizers and ways to use them can be found in these two sources:

PERESICH, M. L., MEADOWS, J. D., & SINATRA, R. (1990). Content area cognitive mapping for reading and writing proficiency. *Journal of Reading, 33,* 424–432.

PITTELMAN, S. D., HEIMLICH, J. E., BERGLUND, R. L., & FRENCH, M. P. (1991). *Semantic feature analysis: Classroom applications*. Newark, DE: International Reading Association.

The importance of purpose in reading comprehension and how various strategies help students set purpose is the focus of this article:

BLANTON, W. E., WOOD, K. D., & MOORMAN, G. B. (1990). The role of purpose in reading instruction. *The Reading Teacher, 43,* 486–493.

In this article you will learn how to write previews for short stories; previews are study guides, tailor-made for short stories:

GRAVES, M. F., PENN, M. C., & COOKE, C. L. (1985). The coming attraction: Previewing short stories. *Journal of Reading, 25,* 594–598.

This book contains a wealth of ideas and variations for the before-reading phase of a content comprehension lesson:

MOORE, D. W., READENCE, J. E., & RICKELMAN, R. J. (1989). *Prereading activities for content area reading and learning* (2nd ed.). Newark, DE: International Reading Association.

The following summarize the research on the theory and teaching of reading comprehension:

ORSANU, J. (Ed.) (1986). *Reading comprehension: From research to practice.* Hillsdale, NJ: Erlbaum.

PEARSON, P. D., & FIELDING, L. (1991). Comprehension instruction. In R. Barr, M. D. Kamil, P. B. Mosenthal, & P. D. Pearson (Eds.), *Handbook of reading research* (Vol. 2, pp. 815–860). White Plains, NY: Longman.

chapter 5

Meaning Vocabulary

Looking Ahead

Knowing the appropriate meanings for the words used to communicate ideas in a content subject is essential for learning that subject. Because many students have not encountered the critical vocabulary for each content area through their general world experience or acquired it through previous schooling, content area teachers are responsible for teaching the meaning vocabulary essential to communicating about their subject. Part of what it means to know biology, geometry, economics, and so forth is to be able to read, write, listen, and speak using their terminology. In order to provide students access to words, good understandings are needed of what it means to know a word, how learners grasp word meanings, and how teachers construct effective word learning opportunities.

Words are used to communicate ideas. You are able to compose or comprehend ideas only when you can associate meanings with the corresponding words. Indeed, studies of what makes passages difficult to read consistently have shown word difficulty to predict passage difficulty. Correlations between students' vocabulary test scores and passage comprehension scores generally are among the highest of any school assessments. There is little doubt that those who do well with individual words also tend to do well reading and writing passages.

These are the key ideas in this chapter:

1. There are many aspects of vocabulary knowledge.
2. Words are learned through direct and visual experience and by making connections.

3. Effective teachers are selective about which words they teach.
4. There is great variety in the strategies content teachers use to teach vocabulary.
5. Polysyllabic words require special attention and strategies.
6. Students become independent learners of words when teachers encourage responsibility, reflection, and self-assessment.

THERE ARE MANY ASPECTS OF VOCABULARY KNOWLEDGE

Given the importance of vocabulary knowledge to academic success, there are many aspects of vocabulary learning to consider. To illustrate, examine the following two sentences:

The avuncular man scratched his philtrum.
She painted all but her lunules.

These are simple sentences. You probably gained a general idea that a "certain" man scratched "something" that belonged to him, and that the woman painted all but some specific "things" that belonged to her. Because you probably lack meanings for some key words, however, your comprehension of these sentences is impaired. If you looked for dictionary definitions of these key words, starting with *avuncular*, you found that it meant "acting like an uncle." Depending on your experiences with uncles, you then conjured up a meaning for the previously unfamiliar word, *avuncular*. You also discovered that you have both a philtrum (groove in the middle of the upper lip, below the nose) and lunules (moon-shaped white areas at the base of the fingernails that at one time were fashionable for women to leave white while painting the rest of their nails).

Notice that you did not lack meanings for the three words in this example. But you were unable to connect the meanings with the words. Psychologists would say that you had the concepts—how uncles behaved, the groove in the middle of your upper lip, the moon-shaped white areas at the base of your fingernails. What you didn't have was these particular labels, or words, for the concepts. Having concepts and labels for concepts are two aspects of vocabulary knowledge.

Consider another example:

The pharmacist needed lupulin and lupulone.

Again, you know that the pharmacist needed two "things." But which two things? When you look up *lupulin*, you discover that it is the "glandular hairs of the hop." Lupulone is "a white or yellow crystalline solid." These meanings are not very informative because you probably do not know what the meanings mean. In this example, you probably lack the labels as well as the concepts. Dictionaries are very helpful when we have a concept but not the particular label by which it is being called. Dictionaries have limited usefulness when we lack both the labels and the concepts.

As you consider how to teach word meanings, keep in mind the aspects of labels and concepts. If the word to be taught is one for which students already have the appropriate concept and lack only the label, the teaching task is relatively simple. If, as is more common during subject matter study, students lack both the concept and the label, the task is more difficult.

Years ago Burmeister (1978) pointed to other aspects of vocabulary when she suggested that knowing a word is like knowing a person. Asking "How many words do you know?" is like asking "How many people do you know?" If we ask the latter question, you will probably look askance at us and not respond, thinking that we could not be serious. If we persist, however, you might answer with a question of your own: "What do you mean by *know?*" There are many aspects to knowing word meanings.

There are many people whom you know only by name. There are also many words for which you have the label but whose concept remains vague. *Truffles* is a word known to many people, but perhaps the whole extent of your meaning for *truffles* consists of "I think you eat them." Your meanings for the word *potatoes,* on the other hand, probably could fill pages. You might call up your knowledge that potatoes are "vegetables," "underground tubers of a plant," "sometimes covered with eyes," "grown in great quantities in Idaho," "eaten in many forms: baked, mashed, french fried," "the crop that failed during the Irish famine of the 1840s," and so on.

Knowing a word is complicated by the fact that words have not only literal, factual meanings upon which almost everyone can agree, but also personal, evaluative meanings that vary from person to person. Literal meanings are generally found in the dictionary and are referred to as denotations; evaluative meanings are referred to as connotations. Some people's meanings for potatoes include connotative ideas such as "boring" and "greasy." Returning to our analogy between words and people, we see that the mention of a person's name also calls to mind both connotations and denotations. Richard Nixon, for example, was born in 1913, was a Republican, and was the thirty-seventh president of the United States. These are all denotations for Nixon. If you saw Nixon's name and thought "crook" or "beleaguered," then you produced connotative meanings for Richard Nixon.

Recognizing that words have the aspects of connotations as well as denotations is an important part of vocabulary instruction. We want students not only to understand what they read but also to evaluate it. When we say that we want our students to develop their evaluative thinking process, we often mean that we want them to have a sense of the connotative meanings of words.

Just as most names stand for many different people, some of whom are related and some of whom are not, most words stand for many different meanings, some related, some not. Look up *root,* for example, and you will find many meanings. Plant roots, tooth roots, root words, and square roots all share a common concept, the idea of a basic part, often hidden, from which other parts, usually visible, emerge and grow. The related meanings of a word may be compared to related people who share the same name. Such people often share a family resemblance: physical (red hair, big bones) or behavioral (mannerisms, gestures, idiosyncrasies of speech). In some families, these resemblances are striking. In others, only the most astute observer would be able to detect family resemblances. So it is with words. The relationship among the many meanings for some words is apparent to everyone; other words reveal their kinship only to philologists. Thus, most students need a teacher's help to perceive the family aspect of words.

Now let us consider the meaning *root* has when we say, "She rooted for the Demon Deacons." This meaning may at one time have had some relationship to other meanings for *root*, but this relationship is no longer apparent. Thinking of these other meanings would hinder rather than help the reader trying to make sense of the sentence: "Does it mean she looked for the Demon Deacons under the ground?" Students must learn that, while words may have related meanings, not all meanings of a word are related. The bear in the forest does not bear fruit. Coat checkers in restaurants might wear checkered jackets and play checkers during offhours. Words with a large number of distinctive meanings are termed *multimeaning* words. The context in which we read a word usually allows us to determine its appropriate meaning.

Finally, we must be concerned with some terms not usually considered *words*. A few examples should illustrate this point:

The FBI and CIA directors met last week.
AB = CD.
N.Z. is ESE of Australia.
The president of ASCAP was a member of the CORE.

Phrases, symbols, abbreviations, initials, and acronyms all occur in the material students read in content areas. While these terms are not technically "words," they are entities for which meaning must be built, and teachers should remember to teach meanings for any symbols that students will need to understand in order to read and write effectively in a particular content area.

In summary, a teacher who is concerned about student vocabulary should keep in mind the many aspects of words. Understanding vocabulary requires a grasp of concepts and labels for concepts (think of the difference between learning *philtrum* and learning *lupulone*). Other important aspects of word learning involve depth of meaning (think of your knowledge of *truffles* versus your knowledge of *potatoes*) and word connotations (think of *Richard Nixon*). Flexibility in choosing appropriate meanings for multimeaning words is another important aspect of vocabulary knowledge (think of possible meanings for *root*). Finally, meanings must be developed not only for words but also for those symbols and abbreviations that stand for words (think of *FBI*).

WORDS ARE LEARNED THROUGH DIRECT AND VISUAL EXPERIENCE AND BY MAKING CONNECTIONS

Think of a person whom you know very well. Try to recall how you learned all the things you know about that person. You may be able to remember particular instances in which you learned specific bits of information. Perhaps you recall learning that your friend was allergic to chocolate on the evening of the day you spent making chocolate mousse. You may recall learning that he or she had an identical twin after jovially greeting the look-alike on a busy street. For the most part, however, you probably do not remember how you learned all the things you know about your friend. You do realize that you got to know this person during many different encounters in various contexts over an extended period. Now, when did you learn this person's name? You may have learned the name the first time you were introduced, or perhaps you had several casual encounters first. Even if you heard the name when you were introduced, you may have forgotten the name but remembered a lot about the person. As time passes, you are continually adding to your understanding of the type of person your friend is. Your friend's name comes to represent your constantly expanding concept of what sort of person he or she is.

How does this apply to words and their meanings? Imagine that you are a child at a museum and see a giant telescope. You ask your friend, "What's that huge thing?" "It's a telescope," she responds. "Oh, really! How does it work?" Your friend may explain how a telescope works. At this point you have a little bit of meaning for telescope, as well as the word that labels that concept. The next time you see a telescope, you will remember that you saw one before and perhaps some of what your friend told you. You may or may not remember the name *telescope*. Imagine, however, that you become an avid astronomer as a teenager. You will use various types of telescopes, read about them, and perhaps build or modify one. Soon your meaning for the word *telescope* will be an enormous network of ideas. You probably will not remember all the many different encounters from which you developed your concept for telescope, but one day, as a famous astronomer, you may reflect, "When I was eight, I had to ask someone what a telescope was!"

Most of the people whose names you know are people with whom you have interacted over a period of time. You have had firsthand, direct experience with them. Many of the words for which you have meanings are also words with which you have had direct experience. If you have actually seen a tiger in the wild or at a zoo, your meaning for the word *tiger* is based partly on direct experience. If you have run a marathon or played tennis or basketball, your meanings for these words are rooted in this direct experience. When you experienced fear, love, or sorrow, your meanings for these words are based on that experience.

However, you have not directly interacted with all the people whose names you know, nor with all the meanings whose words you know. You know a lot about Ronald Reagan, Elizabeth Taylor, and George Washington, with whom you have probably not had firsthand experience. But you probably have seen them in pictures or films or on television. You "know" these persons through visual experience. The meanings for some of the words you know are also based on visual rather than direct experience. You know what pole-vaulting is because you have watched it on television, even though you may never have actually done it or been there watching someone do it. There are places you have never visited but have seen pictures of; thus, you have meanings for words such as *Jerusalem* and *Andes*.

Finally, you know some people whom you have neither met nor seen. These real or fictional people are ones you have read about in novels or historical literature. While you have never met these people, you use the knowledge gained from all the people you have met to understand the unknown people about whom you are reading. So it is with words. Imagine that you are reading this passage about the game of cricket:

> The batsmen were merciless against the bowlers. The bowlers placed their men in slips and covers. But to no avail. The batsmen hit one four after another along with an occasional six. Not once did a ball look like it would hit their stumps or be caught. (Tierney & Pearson, 1981, p. 56)

Now, imagine that you have never played cricket nor seen it played, but you call up what you do know to help you build meanings for the word *cricket* and other words in the passage. "Baseball is a lot like cricket," you might think. "The bowlers must be like pitchers. The batsmen are obviously the batters. Maybe the stumps are bases." You use what you know to predict meanings for words. In situations where you build meanings for words without any direct or visual experience with what the words represent, you still draw on your direct and visual experience, but you do so through comparisons: "It is like this known thing in these ways—but different in these ways." We refer to this way of learning as learning by connection.

Try It Out

Words and meanings, like names and people, are learned through direct experience, visual experience, and connection. List three people and three word meanings you have learned through direct experience—people and concepts with whom you have actually interacted. Then list three people and three word meanings you have acquired through visual experience—people and concepts you have not actually met or experienced but that you feel you know through the power of the visual media.

Finally, list three people and three words that you have learned by connection. These people and words were learned by calling up your direct and visual experience in similar situations and connecting those experiences to the new names or words to build meaning.

EFFECTIVE TEACHERS ARE SELECTIVE ABOUT WHICH WORDS THEY TEACH

Imagine that you have a friend moving into town and want to introduce him to some people. Which people would you choose? You surely cannot introduce him to all the people in your community. You do not even know them all. First, you think about the people you know, considering which of these your friend would like or need to meet. You draw up a list. Carl and Carol are on the list because they share skiing and guitar interests with your friend. You put Juan and Suzanne on the list because, like your friend, they are accountants and might help your friend make some professional connections.

Once you have made your list, you arrange a first meeting. A party is planned to which you invite all the potential friends as well as the Boyds, the only people besides you whom your friend already knows. In addition to the party, at which initial introductions are made, you plan several smaller events. Lunches, football games, and bridge foursomes are all opportunities for your friend to get to know these new people better. After several months, your friend continues to interact with some of the people to whom you introduced him, without your arranging the get-togethers. He also hears about some people you know whom you had not thought he might want to know, so he asks you to introduce him or arrange a way for him to make their acquaintance.

You can decide which words to teach your students in much the same way that you would decide which people to introduce a newcomer to. The content area is the new community. There are many more words in this new community than anyone could possibly come to know immediately; so you select the words that the new learner might like to know because they are so interesting. You also select some words that the new learner needs to know if he or she is going to "get around" successfully in this new community. You sit down and make a list of these new words, then plan get-togethers in which students are introduced to the words. After initial encounters, students continue to learn more about the words as they read and hear them in a variety of contexts. As students become more familiar with the new content, they might preview the materials to be read and suggest words they would like to get to know. You can then either arrange encounters for your students or suggest ways your students might independently get to know these words.

Thus, in selecting words to teach, teachers of content areas should follow these commonsense rules:

1. *Consider the unit you are presenting and list all the key words.* As Chapter 2 indicated, much instructional decision making occurs when planning units of instruction. When planning units, be selective about the vocabulary you intend to teach. Begin by identifying key words. Key words are words that unlock the meaning of a passage. Be sure to include multimeaning words, such as *root*, for which the students might know a meaning that is not appropriate. Do not include words that are already known by most students. If your unit is on plants, *plants* would be a key word but would not need to be taught to most students. You would include such known words in your teaching activities, just as you invite known people in the new community to the party, but you would not spend valuable time building meaning for them.

2. *Pare down this initial list by setting priorities.* Determining how many words to teach is a difficult task, but research seems to indicate that ten new words per week per class is the outside limit of what we can expect students to learn. Ten words per week may not sound like much, but consider that it means 360 new words per year! Furthermore, if a student is studying five subjects and each subject includes 10 new words each week, that would add up to 1,800 new words per year—a considerable increase in vocabulary.

To pare your list, first select the words that are important not only to the unit of study but also to the whole understanding of the content area. The word *cell* in a science unit on plants should be kept because it is crucial not only to understanding plants but also to the whole study of biology. Likewise, the word *angle* is crucial to the whole study of geometry. In addition to words crucial to the whole discipline, keep on your list words that occur repeatedly in the unit of study and that are crucial to understanding it. A word appearing only once is probably less important than a word that occurs frequently throughout the unit.

3. *Include words that will be of particular interest to your students.* Sometimes, there is a word or two which are not critical to your discipline but which are interesting words. Including these words will increase the engagement of your students and help convince them that words are wonderful!

Try It Out

Select a unit of study you might teach to a group of students. Consider what you want them to learn. Preview laser disks, CD-ROMS, videos, and other teaching aids you might use. Read the text chapters and other sources students might read. As you think, preview, and read, list all the key words. Be on the lookout for multimeaning words. These are hard to spot because when we know the appropriate meaning, we often forget that students may only know the more common meanings.

Once you have listed your key words, cut the list to a reasonable number (no more than ten per week) following the guidelines given. Assume your unit will last three weeks, and cut your list of words to teach down to thirty.

Finally, think about which of your words probably represent concepts students already have for which you only need to help them link up a new label (like *lunules, avuncular,* and *philtrum*) and which are new concepts that will have to be developed (like *lupulin* and *lupulone*). There should be a balance of both on your list. Since content area instruction is designed to build concepts, you should expect to have some words for which you must provide direct or visual experience which will help students develop these new concepts. Other words, which will be quicker and easier to teach, will be new labels for concepts students already have.

THERE IS GREAT VARIETY IN THE STRATEGIES YOU CAN USE TO TEACH VOCABULARY

As you move through units of study, you can use numerous strategies for presenting the key words you have selected. How we teach something should parallel how something is learned. Since we remember best the things that we do, direct experience with the concept represented by the word is the most powerful and lasting way to teach. Providing this real experience, however, is not always possible, and thus we often look to the next best thing, visual and symbolic representations. We also can teach new words by helping students see the relationships between new concepts and already known concepts.

Remember that effective settings for learning include meaningful and connected situations in which learners are actively involved and well supported. And cycles of instruction occur during which teachers plan, introduce, guide, and culminate learning activities. Such settings and cycles apply to learning words. This section presents a variety of teaching strategies based on principles of instruction that apply to learning in general and word learning in particular.

The Real Thing

The Real Thing is exactly what it sounds like. You want the students to develop a meaning for a word, so you put them in direct contact with the thing that the word represents. Field trips are often good ways to show students the real thing. If you have ever taken a field trip to a state capitol to watch the legislative process, your teacher was providing you with real experience for a number of words: *capitol, legislature, gavel, quorum, debate, adjourn.* Field trips are one of the best ways of providing students with direct experience on which to base meaning for new words, but they are expensive and time-consuming, and often the things you need to show students are not available at a reasonable distance from the school.

When you cannot take the students to the real thing, the next best option is to bring something to the students. Learners at all levels learn something best when they have actually seen it, touched it, smelled it, listened to it, or even tasted it.

Sometimes the actual subject of study could never be available for students to interact with, but a model could. Models of the human heart, a pyramid, or a DNA molecule, while differing in size and other features from the real thing, are still three-dimensional representations that can be explored by the senses. Computer programs now offer simulations which allow students to experience science and mathematical phenomena impossible to provide in pre-technological revolution days. Teachers sometimes think that they can provide students with direct experience only when the word for which they are building meaning represents an actual "thing." That is simply not true. You can provide students real experience with verbs like *cringe, catapult,* and *pontificate* by demonstrating these actions, then letting students act them out. You provide students with real experience with such concepts as *assembly line* and *electoral process* by simulations in which each student takes part as the class manufactures something assembly-line style or participates in a mock election. Because of time and other constraints, not all meanings can be developed through this method. But the time and effort involved in providing the real thing must be weighed against the depth and the permanence of the learning and excitement that this method generates.

During field trips and classroom events, such as special guest talks or simulations, the meanings for many words are being developed. Consequently, preparation and follow-up are required. In order to make the most of providing the real thing, follow these guidelines:

1. *Help students figure out what they already know.* Conduct a "What Do You Know?" discussion in which you make a list of what students know, based on their responses to questions such as the following: "What things will we probably see happening when we visit the legislature?" "What do you think Dr. Horsey will tell us about what a veterinarian does?" "How do you think an assembly line works?"

2. *Help students figure out what they would like to know.* Have students work together to prepare a list of questions to be sure to try to answer. Designate different students to write down or be responsible for certain questions to make sure they all get answered.

3. *Make a list of all the words for which you want to develop meanings.* Have students write down these words. As you see and hear things that develop concepts for these words, be sure the students understand how to match words with meanings. You may want students to make notes next to the word, or at least check off each word as meaning for it is developed. Younger children can each be responsible for a word or two.

4. *Follow up with a discussion guided by the questions.* If some questions are not fully or satisfactorily answered, this is an excellent time to have students turn to resource books to get more information.

5. *Discuss what students saw happening for each of the words.* Formulate definitions that are based in this experience, rather than in dictionary style. For ex-

Stitchery provides direct experience during a unit on colonial life.

ample, "The quorum was when they called the roll and saw that there were enough senators there. The quorum had to be at least two-thirds of the senators." You may want to record these experience-derived definitions to display for the class or have students write them in their notebooks.

Skits

Skits are actually a special version of the real thing. Because they require special preparation, we have chosen to give them a separate name and discuss them separately. A *skit* is a short drama. Generally, the teacher writes a short description of the skit, including the number of actors needed, a sentence containing the word whose meaning is to be acted out, a short description of what the actors should try to get across, and questions the actors should ask the audience after completing the skit.

Here is an example of a skit lesson plan to teach the word *controversy* and its meaning:

Example sentence: All parties had something to say in the controversy about whether athletes deserve special privileges.

Skit: (Actors needed: 3) Two students are standing in the cafeteria line when the star football player goes to the head of the line, gets his plate filled with specially prepared food, and takes his tray over to the "athletes' table." "I just don't think it's right," says the first student. "Athletes in this school get all kinds of special treatment." "Well," says the second student, "I don't see

what the controversy is all about. Athletes are special people. They need more and better food. After all, they earn their special privileges." The two students continue to discuss the pros and cons of the controversy while the football player eats his lunch, oblivious to the discussion.
Questions to ask audience: What did controversy mean in our skit? Have you ever been involved in a controversy?

The teacher prepares for the lesson by writing out a skit card similar to that shown above and giving the card to the actors so that they have time to prepare. A teacher might have a skit day and divide the whole class into teams of two to four members, giving each team a skit card and allowing five minutes for each team to prepare. As each group of actors comes up, one of them writes the target word on the board and pronounces it. They then do their skit, trying to sneak in the target word as often as possible. If the actors have done a good job, the watchers should be able to answer the question, "What did the word mean in our skit?" The second question, "Have you ever . . . ?" is intended to help the watchers access any experience they might have had with the target word and to attach the word to the experiences.

Skits are especially valuable when you are trying to teach an unfamiliar meaning for a multimeaning word. Most students know what fog is, but many do not know what it means to be in a fog. A skit in which this use of the word fog is demonstrated would help students to learn the new meaning.

Skits are strategies for building meaning because watching the skit provides the watchers with visual experience of a concept. For students who have not had the experience represented by a particular word, the skit is the basis of their new understanding. Other students may have experienced controversies but did not know the word that stood for what they had experienced. These students did not actually need the experience of the skit, but only needed the appropriate meaning to be accessed and attached to the new word. For these students, the question, "Have you ever . . . ?" helps them find the appropriate experience to connect with the new word. Classes always contain a wide variation of ability and experiences.

A Picture Is Worth a Thousand Words

Visuals provide us with "the next best thing to being there." All of us have numerous concepts that we have not experienced directly but have developed through movies, television, photographs, paintings, diagrams, or maps. Imagine trying to explain the Grand Canyon to someone who has never seen it, describe with words the color teal, what fencing looks like, or life at the bottom of the ocean. Your words are meaningful only to those who have seen what the word represents.

Fortunately, we are surrounded by visual stimuli. Television programs offer great possibilities for content teachers. Most school system media centers contain many laser disks, videos, CD-ROMs, slides, and other visual aids that

Two students complete a skit for the word *conciliation*.

suffer from underuse. As you consider how to build meaning for words, ask yourself, "Where could I find a picture of this?" Often, the answer is as close as your textbook.

When you have your list of words for which you must build meaning, look at the textbooks and other books you have available. Note page numbers where various concepts are portrayed visually. You can introduce these concepts by writing the word on the board, pronouncing it and having students pronounce it with you, and directing their attention to the appropriate text visual.

To make the most of videos, laser disks, and other visuals, follow the guidelines given above for field trips and classroom events. Students who have listed what they know and which questions they want answered and who have been alerted to words for whose meanings they are looking will get more than just enjoyment (or boredom!) out of watching a video. When you have many concepts to develop, you will probably want to show the video more than once. The second time, stop the video at appropriate points to discuss questions or develop meanings for words. Record answers and definitions on a chart or have students record them in their notebooks.

In the case of visuals, if one is good, two are twice as good. Remember that developing a concept is not a matter of "one time—now you've got it." Your meaning for *mountains* is not based on having seen just one picture of one mountain. If your students see several visuals, the depth of their meaning for

This teacher is using a picture to build meaning for words.

the word will be much greater than if they see only one. In addition to broadening their concepts, each visual provides review of the meaning represented by the word.

Scavenger Hunts

Have you ever had firsthand experience with a scavenger hunt? Have you actually gone to gather assorted items, competing to be the team that found the most in a limited time? If you have not, perhaps you have had visual experience of watching others go on one. Scavenger hunts are fun because they develop both competition and a sense of team spirit. For a scavenger hunt that helps your students build word meanings by collecting real things and pictures, follow these steps:

1. *Make a list of the items for which you want students to scavenge.* Include anything for which students might be able to find a real object, model, or picture, but make sure to include items represented by those words for which you need to build meaning. Be sure to add some well-known, easy-to-collect items so that some of the finds will be easy and immediately satisfying. Here is a list used for a scavenger hunt before beginning a unit on the desert:

sand	woodpecker	cactus	vulture
skunk	dune	fox	kangaroo rat

| mesquite | dates | oasis | nomads |
| roadrunner | coyote | yucca | |

2. *Divide your class into teams of three or four.* Ask students to share experiences with scavenger hunts. If necessary, explain how scavenger hunts work. Be sure students understand that they must bring in objects and pictures by a certain date and that each team should keep secret which items were collected and from where the items came.

3. *Let the team have an initial planning meeting.* Tell the team that they get two points for each object or model and one point for each picture. Pictures include drawings and tracings (you may want to make tracing paper available). Only one object and one picture can be counted for each word. Let the team choose a leader or appoint one yourself. Have the leader read the list and lead the group in a discussion of who thinks they can find what and where. Set a date for students to bring objects and pictures to school. One week is a reasonable amount of time. Do not allow objects and pictures to be displayed before the due date.

4. *Allow the teams to meet briefly once or twice more.* Teams should check things off their lists and see what is still needed. Be sure to promote an atmosphere of secrecy and suspense. If students protest that "No one could find a . . . ," assure them that "No one could possibly get objects or pictures for everything. The goal is to collect as much as you can." This will generally result in some students making sure that they have a picture, if not an object, for everything, just to prove you wrong.

5. *On the appointed day, have teams bring their finds.* Let teams meet to go over their findings and tally up their points. Double-check the teams' figures. Count drawings and tracings only when they actually represent the thing and are not merely "thrown together." The winner is the team with the most points.

6. *Reward the winning team by allowing them to display their findings.* Cards on which each word is printed might be attached to a bulletin board and all the pictures representing that object can be arranged in collage fashion around the word. Objects that are not alive, dangerous, or valuable can be labeled and placed on a table near the bulletin board. Be sure to include the names of all the winners next to the display.

Scavenger hunts are fun and, more importantly, involve students in the preparation for the unit. These hunts are best done a week or two before you actually begin the unit for which the objects are being collected. That way, by the time you are ready to explore the topic with your students, they already have a lot of information about and interest in the subject. In addition to learning what the words on the list mean, students often pick up incidental information as they peruse magazines looking for pictures or talk to people whom they hope will have objects to loan. In one class where Mexico was the scavenger hunt topic, a student had an uncle in California who had been to Mexico often. He called his uncle, who sent a box containing many of the objects on the list as well as some other objects. In addition, the uncle wrote a long letter describing Mexico and comparing it to the United States, and he sent along many photos he had taken. A scavenger hunt on the weather once included the word *meteorologist*. A student who lived next door to the local television meteorologist brought the woman along as one of the "objects." The meteorologist, of course, brought many of the objects on the list as well as other weather-related paraphernalia and talked to the class about forecasting the weather. You can imagine how interested the students in those two classes became in their units! While these two instances are somewhat unusual, students do become good at digging up objects and pictures. They develop some sense of ownership in the unit to be studied and generally begin the unit with more enthusiasm.

One final benefit of scavenger hunts is the ratio of teacher work to student work. For a scavenger hunt, the teacher makes the list, forms the teams, arranges for them to meet a few times, and checks their tallies of the points. The students do the rest—including the often onerous and neglected task of making a bulletin board.

Creating Analogies

Analogies help students develop a concept for a word that you cannot represent with firsthand or visual experience. You think of something students know that is like the unknown thing you wish to teach them. The idea that cricket is a lot like baseball is an analogy. (Analogy is sometimes used narrowly to denote statements such as "Summer is to hot as winter is to cold"; we use the word in a broader sense.)

To create an analogy, think of something your students are apt to know that is like the thing they do not know. It is very important that students be familiar with the concept being used to teach the unknown concept. Telling you that cricket is a lot like rounders is not helpful if you do not know rounders either. Once you have decided which analogy to make, consider the similarities and differences between the familiar and unfamiliar concepts.

To present the analogy to the students, first ask them what they know about the familiar concept. Highlight the relevant traits, adding to the information they give you as necessary. Next, tell them that this familiar concept is a lot like another, unfamiliar concept and point out the similarities. Finally, tell students how the new concept is different from their known concept. Here is an example from social studies:

Imagine that you want to teach the students about taxation without representation and its relationship to the Revolutionary War. You decide to compare this concept with the idea of belonging to a club to which you have to pay dues. You do not mind paying the dues, even though the club founders meet each year and decide how the dues are to be spent. After a while, it occurs to some club members who are not founders that since the dues are partly theirs, they should have some say in how the dues are spent. The founding members will have no part of this and insist that the power to spend dues is theirs, as is written in the club's bylaws. Once you have gotten from students what they know about clubs and dues, you may have to interject the notion that founding members could have control of the dues since this may not be in the experience of most students. Then, explain that taxation is like dues and that representation, in this case, means the power to decide how something is spent. A difference that should be pointed out is that you as a club member always have the right to quit the club and stop paying dues. When the colonists quit and stopped paying taxes, a war ensued.

Capsule Vocabulary

Capsule Vocabulary (Crist, 1975) is a strategy in which students listen to, speak, write, and read words related to a particular topic. These topically related words (using approximately six words works best) are presented by you one at a time. Write each word on the board, briefly tell the students of an experience with the word, and let students share their own experiences. In addition to words for which students have meaning but not the word, include some words already well-known to students and perhaps some for which you have already built meaning in previous lessons. After all the words have been introduced and all the experiences shared by you and students, have each student copy the words from the board onto a sheet of paper. Pair the students and give each pair a limited time (three to five minutes) to try to use the words in a conversation about the topic. Students should check off the words as they are able to sneak them into the conversation. (Use a timer or appoint an official clock-watcher to announce when the time is up.) Finally, have students write a paragraph about the topic in which they use as many of the capsule words as possible. Form students into groups of four or five and let them share their paragraphs. Then collect the paragraphs and select several to read to the entire class.

Word Boards

Many teachers reserve one of the bulletin boards in the room to display the important words associated with a unit. Sometimes these words are part of a graphic organizer such as a web or a chart. Other times the words are displayed with pictures which help to clarify their meanings. Still other times, they are simply written on index cards and attached to the board. Some teachers put all the important unit words up at the beginning of the unit and refer to these words throughout the unit, periodically asking students what else they have learned about these important words. Other teachers prefer to add words gradually as the words occur and do some culminating activities at the end of the unit to help students tie all the words together.

Word Books

Many teachers like to have students make word books—vocabulary notebooks in which to record the words they are learning. Students may use a notebook or sheets of paper stapled together and decorated with an interesting cover. Words are then usually entered according to their first letter, but in the sequence in which they are introduced, alphabetical by first letter only. Depending on the age of the students and the type of word being studied, different information can be included with each word. Many teachers like students to write a personal example for each word ("Frigid is a February day when the thermometer hits 20°F.") as well as a definitional sentence ("Frigid means very, very cold."). Although students may consult the dictionary for help, it is best not to let them copy dictionary definitions since this requires little thought or understanding. In addition to the example and definitional sentence, other information may be included when it is helpful. A phonetic respelling may help students remember how to pronounce words. Sometimes, a common opposite is helpful in remembering the word. If the word has a common prefix, root, or suffix that will jog students' memory of its meaning, this can be noted. For some words, students can draw pictures, diagrams, or cartoons.

In the next chapter on writing, we discuss having students keep content journals. Many teachers who have students create journals reserve special pages in those journals as a word book section. Students add new words and their own personal definitions as each unit is studied.

Context Power

Often the surrounding words, or context, help us access known meaning and put it with a new word. Do you know what a jingo is? Imagine that you are reading and come across the unknown word *jingo* in this context:

> All he ever talked about was war. His country was the best country, and anyone who disagreed should be ready to fight in battle. He was really quite a jingo!

You could now infer that a jingo must be a militaristic person ready to defend his or her country (or have someone else defend it) at the drop of a hat. The word *jingo* may have been unfamiliar, but if you have had experience with nationalistic, militaristic people, the concept was not. The context helped you associate your old meaning with a new label. Context is a valuable tool for associating meaning with words, because once you learn how to use context, you can do so independently without a teacher's help. Many students, however, do not make use of context. They do not know that the surrounding words often give clues to an unfamiliar word and sometimes do not understand how our language gives these clues.

To prepare for a lesson in which you teach students to use context clues, select some words for which students have the meaning but not the word and use them in a few sentences that give clues to their meaning. It is best to use the actual context from the book when that context makes the meaning clear. There is a variety of context clues, and you should try to use all the common types so that students become familiar with them. Common types of context clues include explanatory sentences, as in the jingo example above; synonyms ("mean, cruel, and truculent"); antonyms ("Some things are easy, others are arduous"); similes and metaphors ("as fervid as a stove"); and appositives ("the pandowdy, a pudding made with apples"). Once you have chosen the words and written the sentences with their context clues, the steps of the lesson are as follows:

1. *Display the words without the context clues and have students guess the meaning.* Pronounce each word and have students pronounce it with you. Have students write down a meaning for each word. If there are more than two words, let each student pick two or assign two words to each student. If students actually know a meaning, they can write it down. If they do not know the meaning, they should make something up. They can also make something up if they know the meaning but want to fool everyone. Once everyone has written something down for two words, call on volunteers to tell you what they have written. Ask them to give their answers as if they are absolutely convinced that they are right. Often students will make up a definition that sounds like the word. For the word *manticore,* for example, students have made such guesses as these: "the pit of the manti fruit," "a manicure for an apple," and "the heart of a mantelope!" The guesses are fun, but more importantly, they help students see that they don't know the meaning for the word. Often when a word's context helps us to access meaning, we grasp the meaning so quickly that we think we knew the word all along. Students will see how helpful context is only if they realize that they did not know the word until they saw it in context.

2. *Display the word in its context and have students guess a second time.* Emphasize that context only gives us clues to words, and sometimes these clues can lead us astray. Our ideas about what a word means when we see it in context should be considered tentative. Our context-based guesses, however, are more likely to be right than the guesses we make without any context.

3. *As students guess what words mean based on context, have them explain how the context clues helped.* Do not settle for "It said so." Students who do not understand how context clues are contained in language do not see what is obvious to those of us who do know how our language system gives clues. Through your questions, get students to explain the obvious: "Mean and cruel mean almost the same, so truculent probably does, too." "Stoves are hot; if something is as fervid as a stove, it must be hot, too." "The commas around 'a pudding made with apples' tell you that it is the same as pandowdy."

4. *As each word is guessed from context and the reasoning behind the guess is explained, have a volunteer look up the word in the dictionary and read the appropriate definition to the class.* This reinforces the notion that minimal context gives only clues, not certain answers, and it models for students using the dictionary to check hunches and gain more precise information.

5. *Have students apply the context strategy by finding some unfamiliar words in their books and deriving meanings from the book context.*

In addition to these lessons, content teachers have the opportunity on a daily basis to model for students how context helps you figure out meaning for words. When you and your class encounter a word whose meaning even you—the teacher—are not absolutely sure of, that is a perfect opportunity to model authentically how you use context as your first line of attack on a new word. (Some teachers even pretend that they don't know the meaning of an occasional word so that they can model how context gives you clues.) In the next section of this chapter we discuss the big role that morphemes play in figuring out meaning for big words. Context and morphemic sophistication are a powerful combination for adding new word meanings to your vocabulary.

POLYSYLLABIC WORDS REQUIRE SPECIAL ATTENTION AND STRATEGIES

Ten thousand new words—words never before encountered in print—is the number of new words the average student probably encounters each year in school from fifth grade on (Nagy & Anderson, 1984). Most of these new words are big words, words of seven or more letters and two or more syllables. These polysyllabic words occur infrequently but they are very important because they carry the message or ideas in that passage. Many students do not immediately recognize these words and may just skip over them or quit reading in frustration. Here is the first sentence from a *USA Today* article in which all the words of three or more syllables have been replaced with X's.

French XXXXXXXXX are XXXXXXXXX ways to XXXXXXXXX should the United States enforce laws XXXXXXXXXXX XXXXXXXXXXXXX trade with Cuba, Iran, and Libya.

You can easily see that without some ability to pronounce and access meanings for these words, comprehension would be impossible. Now, read the sentence again and put these words where the X's were: officials, exploring, retaliate, restricting, international.

Imagine that you are teaching a unit in economics class on international trade, and you want your students to write a letter to the editor expressing their opinions related to this topic. Writing a sensible letter would be impossible unless they could use some of these big, specific words in their writing. Even if you allow them to spell the words as best they can on a first draft and then fix them on a final draft, they must be able to remember the words and make some attempt at spelling them or their writing will not reflect the kind of thinking you want them to do.

The simple truth is that learning about any content-area topic requires students to learn to speak, understand, read, and write a new vocabulary. Throughout this chapter, we have emphasized strategies you can use to teach new vocabulary, but your students are going to meet many more words than you can possibly teach and if they have a "skip it" or "quit reading" reaction to text with lots of big, not-immediately-familiar words, they are not going to be able to read much independently. This sets off a vicious downward cycle because vocabulary is developed primarily through wide reading, and students who avoid reading are cut off from this most important source of vocabulary development.

Let's look again at those five polysyllabic words your students might not have immediately recognized:

officials, exploring, retaliate, restricting, international

Two of these words, *exploring* and *restricting,* are what linguists call "morphologically transparent," that is they are related to smaller words and would be almost instantly identified by a reader who knew the words *explore* and *restrict.* Two other words, *officials* and *international,* also have related words but it requires a level of "morphological sophistication" to recognize the similarities. The word *officials* is related to the words *office* and *officers* and also to words such as *nationals* and *professionals. International* is related to the word *nation* and also to *interstate* and *intersection.* The only word for which many readers would not have some related words to help them figure out its pronunciation and meaning is *retaliate.*

English is the most morphologically related of all the languages. (*Morphemes* are meaning-bearing parts of words, including suffixes, prefixes, and roots.) Linguists estimate that for every word you learn, you can transfer some part of its pronunciation, spelling, and meaning to seven other words! That is the good news. The bad news is that in order to do this transferring you have to notice the letters, sounds, and meanings that words share! Research demonstrates that even many high-school students have not noticed common word parts!

Of the 10,000 new words students from fifth grade and up encounter in school each year, only 1000 are probably truly new words, not related to other more familiar words. If we can help our students become more morphologically sophisticated, they will be able to take advantage of these morphological relationships when reading on their own. Word detectives is an activity designed to help students notice these relationships.

Word Detectives

To help students become aware of the helpful links words share, there are two questions you should try to get them in the habit of asking themselves:

"Do I know any other words that look and sound like this word?"
"Are any of these look-alike/sound-alike words related to each other?"

The answer to the first question helps students with pronouncing and spelling the word. The answer to the second question helps students discover what, if any, meaning relationships exist between this new word and others in their meaning vocabulary stores. These two simple questions can be used by every teacher in every subject area. Imagine that students in a mathematics class encounter the new word/phrase:

improper fraction

The teacher demonstrates and gives examples of these fractions and helps build meaning for the concept. Finally, the teacher asks the students to pronounce and look at both words and see if they know any other words that look and sound like these words: For *improper*, students think of:

impossible, important, impatient, imported
property, properly, proper
super, paper, kidnapper

For *fraction*, they think of:

fracture, motion, vacation, multiplication, addition, subtraction

The teacher lists the words underlining the parts that are the same and has students pronounce the words emphasizing the part that is pronounced the same. The teacher then points out to the students that thinking of a word that looks and sounds the same as a new word will help you quickly remember how to pronounce the new word and will also help you spell the new word.

Next the teacher explains that words, like people, sometimes look and sound alike but are not related. If this is the first time this analogy is used, the teacher will want to spend some time talking with the students about people with red hair, green eyes, and so on who have some parts that look alike but are not related and others who are.

"Not all people who look alike are related but some are. This is how words work too. Words are related if there is something about their meaning that is the same. After we find look-alike/sound-alike words which will help us spell and pronounce new words, we try to think of any ways these words might be in the same meaning family."

With help from the teacher, the students may discover that *impossible* is the opposite of *possible*, *impatient* is the opposite of *patient*, and *improper* is the opposite of *proper*. *Proper* and *improper* are clearly relatives! *Impossible, impatient,* and *improper* are probably "distant cousins" because they all have *im* making it the opposite. Depending on their word sophistication, someone might be able to point out that a *fracture* is a break into two or more parts and that *fraction* also involves parts.

Imagine that the students who were introduced to improper fractions on Monday by their math teacher and were asked to think of look-alike/sound-alike words and consider if any of these words might be "kinfolks," have a science teacher on Tuesday who is beginning a unit on weather and does some experiments with the students using *thermometers* and *barometers*. At the close of the lesson, the teacher points to these words and helps them notice that the *meters* chunk is pronounced and spelled the same and asks the students if they think these words are just look-alikes or are related to one another. The students conclude that you use them both to measure things and the *meters* chunk must be related to measuring, as in *kilometers*. When asked to think of look-alike/sound-alike words for the first chunk, students think of *baron* for *barometers* but decide these two words are probably not related. For *thermometer*, they think of *thermal* and *thermostat* and decide that all these words have to do with heat or temperature.

Now imagine that this lucky class of students has a social studies teacher on Wednesday who points out the new word *international* and asks the two critical questions, an art teacher on Thursday who has them do some *sculpture*, and an English teacher on Friday with whom they encounter the new word *foreshadowing*.

Throughout their school day, our students from the intermediate grades on up encounter many new words. Because English is such a morphologically related language, most new words can be connected to other words by their spelling and pronunciation and many new words have meaning-related words already known to the student. Some clever, word-sensitive students become word detectives on their own. They notice the patterns and use these to learn

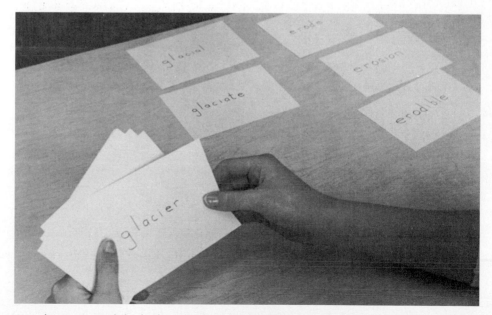

A student sorts cards by looking for the words with the same root.

and retrieve words. Others, however, try to learn to pronounce, spell, and associate meaning with each of these words as separate, distinct entities. This is a difficult task which becomes almost impossible as students move through the grades and the number of new words increases each year. Asking the two critical questions for key vocabulary introduced in any content area adds only a few minutes to the introduction of key content vocabulary and pays students back manyfold for that time.

Do It Together

In a small group or pair preparing to teach the same content subject, discuss the meaning vocabulary teaching and practice strategies described in the last two sections. Choose three of the strategies that your group or pair would be most likely to use with students during content instruction and write a one-sentence rationale for choosing each. Compare your list and rationales with other groups or pairs who have engaged in the same activity. Did different groups or pairs pick different strategies for different reasons? Is a variety of meaning vocabulary strategies called for?

STUDENTS BECOME INDEPENDENT LEARNERS OF WORDS WHEN TEACHERS ENCOURAGE STUDENT RESPONSIBILITY, REFLECTION, AND SELF-ASSESSMENT

So far, this chapter has stressed teacher-directed vocabulary instruction. The teacher selects words. The teacher finds laser disks and videos. The teacher creates context sentences. The teacher draws student attention to a word and asks if they know any other look-alike, sound-alike words and if they think these words might be relatives. Some of these activities, though teacher-directed, do move students toward becoming independent students and lifelong learners. Students who become good users of context and morphologically sophisticated word detectives are well on their way to being able to add to their vocabulary stores whenever they read.

To help students become truly independent word learners, however, teachers must encourage student responsibility, reflection, and self-assessment. Here are some ways successful teachers accomplish these lofty—but obtainable—goals.

Model Word Wonder

Are you a logophile? Do you love words? Were you intrigued earlier in the chapter to realize that you have both a philtrum and lunules? Teachers who are most successful at helping their students become word wizards are teachers who themselves find words fascinating. When helping students learn a new meaning for a familiar word or use context to figure out an appropriate meaning or analyze the morphemes in a word, they don't just point these things out. Rather they communicate—sometimes with words but more often with the enthusiasm in their face and voice—that words are fascinating! To word lovers, encountering a new word is not something dreaded that must be learned but rather an opportunity to add a new treasure to their powerful arsenal of words.

If you are fascinated by words, you need to realize that you probably developed that sense of wonder by interacting with someone—a parent, teacher, friend—who communicated his or her love of words. That gift is now one that you can pass on to your students, regardless of what subject you teach. If you have not yet developed an appreciation for words, it is never too late! Put *The New Shorter Oxford English Dictionary* on your holiday wish list. Read a few word wonder books such as Isaac Asimov's *Words of Science and the History Behind Them,* John Ciardi's *A Browser's Dictionary,* Willard Espy's *Have a Word on Me,* or William Safire's *What's the Good Word?* These and other sources will help you overcome any lingering logophobia and help you and your future students become logophiles!

Let Students Select the Words to Be Learned

M. R. Haggard (1982) suggests a vocabulary self-collection strategy in which students preview materials to be read with the purpose of listing two words they consider important and relatively unknown. Help students to define *important* as occurring many times in the material to be read. Help them also to consider whether the word is unknown not by their ability or inability to pronounce it but by their "I wonder what that word means" reaction. The list of words that students suggest should be modified by the teacher to fit the criteria for choosing which words to teach offered earlier in this chapter. Of course, you should add words not suggested by students if these words are crucial to the discipline or the unit.

Let Students Plan a Lesson to Teach the Words

After you have directed the students' lessons, students should know that we can build meanings for words by providing direct experience, visual experience, or an analogy. Students can work individually or in pairs to prepare their lessons, which might include bringing in the real thing or a model; finding a picture, including films, filmstrips, and slides; creating a skit for a word; and creating an analogy. Students will, of course, need some initial help with this work, but as time goes on, they should become more independent. As students teach their lessons, you should remind them that they can perform some of these activities whenever they meet a word for which they do not have meaning. "Where could I find a picture? I wonder if there is one in my text?" "Maybe if I read the sentence again, the context will give me an idea about what this word means" and "Is this word like any other words I already know?" are models for how students should think when faced with an unknown, important word.

Move Students Toward Independence in the Lessons You Teach

Earlier in this chapter, we described how creating an analogy helps students make connections. Once students understand how analogies help them learn, they need to take on the responsibility for thinking of the analogies.

"Today, you will be reading about circuits and how electrons move only through a complete circuit. As you read, try to think of how open and closed circuits are a lot like something you already know. When you have finished, we will share all our ideas for what circuits are like."

When students finish reading, you should accept all reasonable analogies, helping students to state how their analogies are similar to and different from the new concept. As the teacher, you can, of course, share your own analogy with students, but be sure not to give them the idea that there is only one right analogy.

This process of moving students toward independence can be applied to all teaching strategies. For example, in context power, students guess word meanings first without, then with, context sentences. To move students toward independence, ask them to use the context provided in the textbook rather than sentences you write. In that case, students would guess without context, then be directed to a specific part of a page that contains the new word. Students figuring out meanings from the context in their books are moving toward greater independence. Ultimately, students could be alerted to several words before they begin reading and then asked to use the text's context clues to figure out meanings. After completing the reading, various students could suggest meanings and show where and how the text gave them clues.

Teach Students How People Really Use the Dictionary

As you began this chapter on vocabulary, did you expect to find a chapter full of dictionary activities? That expectation is reasonable when you consider the experience you have probably had with vocabulary activities throughout your schooling. The most common vocabulary activity in classrooms at all levels is to assign students to look up words and write their definitions. This frustrating practice is like expecting that you could get to know some new people by looking them up in *Who's Who* and writing down their distinguishing characteristics. Such an activity is helpful only if you already know something about the people and want to find out more. In the same way, dictionaries are wonderful resources for adding to or clarifying a word's meaning.

Students need to see how real people use the dictionary. Real people do not look up lists of words and write definitions that they memorize for a test. Real people consult a dictionary when they cannot figure out the meaning of a word they encounter in their reading. They look up a word they know a little about when they meet it in a new context and need some clarification or elaboration on its meaning. Sometimes a dictionary is used in the real world to check the spelling of a word needed in writing.

All teachers should keep a dictionary handy and model its real use. When students meet a new word and ask what it means, you may respond with a little information and then say, "I don't really know exactly what that means. Let's look it up and find out." As described in the context power lesson, you can have children use the dictionary to check or flesh out a meaning derived from context. When you are at the board recording a brainstormed list or some other student-generated responses, they can model how to check the spelling of a word of which you are unsure. Showing students that you, the teacher, see the dictionary as the natural tool to discover and clarify meanings and check spelling will go a long way toward making them independent vocabulary learners.

Help Students Develop Self-Assessment Strategies

Assessment is an important part of the learning cycle. Every content teacher has the responsibility to assess how well students are learning. When you assess how well students are learning your content, you are of necessity assessing their understanding of the key vocabulary included in that content. As students think about, discuss, and write about the subject, they are doing what you want them to with vocabulary—using the important words that form the communication base for your subject. Contrast this with the unfortunate practice of testing students on the definitions. Most of us have had the experience of memorizing the definitions for a vocabulary test, without incorporating those words into our listening-reading-speaking-writing vocabularies. When you teach the important words so that they will be used rather than memorized, your assessment should reflect these priorities.

Helping students self-assess is one of the major ways of helping them develop responsibility for their own learning. Letting students select the words to be learned is one type of self-assessment because in selecting they are deciding that these are relatively unknown words to them and that these words are likely to be important to the unit under study. You might also help students self-assess by presenting them with a scale such as the following and have them put various unit words on that scale at the beginning and end of the unit. Students could then add up the number of points they have moved and have tangible proof of their vocabulary growth in your content-area.

Vocabulary Self-Assessment Scale

0 = I never heard of that word in my whole life.

1 = I heard it but I have no idea what it means.

2 = I couldn't tell you what it means but I might be able to pick the right meaning from four choices.

3 = I can tell you a little about that word.

4 = I could put that word in a good sentence that would show its meaning.

5 = I could use that word correctly in discussion and writing.

Listen/Look and Learn

Interview three of your friends about their vocabulary remembrances: Are they logophiles or do they suffer from logophobia? Do they remember teachers who were word wizards? Do they remember looking words up and writing the definitions? How did this affect how they felt about the dictionary? Do they use a dictionary now and how do they use it? Ask them also if they remember teachers that let the class choose the important words and let students plan lessons to teach the words. What did they think of these activities? If they never experienced this, ask them to decide if they thought these types of experiences would have made them more independent word acquirers.

Specific Content Area Applications

● VOCABULARY IN THE ENGLISH/LANGUAGE ARTS CLASSROOM

Two primary goals of reading novels, short stories, plays, and poetry is to gain insights into the human condition and to participate vicariously in the text worlds authors create. To accomplish these goals, readers must understand the words they encounter. Understanding vocabulary, then, is the means to the end of literary insights and experiences. Understanding vocabulary is not the end.

Effective English teachers perform a balancing act when addressing vocabulary: they work at developing word understandings while keeping those understandings subservient to the larger purposes for which students read. They achieve balance before students read by teaching the specific word meanings needed to grasp overall passage meanings. Effective English teachers achieve balance after reading by focusing attention on the key words that elicited the messages and experiences students gained. This balancing act fits situations involving single passages as well as multiple passages.

Single Passages

To consider effective ways to promote vocabulary when students are reading a single passage, think of *Shabanu, Daughter of the Wind,* the novel addressed in Chapter 4 (pages 137–139). Vocabulary learning readily can be folded into the study of this piece of literature.

Before students read *Shabanu,* introducing unfamiliar words that are crucial to understanding a section but are not fully explained is a good way to balance vocabulary and passage understandings. To illustrate, desert *oases* play a large role in *Shabanu.* Readers who lack clear and extensive understandings of this term risk substantial difficulties with the novel because it assumes readers already know about oases. Presenting the word in depth to students before they read the book is appropriate. As part of the introduction to the novel, you display *oasis* before the class and call attention to its pronunciation, then develop in-depth knowledge of its meaning. You ask students to call up what they already know about oases, present pictures and videos of them, and create analogies. You connect this individual term to the overall novel by explaining how it is a central part of the setting.

Folding vocabulary instruction into the study of *Shabanu* also can be done in the during- and after-reading phases. Asking students, "What is the most important word in this section?" and discussing their choices goes far in promoting active comprehension and in-depth vocabulary learning. A student who selects *storm* for the scene in which Shabanu's grandfather dies might focus on the denotations and connotations of this word. What exactly is a storm? Does *storm* refer to a physical weather disturbance or to characters' turmoil? How can personal relationships or the course of one's life be stormy?

If students are maintaining response journals for *Shabanu,* some of the writing prompts can highlight vocabulary. Offering a menu of prompts allows readers to select a vocabulary response format they find most productive. For instance, students illustrate the meanings of three words from a chapter (e.g., show people wearing *chadrs* and *turbans* or having their bodies painted with *henna*). They present word families (pilgrim, pilgrimmage; nomad, nomadic). They maintain a list of "words I should learn more about" for weekly follow-ups, or they complete vocabulary self-assessment scales of words that peers select. Students maintain a *"language gems"* section in their journals for recording vivid comparisons, strong verbs, and other phrases they find compelling.

Multiple Passages

A standard recommended practice for increasing vocabularies is for students to read widely in materials that are within their capabilities. This recommendation is based in part on realizations of the inefficiency of teaching isolated terms in a word-by-word fashion. A large volume of reading provides students opportunites to encounter the thousands of new terms they need to develop their vocabularies.

English teachers who stimulate their students to read widely for pleasure and for academics certainly assist vocabulary development, but additional actions are needed to enhance the impact of this practice. Since it is impossible to introduce unfamiliar words that are crucial to understanding a section when each student selects his or her own materials, focusing on vocabulary in the during and after phases of self-selected reading is appropriate.

A good way to incorporate word study while students are reading on their own is to have them maintain journals with a section devoted to vocabulary. Students select their own materials for silent reading, and they enter into their journals sections of text that contain words or phrases they find appealing, that they want to remember, and that they believe deserve sharing with classmates. They might cite author, title, and page number for each section they record. About once a week students share what they have recorded, and they engage their peers in a discussion of the passage context and meaningful word parts (if any) that determine the word's meaning. Students might first meet in groups to nominate one they consider most important for class consideration. When group representatives present their words to the class, they explain why they believe others should know it by articulating its contribution to the unit of study being conducted. Favorite sections might be gathered, posted on a bulletin board, and published every few weeks in a class anthology.

● VOCABULARY IN SECOND-LANGUAGE CLASSROOMS

Understanding the words of a second language is only part of understanding the second language, but it is a crucial part. Here are some ways to build on the suggestions presented in this chapter when teaching word meanings to learners of a second language.

Scavenger Hunts

Realia and visual aids are used in many second language classrooms to teach vocabulary meaningfully. One way to add to these concrete teaching tools is by enlisting students' help through scavenger hunts. Present a list of terms for each instructional unit, and have students individually or in groups bring in concrete objects, models, pictures, and illustrations that represent the terms. Afterwards, you have an almost instant bulletin board or display table for introducing and practicing vocabulary.

Looking beyond obvious sources and representations is a good way to extend what you gather during scavenger hunts. For instance, children's action figures, dolls, and other toy people often come with physical settings such as dollhouses, forts, and farms. Leading your class to describe the locations and actions of scenes ("The man is hiding behind the large house hoping to surprise the enemy") can result in active participation and meaningful applications of terms. You also might provide well-illustrated magazines for students to scavenge during class time. Calendars, catalogs, and newspapers are other frequently untapped teaching aids that provide useful tools for promoting second-language vocabularies.

Capsule Vocabulary

The Capsule Vocabulary teaching strategy presented in this chapter provides students good practice using the vocabulary of a second language. In this strategy you first present the pronunciations and meanings of topically related words (e.g., fruits), then students use these words (e.g., apples, oranges, bananas) while conversing with each other. This strategy is most productive when the terms refer to common concepts that require little explanation because the emphasis here is on students practicing and applying new terms in a supportive setting. Capsule Vocabulary stresses attaching labels to concepts already understood more than developing conceptual knowledge.

Several options are available for practicing the Capsule Vocabularies that are introduced. Using the words in oral conversations certainly is appropriate. In written conversations, or buddy journals, students take turns composing notes to each other in a manner similar to the surreptitious note passing that sometimes occurs during class. Written conversations are like pen pal situations; however, the pals are in the same classroom and they are using certain terms associated with units of study.

Another Capsule Vocabulary practice option is for students to write one term each on a card and categorize the cards in whatever groupings come to mind. Additionally, students might write sentences with each one containing two or three target terms. The class could play Twenty Questions in the second language, a game in which one word is selected and players try to determine what it is by asking yes-no questions ("Is it an animal?" "Is it four-legged?" "Is it domestic?"). Charades and Password are two other games appropriate for practicing Capsule Vocabulary terms.

Using Cognates

Successful readers of second languages often apply their knowledge of word cognates when they encounter unfamiliar vocabulary. Cognates are words derived from a common earlier form. Spanish and English have especially large numbers of cognates due to their historical bases in Latin. Here are some Spanish-English cognates:

naturalmente	naturally	novelas	novels
clima	climate	decidir	decide
curioso	curious	farmacia	pharmacy

Using cognates to help understand and remember unfamiliar words involves several mental operations. Learners identify unfamiliar words that justify the time and energy to be figured out, they examine target words' spellings and pronunciations to determine if they might be cognates of known words, and they test possible meanings for the unfamiliar words in the contexts of the passages to decide upon specific meanings.

Teaching students to transfer their knowledge of word meanings in one language to help in another can be done according to the recommendations in this chapter for teaching morphological sophistication. Indeed, a shared morpheme is what makes up a cognate pair. In essence, students act as detectives when figuring out word meanings, and cognate relationships are powerful clues to solving the mystery of what many words mean. When attention is directed to long unfamiliar words, remind students to ask themselves,

"Do I know any other words that look and sound like this word?"
"Are any of these look-alike/sound-alike words related to each other?"

And when meanings are suggested through possible cognates, have students ask themselves,

"Does my understanding of this word make sense in this passage?"

Consider the following description by a Mexican-American woman of one of the healing plants in her garden:

"Estas hojas tienas se hiervan para hacer un te. Este te es para los diabeti-cos. Ellos lo toman para su enfermedad." (These tender leaves are boiled to make a tea. This tea is for diabetics. They drink it for their illness.) (Brozo, Valerio, & Salazar, 1996, p. 164)

Te-tea and *diabeticos-diabetics* are two word pairs with obvious cognate relationships. Students could be expected to capitalize on these relationships when assigning meaning to what they read. Somewhat more obscure relationships are apparent in *un-a* and *enfermedad-illness*. Explaining that the *un* in *unit*, *unite*, and *union* refers to *one* or *single* and that *infirmity* is a synonym for *illness* would offer students powerful clues for understanding and remembering the meanings of *un* and *enfermedad*.

● VOCABULARY IN THE MATHEMATICS CLASSROOM

When most people think of mathematics they think of numbers, but math is a subject with its own very particular vocabulary, and if you don't know precisely what its words and symbols mean, you just can't do mathematics! Here are some activities teachers use which help students master the language of math.

A Symbol Board

Cover a bulletin board or attach a banner to your wall and add symbols to it as they are introduced. Put the symbol and a "class-created, user-friendly" definition. Add pictures and opposites as appropriate. Use different colored markers and make it as appealing as possible

Math Morphemes

The Word Detective activity in which you ask your students if they know any other words that look and sound like a new mathematics term and if they think any of these words might be related will help your students become more morphologically sophisticated. In addition, you have the unique opportunity to teach your students the meaning for some morphemes that occur most commonly in mathematics words. Seize this opportunity when introducing one of these words because your students might not meet these morphemes in any of their other classes:

Morpheme	Math Usage	General Usage
bi (two)	bisect, binomial, bimodal	bicycle, bifocals, bilingual
cent (hundred)	centimeter, percent	century, centipede
circu (around)	circle, circumference	circumvent, circumstances
co, con (with)	coefficient, cosine, collinear	cocaptains, coordinate, concurrent
dec (ten)	decimal, decagon	decade, decibel
dia (through)	diagonal, diameter	dialogue, diagram
equi (equal)	equilateral, equiangular	equator, equinox, equitable
inter (between)	intersect, interpolate	interception, international
kilo (thousand)	kilometer, kilogram	kilowatt
milli (thousand)	millimeter, milligram	millenium, million
peri (around)	perimeter	periphery, periscope periodontal
poly (many)	polygon, polynomial	polygamy, polyunsaturated
quadr (four)	quadrant, quadruple	quadrangle, quadruped
tri (three)	triangle, triple	tricycle, tripod, trilogy

Multimeaning Luck

Math has more than its share of words such as *base, product, power, point,* and *ray* for which students have one meaning but for which they need to develop a math-related concept. Multimeaning Luck is a fun activity to review the mathematical meaning for these words. Prepare for the lesson by writing down each word, with one math-related and one nonmath-related definition. (Overhead transparencies work best for this lesson, but you can also write the words on the board.) On the bottom of the transparency or on a part of the board you can cover temporarily, write one sentence for each word. Be sure to include in these sentences both math-related and unrelated meanings, as students will have to guess which definition your sentence uses. If you use only math-related meanings, they will easily figure out the system. Here is a sample lesson:

Begin the lesson by displaying the words and their two definitions:

times	1. multiplied by
	2. periods of life
gross	1. disgusting
	2. 12 dozen
line	1. a piece of rope, cord, wire, or string
	2. the shortest distance between two points
mean	1. unkind
	2. average
face	1. front part of the head
	2. any surface of a solid figure

As you read each word and its two definitions, have each student write the word and a 1 or 2 to indicate a guess of which meaning you have used in the covered sentences. Be sure to tell students that doing well on this part of the lesson is simply a matter of luck. You may want to tell students this is a way to find out how their luck is running today.

When all students have made their guesses, display the sentences one at a time. Have students give themselves five points for every lucky guess and deduct five points for every unlucky guess. The person with the most points is the lucky person for the day. Once lucky and unlucky persons have been applauded or commiserated with, review the math definitions and remind your students that they will often find words in math for which they have other meanings and that they must not let those words lead them astray but must try to figure out and remember the mathematical meaning.

Are you curious as to how you did with your guesses? If so, you will see one of the advantages of Multimeaning Luck. Once you have made a guess, you want to know how you did. You care about and pay attention to which meanings the multimeaning words had. Here are your sentences.

We had some good times together.
She ordered a gross of pencils.

I've got a huge fish out here on my line.
The mean temperature for Hawaii in July is 84 degrees.
My aunt is in the hospital having a face-lift.

Give yourself five points for every lucky guess and subtract five for every unlucky guess. Are you having a lucky day? Did you pick only the math-related meanings even though we told you to include others?

● VOCABULARY IN THE SCIENCE CLASSROOM

Could You Say That in English?

Each content area has unique vocabulary but the technical vocabulary load in science is probably greater than in any other subject. Look at the "key vocabulary" listed for each chapter and you will often find 30–50 words. If you are going to follow the 10-words-a-week guideline, you would need about a month to teach each chapter and the typical textbook contains 30 or more chapters! It can't be done! Another problem is that much of the vocabulary used in science falls into the lupulin/lupulone category—students know neither the word nor the concept—rather than the lunules/philtrum/avuncular category in which students have the concept but simply lack the label. One advantage that science teachers have is that much of their class time is spent with hands-on activities and experiments which are intended to provide the direct experience essential for building meanings for these completely new concepts. Generally, the hands-on experience should occur first and then students should be led to attach the associated vocabulary with the phenomena experienced.

Science teachers must be ruthless about limiting the number of words following guidelines listed earlier. Textbook and curriculum guide writers often list all words not apt to be known by students without consideration for the fact that some listed words only occur once and are not essential for understanding the unit much less the whole discipline. Once you have identified the key vocabulary, it is a good idea to let students know exactly which words it is critical to master. One way to do that is to post critical vocabulary on a board along with a "plain English" translation and/or picture or diagram whenever possible. It is also helpful to show the phonetic pronunciation next to each word because many students have difficulty pronouncing these strange big words. Psychologists believe that while we can put concepts in our long-term associative memory stores without pronouncing them, retrieval from that memory store often follows an auditory route. Students who cannot pronounce the critical vocabulary may understand what they are reading and what you are telling and demonstrating for them. But they may lack the auditory route to retrieve that information if they have not said the critical words.

Science Morphemes

The Word Detective activity, in which you ask your students if they know any other words that look and sound like a new science term and if they think any of these words might be related, will help your students become more morphologically sophisticated. In addition, you have the unique opportunity to teach your students the meaning for some morphemes which occur most commonly in science words. Seize this opportunity when introducing one of these words because your students might not notice these morphemes in any of their other classes:

Morpheme	Science Usage	General Usage
astro (star)	astronomy, astronaut	astronomical, asterisk
bio (life)	biology, biome, biosphere	biography, antibiotic
chlor(greenish)	chlorophyll, chloroplast	chlorine
eco (habitat)	ecology, ecosystem,	economy
hydro (water)	hydrogen, hydroelectric	hydrant, hydroplane
hypo (under)	hypothermia, hypodermis	hypodermic
hyper (too much)	hyperglycemia	hyperactive, hypertension
meta (change)	metamorphosis, metabolism	metaphor
micro (small)	microscope, microorganism	microphone
logy (science)	biology, geology, physiology	psychology
photo (light)	photosynthesis, phosphorescent	photograph
sym, syn (together)	symbiosis, symmetry	symphony, synchronize
therm (heat)	thermometer, thermal	thermos, thermostat
vor (eat)	omnivore, herbivore, carnivore	devour, voracious

● VOCABULARY IN THE SOCIAL STUDIES CLASSROOM

Fighting Words

In social studies, more than any other subject area, students have to become attuned to the connotations as well as the denotations of words. In describing various events, the point of view of the writer colors the reporting and interpretation of these events, and this point of view is usually evidenced by the words used. To help students become sensitive to word choice and to review important vocabulary, give students lists of words/terms and have them indicate with a plus, check, or minus sign whether they think the word generally has positive, neutral, or negative connotations. After students complete this activity separately, have them get together with peers and discuss their decisions. This is an activity in which you want them to use the evaluate thinking process. Don't expect everyone to agree since their point of view will affect their decisions. But, considering the different connotations of common social studies terms will help them be more critical readers and better understand and retain the word meanings. Here are some starter words/terms. Pick similar words from your units:

liberal	conservative	Stars and Stripes
hawk	dove	AFL-CIO
corporation	pro-choice	pro-life
John Bircher	revolutionary	capitalist
reactionary	hillbilly	feminist
media	minority candidate	third world

Social Studies Morphemes

The Word Detective activity in which you ask your students if they know any other words that look and sound like a new social studies term and if they think any of these words might be related will help your students become more morphologically sophisticated. In addition, you have the unique opportunity to teach your students the meaning for some morphemes which occur most commonly in social studies words. Seize this opportunity when introducing one of these words because your students might not notice these morphemes in any of their other classes:

Morpheme	*Social Studies Usage*	*General Usage*
anti (against)	antitrust, antislavery	antibody, antisocial
com, con (with, together)	community, congress, conspiracy	compile, committee, company, conform
counter, contra (against)	counteroffensive, counterintelligence	counterfeit, contradict
ex (out)	exports, explorers	expedition, exit
form (shape)	conform, reformers	deformity, formula
geo (earth)	geography, geopolitical	geometry, geology
im, in (in)	imports, immigration, invasion, inauguration	implant, impoverish, indent, intruder
im, in (opposite)	immoral, independence	impatient, inefficient
inter (between)	international, intervention	interrupt, interfere
ism (state of)	communism, capitalism	patriotism
ist (person)	communist, nationalist	pianist, scientist
mono (one, same)	monarchy, monopoly	monorail, monastery
non (opposite)	nonviolence, nonpartisan, nonproliferation	nonprofit, nonstop
sub (under)	subcontinent, subcontinent	subway, substitute
trans (across)	transAtlantic, transcontinental	transport, transfer
uni (one, same)	unilateral, unified, universal,	uniform, united

Acronym Board

Cover a bulletin board or attach a banner to your wall and add acronyms to it as they occur in your study. List the acronym and the word for which it stands. Have your artistically talented students draw something to symbolize each acronym. Here are some examples of common social studies acronyms:

AID—Agency for International Development
CARE—Corporation for American Relief Everywhere
CORE—Congress of Racial Equality
ERA—Equal Rights Amendment
SADD—Students Against Drunk Driving
HUD—Housing and Urban Development
MIA—Missing In Action
SNCC—Student Nonviolent Coordinating Committee
VISTA—Volunteers In Service To America
WHO—World Health Organization

● VOCABULARY IN THE "ACTIVITY" CLASSROOM

In many subjects, the emphasis is on doing rather than on reading and writing. In order to do anything successfully, however, you have to develop the vocabulary—the lingo—of that area. Whether you teach physical education, music, art, a vocational subject, or some other activity-oriented course, your students will learn more and like it more if you expend a small amount of time and effort identifying the key vocabulary in your area and making sure your students attach the appropriate meanings to the words and symbols. Here are some specific activities teachers in nontextbook courses have used to develop meanings for critical words.

Multimeaning Luck

In every field there are words with a subject-specific meaning for which students have a more commonly used meaning. Music class can be pretty confusing when the teacher is talking about *keys, scales,* and *notes,* and the students are picturing car keys, bathroom scales, and messages to their friends! Common words such as *rack* and *tolerance* have very specific meanings when used in a mechanics class. Students who are becoming computer experts must realize that you can't fish with this *net,* bet with this *chip,* and shouldn't scream at this *mouse!*

Multimeaning Luck is a fun activity to review the content-specific meaning for words. Prepare for the lesson by writing down each word, with one math-related and one nonmath-related definition. (Overhead transparencies work best for this lesson, but you can also write the words on the board.) On the bottom of the transparency or on a part of the board you can cover temporarily, write one sentence for each word. Be sure to include in these sentences both subject-related and unrelated meanings, as students will have to guess which definition your sentence uses. If you use only subject-related meanings, they will easily figure out the system. Here is a sample lesson from a computer class. Begin the lesson by displaying the words and their two definitions:

menu	1. list of available foods
	2. options in a computer program
boot	1. footwear often used in rain or snow
	2. load an operating system into a computer
ram/RAM	1. Random Access Memory
	2. crash into
virus	1. an infection from a submicroscopic organism
	2. a computer program that can attack other programs
bug	1. error in a program
	2. small insect

As you read each word and its two definitions, have each student write the word and a 1 or 2 to indicate a guess of which meaning you have used in the covered sentences. Be sure to tell students that doing well on this part of the lesson is simply a matter of luck. You may want to tell students this is a way to find out how their luck is running today.

When all students have made their guesses, display the sentences one at a time. Have students give themselves five points for every lucky guess and deduct five points for every unlucky guess. The person with the most points is the lucky person for the day. Once lucky and unlucky persons have been applauded or commiserated with, review the subject-related definitions. Remind your students that they will often find words in your subject for which they have other meanings and that they must not let those words lead them astray but must try to figure out and remember the appropriate meaning.

Are you curious as to how you did with your guesses? If so, you will see one of the advantages of Multimeaning Luck. Once you have made a guess, you want to know how you did. You care about and pay attention to which meanings the multimeaning words had. Here are your sentences:

You can check your spelling by pulling down the edit menu.
The only clue at the scene was a size 11 boot print.
I was just sitting there and I saw this car ram right into the house!
I found a virus on my computer.
There must be some kind of bug in this program.

Give yourself five points for every lucky guess and subtract five for every unlucky guess. Are you having a lucky day? Did you pick only the computer-related meanings even though we told you to include others?

Word/Symbol/Picture Board

Fortunately, many of the new meanings which students must learn in activity courses are words which represent concrete, real things. Leanings the names of the parts of the lathe becomes a much simpler task when a picture or diagram is displayed with these parts labeled. Coaches have long made use of diagrams for various plays and positions. A music board might display the symbols for *sharp, flat, note, repeat,* and so forth along with the words for which they stand. A display of art labeled for its style and media catches the eye while simultaneously giving reality to confusing terms such as *impressionist, neoclassical,* and *acrylic.*

Word Detectives

Just as in all areas, many of the new words your students will encounter are big words for which your students have other words which will help them figure out and remember pronunciations, spellings, and meanings. Students in an art class who are dealing with the concepts of *foreground* and *background* and whose attention is drawn to words such as *forehand, forehead, backhand,* and *backpack* should have no trouble understanding and using the new art terms. The strange new words *micrometer, variometer,* and *magnetometer* are not so strange when connected with *speedometer, thermometer, microscope, variations,* and *magnetic.* With a little help, students can even be lead to see the "strong" relationship in such words as *fortress, fortitude, fortify,* and *fortissimo.*

When you are on the lookout for these morphemic relationships between words and point them out to your students, your students benefit in two ways. The obvious benefit is that they can more easily learn your new vocabulary and retain it fairly effortlessly. Less obvious—but actually more important in the "scheme of things"—you help your students become "word detectives" who, whenever they encounter a new word, are apt to look for clues in already-known words and thus can grow independently in vocabulary knowledge from all the reading they do. Not a bad return on a small investment of time and energy!

Looking Back _____

Having a thorough knowledge of the key words is essential to learning in any content area. The vocabulary of each content area is specific to that area and not apt to occur in normal conversation, recreational reading, or television viewing. All content area teachers must teach the vocabulary essential to communicating about their subject. These are the key ideas you explored in this chapter: (1) There are many aspects of vocabulary knowledge; (2) words are learned through direct and visual experience and by making connections; (3) effective teachers are selective about which words to teach; (4) there is great variety in the strategies content teachers use to teach vocabulary; (5) polysyllabic words require special attention and strategies; and (6) students become independent learners of words when teachers encourage student responsibility, reflection, and self-assessment.

Add to Your Journal

Reflect upon the six key ideas in this chapter and decide what you think: Do you remember learning words through direct and visual experience? Can you think of words for which you have had no experience and which you learned by connecting them to known words? Do you remember teachers who worked hard to provide you with direct experiences? Do you remember taking field trips? Engaging in simulations? Building models? Do you remember teachers who used films and videos effectively? Can you think of ways in which teachers tried to develop abstract concepts by creating analogies to real situations? Did any teacher help you learn to use context or become morphologically sophisticated? Think about the teaching strategies described. Which ones could you most profitably use in your content area? Finally, think about independence. Students will not always have you there to ferret out the critical words and devise nifty ways to learn them. What will you do to make your students independent word learners?

REFERENCES

BROZO, W. G., VALERIO, P. C., & SALAZAR, M. M. (1996). A walk through Gracie's garden: Literacy and cultural expectations in a Mexican American junior high school. *Journal of Adolescent and Adult Literacy, 40* (3), 164–170.

BURMEISTER, L. (1978). *Reading strategies for middle and secondary school teachers* (2nd ed.). Reading, MA: Addison Wesley.

CRIST, B. I. (1975). One capsule a week—a painless remedy for vocabulary ills. *Journal of Reading, 19,* 147–149.

HAGGARD, M. R. (1982). The vocabulary self-collection strategy: An active approach to word learning. *Journal of Reading, 26,* 203–207.

NAGY, W., & ANDERSON, R. C. (1984) How many words are there in printed school English? *Reading Research Quarterly, 19,* 304–330.

TIERNEY, R. J., & PEARSON, P. D. (1981). Learning to learn from text: A framework for improving classroom practice. In E. K. Dishner, T. W. Bean, & J. E. Readence (Eds.), *Reading in the content areas.* Dubuque, IA: Kendall/Hunt.

ADDITIONAL READINGS

Books which will help you develop your word wonder include:

ASIMOV, I. (1969). *Words of science and the history behind them.* New York: New American Library.

CIARDI, J. (1980). *A browser's dictionary.* New York: Harper & Row.

ELSTER, C. H. (1996). *There's a word for it.* New York: Scribner.

ESPY, W. (1981). *Have a word on me.* New York: Simon & Schuster.

SAFIRE, W. (1982). *What's the good word?* New York: Crown.

Approaches to developing vocabulary in general with a special chapter for content area vocabulary can be found in this book:

JOHNSON, D. D., & PEARSON, P. D. (1984). *Teaching reading vocabulary.* New York: Holt, Rinehart & Winston.

Research on the use of analogy to develop unfamiliar concepts in a health textbook are reported in the following article; the methods described are applicable to any content area:

VOSNIADOU, S., & ORTONY, A. (1982). The influence of analogy in children's acquisition of new information from text: An exploratory study. In J. Niles (Ed.), *Searches for meaning in reading/language processing and instruction* (Thirty-First Yearbook of the National Reading Conference) (pp. 71–79). Rochester, NY: National Reading Conference.

Chapter 8 of this book will provide you with lots of information about prefixes, suffixes, and roots and may increase your morphological sophistication!

BEAR, D., INVERNIZZI, M., TEMPLETON, S., & JOHNSTON, F. (1996). *Words their way: Word study for phonics, vocabulary, and spelling instruction.* Englewood Cliffs, NJ: Prentice-Hall.

This is a scholarly account of the role of morphemic analysis in vocabulary development:

ANGLIN, J. M. (1993). Monographs of the Society for Research in Child Development, *Vocabulary development: A morphological analysis. 58*(10) (Serial No. 238), 1–186.

Suggestions for using content-word boards including review activities can be found in this book:

GREEN, J. (1993). *The word wall: Teaching vocabulary through immersion.* Markham, Ontario: Pippen and Portsmouth, NH: Heinemann.

Practical approaches to vocabulary instruction that could be used in any content area are included in the following articles:

BLACHOWICZ, C. L. (1985). Vocabulary development and reading: From research to instruction. *The Reading Teacher, 38,* 876–881.

CARR, E. M. (1985). The vocabulary overview guide: A metacognitive strategy to improve vocabulary comprehension and retention. *Journal of Reading, 28,* 684–689.

IRVIN, J. L. (1990). *Vocabulary knowledge: Guidelines for instruction* (What research says to the teacher). Washington, DC: National Education Association.

MARZANO, R. J. (1984). A cluster approach to vocabulary instruction: A new direction from the research literature. *The Reading Teacher, 37,* 168–173.

NAGY, W. E. (1988). *Teaching vocabulary to improve comprehension.* Newark, DE: International Reading Association.

Some good syntheses of research on meaning vocabulary instruction and learning include the following:

BAUMANN, J. F., & KAMEENUI, E. J. (1991). Research on vocabulary instruction: Ode to Voltaire. In J. Flood, J. M. Jensen, D. Lapp, & J. R. Squire (Eds.), *Handbook of research on teaching the English language arts* (pp. 604–632). New York: Macmillan.

BECK, I., & McKEOWN, M. (1991). Conditions of vocabulary acquisition. In R. Barr, M. L. Kamil, P. B. Mosenthal, & P. D. Pearson (Eds.), *Handbook of reading research* (Vol. 2, pp. 789–814). White Plains, NY: Longman.

BLACHOWICZ, C. L. Z., & FISHER, P. J. L. (1994). Vocabulary instruction. In A. C. Purves, *Encyclopedia of English studies and language arts* (A Project of the National Council of Teachers of English) (pp. 1244–1246). New York: Scholastic.

GRAVES, M. F. (1994). Vocabulary knowledge. In A. C. Purves, *Encyclopedia of English studies and language arts* (A Project of the National Council of Teachers of English) (pp. 1246–1248). New York: Scholastic.

KLESIUS, J. P., & SEARLS, E. F. (1990). A meta-analysis of recent research in meaning vocabulary instruction. *Journal of Research and Development in Education, 23,* 226–235.

RUDDELL, M. R. (1994). Vocabulary knowledge and comprehension: A comprehension-process view of complex literacy relationships. In R. B. Ruddell, M. R. Ruddell, & H. Singer (Eds.), *Theoretical models and processes of reading* (4th ed.) (pp. 414–447). Newark, DE: International Reading Association.

SCOTT, J. A., & NAGY, W. E. (1994). Vocabulary development. In A. C. Purves, *Encyclopedia of English studies and language arts* (A Project of the National Council of Teachers of English) (pp. 1242–1244). New York: Scholastic.

chapter 6
Writing

Looking Ahead

Writing is thinking you do with a pen, pencil, or word processor. Because writing is primarily thinking, you use some or all of the thinking processes as you write. Students who write about what they are learning are engaged in thinking. In order to write, students call up what they know and even seek out more information or clarifications. They show the connections they have made. They organize information in new ways. They share their images, generalizations, and opinions. Writing is an application of new knowledge. As people write, they monitor what they know, what they think, and how well they are communicating. Teachers support students' thinking by planning and carrying out lessons in which the writing tasks are made clear and the fulfillment of these purposes is ensured by group sharing and feedback.

As you no doubt understand by now, learning requires thinking, and thinking usually begins with calling up past experiences. In this chapter, you will learn how to use writing to help students learn. In order to learn about writing, you must think about writing. Your past experiences with writing will be the starting point for your thinking and learning. To determine where your past writing experiences have gotten you, complete this writing attitude self-appraisal. Place yourself on a 1 to 10 scale between these polar statements:

I really hate to write.   I really like to write.

  1   2   3   4   5   6   7   8   9   10

I write only when I have to.

| 1 | 2 | 3 | 4 | 5 | 6 |

I write for my own pleasure.

| 7 | 8 | 9 | 10 |

All of my school writing
   was for a paper or test.

| 1 | 2 | 3 | 4 | 5 | 6 |

All of my school writing was to
help me express my thoughts.

| 7 | 8 | 9 | 10 |

All school writing was graded.

| 1 | 2 | 3 | 4 | 5 | 6 |

No school writing was graded.

| 7 | 8 | 9 | 10 |

Most students are
   terrible writers.

| 1 | 2 | 3 | 4 | 5 | 6 |

Most students are
wonderful writers.

| 7 | 8 | 9 | 10 |

Writing should not be used
   because students cannot
   do it.

| 1 | 2 | 3 | 4 | 5 | 6 |

Writing should be used in
every class so that students get
better at it.

| 7 | 8 | 9 | 10 |

In a content class, all writing
   should be graded for both
   content and mechanics.

| 1 | 2 | 3 | 4 | 5 | 6 | 7 | 8 | 9 | 10 |

In a content class, writing
should not be graded.

Now look at your ratings and see where your past experiences with writing have led you. If you rated yourself a perfect 10 on every statement, you have an incredibly positive view of yourself as a writer, others as writers, and the potential of writing as a tool for learning in your classroom. If you rated yourself 1 on every statement, writing for you as an individual and as a teacher is going to be quite a challenge!

Most teachers rate themselves someplace between 1 and 10, often on the low side. Writing for many of us is not something we feel particularly good at, not something we choose to do, and not something we see as a tool that can help students learn the content we need to teach. Consequently, both research and classroom observation confirm that not much writing happens and that the writing that does happen is often for a test or paper. Unfortunately, writing in many classrooms is not a road to learning but an assessment of what has been learned.

In this chapter, we hope to convince you to use writing in your classroom because it is not "one more thing you have to do" but rather an often-overlooked and readily available resource for helping your students think and learn more. We know, however, that your past experiences with writing, your attitudes toward yourself as a writer, and your confidence that students can and will write may be less than positive. If your past experiences have left you with negative attitudes, we ask you to read and think with an open mind and reconsider the potential writing holds for you and your students.

These are the key ideas in this chapter:

1. Informal writing experiences promote student thinking and learning.
2. Planning a writing lesson includes deciding on clear writing tasks, background knowledge, and motivation.

3. Writing lessons guide students through the before, during, and after phases of writing.
4. There are many variations within the writing lesson framework.
5. Students become independent learners when teachers encourage student responsibility, reflection, and self-assessment.

INFORMAL WRITING EXPERIENCES PROMOTE STUDENT THINKING AND LEARNING

Writing is best defined as "thinking made external." When we write, we put down our thoughts and discover new thoughts. Writing, like reading, has before, during, and after phases. Thinking pervades all these writing phases. If you come upon someone who is sitting with a pen in hand or fingertips poised over the keyboard and staring at the blank page or screen, you might ask, "What are you doing?" The person will often respond, "I'm thinking."

Continuing to observe, you will see the person eventually move into the writing phase, but the writing is not nonstop. If you are rude enough to interrupt during one of these pauses and ask, "What are you doing?" the writer will probably again respond, "I'm thinking." Eventually, the writer will finish the writing, or more accurately finish the first draft. The writer may put the writing away for a while or ask someone to "take a look at this and tell me what you think." Later the writer will return to the writing to revise and edit. Words will be changed and paragraphs added, moved, or deleted. Again, the writer will pause from time to time during this after-writing phase; if you ask the writer what he or she is doing, you will likely get the familiar response, "I'm thinking!"

We offer this common scenario as proof that writing is at its essence thinking (even the most naive writer knows this). Because writing is thinking and learning requires thinking, students who write as they are learning think more and thus learn more.

In addition to being thinking (or perhaps because it is thinking), writing is hard. It is complex. There are many things to think about all at the same time, such as

What do I want to say?
How can I say it so that people will believe it?
How can I say it so that people will be motivated to read it?
Who are the people whom I want to read it? What do they already know, think, and believe about this subject?

In addition to these major issues, there are a host of smaller, but still important issues:

How can I begin writing in a way that sets up my ideas and grabs the reader's attention?

Which words best communicate these feelings and thoughts?
What examples can the reader relate to?
Do I need to clarify here or include more detailed information?
How can I end it?
What would be a good title?

As if these grand and less grand issues are not enough, there are all the minor details. Sometimes these are taken care of during the after-writing phase, but often writers think about them as they write. These are some examples:

Should I begin a new paragraph here?
Do I capitalize state when it refers to North Carolina?
What is the correct spelling of Beijing?
Does the comma go inside or outside the quotation marks?

We have not included this sampling to discourage you. We included it to convince you that students need effective instruction, with special attention to academic and social support as presented in Chapter 1, if they are going to be able and willing participants in writing.

We organize writing activities into two categories, informal writing and writing lessons. Both should occur regularly during every unit of study in which students participate. Informal writing can take just a few minutes but can help students focus on what they know, what they don't know, and what they think. In some classrooms, students keep daily journals which record their ideas, questions, and feelings throughout a unit. On the other hand, writing lessons require substantial planning and class time and are used when teachers want students to explore specific topics and learn to write specific forms. Writing lessons can consist of short tasks which take only a day to complete, or they can be extensive projects that help students synthesize large amounts of information and culminate units. Writing lessons are the subject of the following three sections. In this section we describe two types of informal writing, quick writes and content journals, that can occur on a daily basis in almost any class and that serve a multitude of purposes.

Quick Writes

1. We are about to begin learning about desert habitats. Take thirty seconds and write down all the words you think of when you think of desert. The clock starts now!
2. Before we begin our exploration of matter, write down everything you know about matter. You have one minute.
3. We have been talking about communities today. Write one sentence in which you come up with your own definition for community. Try to include the big ideas we have talked about.
4. We have been learning about habitats. List as many habitats as you can in 30 seconds.

5. Today's math lesson had some difficult concepts. We will work more on this tomorrow. List at least one thing you don't think you understand.
6. I didn't hear from many of you today and I am wondering what you are thinking. Tell me in a sentence or two what you thought of today's activity.
7. The topics of race and prejudice are emotional ones. Tell me in a few sentences how you are feeling about the difficult issues we have talked about today.

These are all examples of quick writes used in content area classrooms. Quick writes are the least formal kind of writing and in some ways the easiest ones to fit into a crowded content curriculum. Quick writes are used for a variety of purposes. Examples 1 and 2 were previewing quick writes, intended to help both students and teacher assess the entry-level knowledge of the class about a new topic. Examples 3 and 4 were quick writes which help students synthesize the day's learning and let teachers know how well the concepts were understood. Examples 5, 6, and 7 were self-assessment quick writes. Students had to assess their understanding, their involvement, their attitudes, and their emotions. By reading these quick writes, teachers could determine common confusions, evaluate the success of the activity, and determine if an emotional topic under consideration was at or beyond students' comfort level.

What you do with quick writes depends on why you did them and how much time you have. If the quick writes are like examples 1 and 2 and intended to get students accessing prior knowledge and thinking about a topic, you may want to have students tell what they have written down as you list this on the board and point out that this is the starting point, the "what we know" from the KWL comprehension lesson framework in Chapter 4. You may also ask volunteers to share what they have written in response to examples 3 and 4 in order to let students see how others defined *community* or how many habitats they have listed. This helps students self-assess their learning and monitor their level of understanding. Sometimes teachers collect the quick writes, telling students that these will help guide the planning of tomorrow's activity. In this case, you may want to ask students not to put their names on quick writes to make sure students know you are evaluating the lesson, class learning, mood, and so forth and not individual students. Many teachers hand students small index cards for these assessment quick writes. Because of their size and their "real world" uses, index cards are unintimidating and help students to view this writing as different from some of the other more formal class assignments.

Content Journals

We hope that you have been keeping the journal suggested at the end of each chapter. This is just one example of a content journal. A content journal is a place for students to record their personal insights, questions, confusions, disagreements, and frustrations about what is being learned. (Some teachers call these journals *learning logs.*) Journal writing is primarily writing students do for themselves; it helps them sort out what they think about what they are learning.

Content journals may have a great deal of structure or very little. When there is little structure, students choose what to write about. One student might write a diary-style account of what was learned, while another might write a letter to the teacher, complete with visuals, explaining his or her reaction to what is being studied. When students have control over the specific content they are writing about, the journals are said to have *low structure.*

With *high-structure* content journals, the teacher requires students to react to specific ideas they are exploring in class. Students may be asked to explore some controversial issue associated with the content. For instance, if westward expansion were the unit of study in American history, students might be asked to record their impressions of the similarities between nineteenth-century movement by U.S. citizens into Texas and twentieth-century movement by Mexican citizens into Texas. Students could be asked to call up impressions they had before beginning the class and compare them to their current impressions. They might be asked to summarize chapters or articles they are reading. The structure is high because the teacher assigns the writing task, students have little say about what they are to write.

Typically, students are expected to write in their journals from five to ten minutes each day. Some teachers begin class each day with a five-minute journal writing time. During the five minutes while students are completing their journal entries, teachers do the routine chores of attendance taking, talking to a student who was absent yesterday, and so on. On some days, a high-structure entry is required and prompted by a sentence or two written on the board. On other days, students write whatever they want related to the topic being studied. Teachers who establish this five-minute beginning-of-class journal writing routine report that journal writing does not take away from their teaching time since they must spend a few minutes at the beginning of each class with routine chores and that students settle in and get back into the content of the class much more readily when they have this daily journal writing time.

Journals are collected several times a term in order to make sure that students have been writing regularly, and in order to determine whether students are learning course content and reacting thoughtfully to the ideas they are encountering. While reading the journals, some teachers write comments to the students, creating a written dialogue, about how well students are learning the course material and how clearly they express what they have learned. Students' attitudes and efforts regarding journal writing seem to be directly related to the frequency and quality of a teacher's comments in the journals. Weekly reactions are ideal, although biweekly or monthly input is generally more feasible. Most teachers don't grade each journal entry but they do give

Students explore their feelings and reactions to classroom experiences by writing in journals.

students points for keeping their journal up-to-date and for demonstrating good thinking.

Try It Out

Think about a unit you will be teaching. Come up with three quick writes, one each for previewing, synthesizing, and self-assessment. Write down each including how much time you would give students or how many words, sentences, and so forth you want them to write. Next come up with three prompts for high-structure journal entries which your students could complete in five to ten minutes.

PLANNING A WRITING LESSON INCLUDES DECIDING ON CLEAR WRITING TASKS, BACKGROUND KNOWLEDGE, AND MOTIVATION

Writing lessons clearly follow the steps of an instructional cycle. There are distinct times for planning, introducing, guiding, and culminating, and assessment and reflection occur throughout the process. With regard to planning, as we said about comprehension lessons in Chapter 4, you must decide on clear learning purposes and decide what background knowledge and motivation students would need to achieve these purposes. When planning a writing lesson, you follow similar steps.

Deciding What You Want Students to Think About as They Write

Once you become convinced that the main purpose for writing in a content area classroom is to get students thinking about content topics, then you must decide what you want them to think about. For every unit of study, there is a host of possibilities. Imagine that you are teaching about twins and the incredible similarities that exist between identical twins separated at birth (see Holden, 1990, for a fascinating presentation of this topic). Here are some issues that you might consider important and that deserve your students' attention:

1. What genetic traits do twins share?
2. What are the advantages and disadvantages of having a twin?
3. What personality traits seem to be most and least accounted for by heredity?
4. How does research on twins help us understand the heredity versus environment issue?
5. Should the findings of research on twins influence your decision about whom to marry?
6. How are you similar to and different from members of your own family?
7. What is there about being a twin that makes someone less likely to become famous?
8. How are twins portrayed in literature?

There are many different issues and questions about which you might want students to think. In doing so, they will use different thinking processes. Almost all writing tasks require students to call up what they know and connect new information. Likewise, students must monitor what they know and are communicating as they write. Students' use of the other thinking processes will depend on what you want them to focus on and the writing task you set for them.

Designing a Writing Task That Will Stimulate Students to Think About Important Aspects of the Topic

In Chapter 4, we noted that once you decide what you want students to learn, you should design a task that will focus their attention. When writing, once you know what you want students to think about, you design a writing task that focuses their attention. A writing task has four major components: topic, form, audience, and role.

Topic   The topic is both the "what?" and the "what for?" of writing: the content and the intent. The topic chosen can include what the students will write about and the purpose the writer should attempt to accomplish during writing.

In a content class, the topic is selected so that students focus their thinking. If you want students to think about what genetic traits twins share, for example, your topic might be this:

> Describe a restaurant meeting between you and your identical twin, who was separated from you at birth 20 years ago, including details about what each of you is wearing; what each of you orders; what pictures of family, friends, pets, and houses you share; and how each of you reacts when the food served is not what you ordered.

The topic can be very broad, but the best writing topics are narrowed so that the writer knows how to focus attention. By assigning topics with specific content, teachers often narrow the topic to help students know better how to plan their writing.

Teachers sometimes narrow the content of a writing task by specifying the approach the writer is to take. There are five general approaches writers can take:

1. Compare and/or contrast.
2. Give the sequence.
3. Make a list.
4. Relate cause(s) and effect(s).
5. State the solution to a problem.

Another way teachers sometimes narrow the topic is by specifying the intent or aim of the writing. Here are some possible intents for writing:

1. Describing
2. Explaining
3. Expressing feelings
4. Narrating
5. Persuading

Form   Form is the medium of writing. How are students going to write about the topic? Are they going to write a poem, a story, an essay, or a newspaper article? Writers use a variety of forms, and their choice of form is related to their topic. For example, your writing on the sample topic above might take the form of a play, a letter, a short story, or even a comic strip.

Specifying the form of a passage usually includes specifying its length. Knowing the approximate length of their writing helps students understand how much information to include. Imagine that you are assigning a paper describing the metric system. Do you expect the paper to be one page or five pages long? A one-page paper would leave space for few examples, but a five-page paper would need many examples. Assigning approximate lengths for writing helps clarify the depth of discussion you expect to find in the writing. Often, the teacher will have more success by setting a maximum length than a minimum one. For students to have to meet the demands of the topic within a constraining length, they will have to plan carefully before writing.

Much school writing is limited to a few forms—paragraphs, stories, letters, poems, and reports. Actual writing, however, contains countless forms. In the real world, people write lists, journal entries, and directions. The list below gives just a sampling to get you thinking about the possibilities for writing forms:

A Sampling of Some Writing Forms

ads	lab reports
allegories	letters
announcements	lists
autobiographies	magazine articles
biographies	memoirs
book jackets	memos
book reviews	mysteries
brochures	myths
campaign speeches	newspaper articles
character sketches	newspaper columns
comic strips	obituaries
commercials	observational notes
contracts	plays
debates	poems
diaries	position papers
directions	questionnaires
editorials	recipes
encyclopedia entries	reports
epitaphs	reviews
essays	scenarios
fables	scripts
grocery lists	song lyrics
interviews	stories
journals	summaries

Audience   Imagine this vignette:

It was a dark and foggy night, and you were driving home from class. You did not stop at a STOP sign that had only recently been installed at a familiar intersection. Fortunately, there were no other cars in the intersection, so you got through safely. Unfortunately, a police officer was parked along the curb ahead. You were given a ticket for running the STOP sign.

Now imagine that you are going to write a letter about this sad incident to a 7-year-old cousin, your best friend, your father (in whose name the car is registered), and the judge who will decide on your fine. The topic and form will be the same for all the letters, but the audience for each is quite different. Think about how the four letters would be different.

Audience, one of the "who's" of writing, refers to the person or persons who might read your writing. Sometimes the audience is real. For example, students write pieces to be read by their classmates, students in other classes, younger children, pen pals, parents, school personnel, newspaper readers, and public officials. Sometimes the audience cannot really read the piece, but the writer writes as if the audience could. For example, letters are written to George Washington, or descriptions of life as it is today are put into time capsules for some possible readers, years or even decades into the future.

Often writers write for themselves. People keep diaries and journals; make lists, schedules, and notes; and write to clarify their own thinking rather than to communicate that thinking to others.

In schools, the most common audience is the teacher, probably the hardest audience for whom to write. Students who know that their teacher will be the only reader often leave important data unstated because they know that the teacher already knows the information.

Having a real audience other than the teacher has been shown to improve greatly the quality of student writing. Students write more clearly and use more examples when they know that someone who really needs the information is going to read it. Whenever possible, students should write for a variety of audiences, including themselves, their classmates, and other people in the real world. Before students begin to write, they should be clear about who will be the audience for that piece of writing.

Returning to our twins example, the students could write to a friend, to the mother who gave the twins up for adoption, to the person who arranged the meeting after 20 years, or to an audience of magazine readers.

Role   The other "who" of writing is the role you take as a writer or the perspective you take. Often we write from our own perspective so that we do not think about our role; sometimes we write from different perspectives. Assuming different roles helps students produce clear, interesting writing.

Students could write to Abraham Lincoln, and thus Lincoln would be the audience; or they could write what they think Abraham Lincoln would say in a speech today, and thus they would assume the role of Lincoln. For actors, getting into the part, believing they are who they are portraying, is crucial for believable acting. For writers, assuming different roles helps them write more vividly.

Returning one more time to our twins example, students could write from the role of either twin, the role of the restaurant waiter, or even the role of a nosy eavesdropper at the next table.

A writing task thus has four components: RAFT (Holston & Santa, 1985) is a mnemonic device for remembering the four components:

Role—Who seems to be doing the writing?
Audience—For whom are you writing?
Form—How will you write about the topic? How long will your writing be?
Topic—What are you writing about and for what aim?

When teachers design a writing task for a content area class, they most commonly think about the topic first and then the forms, audiences, and roles that would help students think about the topic. Sometimes, however, you may wish to focus students' attention on a particular form or audience. Form would be the component getting the most attention if the lesson purpose were to learn to write a poem, a mathematical word problem, a first-person historical account, or a lab report. Role or audience would be the focus if you were helping students learn about Lincoln by writing to him or assuming his role.

When planning a writing task, you first decide about what the writing is going to get the students thinking. This can be a topic, a form, an audience, or a role. Once you have done so, you make decisions about the other three components so that they will support the emphasis on the other component by not being too new or difficult.

Writing tasks have these four components, but you do not have to specify all four. Sometimes you may want to decide on the topic and form but let students choose their audience and role; other times you may want to specify the topic and audience and let students decide on the form.

Considering the four possible components of a writing task in light of what you want students to think about while writing guides your thinking as you plan writing tasks. It is important to remember, however, that planning effective writing tasks cannot be done mechanically. Teachers need a sense of what students like and can do. This is the "art part" of writing lesson planning. You can develop this by actually planning and teaching writing lessons. Mixing experience with a knowledge of the four components of a writing task will eventually lead you to the professional skill of constructing writing tasks that simultaneously focus on important ideas and engage learners' attention and actions.

Here are some examples of writing tasks that get students to think about the twins' issues:

1. *Think about:* What genetic traits do twins share?
   Task: Write a two- to three-page scenario to be shared with your classmates describing the following scene: Imagine that you had an identical twin who was separated from you at birth. You meet 20 years later at a restaurant. What kind of clothes are each of you wearing? What kind of food do you order? What is shown in the pictures (family, friends, pets, houses) you share? When the waiter brings the wrong food order, how do each of you react?
2. *Think about:* What are the advantages and disadvantages of having a twin?
   Task: Locate a twin to interview about the advantages and disadvantages of being a twin. Write a one-page magazine article summarizing your interview, which will be compiled with others into a special class magazine on twins.
3. *Think about:* What personality traits seem to be most and least accounted for by heredity?
   Task: First, describe your major personality characteristics. Then compare and contrast your major personality characteristics with

those of family members or ancestors. Finally, explain which of your major personality characteristics you believe to be most attributable to heredity. You will share your description and conclusions with classmates.

4. *Think about:* How does research on twins help us understand the heredity versus environment issue?

   Task: Imagine that you are a scientist who is thinking about how you might use twins in research to shed light on the heredity versus environment issue. You are talking on the phone to a scientist from another country and seeking advice on how to proceed. Write what each of you might say in this conversation. Remember that international calls are very expensive, so limit your conversation to five minutes.

5. *Think about:* Should the findings of research on twins influence your decision about whom to marry?

   Task: Write a 30-second public-service TV commercial in which you try to convince teens and young adult singles to consider the personality traits of their boyfriend's or girlfriend's family when making a decision to marry.

6. *Think about:* How are you similar to and different from members of your own family?

   Task: Write to a pen pal (or a key pal if using e-mail) a letter in which you describe yourself and your family, and tell about how you are similar to and different from each other member.

7. *Think about:* What is there about being a twin that makes someone less likely to become famous?

   Task: You are a freelance writer working on an article entitled, "History's Missing Famous Twins," for submission to a popular magazine. Describe how small is the number of famous people who are twins when they are compared with their actual numbers in the population. Speculate on why twins might be less likely than nontwins to become famous.

8. *Think about:* How are twins portrayed in literature?

   Task: Think about the stories and books you have read in which twins were major characters. Were they realistically portrayed, given what you have learned about twins? Write for a literary publication an essay in which you compare twins' portrayal in literature with what you have learned about twins.

Note that we use the phrase *think about* in the writing tasks listed above. Many educators would prefer terms such as *outcome, objective,* or *learning target* in place of *think about.* For the above writing task number 1, instead of saying "*Think about:* What genetic traits do twins share?" some educators might say, "The learner will describe three genetic traits that twins share." We prefer our format because it seems to foster meaningful engagement with subject matter. Using preset, overly defined objectives risk causing learners to narrow their thinking and reproduce only what they think already is in teachers' minds.

Try It Out

Read the writing tasks and decide what the topic, form, audience, and role is for each. For example, for the first writing task, the topic was a restaurant meeting with an identical twin who had been separated at birth, the form was a scenario, the audience was classmates, and the role was yourself. For the second task, the topic was the advantages and disadvantages of being a twin, the form was a magazine article, the audience was class magazine readers, and the role was you as an interviewer. (Remember that not all of these must be specified in every writing task. The third task, for example, does not specify the form.) Choose two of the tasks and change one or more of the components (topic, form, audience, or role) to create a new writing task. Be sure, however, that your new writing task is still getting students to think about what you want them to think about.

Building Background Knowledge and Motivation

Once you know what you want students to think about and what writing task they will perform, you can decide what background knowledge and motivation you need to build to enable them to carry out the task. Building background knowledge for writing is no different from building background knowledge for reading. Ask yourself what students need to know to complete the task, then think about how most efficiently to build that knowledge. Consider providing direct and visual experience when needed and possible and trying to help students make connections with things they already know. Often a reading or listening comprehension lesson becomes the source of background knowledge for writing. Sometimes writing and sharing writing is a way of building background knowledge for reading. Sometimes students are required to do independent library research or reading as a means of building their own background knowledge for the content of their writing.

Background knowledge for writing usually includes content related to the topic but may also include how to write the form. Students cannot successfully write a letter, an essay, or a TV commercial if they do not know the way in which this particular form is written. Modeling of the form and/or examples may be required.

Building motivation for writing shares some traits with building motivation for reading. Students are motivated to write when teachers use analogies, share personal anecdotes, or present a puzzle, a problem, or an apparent contradiction. We also suggest you focus more of your attention on the thinking in which students engage and less on the writing product.

Helping Students Plan What They Will Write

Once you have built background knowledge for the task, presented the task, and helped students do any required research, are they ready to write? Not

This teacher is building background knowledge.

quite. Their writing will be better if they plan what they are going to say. This is the point at which students prepare outlines or webs, jot down words or reasons or names of people or places they may include, discuss with others what they want to say, develop a working title, or compose a final sentence.

You should help students plan before they begin writing. Have them engage in some class activity that will involve them in the planning. If research is involved, help them organize their findings into a writing plan before they begin their paper. One caution: Because writing is a discovery process, do not insist that students follow their plan too closely, even though there will obviously be some relationship between the plan and the paper.

WRITING LESSONS GUIDE STUDENTS THROUGH THE BEFORE, DURING, AND AFTER PHASES OF WRITING

Like a good comprehension lesson, a good writing lesson is fairly easy to teach once it has been well planned. The instructional cycle of introducing, guiding, and culminating is apparent in writing lessons just as in comprehension lessons. Before students write, build their motivation and background knowledge, make clear the writing task they will complete, and help them plan. After students write, lead them to share what they have written and/or give feedback on how well they have completed the task. If what they wrote is to be shared with someone outside the classroom, they should be helped to revise their first draft.

The following is an example of a lesson based on the following topic and task from our twins unit:

Think about: What personality traits seem to be most and least accounted for by heredity?

Task: First, describe your major personality characteristics. Then compare and contrast your major personality characteristics with those of family members or ancestors. Finally, explain which of your major personality characteristics you believe to be most attributable to heredity. You will share your description and conclusions with classmates.

Before Writing

Assume that this writing task is being done in the middle of a unit on twins. Students have already learned about how research with identical twins who were separated at birth is providing insight into the heredity versus environment issue. They know that scientists at the University of Minnesota Center for Twin and Adoption Research have found amazing similarities between identical twins who were separated at birth.

Since the writing task for this lesson requires students to think about which personality traits seem to be more or less accounted for by heredity, specific background knowledge building for this task requires that they know what personality traits are and which ones are believed to be most influenced by heredity. Present them with data from the Minnesota Twin Studies, which indicate that leadership, cheerfulness, optimism, imaginativeness, stress vulnerability, and risk avoidance are strongly influenced by heredity. Other traits, such as the ability to establish emotional intimacy and the propensity to be sensible and rational, appear to be less influenced by heredity.

Write these traits on the board in two columns under the headings: *Personality Traits Most Influenced by Heredity* and *Personality Traits Less Influenced by Heredity*. Next, have the class brainstorm other personality traits, such as these: hot-tempered, impatient, cooperative, laid-back, high-strung, nervous, and cautious.

Write these traits on the board also but not under either heading, then explain that some personality traits seem to be more influenced by heredity than others, but we do not know which. Students will write a self-description in which they compare their personality traits with those of their family members and try to conclude, based on their own family experiences, which traits they seem to share with other family members. Remind them that because they have shared the same environment with many of these family members, the traits they share are probably attributable to both heredity and environment; however, it will be interesting to think about from where their personality characteristics come.

Then suggest that the paper should be about two pages long and that they can first describe themselves and then compare themselves to other family members or that they can concentrate on one personality trait, then another, and so on as they go along. Finally, tell them that after writing, they will read their self-descriptions to others in a small group and the group will see if any conclusions can be drawn about shared personality traits based on that group's self-descriptions. Each group's information will then be compiled, and the class will decide if they can draw any generalizations from the separate experiences of all the class members. After this introduction and guidance, move to the writing phase of the lesson.

Writing

Now the students write. They are motivated because the topic, themselves, is of universal interest. They are also motivated because they know that small-group sharing will be what happens after they write. Background knowledge comes from what they have learned about the heredity versus environment issue and about personality traits combined with the firsthand knowledge they have of themselves and their families. The first two parts of their task, to describe their own personalities and compare them to those of other family members, are clear and easy to do for most students. Make sure that students have enough time to write but not so much time that they will not stay on the task.

Students record their thoughts in the during writing phase.

After Writing

Put the students in groups of three or four and give them about twenty minutes to share their writing. When all students in the group have had a chance to read what they wrote, the group lists all the different personality traits discussed in all the papers and tries to classify them as more or less attributable to heredity. The whole class then reconvenes to culminate the lesson. You record the small-group decisions on the board, and you lead the class to see if there is any agreement across the groups.

Listen/Look and Learn _____

Visit a classroom to observe a writing lesson or watch a videotaped writing lesson. Summarize what you saw during each phase of writing. Evaluate the lesson based on what you have learned so far in this chapter. What worked? What might the teacher have done differently?

THERE ARE MANY VARIATIONS WITHIN THE WRITING LESSON FRAMEWORK

We hope that you now have a good idea of how writing promotes thinking; how you plan a writing task; and what the before, during, and after phases of a writing lesson might look like. Of course, each writing lesson is unique because background knowledge and motivation demands before writing differ and ways to organize for sharing and feedback after writing are numerous. In this section, we suggest some of the possibilities for the three phases of a writing lesson.

Before-Writing Variations

The before-writing phase is sometimes called *prewriting.* In the South, some people call it "fixing to write." D. Kirby and T. Liner (1981) call it "getting it together." There are various ways that teachers help students get ready to write. We have already talked about the importance of providing adequate background knowledge and motivation. Background knowledge is often built through such activities as these:

brainstorming	charting
reading	viewing
role-playing	interviewing
webbing	outlining
listening	discussing
researching	drawing

Sometimes these activities for building background knowledge are done with the teacher directing the whole class, but small groups using the above activities allow for much more participation of each student.

Motivation to write is related to background knowledge because writing is hard enough when you know a lot and just about impossible when you do not know much. As you learn information, you not only have "something to say" but also become more interested in the topic. Students who are engaged in reading, researching, and brainstorming are sometimes overheard to make comments such as, "Hmmm, this is really interesting," and "Wow! I didn't know that!"

Motivation is also related to the writing task. Contrast these two writing tasks in terms of their motivation potential:

Task: Write three paragraphs summarizing what you have learned about personality characteristics and heredity from the twin research.

Task: First, describe your major personality characteristics. Then compare and contrast your major personality characteristics with family members or ancestors. Finally, explain which of your major personality characteristics you believe are most attributable to heredity. You will share your description and conclusions with classmates.

Both tasks require the writer to think about the relationship between personality and heredity, but which would you be more motivated to write? Most people would choose the second topic because it involves applying what is learned rather than just recalling. Often, we use writing to "find out what students know." Writers, on the other hand, usually write to "tell what they think." Writing tasks communicating that you are interested in students' thinking will result in more motivated writers.

Finally, motivation is related to what students believe will be done with what they write. Variations in what you can do with students' writing will be discussed in the after-writing variations section, but student motivation to write will be increased if you let them know beforehand what will be done with it. Consider how motivated students would be given the following after-writing possibilities:

- Your paper will be graded for both content and mechanics, and points will be deducted for each misspelled word.
- Your paper will be graded, and you will rewrite it and turn it in again.
- Tomorrow each person will stand and read his or her paper to the whole class.
- You will work with a classmate to revise your first draft before turning it in for grade.
- You will read your paper to a small group and then compile the best ideas from all group members.
- This writing is just for you. I will read it to see what you think and give you a point for good effort, but I will not grade it.

Once students have sufficient background knowledge and motivation to write, you must make sure that they understand the task. If students do not understand how to write a particular form, you will have to teach it. Students cannot write a lab report, TV commercial, or brochure if they do not know the form.

The most efficient way to teach students the form is usually demonstration. Using the overhead projector, a science teacher can write up the lab report while thinking aloud. As students watch and listen, the teacher talks about what is important to include where and does the actual writing. It is helpful if the teacher makes some mistakes and false starts. These can then be fixed either immediately or when the teacher demonstrates how to reread the whole thing before turning it in.

This teacher demonstration is called *modeling* and has been shown to be an effective and straightforward way of teaching. Teacher modeling is more effective than just presenting students with an already completed model because when students watch teachers write and listen as teachers think aloud, they learn how the product is produced.

Already done models are, however, another way of showing students forms. These already done models are quicker than teacher modeling and are best used when students need just a quick review or a reminder of a form with which they are familiar. Showing students a letter or brochure and pointing out the salient features that all letters or brochures share may suffice to enable them to produce the desired form. Whenever possible, these already done models should be student-produced, and you should provide several. Multiple models help students find their own writing style and make it clear that there is never just one right way to write. Students are more motivated if they see something similar done by last year's class. Some students are even challenged to excel as they respond to last year's models with a "We can do it better!" attitude.

All or any combination of activities can go on during the before-writing phase. The intent is to engage students actively in meaningful writing experiences that offer academic and social support. Prewriting sometimes takes two minutes, sometimes two days. This prewriting time does not take away from content learning, however, because most of it involves students thinking about the content they are learning.

During-Writing Variations

If prewriting is "getting it together," writing is "getting it down." What happens during the writing phase ought to be fairly obvious. Still, there are some questions teachers must think about and some decisions they must make. The first major decision is whether students will write alone or communally.

Writing is usually conceived of as an individual activity, but in the real world many excellent pieces of writing (this textbook, for example) are group-written. Students often achieve much and enjoy learning when it is arranged in some kind of cooperative learning format. This is especially true of writing. When you want students to write communally, you have available a variety of classroom grouping patterns.

Students might work in a group of three or four with one person recording the ideas of the entire group. This communal writing seems to work best if everyone contributes ideas and one student acts as scribe and produces a first draft and reads it to the group. All group members can suggest ways to make the writing better and clearer. Alternately, students might work with a partner and switch the roles of thinker and writer.

For a lengthy piece, students might divide up the sections (as we did with the first draft of this book). They would first plan which part each would write and set some guidelines about content to be covered and writing style to be used. Each person would then write his or her part to which everyone in the group would respond. The group would work together producing a draft to which they all had contributed. Another decision you must make is what students are going to write about and what they will use to do so. Do not assume that all writing must be done with a pencil or pen and a sheet of notebook paper. Variety here is important, too. Students are sometimes motivated to write when they are given an index card and asked to write a brief description. Somehow the small index card is less intimidating than a huge piece of notebook paper. Students can write with nonpermanent markers on transparencies that can then be projected and shared with the class. Students can write with markers on discarded roles of wallpaper, with chalk on sections of the chalkboard, or with colored pens on stationery.

In many classrooms today, students write using computers. Those who have regular access to computers for word processing are more willing to write, write more, revise more, and feel more confident in their writing. Writing on a computer frees you from many of the first-draft mechanical, spelling, and formatting concerns because you can fix your writing without copying it over. Many word processing programs have spelling and grammar checkers that actually make editing an entertaining process (relatively speaking). As computers become more available in classrooms, we envision a future in which writers and teachers will find it easier to focus on the ideas and the thinking and let the computer take care of some details.

Elementary-school teachers who want to use computers to help children write should get a copy of *From Scribblers to Scribes: Young Writers Use the Computer* (Katzer & Crnkovich, 1991). It is clear that these authors are real teachers who have worked out most of the nitty-gritty details for using computers with children. The book not only contains lots of easy-to-follow sample lesson plans and suggestions for scheduling and organizing, but also has a whole chapter on using computers with "challenged learners," which includes at-risk students as well as students with visual and physical impairments.

In addition to a normal word processing program that allows the students to write, edit, check spelling, and so forth, there are some writing programs that support writing in specific ways. A whole generation of desktop publishing software including *Publish It! The Children's Writing and Publishing Center, Kid Pix Slide Show,* and *PageMaker* allows students to create professional-looking newsletters, reports, and announcements. Other software such as *Cricket Graph* and *MECC Graph* can produce charts and graphs. A few programs allow students to scan pictures and place them in their writing. Tools such as *Book Workshop, Storybook Weaver Deluxe, Print Shop Deluxe,* and *Superprint* contain artwork files that allow students to select illustrations, logos, and other visuals to spice up stories, news reports, or other projects.

Finally, you must decide what you are going to do while the students write. Some teachers conduct "miniconferences" with students, stopping for a minute at each desk to say some encouraging words and perhaps make a suggestion. While this seems often to work very well, some students find that this teacher input during first-draft writing hinders their concentration and interrupts their flow of ideas; it also seems to tempt some students to become or remain overly dependent on the teacher.

Some teachers circulate and spell problem words. While students seem to appreciate this support, it is probably not a good idea in the long run. Classroom observation shows that when teachers circulate and respond to raised hands by spelling words, students write much less than they would if left to spell words as best they can. Some students will just wait until the teacher spells their word and spend more time waiting than writing.

Spelling, of course, is a concern for writers and teachers, but it seems best to underemphasize it during first-draft writing. Students should be encouraged to brainstorm lists of words, use a dictionary (if they know how and want to), and write words as best they can. Some teachers encourage students to leave blanks for letters about which they are uncertain or put an asterisk in the margin where they think their spelling is probably wrong.

The procedure just described sounds easier than it is. Because students are afraid of misspelling words, teachers feel a natural tendency to want to help. But, students will write longer drafts and use more sophisticated words if they are freed up from real or perceived "perfect spelling" demands on their first-draft writing. Students should learn that perfect spelling is not required for them to share their work with a small group and that when their writing is to be publicly displayed or graded, they will be given time and help to fix the spelling.

Fixing spelling, and many more substantive "fixings," is what some teachers do while students produce their first drafts. In some classrooms, teachers work with individuals or small groups who are revising an already completed first draft while the rest of the students are writing their first drafts. These writing conferences are usually conducted quietly in a corner of the room so that the writers are not disturbed.

Some days, while students are writing, you may want to write a piece yourself. Students rarely watch adults write, and thus they often see writing as something adults "make students do." By writing as the students write and then sharing what you have written, you provide an often-absent model of an adult in the act of writing. If you do write, show your mistakes, cross some things out, and mark some words for a later spelling check. Students need proof that writing is complex and that perfect first-draft writing is not possible; you have the perfect opportunity to present them with a firsthand example of nonperfection.

After-Writing Variations

During the culminating after-writing phase, possibilities range from doing nothing to sharing the writing by reading it aloud to revising, editing, and publishing it. Let's consider the doing-nothing option first. If your major purpose for having students write is to promote their thinking about content, you may have accomplished that goal with the thinking engaged in by the students before and during writing. In this case, you would simply check to see that the writing was indeed done and that a sufficient effort was made.

The problem with the doing-nothing response is that students do not get any feedback on how well they performed. This feedback can be provided by you, by the person who wrote the piece, or by classmates. You can assess how well each student has done and make some notes on the writing about what the student might have misunderstood or might need to clarify. You can have a short conference with each student and give feedback in this setting. Some teachers use a writing guide to structure the feedback they give about how well writers have completed the task. Since writing guides and scales play a large role in helping students become independent, reflective writers, their use will be discussed in the next section of this chapter.

When the writing is a culmination to a consequential project that will be displayed or publicly shared in some way, the after-writing phase becomes more extended and more complex. (If you have used Kirby and Liner's terms "getting it together" and "getting it down" to help students conceptualize the after- and during-writing phases, you might want to tell them that now they are engaged in "getting it right.") Here again, students could work with a partner, a small group, or the teacher to do the revising and editing process. This help needs to address both the message contained in the writing and the mechanics. The message should be dealt with first, then attention should focus on mechanics. B. Lyons (1981) suggests that PQP (praise, question, polish) is a nifty mnemonic to help students remember how to help one another.

Each writer should read his or her paper aloud to a willing listener or listeners (teacher, partner, or small group). When the writer finishes reading, the writer elicits praise by asking something like this: "What did you like about it?" The listener or listeners then provide some positive comments:

> "You really learned a lot by interviewing two sets of twins."
> "Your reasons for why twins might not become famous really made sense to me."
> "Your conversation with the other scientist sounded like a real phone conversation, and you had some good ideas for using twins in research."

Next, the writer should elicit questions by asking, "Do you have any questions?" or "Was there anything you didn't understand?" These are sample responses:

> "I didn't understand if the twins finally thought it was better or not to have been born twins."

A writer getting editing help from a friend.

"You lost me in the middle part."
"How would you find the twins for your research?"

Finally, the writer should ask the listeners to help polish the paper. The writer might ask, "Can you think of ways to make the writing more interesting, informative, or compelling?" Using the comments, the writer has some concrete things to do in order to revise the message of the piece.

The next step is editing for mechanics, with which students and teachers can help. The most important thing for everyone to remember is that "perfect writing just doesn't exist." Even textbooks such as this one (which has been revised and edited by all four authors and an editor from the publishing company) will still contain some errors when published. (Everyone, however, wants their writing to be perfect, so if you find errors in this textbook, please jot them down and send them to the publisher so that we can correct them on the next printing.) The goal of editing is to produce a finished product of which the writer can be proud. How perfect that needs to be depends on the age and ability of the students and the expectations of the audience who will read the final copy.

Once the writer has had help revising the message and editing for mechanics, the piece should be recopied, retyped, or reprinted on the computer. This finished product should then be displayed or published, since the reason for revising and editing first drafts is to make them more readable for a new reader.

The final after-writing variation has to do with grading. As we suggested early in this chapter, this is a very controversial issue, but it is one on which

A writer getting editing help from a teacher.

you must take a stand. Some teachers grade every piece of writing for both content and mechanics because they believe that students will not improve their writing if it is not graded. Other teachers do not assign any "quality grades" but give students points for good effort. Other teachers give points for good effort for all first-draft writing and grade only those pieces that students have had ample opportunity and help to revise and edit. For writing, the grading issue is complex, and you must make decisions based on what you believe will best motivate your students. Whatever you decide, make your grading policy clear to students so that they know for what they will be held accountable.

Try It Out

Plan a writing lesson. Make a sheet like the one in Figure 6.1 and fill in what you will do during each phase.

```
Before writing:
    What I want students to think about:
    The task:
        Topic:
        Form:
        Audience:
        Role:
    Background knowledge motivation:
    Individual planning activity:
During writing:
    Write alone or communally:
    Write on what and with what:
    What I will do while students write:
After writing:
    Feedback given by me, themselves, classmates: How?
    Revising and editing:
    Grading
```

Figure 6.1 Planning a Writing Minilesson

STUDENTS BECOME INDEPENDENT LEARNERS WHEN TEACHERS ENCOURAGE STUDENT RESPONSIBILITY, REFLECTION, AND SELF-ASSESSMENT

Just as with comprehension and vocabulary, our ultimate goal is to have students use writing as a tool to becoming an independent student and a lifelong learner. To produce independent lifelong writers, teachers need to encourage responsibility and reflection and help students develop self-assessment strategies

Once students understand that a writing task has four components—topic, form, audience, and role—they should be given some responsibility for deciding on appropriate writing tasks. Returning to our twins example, you may decide that students should think about the advantages and disadvantages of being a twin. This topic might be given to the students, then the students might decide what would be an appropriate form, audience, and role. Here your responsibility is not to specify but rather to lead students to consider the possibilities. Questions such as the following help students begin to make the kinds of decisions real writers make:

- In what different forms might your ideas about the advantages and disadvantages of being a twin best be described?
- For whom are you going to write this? Will you write it for adults, twins, or parents expecting twins? All kinds of people might read this, but a good writer often has a specific reader in mind; picturing this audience helps the writer to write clearly and use appropriate examples.
- What role will you take on as the writer? Will you be a twin? Will you

be two twins, each with a different opinion? Will you be an anonymous observer?

Questions such as these help students become independent in deciding how their writing can be most effective. Once students have a writing task in mind, they need to reflect upon their own background knowledge and what additional knowledge they might need. Again teachers help by making suggestions:

- What do you need to know?
- How could you find out more about twins?
- Do you know any twins?
- Would it help to interview some twins?
- Where could you find some more information about how twins feel about being twins?
- If you were a twin, how would you feel?

Finally, if students are to become independent writers, they must learn to reflect upon their own writing and assess their own writing products. Some teachers provide students with a reflection sheet they can use to evaluate any piece of writing they do. The reflection sheet might include questions such as these:

- What do I like best about what I wrote?
- What is not clear? How can I make it clearer?
- Do I need some more examples?
- Will the reader be interested in reading it?

Many teachers use scoring guides including checklists and rating scales to help student learn to assess their own writing. Scoring guides fit specific writing projects or tasks and may take the form of checklists in which questions are answered with a "yes" or a "no."

- Does the paper give a clear and accurate definition of anxiety?
- Does the paper give a clear and accurate definition of fear?
- Does the paper state at least two different and accurate commonalties between anxiety and fear?
- Does the paper make at least two different and accurate distinctions between anxiety and fear?

Rating scales cover degrees of proficiency. (For an example of a rating scale, see Figure 8.6 in Chapter 8, "Student Inquiry").

Writing guides are usually explained to students before they write. After writing, students work with a peer to evaluate their paper according to the criteria set up in the guide. Some teachers send the writing guides home and ask parents to help the writer read the piece to determine if the criteria are being met. The essential factor with writing guides is that the students are taught how to use them to improve their own writing.

While reflection sheet and writing guides do help students learn what is expected in their writing and how to assess their own writing, there is a danger that students will become too dependent on these devices and "write to the formula." The most successful teachers use these devices but gradually help students to determine what the criteria on these assessment devices should be and eventually help students reflect upon and assess their own writing based on their own criteria of what they are trying to accomplish.

Do It Together

In this chapter, we give you suggestions for what students might write; for how you can guide, support, and encourage that writing; and for how you can help them become more independent in their writing and learning. As you think about how you can use writing to increase thinking and learning in your classroom, we would like you to consider our content writing guidelines:

1. Because writing is difficult, most students will write more willingly and learn more if they write several short pieces than if they write one long piece.
2. Because it is impossible to write about what you do not know much about, writing should be on topics about which students are learning.
3. Because writers often find they do not know enough, they should be encouraged to read and use other sources of information as they write.
4. Because everyone likes variety, students should write in many different forms, for different purposes, and for different audiences.
5. Because much thinking occurs during the prewriting and writing phases, much of what students write should not have to be revised and turned into a final draft.
6. Because students learn more content and become better writers when they share what they have written, small-group sharing and feedback should be the most common after-writing activity.
7. Because all published writing requires editing, students should get help from other students and/or the teacher when they need to produce a displayable final draft.
8. Because red marks discourage writers, no red marks should be put on papers.
9. Because the purpose of writing in a content class is to have students think about what they are learning, most writing should count for the grade but not be graded. Everyone who makes a good effort should be given points for engaging in the thinking required to produce the writing.
10. Because writing and sharing writing involve risk, teachers should show themselves willing to take those risks by occasionally writing and sharing what they have written.

These ten guiding principles for content area writing are controversial. Not everyone will agree with them. Many people believe, for example, that every piece of writing should be graded for both mechanics and content because students may get "sloppy" and never learn to write well. The flip side of this argument is that student resistance to writing is directly related to their awareness that they do not write perfectly and their certainty that they cannot "make the grade." Discuss each of these ten guiding principles with two or three colleagues. Decide which ones you can accept and which you cannot. After the group discussion, work by yourself to write guidelines that you can follow.

Specific Content Area Applications

● WRITING IN THE ENGLISH/LANGUAGE ARTS CLASSROOM

Countless opportunities exist for writing in English/language arts classes. Indeed, if you review the English/language arts classroom suggestions for comprehension and vocabulary in the preceding chapters, you will see writing activities already incorporated (e.g., maintain a response journal, compose a resolution to the central question, record passage sections containing words worth remembering). The following suggestions go beyond the ones already presented, building on ideas introduced in this chapter specifically related to quick writes, journals, and lesson tasks. The following would be appropriate for students engaged with the novel *Shabanu, Child of the Wind.*

Quick Writes

Quick writes help when calling up prior knowledge on a topic. Students might produce quick writes in response to the following:

> What three things should nomadic people do when desert sandstorms occur?
> What wedding customs have you seen or heard of?

To have students predict what comes next in Shabanu, you might offer these prompts:

> What will happen to Shabanu's betrothal to Rahim-Sahib?
> What will happen in the next chapter?

Synthesizing ideas about the novel can be elicited by having students write in response to these items:

> What Islamic customs differ from the ones you are used to?
> List the similarities and differences you can think of so far between Shabanu and her sister, Phulan.

To help students reflect on their processing of *Shabanu,* they might write briefly on the following:

> What part of *Shabanu* has been confusing?
> Why is *Shabanu* maintaining—or losing—my interest?

Journals

Journals contain writings that take numerous forms. Indeed, students might maintain reactions to the quick write prompts listed above in their journals. As noted in Chapter 3, students might have available a menu of generic prompts from which to react. Here are some generic prompts we have found to be productive that would fit *Shabanu*:

What have I learned from reading this passage?
What images did I experience while reading this passage?
What do I not really understand so far?
What did this passage remind me of?
What would I like to see changed?
How did I feel when reading this passage?

Designing Tasks for Lessons

Thinking of RAFTs (roles, audiences, forms, and topics) when designing tasks for writing lessons helps produce meaningful and connected learning opportunities. Students tend to find writing tasks explicitly based on RAFTs more engaging than traditional ones. If the topic you are addressing is the wedding of Shabanu's sister, Phulan, here are some ways RAFTing could be done to transform conventional writing tasks.

Modifying Forms

Students benefit from modifying forms of expression while maintaining essentially the same role and audience. We call this practice *translation writing*. After students read the passage describing Phulan's wedding, they might rewrite the description of it in a form selected from the following:

play	song lyrics
interview script	newspaper article
illustrated strip	diary
poem	contract
personal letter	

Modifying Roles

Considering different roles that writers might assume also contributes to the design of writing tasks. For instance, if students decide to produce a poem or a set of diary entries centering on Phulan's wedding, they might consider the multiple perspectives that are available. They might write a wedding poem while acting in the role of Phulan, Shabanu, the girls' mother, or the girls' father. They might write poems from the points of view of all four story characters.

Modifying Audiences

When thinking about possible wedding poem audiences, students again have several options. They might write for those in attendance, for Phulan's husband, for other members of the family, for younger children, or for readers of a literary journal. Associating different roles and forms with different audiences as we have done here produces writing task possibilities with space for most students' interests and abilities.

Supporting Writing

The tasks listed above provide good momentum for students writing about *Shabanu* in English classrooms, but there certainly is more to writing instruction than this. Students require support, or scaffolding, to accomplish goals along with opportunities to reflect on and assess their writing performance. This section concentrated on tasks for writing because teaching and learning are greatly facilitated when there are clearly stated engaging tasks guiding the attention and action of teachers and students.

● WRITING IN SECOND-LANGUAGE CLASSROOMS

Writing in second-language classrooms is much the same as writing in first-language classrooms. Students plan what they will write, produce written drafts, and sometimes revise what they have written. The main difference between writing in one's first language and in one's second language involves the support that is required. Effective teachers support second-language writing in several ways.

Connections

Writers who easily sustain a line of thinking are able to concentrate on overcoming the word choice, grammar, spelling, and other such challenges a second language presents. One way effective teachers support second-language writers and help sustain their lines of thought is by offering them access to life experience topics that have personal connections.

Topics from life experiences enable writers to focus on expressing themselves. Life experience topics that promote ready connections include such student favorites as:

foods	books/comics/magazines
clothes	weekend activities
sports	adventures
games	pets/animals
hobbies/collections	television shows/movies
friends	songs/musical groups

Teachers often suggest topics such as one's preferences for food, entertainment, and clothing, and students go into depth on particular ones. Producing a personal crest that heralds one's identity and explaining the crest is another common practice that capitalizes on personal connections. Of course, when describing one's personal background or family history, students should realize they are free to decide how much they will reveal about themselves.

Oral history projects with family or community members are good ways for second-language learners to capitalize on life experiences and personal connections. When students interview parents and grandparents, aunts and uncles, and neighbors and business people in their communities, they are connecting the stories of others' lives with their lives. They can see how past actions might have affected their lives and how conflicts and circumstances from the past might be similar to those of the present. Writing comes into play during oral history projects when students research the times in which people lived, prepare questions, record interviewees' responses, and write up reports.

Finally, writers who address topics associated with their cultures also have ready access to personal connections. Practically everyone has personal experiences and understandings of distinctive holidays, foods, ways of dress, and pastimes. Addressing such topics allows writers to concentrate on expressing themselves, and it provides opportunities to honor and celebrate differences in culturally diverse classrooms. Teachers who share their interest and respect for others' cultures model ways that students can do the same.

Collaboration

Promoting collaboration is another good way to support students who are writing in a second language. Collaborative writing projects call for students to work together in whole-class, small-group, or paired situations. Students with high proficiency and those with low proficiency in the second language might collaborate sometimes, and those with similar levels of proficiency might collaborate other times.

One key to the success of collaborative writing is the instruction students receive about how to act. Teachers typically demonstrate positive face-to-face interactions (e.g., praising others, encouraging participation, finding common ground) so students will do the same when they interact. Teachers often specify particular interactions, then they and the students reflect on the behaviors during and after collaborative work.

Collaboration during the planning, before-writing phase occurs many ways. If students are writing in their second language about particular life experiences, they first might jointly brainstorm possibilities. They could list key words that are related to what each plans to write. They could help each other decide on terms that would most appropriately articulate what they want to say. They could talk about the order in which they would use the words, stating orally what they plan to express in print. They could figuratively step back and talk with each other about what they want to write.

When students are getting their writing down, they still can benefit from collaboration. They might request a partner's help with a particular term or a grammatical form (How do you say, "May I help you?"), or they might consult about the spelling of a word. Writers who cannot produce a particular word or phrase in their second language might insert a few words from their first language to get past the difficulty, later getting help to replace the native language terms.

Collaboration also is appropriate in the after-writing phase. Students can read their writing orally to a single partner or to a small group, and all concerned individuals can listen for points to praise and to question. Rather than listening, partners and small-group members can read what one has written, looking for points to praise and to question. Teachers typically model before a whole class the dynamics of small-group revisions. They demonstrate how to attend to specific features of writing as well as how to comment appropriately when they spot difficulties.

● WRITING IN THE MATHEMATICS CLASSROOM

For many of us, writing was not a part of how we learned in a mathematics class. Recently, however, all content areas have become concerned with students' ability to think and communicate and writing is one of the major ways of promoting both of these. Here are some specific ways that math teachers use quick writes, journals, and word problems to help students think and communicate mathematically.

Quick Writes

As previewing activities, math teachers ask students to

> List as many kinds of different triangles as you can in 30 seconds.
> Draw and label three shapes that have different names.
> List ways you use decimals in real-life activities.

To synthesize what was learned at the end of a class, ask students to

> Define in your own words what parallel lines are.
> Write in words what this formula means.
> Use the symbols =, <, and > to write three true sentences.

To help students self-assess understanding, attitudes, and so on, ask

> What did you not understand about today's lesson?
> List one or more terms you cannot clearly define.
> I have the feeling many of you are not "with me" on this topic. Write what you are feeling about what we are doing and if there is anything I could change to help you feel more involved and successful.

Journals

Journals call for more extended entries than quick writes and are most successful if used on a daily basis. Both high-structure and low-structure journals can be used in math class. Here are some examples of high-structure journal prompts math teachers use:

> Draw and label pictures that will help you remember each of the shapes we have studied so far.
>
> Write a paragraph using as many of the following words as possible. (List math terms you are studying.)
>
> Analyze the mistakes made on your homework (or in-class work). What have you learned that will help you avoid making these same mistakes again?
>
> Write an explanation of why we need to study _____, which would make sense to a younger friend who hasn't yet taken this course.

Word Problems

Solving word problems is an essential math skill but one which presents problems for many students. To understand word problems from the inside out, students are often helped by trying to write some. Most teachers find that since this is a difficult task, it is one which students are more successful at and willing to tackle if they write cooperatively as a team of two or three members. Team members are asked to write word problems similar to the ones they have been trying to solve, and then two teams are paired to try to solve each other's problems. The solving team points out any missing information or unclear language and the writing team rewrites. Finally, the combined team picks its "best" and most challenging problem for the whole class to solve.

Aggie Azzolini (1990) presents some excellent guidelines for changing word problems into harder and easier ones. Her suggestions (adapted) for making problems easier include

> Using fewer words
> Using shorter sentences
> Using smaller numbers
> Using simpler figures
> Having fewer steps or operations
> Putting the information in the order it will be used
> Including a chart or diagram
> Suggesting the use of manipulatives

Should you want your students to try to make a word problem harder, she suggests you do the opposite of the relevant suggestions.

● WRITING IN THE SCIENCE CLASSROOM

Many students (and teachers!) don't see many connections between science and writing. But scientists are inveterate writers. They write down hunches and sketch possible arrangements of whatever they are studying. They observe carefully and write down their observations. They conduct experiments and write down what they think will happen as well as what they actually observe. Writing and sketching are important tools real scientists use to help themselves think. Here are some specific ways that science teachers use quick writes, journals, and lab reports to help students think and communicate.

Quick Writes

As previewing activities, science teachers ask students to:

> List as many different animals with backbones as you can in 30 seconds.
> Draw and label the parts of a tomato plant.
> List ways that chemistry is important to us in real-life activities.

To synthesize what was learned at the end of a class, ask students to:

> Define in you own words what an ecosystem is.
> Your book says, _____. Write what that really means in English.
> Use the words _____ and _____ and _____ to write a true sentence.

To help students self-assess understanding, attitudes, and so forth, ask:

> What did you not understand about today's lesson?
> List one or more terms you cannot clearly define.
> I have the feeling many of you are not "with me" on this topic. Write what you are feeling about what we are doing and if there is anything I could change to help you feel more involved and successful.

Journals

Journals call for more extended entries than quick writes and are most successful if used on a daily basis. Both high-structure and low-structure journals can be used in a science class. Here are some examples of high-structure journal prompts science teachers use:

> Draw and label the parts of the digestive system.
> Arrange the following words into a web that shows their relationships.
> Analyze how you did with today's experiment? Were you able to follow the directions? Did the experiment turn out as you had predicted?
> Explain to a younger person (brother, sister, cousin) why it is important for everyone to understand about toxins in our environment.

In addition to content-oriented journal entries such as these, science teachers may want to use "personal history" journal entries early in the year to help students come to terms with their science "attitudes." Many students have not had good experiences with science and in spite of all the recent efforts to have science classes be "hands-on" active learning environments, many students associate science with hard-to-read textbooks and big unpronounceable words to memorize. If students see themselves as inadequate and uninterested learners in science, their attitudes will affect their motivation, learning, and thinking. Science teachers can engage students and begin to alter self-concepts in a number of different ways including having students reflect on their own personal science histories.

To use journal entries in this way, tell students that we all have personal experiences in all areas of our lives that affect how we feel about things. Use a few examples to which your students can relate, perhaps telling about some of you life experiences which helped you to feel positively about something and negatively about something else.

> "My mom made me take piano lessons for four years and I hated it. I generalized that hate to all music and only in recent years have I learned to enjoy jazz and some other types of music."

> "When I was your age, I had a friend who was a great baseball player. All he ever talked about was baseball. Eventually, I got interested in baseball too, even though I didn't play well. I still love baseball."

Let students share some of their earlier experiences with real life—not science—topics and then tell them that since your job is to teach them science and their past experiences with science will affect their attitudes, you would like to know about those experiences. Explain that each day for a week or two you will ask them to write about specific science experiences. After students write, you can let them tell about what they have written, either to the whole class or in small groups or you can collect their journals and read them so that you get to know their science stories. Be sure that if you read them, the students know that the entries won't be graded (although doing them may add some points to their grade) and that you want to know both the high points and the low points of their experiences. Here are some possible prompts that could be used across several days of journal writing time:

> Of all the school subjects you study, is science one of your best or one of your worst? Rank it on a 1 (worst) to 10 (best) scale and explain why you chose the number you did.
>
> Regardless of how much you like science, some of your science teachers/classes were probably better or worse than others. Write what you remember about your worst science teacher/class. What grade were you in? What made it so awful? How did things work in the class? Change the name of the teacher of that class to X to protect the guilty.
>
> Today reflect on your best science teacher/class. What grade were you in? What made it good? How did things work in this class? No need to change the name of this teacher!
>
> How do you feel about science experiments? Can you usually do them? Do you like to do them? Do they help you learn?
>
> Have you ever done projects for the science fair? What did you do? Did anyone help you? Did you like doing this? (If you never did, talk about why not and tell about your feelings about science fairs in general.)

Do you do anything out of school that is science related? Do you like sci-fi TV shows, movies, books? Do you like to read *National Geographic* and similar magazines? Do you like any science/nature shows on TV? Have you ever belonged to the scouts, 4H, or another group through which you had any wilderness experiences? Do you have a microscope, telescope, or other science paraphernalia?

While recognizing, expressing, and taking ownership of attitudes will not alter these attitudes, it is a first step. Students who don't like science will enjoy telling you why, "ranting and raving" about their awful experiences. They will get it out of their system and be amazed that you, a science teacher, know and accept the fact that some of them don't like science. If you let them share their responses, they will discover that others have had different experiences with science and begin to realize that with different experiences, they might have developed different attitudes. Science teachers are always concerned with helping students recognize their misconceptions. If your students have misconceptions about science, spending some of your journal time exploring personal science history issues will help you and them begin to change those misconceptions.

Lab Reports

Many students feel about lab reports the same way they feel about book reports. They don't mind the lab (book) and even enjoy it sometimes, but they detest writing it up. Successful science teachers find ways to make the writing of the lab report less tedious and more successful. They usually begin by modeling at the overhead or chalkboard the writing of the report. This is not the same as giving the students an already completed model because as the teacher writes, he or she "thinks aloud," allowing students to see how the teacher decided what to include and how to word it. Most teachers do the modeling and thinking aloud themselves several times and then continue modeling but asking students to give them ideas of what to write next and how to write it. Once students are participating in the writing being modeled by the teacher, many teachers move to a small-group writing format. One person in each group is appointed as writer, but all group members share in deciding what to write and how to write it.

Once students have had lots of experience watching and helping the teacher model the writing of a lab report and participating in group writing, many teachers like to have the class create a frame for a lab report which can then be displayed in the room (and/or duplicated for their science notebooks) and will serve as a reminder of the form and essential elements of a lab report. This frame is most useful if it is constructed by the class after teacher modeling and group work. A generic frame is given here but should only be considered as an example and not as *the* frame for lab reports. Frames more specific to the particular area of science being studied, the age, and scientific sophistication of your students will support student writing of lab reports.

Laboratory Report

Problem
> Why does . . . ?

Hypotheses
> I think that . . .

Materials
> (List materials used.)

Procedures
> (List in order what you did)

Data
> (List what you observed, including numbers, pictures, etc. as appropriate)

Conclusions
> My problem was . . .
> The results showed that . . .
> These results supported (did not support) my hypotheses because . . .

● WRITING IN THE SOCIAL STUDIES CLASSROOM

Writing in social studies is more common than in many other content areas. Because you are studying about people and events, there are endless opportunities for students to "think things through" while writing.

Quick Writes

As previewing activities, social studies teachers ask students to:

> List as many names of people important in the Civil War as you can in 30 seconds.
> Write down one question you have about our federal budget.
> List three major inventions of the twentieth century.

To synthesize what was learned at the end of a class, ask students to:

> Define in your own words what a democracy is.
> List two things that changed after the *Brown vs. The Board of Education* ruling.
> Use the words *interest rates, inflation,* and *stock market* to write a true sentence.

To help students self-assess understanding, attitudes, and so forth, ask:

What did you not understand about today's lesson?

List one or more terms you cannot clearly define.

I have the feeling many of you are not "with me" on this topic. Write what you are feeling about what we are doing and if there is anything I could change to help you feel more involved and successful.

Journals

Journals call for more extended entries than quick writes and are most successful if used on a daily basis. Both high-structure and low-structure journals can be used in a social studies class. Here are some examples of high-structure journal prompts social studies teachers use:

We have been studying the controversial topic of our welfare system and the law which limits welfare benefits. Are you for or against this law? On balance, is it going to make us a better or worse society? If you could have voted on this issue, how would you have voted? List three reasons to justify your vote.

Arrange the following words into a web that shows their relationships.

Explain to a younger person (brother, sister, cousin) why it is important for everyone to understand the concept of global interdependence.

In addition to content-oriented journal entries such as these, many social studies teachers use "historical figure diaries" to help students relate to events often far away in time and space. While studying about the Vietnam War, students may become major players such as John F. Kennedy, Lyndon Johnson, Henry Kissinger, Ho Chi Mihn, Ngo Dinh Diem, or "little people" such as a marine sent to Vietnam, a college student with a draft deferment, a soldier in the Viet Cong, a civilian living in North Vietnam, and the child of an American soldier left in Vietnam. Teachers may let students choose their character or have them pick a character "from a hat" so that all points of view are represented. As the unit continues, characters write each day "diary style" what they are doing and thinking. If two people have the same character, they can write separately or can collaborate on a joint entry. To make this more effective, have the "little people" characters name themselves and decide on their personal characteristics (age, occupation, family status, etc.) before beginning. From time to time, let characters share their diary entries with the whole class or in small groups.

Getting students involved in events that occurred long before their birth is not easy. Having students assume the role of a person in a historical setting promotes their use of the imaging and evaluating thinking processes. Keeping a diary is a real-world writing task. Anne Frank kept one, as did Richard Nixon! Incorporating historical figure diaries into your social studies routine increases student motivation and engagement and gives students a real purpose for writing.

Oral History Projects

Oral history projects use interviews with real people who have experienced an event as the primary source of information. They can be used anytime the event or phenomenon being studied is one which friends and relatives of the students have experienced. Many teachers use oral history projects when studying about immigration or societal changes. Often the oral history project begins in the middle of the unit when the students have enough background information to construct good questions. The first time this project is used, it is probably best to lead the class as a whole to construct the questions. As this format is incorporated into other units, students can work in small groups to construct questions and finally construct their own questions. Students may conduct the interviews individually or with a partner. After conducting the interview, students can report to the whole class about what they learned. In many classes, students write a book in which each interview is summarized and printed, perhaps with a picture of the person being interviewed.

Oral history projects make history come alive for students. Learning about the flood of immigrants that arrived after a particular war and the personal and societal upheaval that accompanies immigration takes on a whole different dimension when someone you actually know was one of these immigrants. Students develop new respect (and sometimes even awe!) for neighbors and relatives often previously ignored. Teachers of two-language children and newcomers find that incorporating oral history projects into their social studies classrooms is a way of involving and validating the experience of students struggling with English and with a new culture. Of course personal involvement increases motivation and engagement, and writing becomes a tool for thinking as students write down the questions, write down the answers, and construct the written summary of what was learned. The name "oral history" refers to how the student gathers the information but, for the student, oral history projects involve a lot of purposeful, focused writing.

Writing Your School's History

Beverly Fazio (1992) describes a wonderful social studies writing project in which U.S. history students began their study of history with their own school. Using old school yearbooks, newspapers, minutes of school board meetings, and interviews with community members, students studied the history of the 84-year-old school. One of the respondents to their advertisement in the local newspaper soliciting information from bygone days was a 1918 graduate who told the students that their high school in her day had three grades and three teachers—one for each grade. The building which housed the high school had neither electricity nor plumbing. Men who had left school in the 1940s to fight the war came forward to decry the fact that they couldn't graduate and to explain the lack of a football team during the war years—not enough male students left in school! (The article describing this school history project gives many details about how to proceed, along with other fascinating tidbits.)

Doing the school's history involved oral history along with lots of other research using primary sources. Writing was involved in all stages of this project, which culminated in the printing of a real book, eagerly bought by students past and present. History and how historians "do" history was directly experienced by these lucky students of American history.

● WRITING IN THE "ACTIVITY" CLASSROOM

Many students (and teachers!) don't see connections between art, music, physical education, vocational subjects, and writing. But all teachers are constantly seeking ways to get students to think more deeply about their subjects, and writing is one way to focus and organize thinking. In addition, almost all jobs require an astonishing amount and variety of writing. Here are some specific ways that teachers of activity courses use writing to help students learn and think.

Quick Writes

As previewing activities, ask students to:

> List as many different materials sculptors might use as you can in 30 seconds.
> Sketch what you think a miter box looks like.
> List reasons that knowing first aid is important to us in real-life activities.

To synthesize what was learned at the end of a class, ask students to:

> Define in your own words what syncopated rhythm is.
> Draw a stick figure to show what the backhand position looks like.
> Use the words _____ and _____ and _____ to write a true sentence.

To help students self-assess understanding, attitudes, and so forth, ask:

> What did you not understand about today's lesson?
> List one or more terms you cannot clearly define.
> I have the feeling many of you are not "with me" on this topic. Write what you are feeling about what we are doing and if there is anything I could change to help you feel more involved and successful.

Journals

Journals call for more extended entries than quick writes and are most successful if used on a daily basis. Both high-structure and low-structure journals can be used in activity classes. Here are some examples of high-structure journal prompts:

> Draw and label a _____.
> Arrange the following words into a web that shows their relationships.
> Analyze how you did with today's activity? Were you able to follow the directions? What problems did you experience? What did you do to help yourself understand?
> Explain to a younger person (brother, sister, cousin) why it is important for everyone to know how to do CPR.

Interviewing Real People About On-the-Job Writing

Many students have the idea that once they are done with school, they won't need to write anymore! In today's advanced society, this is hardly ever true. Mechanics, technicians, computer specialists, and store managers expend a huge amount of time and effort writing everything from letters to orders to e-mail messages to reports. Every student needs to see writing as an important part of any job to which they aspire. Of course, preaching this to them is rarely effective. Some teachers of activity-oriented courses send the students out to find out for themselves. Students select some people in a variety of nonacademic jobs and then interview them to find out specifically what they write. When all the information obtained from these interviews is compiled and shared with the whole class, students may develop some real-world motivation for learning to write clearly and well.

Writing Directions in Plain English

Everyone knows that directions are hard to read. Students who experience frustration reading directions feel better if teachers demonstrate a "It's not your fault, they should write them more clearly" attitude. Students are more willing to work through a set of directions and try to make sense of them when they realize that not being able to follow the directions easily says more about the writer of the directions than it does about their own reading ability. One effective writing activity to use when you and your students are faced with complex written directions is to rewrite them "in plain English." When you come across poorly written directions, have the students work together in small groups to first try to follow the directions. Once they have assembled the object or carried out the procedure, have them rewrite the directions so that they are easier to follow. Here are some guidelines for making directions easier to follow:

1. Use shorter sentences.
2. Use "plain" English words instead of technical terms.
3. Include only one thing in each step.

4. Make sure the steps are in logical order.
5. Include a drawing for each step when possible.
6. Include a list of materials/parts with each one clearly labeled.
7. List important "don'ts" at the beginning. (Sometimes, knowing what not to do is more important than knowing what to do!)

Once students have rewritten a particularly difficult set of directions, have another group of students carry out the directions to see how they work. You may want to compile their simplified directions in a resource book for other classes to use. Tell them that they are providing a service to all the students who will follow them in this course and who will not have to wrestle with that particular set of poorly written directions. Students who rewrite directions to make them simpler and clearer become better at reading all kinds of directions—including the poorly written ones they will encounter in the future!

Looking Back

Writing is hard and not something many view as a tool for learning and thinking. Consequently, not much writing occurs in content area classrooms, and the writing that does occur is usually viewed as a way of assessing what was learned rather than as a learning tool. In this chapter, you learned why and how writing should play a role in your classroom and five key ideas about writing in content area classrooms: (1) Informal writing experiences promote student thinking and learning; (2) planning a writing lesson includes deciding on clear writing tasks, background knowledge, and motivation; (3) writing lessons guide students through the before, during, and after phases of writing; (4) there are many variations within the writing lesson framework; and (5) students become independent learners when teachers encourage student responsibility, reflection, and self-assessment.

Add to Your Journal

Reflect upon the five key ideas presented in this chapter and decide what you think. Do you see ways that writing can help your students think and learn in your content area? Does the procedure for planning a writing lesson make sense to you? Do you agree that some writing tasks are more motivating than others and that helping students think about role and audience as well as topic and form can help them focus their writing? Can you imagine yourself guiding students through the before, during, and after phases of writing lessons? Can you apply the variations to writing tasks you think would work best for you? Finally, what do you think about encouraging student responsibility, reflection, and self-assessment as ways to make students more independent learners? Describe your reactions to the five key ideas and generalize about the role of writing in your classroom. What and how large a role do you see for writing in your classroom?

REFERENCES

AZZOLINO, A. (1990). Writing as a tool for teaching mathematics: The silent revolution. In Cooney, T. J., & Hirsh, E. R. (Eds.), *Teaching and Learning Mathematics in the 1990s*. Reston, VA: National Council of Teachers of Mathematics.

FAZIO, B. (1992). Students as historians—writing their school's history. *The Social Studies, 83,* 64–67.

HOLDEN, C. (1990). Double features. In *The 1990 World Book Yearbook* (pp. 140–153). Chicago: World Book.

HOLSTON, V., & SANTA, C. (1985). A method of writing across the curriculum that works. *Journal of Reading, 28,* 456–457.

KATZER, S., & CRNKOVICH, C. A. (1991). *From scribblers to scribes: Young writers use the computer.* Englewood, CO: Teacher Ideas Press.

KIRBY, D., & LINER, T. (1981). *Inside out: Developmental strategies for teaching writing.* Portsmouth, NH: Boynton/Cook.

LYONS, B. (1981). The PQP method of responding to writing. *English Journal, 70,* 42–43.

Computer Software

BOOK WORKSHOP. SUNBURST COMMUNICATIONS, 101 CASTLETON ST., PLEASANTVILLE, NY 10570.

CRICKET GRAPH. COMPUTER ASSOCIATES INTERNATIONAL, 1 COMPUTER ASSOCIATES PLAZA, ISLANDIA, NY 11788.

KID PIX SLIDE SHOW. BORDERBOUND, 500 REDWOOD BLVD., NOVATO, CA 94948.

MECC GRAPH. MINNESOTA EDUCATIONAL COMPUTING CORP., 6160 SUMMIT DR. N, MINNEAPOLIS, MN 55430.

PAGEMAKER. ADOBESYSTEMS, 1585 CHARLESTON RD., P.O. BOX 7900, MOUNTAIN VIEW, CA 94039.

PRINT SHOP DELUXE. BORDERBOUND, 500 REDWOOD BLVD., NOVATO, CA 94948.

PUBLISH IT! MICROSOFT, ONE MICROSOFT WAY, REDMOND, WA 98052.

STORYBOOK WEAVER DELUXE. MINNESOTA EDUCATIONAL COMPUTING CORP. 6160 SUMMIT DR. N., MINNEAPOLIS, MN 55430.

SUPERPRINT. SCHOLASTIC, 730 BROADWAY, NEW YORK, NY 10003.

THE CHILDREN'S WRITING AND PUBLISHING CENTER. THE LEARNING COMPANY, 6493 KAISER DR., FREMONT, CA 94555.

ADDITIONAL READINGS

These books suggest many practical ways to integrate writing into all areas of the curriculum:

ATWELL, N. (Ed.). (1989). *Coming to know: Writing to learn in the intermediate grades.* Portsmouth, NH: Heinemann.

HELLER, M. F. (1991). *Reading-writing connections: From theory to practice.* White Plains, NY: Longman.

KIRBY, D., LINER, T., & VINZ, R. (1981). *Inside out: Developmental strategies for teaching writing.* Portsmouth, NH: Boynton/Cook.

These books address the issues of writing to learn at middle- and secondary-school levels:

ATWELL, N. (1987). *In the middle: Writing, reading and learning with adolescents.* Portsmouth, NH: Boynton/Cook.

FASSLER WALVOORD, B. E. (1982). *Helping students write well: A guide for teachers of all disciplines.* New York: Modern Language Association.

FULWILER, T. (1987). *Teaching with writing.* Upper Montclair, NJ: Boynton/Cook.

GERE, A. R. (Ed.). (1985). *Roots in the sawdust: Writing to learn across the disciplines.* Urbana, IL: National Council of Teachers of English.

OLSEN, C. B. (1987). *Practical ideas for teaching writing as a process.* Sacramento, CA: California State Department of Education.

WILLS, H. (1993). *Writing is learning: strategies for math, science, social studies and language arts.* Bloomington, IN: Edinfo Press.

ZINSSER, W. *Writing to learn.* New York: Harper & Row, 1988.

These books contain practical descriptions of how to use journals in different content areas:

BROMLEY, K. (1993). *Journaling: Engagement in reading, writing, and thinking.* New York: Scholastic Professional Books.

FULWILER, T. (Ed.). (1987). *The journal book.* Portsmouth, NH: Boynton/Cook.

This book includes case studies of seven high-school English, science, social studies, and home economics teachers as they implemented various writing activities in their classrooms; the different writing activities used and the analysis of how they promoted thinking are insightful and thought provoking:

LANGER, J. A., & APPLEBEE, A. N. (1987). *How writing shapes thinking: A study of teaching and learning.* Urbana, IL: National Council of Teachers of English.

This book summarizes the research on writing, particularly the use of inquiry and writing:

HILLOCKS, GEORGE, JR. (1986). *Research on written composition: New directions for teaching.* Urbana, IL: National Council of Teachers of English and ERIC/RCS.

This summarizes the research on the relationships between reading and writing and the benefits to students of connecting the two:

TIERNEY, R. J., & SHANAHAN, T. (1991). Research on the reading-writing relationship: Interactions, transactions, and outcomes. In R. Barr, M. D. Kamil, P. B. Mosenthal, & P. D. Pearson, (Eds.), *Handbook of reading research* (Vol. II, pp. 246–280). White Plains, NY: Longman.

chapter 7

Studying

Looking Ahead

Studying is independently understanding and remembering subject matter. Students in K–12 schooling seldom develop effective and efficient study abilities from merely being required to study. Explicit instruction in how to study is necessary if most students are going to acquire those abilities. Study strategy instruction involves, among other things, teaching students how to take notes, question themselves, and organize what they read. There is no one right way to study or to teach studying. A team approach, in which each teacher helps students learn how to study that subject that year in the way that teacher has found helpful, would be the most effective way for schools to teach studying.

Units of instruction based on integration and inquiry, as discussed in Chapters 2 and 8, go far in developing students' independence as learners. Students who examine a topic as an integrated whole or direct their own inquiries have an opportunity to discover how to learn. However, setting the stage for discovery is only part of a good instructional program for developing independent learners. Because too many students will not learn how to study efficiently and effectively through discovery alone, teachers should also provide regular explicit instruction in studying.

The term *studying* denotes any conscious effort to learn independently. Students study when they deliberate over subject matter, working to understand and, especially, to remember it (Devine, 1991). Studying is something students do for themselves, orchestrating and monitoring their own learning.

Because reading and writing are major tools for learning, almost all studying involves reading or writing or both.

As literacy and learning requirements increase in our complex society and our schools, the need for students to learn how to study increases. Learning how to acquire new ideas and abilities has become as important as learning subject matter concepts. As we noted in Chapter 1, individuals today need to update themselves continually just to stay abreast of changes in their occupations and personal lives. Developing students who are able and predisposed to be lifelong learners is a paramount goal of education for living in a dynamic society.

Research on systematic approaches to studying supports their effectiveness when students use them (Alvermann & Moore, 1991). Research also demonstrates, however, that many students do not use them (Simpson, 1983). This finding is particularly unfortunate since even academically less successful students benefit from instruction in how to study and can transfer what they learn to novel materials (Weisberg & Balajthy, 1989).

This chapter presents four key ideas:

1. Studying is personal, but students benefit from experiencing a variety of ways to study each content area.
2. The ability to study includes several major components.
3. There are important principles of instruction in how to study.
4. Teaching all students how to study requires a team approach across content areas and grades.

STUDYING IS PERSONAL, BUT STUDENTS BENEFIT FROM EXPERIENCING A VARIETY OF WAYS TO STUDY EACH CONTENT AREA

Providing learners with regular explicit instruction in how to study faces three major challenges. In the first place, because studying is something students do for themselves, studying is personal. Students vary tremendously in their strengths, weaknesses, preferences, and peeves. They have different academic histories, including differing opportunities to have experienced successful independent learning. As a result, there is probably no area of strategic functioning with more room for individuality to display itself than studying. It is probably true that no two successful students study exactly alike.

In the second place, studying is particular to the content area being learned. As we discussed in Chapter 1, content teachers can teach content area reading and writing best because different subjects' different perspectives on the world require different literacies, because students are most receptive to receiving help in literacy when they need it to accomplish specific content assignments, and because content teachers know how best to read and write in their subjects. For these same reasons, it is difficult to teach students how to study in a generic way. When students try to transfer generic approaches to a particular content area, they often find that they are unable to get them to work given the specific demands of that subject. For example, being taught how to take notes outside of math class often fails to help students take notes in math because the summarizing one usually uses when taking notes in other subjects ignores the sequential, step-by-step nature of much mathematics instruction.

In the third place, because studying is something you can do rather than something you can talk or write about, it can only be learned by doing. Learning to study is more like learning to play the piano or basketball than it is like learning American history or English literature. We don't expect students to learn how to be soldiers or poets by studying World War II or William Wordsworth. Likewise, we should not expect students to learn how to study from just reading or hearing about approaches to studying that one could take. The only way most students learn how to perform any complex action is through receiving explicit directions in how to perform the action, watching others correctly model the action, participating in successful guided practice, and engaging in successful independent application. Studying can only be taught to most students through those same means.

Studying would certainly be easier to teach if these three challenges were not in the way. If there were only one way to study effectively, if that one way worked equally for all content areas, and if students could learn that one way by just reading or hearing about it, studying would be a breeze to teach. Because of these three challenges, however, students benefit most from experiencing a variety of ways to study each content area as they move up through the grades.

THE ABILITY TO STUDY INCLUDES SEVERAL MAJOR COMPONENTS

Knowing where to begin studying instruction is difficult because the domain of studying is huge. Philosophers have commented on studying throughout recorded history, and U.S. educators have published voluminous research-based and professional reports about it since the 1920s (Moore, Readence, & Rickelman, 1983). This section describes five central components of learning that fall under the rubric of studying: processes, strategies, systems, resource management, and self-regulation. Two components traditionally categorized under studying are presented elsewhere in this book: Locating information is in Chapter 8, pages 286 to 287; and, interpreting graphics is covered by the lesson format presented in Chapter 4 (see pages 121 to 125).

Study Processes

Thinking processes are the building blocks of studying; they are its fundamental elements. The essential thinking processes described in Chapter 1—call up, connect, predict, organize, generalize, image, self-monitor, evaluate, and apply—are also the processes of studying. Students learn more and remember it longer when they think about a subject. The thinking processes are the antidote to the passive rote learning achieved by reading something over and over until it is memorized. With a few important exceptions like multiplication tables which continue to be useful, that which is memorized by rote is usually forgotten soon after the test.

Proficient learners sometimes employ individual thinking processes to understand and remember information, as illustrated by our example in Chapter 1 of learning a driving manual's information. More frequently, those learners employ study strategies that are each a combination of thinking processes.

Study Strategies

Proficient learners merge individual thinking processes into packages called study strategies. The following study strategies are used and recommended often:

Defining Learning Expectations

Previewing
Setting a purpose

Questioning

Answering prepared
   questions
Self-questioning

Organizing Information Graphically

Outline
Time line
Flow chart
Venn diagram
Web
Cause and effect chain

Writing

Study card
Note taking
Summarizing

Learning log/Journal
Essay

Creating Mnemonic Devices

Analogies
Images
Abbreviations
Acronyms
Acrostics
Rhymes
Phrases

Creating Special Word Associations

Meaningful word parts
Idiosyncratic associations
Mnemonic keyword method

Mental Learning

Retelling
Discussing

Test-Taking Strategies

Defining Learning Expectations   Proficient learners define expectations by clarifying what they intend to learn. They create multistep plans for bringing thought into the learning act. One way of defining learning expectations is previewing, when proficient learners look over what they are to learn before examining it closely. They preview printed materials by surveying many sources of information: titles, headings, italic and boldface print, and other typographical aids; illustrations, maps, graphs, and other pictorial aids; introductions, first sentences of paragraphs, summaries, and conclusions; guiding questions, stated objectives, end-of-chapter exercises, and other adjunct aids. Previewing helps learners define learning expectations by establishing a general idea of what a passage has to offer.

Another aspect of defining learning expectations involves setting a purpose. Learners set purposes when they discern what they should acquire from a passage, lecture, video, CD-ROM, or other teaching device. Learners incorporate what they gathered from a preview with their understanding of the learning task to decide what deserves special attention. They attend to their instructors' stated and unstated cues about what they should learn. The age-old tradition of "psyching out" vague instructors to anticipate what should be in a paper or might be on a test exemplifies part of this strategy. When learners set a purpose, they decide what they want to or need to learn and go after it.

Questioning   Students who read and then answer questions tend to learn more than students who only read. Answering prepared questions often seems like busywork to students, but it can be a potent study strategy. Self-questioning taps learners' creativity. To learn how to self-question, students might be encouraged to pattern their questions after the teacher's, use certain stems (What have I learned about . . . ? What should I remember about . . . ?), or ask and answer questions of one another in reciprocal fashion.

Organizing Information Graphically   Graphic representations arrange key terms in order to depict their relationships. Outlines, time lines, Venn diagrams, and webs (which are discussed in Chapter 4, pages 121 to 125) are different formats for graphically organizing concepts. They all show how selected concepts are organized. A graphic representation of the desert, for example, could consist of terms arranged about such topics as climate, location, plant life, and animal life; it would not be an illustrated scene of coyotes and cactuses.

Writing   Although such strategies as defining learning expectations and questioning might involve writing, study strategies grouped under this heading typically refer to other techniques. Writing strategies that promote learning progress from simply recording facts to assimilating and reflecting on bodies of knowledge. These strategies activate thinking when learners compose the message; they also provide a record for review or revision.

Study cards are one kind of writing strategy. Each study card usually contains a question or vocabulary term on one side with a corresponding answer or definition on the other. These cards are especially useful for factual learning. Many students would not have been successful in fact-filled courses without resorting to study cards.

Note taking is another writing strategy that promotes learning. Note taking assumes many forms. Learners sometimes copy definitions and key ideas verbatim from a passage, comment in the margins of texts, paraphrase information, or add personal examples. They benefit from rewriting their notes, clarifying and consolidating information from class presentations and readings.

In order to help students attend selectively to the information that answers their questions, we recommend regular comprehension lessons as described in Chapter 4. Reading for specific purposes is a dominant feature of those lessons, as well as a central feature of research. Producing notes about what one reads is a logical extension of reading for specific purposes; students producing notes record both the targeted information and their initial reactions to it.

A partial outline is a good tool for introducing note taking to students. Teachers give students a partially completed outline or diagram of the content of a reading selection and demonstrate how to complete it. After a few such lessons, teachers provide students guided practice for completing a partial outline on their own. Figure 7.1 shows a partial outline of Chapter 6. By filling out this outline as you read Chapter 6, your attention would be drawn to the chapter's major ideas, to the relationships among the major ideas, and to the relationships among major and minor ideas. Because you are provided with the outline skeleton, your attention does not have to focus on the trivia of making an outline ("Do I need an uppercase or lowercase *a*?"). Because you are given a fixed number of slots to be filled in, you can easily determine how many ideas to list and what the relationship among them should be. A partial outline helps

---

CHAPTER 6
WRITING

I. Content teachers can provide a variety of writing experiences and support which promote student thinking and learning
    A. Quick writes
    B.
II. Planning a writing minilesson includes deciding on clear writing tasks, background knowledge, and motivation
    A. Deciding what you want students to think about as they write
    B.
        1. Topic
        2.
        3. Audience
        4. Role
    C.
    D. Helping students plan what they will write
III. Writing minilessons guide students through the before, during, and after phases of writing
    A.
    B. Writing
    C. After writing
IV. There are many variations within the writing minilesson framework
    A. Before-writing variation
    B.
    C. After-writing variations

Figure 7.1 Partial Outline of Chapter 6

you to focus on selecting the important information from a text. The amount of information provided in the outline and the amount of instruction you need to provide will vary with the sophistication of the students and with time as you fade yourself out of the picture.

Summarizing uses writing to involve learners in selecting and condensing important information. When summarizing, students may abstract important contents. Learning logs/journals are a variation of class notebooks that require summarization. Students summarize when they record information from class presentations, readings, or outside experiences. Later, students sometimes develop their summaries into more lengthy compositions. In addition, they sometimes use learning logs or journals to pose questions or state confusions about what they are learning. Many mathematics teachers have students write—rather than orally ask—questions about their homework in order to clarify the questions. This practice often leads the students to reach independent solutions.

Essays that call for integration of subject matter or persuasive writing from a particular point of view are forms of writing that powerfully promote content learning, even though they are also time-consuming for teachers to read. Most of us still remember papers we wrote in high school and college classes even though we have forgotten much of the rest we learned in those courses.

Creating Mnemonic Devices   Mnemonic devices—memory aids named after the Greek goddess of memory, Mnemosyne—include several disparate techniques. Analogies stress the similarities between phenomena. For instance, the cell structure of a plant might be compared with the factory structure of an industry. Effective speakers, writers, and teachers frequently use analogies to help students use what they already know to help them understand and remember new knowledge.

Images become mnemonic devices when they are used to represent abstract concepts. For example, a visual image of mist coming from a block of dry ice might be used to represent the physical process of sublimation, the change of a solid directly into a gas. Most of us associate personal or public events of the past with certain images that make those events come alive for us even now.

Mnemonic devices also take such forms as abbreviations (FBI, NAACP, NCAA), acronyms (HOMES for the first letters of the Great Lakes), acrostics ("My very educated mother just served us nine pizzas" for the first letters of the planets in order from the Sun), and rhymes ("In 1492 Columbus sailed the ocean blue"). They also can be phrases that help with meaning ("Hang on tight" for remembering that stalactites are on cave ceilings rather than floors) as well as pronunciation ("It's hot again" indicates the accent to Betatakin, a cliff dwelling in Arizona's Navajo National Monument).

Creating Special Word Associations   A set of mnemonic devices that is large enough and important enough to warrant separate treatment involves individual words. Because understanding and remembering subject matter vocabulary consumes a great deal of students' attention, we present word-study techniques both here and, at greater length, in Chapter 5.

Meaningful word parts, or morphemes, are found in derived words with their prefixes, roots, and suffixes. Contractions and compound words also contain these parts. Students often benefit from attending to the meaningful parts of such words as *underground, triangular,* and *immortalize.* Identifying the meaningful parts of words provides control of them and a tool for identifying new words.

Idiosyncratic associations are similar to meaningful word parts, although the word parts are not from our linguistic heritage. Knowing that the principal should be your friend and that latitude runs the same way as the equator represent idiosyncratic associations.

The mnemonic key word method (Pressley, Levin, & Delaney, 1982) requires first an acoustic link, then a visual one. For instance, to remember that a credenza is a piece of furniture like a buffet or sideboard, the students might recode the word to an acoustic link, such as dents. A visual image of someone bumping into and denting the furniture could then be constructed.

Mental Learning   This somewhat amorphous category of study strategies produces no written or visual products (Wade, Trathen, & Schraw, 1990). It stresses learning activities to be done either with others as part of a study/discussion group or inside one's own head. Retelling is one way to initiate mental learning. After reading, students individually or in groups recount what has been learned. They focus on specific information, sometimes repeatedly verbalizing or paraphrasing it and sometimes reading it aloud. When uncertainties occur, proficient learners return to the source to clarify it or make a note to ask the instructor for clarification. Discussing is an open-ended arrangement for students to come together and refine their learning. They might retell particular portions of subject matter, teach it to one another, or ask and answer questions about it.

Mental learning capitalizes on the essential thinking processes. For instance, learners connect known concepts with what they encounter, evaluate the validity and accuracy of the ideas as well as the author's writing style, and apply concepts to their current lives as well as to the future.

Test-taking Strategies   Figure 7.2 contains a list of test-taking strategies that are appropriate for middle-grade and older students. The strategies are best presented following an actual test. Return the papers to your students and direct their attention to specific test items as you explain each strategy. Demonstrate how you would perform each strategy. Point out the questions you think most difficult and explain that you would mark them and return to them later. As with all teaching, fade out your instruction by reminding students of the strategies before the next several tests and then gradually omitting mention of the strategies as your students become proficient with them.

Systems

Just as proficient learners incorporate thinking processes into study strategies, they also can merge study strategies into systems. Study systems are multistep

General Strategies

1. Survey the test. Estimate its difficulty and plan your time for each section.
2. Underline the important words in each question. Be especially alert for closed terms such as *always*, *never*, and *most*.
3. Be sure to answer every required question (unless there is a penalty for guessing).
4. Do not spend too much time on any one question.

Strategies for Objective Tests

1. Answer the easy questions first. Mark the ones you skip and go back to them when you are ready. Remember that information contained in later items can help you answer previous items.
2. Look for the most correct answer when two items seem to be similar.
3. Narrow multiple-choice items to two, then make your choice when you are not sure of an answer.
4. Rephrasing questions and answering questions in your head before inspecting the choices frequently helps.
5. Change your answers only if you misunderstood the question the first time or if you are absolutely sure that your first response was wrong.
6. False items on true or false tests usually contain one essential word that converts the item into an overstatement, an understatement, or a misstatement.

Strategies for Essay Tests

1. Briefly outline all answers before writing. Jot down key terms and then add to those terms while working on your answers.
2. Include only information that you believe is correct.
3. Plan your time for each question and stick to that schedule.
4. Include topic sentences and supporting details in each paragraph.
5. Proofread your writing.

Figure 7.2   Test-Taking Strategies

plans for bringing thought into the learning act. The classic study system recommended in the literature is SQ3R. Since 1946 it has been presented in many study skills courses. Perhaps you were exposed to it. SQ3R consists of the following strategies, performed in order:

Survey—Preview the material to obtain a general overview of what is to come.
Question—Generate questions from the titles, headings, and subheadings to be answered while reading.
Read—Process the print in order to answer the questions just asked.
Recite—Deliberate over the passage contents, questions, and answers.
Review—Look back over the passage to confirm answers and clarify uncertainties.

Some variations of SQ3R are PQ4R (preview, question, read, reflect, recite, review) (Thomas & Robinson, 1972), OARWET (overview, achieve, write, evaluate, test) (Norman & Norman, 1968), and PORPE (predict, organize, rehearse, practice, evaluate) (Simpson, et al., 1988).

The post-reading (or post-listening) graphic organizer (Barron, 1979) is a study system with much research to support it (Moore & Readence, 1984). Graphic organizers are visual displays that use lines and vocabulary terms to create an overview of some topic. (Figures 4.4 through 4.8 on pages 119–124 contain graphic organizers.) Originally, graphic organizers were created by teachers or textbook publishers to be used as advance organizers before students read or listen. While this is still a valid use of graphic organizers, research suggests that graphic organizers make their greatest contribution to learning when the students themselves construct a graphic organizer after reading or listening about a topic. What makes post-reading and post-listening graphic organizers a study system is their multistep nature. First, students are presented with teacher- or publisher-made graphic organizers and helped to interpret them. Second, students learn to complete partial teacher- or publisher-made graphic organizers after reading or listening. Third, students learn to create graphic organizers in small-groups after reading or listening when given a list of key vocabulary for the topic just taught. Fourth, students learn to create graphic organizers individually after reading or listening when given a list of key vocabulary for the topic just taught. Fifth, students learn to create graphic organizers in small groups after reading or listening when they have to decide what the key vocabulary is as a first step. Sixth and finally, students learn to create graphic organizers individually after reading or listening when they have to decide what the key vocabulary is as a first step. When students are adept at independently creating graphic organizers from scratch after reading or listening, they have mastered a study system with the power to help them both remember more details and understand better the relationship among ideas.

Reciprocal teaching (Palincsar, 1994) is a highly acclaimed study system. In reciprocal teaching, students in small groups take turns leading discussions about sections of a piece of reading material they have all read and have open in front of them. The student leader begins the group's discussion of the section by asking questions of the other students about the section's content. After the questioning period, the student discussion leader summarizes the section aloud for the others. The rest of the students in the group respond to this summary and, if there are disagreements, everyone returns to the text until a consensus is reached. After consensus on an oral summary is achieved, the student discussion leader elicits predictions from the others about the content of following sections. The leader may also add predictions of his own. That ends the group's discussion of that section. If another section is to be taught reciprocally that day, another student in the group becomes the discussion leader for the new text section.

Initially during reciprocal teaching, the classroom teacher moves around, keeping students and groups on task. At opportune moments, the teacher models questions, summaries, or predictions for students. The teacher also provides suggestions and feedback. As the students improve in their ability to teach text segments reciprocally, the teacher fades her guidance until each group is functioning independently.

Reciprocal teaching has been investigated in many research studies that, together, provide strong support for its effectiveness as a study system. Its combination of the study strategies questioning/self-questioning, summarizing, and predicting, mixed with mental learning, explain why it has probably been found to be so effective. The power of reciprocal teaching is readily apparent if one attempts to answer the question: Which does reciprocal teaching teach better, study strategies or the content?

Study systems share an important characteristic with teachers' unit and lesson plans: They have a beginning, a middle, and an end. Learners' study systems and teachers' instructional frameworks call for the learner to think deliberately about a passage before, during, and after reading. Preparation is done in the prereading, beginning stage; actual reading is done in the middle stage; and follow-up occurs in the postreading stage. Proficient learners realize this progression when studying with a system.

Resource Management

One of the authors wanted to attend a time management seminar offered during the writing of this book but couldn't find the time. Resource management clearly is easier to talk about than actually to control. You probably will find this to be the case with your students, but we encourage you to continue emphasizing it because of its importance. Principles of resource management related to studying outside of school include the following:

1. *Maintaining a routine.* Establish a consistent time and place to study.
2. *Creating a productive environment.* Establish appropriate levels of noise, light, and temperature. Make sure school supplies are nearby. Have access to food and beverage. Take short breaks.
3. *Completing tasks in an efficient order.* Sequence tasks in an order such as easy to difficult, short to long, interesting to boring, or most favorite to least favorite (or vice versa). Then complete them in the way that is most efficient for you.
4. *Completing tasks on schedule.* Keep up with readings and assignments; do not procrastinate.
5. *Reviewing information at regular intervals.* Conduct frequent short reviews rather than infrequent long ones.
6. *Seeking help when needed.* Contact friends, classmates, or teachers to clarify information. Use tutors or study centers. Initiate study groups or pairs.

Resource management may be the component of studying that is most dependent on home support to develop. While home support may be crucial, teachers can help students improve their resource management by providing occasional opportunities during class for students to share how they study at home. Generally, such sharing reveals to everyone that students who are doing well conform to most of these six principles of resource management, while students who are not doing well conform to few of these principles.

Schools can support students' development of good resource management by sending home a one-page description of resource management, focusing on the six principles, and explaining how important home support is in helping students do well in school. The great majority of parents are interested in helping their children succeed in school and will appreciate clear, practical suggestions on what they can do at home to support their children's education.

Self-Regulation

Proficient learners do what it takes to learn, employing the study processes, strategies, and systems they can use and have found helpful, and managing resources to enhance their learning. They also are self-regulated.

Self-regulated learners control their learning actions (Corno, 1986). If deep understanding of a passage is needed, these students may preview it, take notes, and question themselves about it. If mastery of specific facts is the learning goal, these learners may decide to create mnemonic devices. Furthermore, they probably know whether an abbreviation, acronym, or acrostic is the best type of mnemonic device for the particular set of facts they intend to learn.

When self-regulated learners read, they sometimes move forward at a medium rate, they sometimes skim, and they sometimes slow down considerably. In other words, proficient learners are flexible. They change their reading rate according to the demands of the material and their purpose for reading. If the passage is easy and learners want an overview of it, they read rapidly. If the passage is difficult and learners want to master the contents, they read more slowly, maintaining their focus. Proficient learners monitor themselves as they move through print, centering on ideas that they know to be important. At times, they regress to an earlier point in the passage and reread it to fix it in their minds or to compare it with a later one. These learners also focus on confusing ideas. If they are unclear about something, they return and attempt to clarify it or seek a third source to resolve an apparent conflict. This control of strategies and reading rate is called *metacognitive control.*

Think of a person skilled in a craft such as plumbing. Good plumbers have many tools and use them selectively to accomplish specific purposes. A plumber might size up a situation, they begin working with a socket wrench. If that tool is not getting the job done, she might employ a crescent wrench. When a plumber is at a delicate part of a job, she will slow down to be sure to get it right. Students with metacognitive control use learning strategies like skilled craftspeople use tools (Paris & Winograd, 1990). They plan to use strategies appropriate to specific learning tasks, check on how well they are progressing, and make adjustments as needed. They have well-developed and flexible repertoires.

Along with having metacognitive control, self-regulated learners are motivated. Students might be full of study strategy knowledge, but it will help only if they are motivated to apply it. Habit and will are as important as content and skill. Self-regulated learners have the predisposition to accomplish academic goals (Borkowski, et al., 1990) and persist with tasks even when they

Interviewer _____ Date _____

Student _____ Grade _____

School Subject _____

Note: If students are confused by a question, explain it until they understand. In addition, probe students' responses until they have no more to say about each item.

1. What do you do when you want to learn the information being presented in your (school subject) class? How do you go about understanding and remembering the information you need for this class?

2. How do you prepare for tests in (school subject)?

3. What do you do to understand and remember what you read?

4. How did you learn how to study?

5. When and where do you study?

6. How much reading do you do each week in (school subject)?

Figure 7.3 Study Questionnaire

become difficult. They engage learning tasks with their full attention, blocking out distractions.

Students with little control of their efforts often attempt to escape learning. They may try to distract teachers or make excuses for their performance. They often create highly charged emotional scenes, acting out verbally and physically or withdrawing sullenly. Feelings of frustration and embarrassment rather than confidence and pride influence their actions.

The affective motivational aspects of self-regulation deserve as much instructional attention as metacognitive aspects. The roles of curiosity, persistence, and confidence in learning should not be shortchanged.

Listen/Look and Learn _____

Interview a few high-achieving and a few low-achieving public school students of the same grade level. You may use the study questionnaire presented in Figure 7.3. Describe the similarities and differences between the students' reported approaches to studying. Explain how your beliefs about studying instruction were affected by interviewing the students.

THERE ARE IMPORTANT PRINCIPLES OF INSTRUCTION IN HOW TO STUDY

At this point you probably realize the complexity of studying. Studying has many aspects, and many of these aspects rely on higher-order thinking. For instance, such strategies as note taking, self-questioning, and representing information visually cannot be broken down into a fixed sequence of steps that always produce the same results. Long division can be reduced to such a series, but study strategies usually cannot. Because self-regulation is a major component of studying, the application of study processes, strategies, and systems requires countless decisions about the relative importance of information and the relationships among ideas. The individuality of knowing what some ways of studying are, understanding which ones to employ in particular situations, and being motivated to do so, add to the intricacies of studying. You can and should be explicit when you teach students how to study, but you cannot expect an answer key to help you check students' notes, questions, or visual representations. Their approaches to studying should produce some common outcomes, but students' individual interpretations, preferences, and peeves will also cause these outcomes to vary somewhat.

Try It Out

Compare the complexity of long division with that of study strategies. With a fellow student or teacher, compute an answer to an identical long-division problem; then both of you take notes on an identical passage. Compare both sets.

Given the complexity of studying, the best teachers can do is explicitly present general guidelines for strategy use, resource management, and self-regulation, then structure regularly occurring situations so students construct systems and habits that work for them. The most common study system seems to be the one students internalize for themselves (Simpson, 1983). This section describes some principles of study strategy instruction.

Integrate Study Strategy Instruction with Content Teaching

Ways to study, like other reading and writing strategies, should be presented during content instruction, when students have the need to know them. This practice is known as functional, or content-driven, instruction. Rather than present note taking by itself because a particular textbook calls for it, present note taking when you expect your students to take notes on upcoming subject matter.

Many upper-grade teachers introduce particular study processes, strategies, or systems during the first few weeks of school to help students study better throughout the semester or year. Teachers identify a few preferred ways to study or take ones from a school's curriculum guide, then present them to students immediately. For example, if they expect students to keep learning logs throughout a semester, they will demonstrate how to do so at the beginning. Or, if mnemonic devices make especially good sense to them and are applicable to a subject they are teaching, they will introduce the creation and use of mnemonic devices to students as early in the semester or year as possible.

Ways to study can also be presented after a semester or school year has gotten under way. Different ways to represent information visually might be presented throughout the year as opportunities and students' needs arise. In social studies, time lines might be appropriate during each unit of study, but outlining might be introduced only when students create the table of contents for a term paper. If students are having special difficulty with a portion of subject matter, then self-questioning might be introduced at that point to help them overcome that special challenge.

Follow an Apprenticeship Model with Student Freedom of Choice

For teaching studying, we advocate an apprenticeship model with student freedom of choice. The best teachers of any subject are usually the teachers who are themselves successful students of that subject. It is difficult to teach science well, for example, unless one is interested in science. Learning how to learn any subject is most effectively done when it is conceived of as a classroom of apprentices learning from a master. While a teacher may not wish to see herself as a master student of, say, mathematics in the academic or even adult world, it is certainly appropriate for her to see herself as a master student of mathematics in the world of her students.

When we conceive of studying instruction as an apprenticeship model, we are encouraging teachers to remember back to when they were studying their subject at different grade levels. What study processes, strategies, and systems did you personally use to successfully study your content area? What principles of resource management did you follow? What mental actions did you take to regulate your own learning? Those are probably the processes, strategies, systems, principles, and mental actions that you are most able to teach, most motivated to teach, and best able to integrate with the teaching of your subject. In an apprenticeship model, you are not responsible for teaching the one and only one right way to study your subject. Rather, you are responsible for teaching students the ways you found helpful.

Students should be given choices within an apprenticeship model because your students are not all like you, with your particular strengths, weaknesses, preferences, and peeves. Nor are they necessarily as committed to your subject as you are. Their talents and interests may lie elsewhere.

Fading and Self-Assessment

Fading is a good approach for teaching students ways to study. As we explained in Chapter 1, fading occurs when teachers show students how to perform a reading or writing strategy, then gradually move back so students do it on their own. Teachers fade out, and students fade in.

Fading requires planning on your part to make sure it happens. Teachers often lead students through particular learning procedures, never fading out to relinquish control to students. But think about it: If you always ask the questions, when do students learn to question themselves? If you always present an outline of course topics, when do students learn to outline independently? When teachers always do the questioning and outlining, these procedures are teaching strategies rather than study strategies.

There is no question that teachers should fade out during instruction in how to study, but sometimes teachers can fade too quickly. Sometimes teachers simply tell students to "take notes on the upcoming material" or "get ready for a quiz on Friday," with little or no instruction on how to take notes or prepare for a quiz. Teachers sometimes assume students are proficient with these strategies when they are not. Guard against not fading out and fading out too soon. Plan studying instruction that balances demonstration, guided practice, and independent application.

Demonstration   During the demonstration stage, teachers begin as the dominant figure in the class. Teachers label and define the desired study process, strategy, or system by naming it, presenting a general description of it, and making analogies to it whenever possible. Teachers explain the relevance of the process, strategy, or system by indicating when and why it is useful. They model it by performing it publicly, explaining it as they go along. Finally, they list prompts for it.

When labeling and describing word study cards, you might tell students something like this:

> Today I will present word study cards to you. These cards are ways to focus on the technical vocabulary of this class. They are like snapshots of individuals rather than a total class picture. Word study cards contain a vocabulary term on one side and ways to understand the word on the other. Making these cards will help you understand the terms, and reviewing the cards will help you remember them.

To explain the relevance of the strategy, you might say something like this:

> Using these cards is one way to cope with the terrific amount of new terms you'll be encountering here. Knowing this strategy will help you in other situations, like getting a new job or being on a sports team when you suddenly have to learn a lot of specific new ideas.

As you model the strategy, you could say something like this:

> Watch how I produce word study cards. First, I acquire a stack of index cards. Then I decide which terms to transfer to the cards. I select words in boldface print, ones listed at the end of the passage, and ones that seem important to me. As you can see, I chose *monarch* as one of the words, so I print it on the front of the card. Then I turn the card over and record information that will help me understand and remember this word. I decide to write a definition, "Ruler. A king or queen"; a sentence containing the term, "Queen Elizabeth is the monarch of England"; and a note on word parts "mon = one (monorail)." I could have drawn a picture or produced other examples of monarch, but what I have here seems to be enough.

Now I put this word card into my pile to review later. I might simply quiz myself on the meanings, separate known from unknown words, get with someone else and take turns quizzing each other, or group the words into different categories.

Finally, listing prompts consists of specifying as well as possible the procedure you followed. Prompts are general guidelines; they are not rules that always lead to the same outcome. You might tell your students something like this:

As you saw, I followed the three steps that I posted on the bulletin board:

1. Identify important terms.
2. Record one term on one side of a card and memory aids on the other.
3. Review the cards regularly.

The memory aids you record are the key to this strategy. Remember to use personal experiences, meaningful word parts, and illustrations as much as possible.

Guided Practice After demonstrating the study process, strategy, or system, provide guided practice in doing it. Direct students to use it and provide feedback while they do. You might say, "Now it's your turn to produce your own study cards. Work with a partner or on your own. We'll get together as a whole class in fifteen minutes to check on progress." As you move around to work with students, you can probe their understanding of the strategy, praise and encourage their efforts, remind them of missing steps, and suggest improvements.

Independent Application Showing students a process, strategy, or system, and then having them practice it several times as you provide cues and feedback is a good beginning, but students need to apply the strategy independently and regularly to make it their own. During the independent application stage, teachers plan situations for students to use and refine the strategy; they determine students' grasp of it and reteach what is needed.

Routine attention to study processes, strategies, or systems is needed during the independent application stage. Plan your teaching so that your instructional routines incorporate study processes, strategies, and systems, and so that students succeed in class when they apply them. Open-notebook quizzes exemplify this type of planning. Regularly provide class time for students individually or in groups to take notes from their readings. Then allow students to use these notes, but not the readings themselves, during quizzes. Many teachers also collect students' learning logs or journals, comment on them, and record a plus or minus grade depending on the amount of writing students produced. Representing information visually becomes an instructional routine when every Monday you randomly select a student to share what he or she produced for an assigned reading. You ensure that self-questioning leads to success when student-produced questions appear on quizzes.

Self-Assessment   The necessary complement to your fading is for students to self-assess during studying instruction. Encourage and remind them to ask themselves during demonstrations, "Do I understand what I am seeing well enough to try to do it myself?" During guided practice and independent application, encourage and remind them to ask themselves, "Am I doing this the way my teacher taught me to do it?" and, "Could I do this at home or by myself at the library?"

Try It Out

Select a study process, strategy, or system, and plan an introductory lesson that contains the demonstration and guided practice steps. Conduct the studying lesson with a group of peers or public school students. Evaluate the lesson: Describe what you would keep and what you would change if you were to do it again. Also describe your next steps to follow up this introductory lesson with opportunities for independent application.

Scaffolding

Construction workers use scaffolding to prop up structures and gain access to them as they are being erected; scaffolds are used in various ways until the building can stand on its own. In education, scaffolds are the supports teachers and students use to construct new knowledge. Dialogue among students and their teacher is a central feature of scaffolded instruction (Paris & Winograd, 1990). Students need a nonevaluative setting to verbalize their understandings and beliefs about study processes, strategies, and systems so teachers and other students can suggest the right actions at the right times. Scaffolds also can be teaching tools, such as cue cards, or teaching techniques, such as classroom grouping patterns (Rosenshine & Meister, 1992).

When you plan and present studying lessons through an approach based on fading, decide what scaffolding is needed. Working closely with your students will help you determine the supports to include, gradually decrease, and eventually remove. Thinking about the following types of scaffolding helps you plan what to fade: prompts, analogies, classroom grouping patterns, reading materials, strategy complexity, and process checks.

Prompts   As we described in Chapter 3, prompts stimulate thinking. They are questions or directions that cue learners to the critical features of the strategy. They induce learners to think a certain way.

Like the outcomes of a traditional task analysis, prompts indicate the actions to perform in multistep procedures. The three guidelines for producing study cards, presented above, exemplify prompts (identify important terms; record one term on one side of a card and memory aids on the other; review the cards regularly).

The five steps of SQ3R (survey, question, read, recite, review) cue readers to the actions they should take during this particular study system. Mathematics teachers usually present a multistep strategy for solving word problems with prompts such as the following:

1. Survey the problem.
2. Determine what is given and what is asked for.
3. Determine what operations to use and when to use them.
4. Estimate the answer.
5. Solve the problem.
6. Determine if the solution is reasonable.

The prompts should be recorded for students' reference. They might be placed on a bulletin board, distributed on cue cards, or copied into students' class notes. You should refer to the prompts frequently at first, then begin to fade them out.

Prompts do not specify invariant rules; they signal general actions. The survey part of SQ3R, for instance, involves examining many parts of a passage in no particular order. However, despite their generality, prompts are valuable supports that guide learners.

Analogies   Another form of scaffolding to include in studying instruction is analogies that compare a study process, strategy, or system to something vivid. Analogies can motivate students and make strategies concrete and sensible. They are good vehicles for discussions.

Many types of analogies are available. You can compare word study cards to snapshots, note taking to gold mining or eating digestible bites of food, and representing information visually to sketching a picture or framing a building. Teachers sometimes compare readers to detectives: Both search for clues, form hunches, and support their generalizations.

If you cannot think of an analogy for the process, strategy, or system you are presenting, ask students for one. Their analogies frequently are more vivid and apt than the ones adults produce.

Classroom Grouping Patterns   Adjusting classroom grouping patterns is a good way to scaffold instruction. Students can develop strategies when participating in whole-class, small-group, learning-pair, and individual configurations. Teachers change classroom grouping patterns to keep their instruction fresh, accommodate the type of lesson they are presenting, and promote dialogue.

Teachers often demonstrate ways of studying to a whole class, then begin fading by jointly performing the procedure with students still grouped as a class. After collaborating with students in a whole-class setting, have them perform the process, strategy, or system in small groups or learning teams. Students who take turns teaching the process, strategy, or system to one another go far in refining their knowledge of it. Small-group or learning-pair production of questions, visual representations, or mnemonic devices are clear tasks that fit group work nicely. Individuals can perform strategies on their own and

Students can learn study strategies while working in groups.

then join a group or a partner to share what they produced and receive feed-back. Finally, group support can be removed as students work to internalize the strategy on their own.

Reading Materials   Ensuring that your instruction offers an appropriate challenge is an important feature of scaffolded instruction. The materials you use when introducing ways to study should present minimal difficulties to your students so they can concentrate on that process, strategy, or system. We have seen many studying lessons torpedoed by lengthy difficult reading materials; the students became confused about the material and, consequently, the strategy.

When you introduce a process, strategy, or system, one way to ensure appropriate materials is to use ones already studied in class. Return to a passage that your class knows and show how the procedure applies to it. Another way is to locate very easy topic-related materials. Secondary-school English teachers often introduce such literary elements as plot, setting, theme, and symbolism with children's literature. After introducing a strategy with short easy materials, you can begin increasing the length and difficulty of the materials to meet your students' abilities. Once students have a strategy for identifying the plot of *The Three Little Pigs*, they can begin transferring it to *Charlotte's Web* and eventually *War and Peace*.

Complexity   Another way to control the difficulty of studying instruction involves the process, strategy, or system being taught. Be sure that the prompts are appropriate for your students. If a step in summarizing is "Determine the main idea of the passage," you would need to ask yourself if your students can accomplish this step. Perhaps this main idea prompt should be modified to "Determine the topic of the passage."

You can regulate the difficulty of a multistep procedure by presenting each prompt gradually, giving manageable yet meaningful portions a step at a time. Ensure that students can perform the first step before beginning the second. If students are to ask themselves or one another generic questions, be sure that they understand each question and know how to go about answering it.

Process Checks   A final way to scaffold instruction involves process checks. Process checks are good ways to keep students in pursuit of learning how to study, directing them to maintain what they are learning. Have students take stock of their use of study processes, strategies, or systems at various intervals. When they are preparing to read, ask them, "What are some things you might do to learn this information?" At other times simply remind students of processes, strategies, or systems they have learned: "Remember what you know about imaging when you read this passage."

Questions such as the following check on students' processing:

Before Reading

How will you remember this? What can you do to learn this?

After Reading

What led you to that conclusion?
Why do you say that?
How did you figure that out?
How did you approach this?

Process questions focus students on how they studied rather than on what they learned. If a student claimed that the Spanish conquistadors were criminals rather than heroes, a product-oriented check would be: "What did they do that was criminal? Were the French settlers any more criminal or heroic?" This would be a process-oriented check: "Why do you say that? What led you to that conclusion?"

Motivating

Motivation, another principle to tap while teaching studying, is a learning outcome as well as a principle of instruction. It is a means to an end *and* an end in itself. Motivating students to learn in your class can result in students who remain self-regulated, motivated learners throughout their lives.

Motivating students is one of the most difficult tasks for teachers. Teachers affect motivation in part by the tasks they present to students (Ames & Ames, 1984). Many of the activities and strategies suggested in this chapter and throughout this book help with motivation. In general, teachers motivate students to learn when they ensure success, allow student choice, emphasize meaningful activities, develop student independence, and get everyone actively involved.

Specific to motivating students to learn how to study, the most powerful method we are aware of is that described by Pearson and Santa (1995). Pearson is a high-school teacher who involves her students in an experiment for them to discover which of five study strategies are most helpful to them as individuals. This experiment is integrated with the content learning they are doing anyway. The students read five different text portions as part of their current unit of study. For each passage after the first one, the students are taught to use a different study procedure. After studying each of the five passages, the teacher gives the same kind of test. Each student graphs her performance on the test across the four study strategies and control condition (passage 1). While prior familiarity with passage content makes some difference, individual students see that some study strategies seem to be more helpful to them than others. Pearson finds that this experiment motivates students to want to use the strategies they have found personally beneficial.

We conclude this section by tying it to Chapters 2 and 8. Students who are engaged in integrated units and inquiry have a better chance at motivation than those involved daily in isolated subject matter lectures. Integrated units and inquiry provide a good setting for subject matter instruction and for explicit instruction in how to study that students find motivating. Capitalizing on these opportunities can lead to motivated independent learners.

TEACHING ALL STUDENTS HOW TO STUDY REQUIRES A TEAM APPROACH ACROSS CONTENT AREAS AND GRADES

Students benefit most from experiencing a variety of ways to study each content area as they move up through the grades. As we have explained, studying is particular to the content area being learned. Just because one is good at studying English does not mean one is good at studying science. Different study processes, strategies, and systems tend to be emphasized by successful students in different disciplines. In addition, the ability to study develops over many years. Students cannot be expected to combine thinking processes together to form study strategies if they cannot perform those thinking processes; they cannot be expected to combine study strategies together to form study systems if they cannot perform those study strategies. Principles of resource management and the ability to self-regulate are highly related to aspects of general maturity that take all of childhood and many successful experiences to develop. Finally, study procedures are best learned when students have a need to know them—when students are motivated and apprenticed to learn them.

If we consider the full domain of studying—processes, strategies, systems, principles of resource management, and self-regulation—in light of how students best acquire them, it is no surprise that few schools can rightfully claim to be teaching their students how to study (Jackson & Cunningham, 1994). Certainly, our students over the years at the university have often complained to us that they graduated from high school without really knowing how to study. Yet, their knowledge of ways to study were surely ahead of most of their fellow graduates who did not attend four-year colleges. When high-school graduates who go on to enter four-year colleges seem not to have been taught how to study, it is likely that few others were either.

What should or can be done to help students acquire the skills for lifelong learning in a dynamic society? We believe that the key to progress in teaching studying is for each content area at each grade level to have a few useful ways of studying that are seen by everyone as part of what is to be learned that year in that subject.

The Tension Between an Apprenticeship Model and the Need for a Team Approach

We advocate an apprenticeship model, with freedom of choice, for teaching students how to study each subject because it maximizes student learning of both content and studying, and it minimizes the time and effort that must be expended in both the teaching and the learning. There is, however, an inevitable tension between each teacher selecting the ways to study that he has found most helpful in his subject, and the need for a team approach to ensure that students learn all the study processes, strategies, and systems they need to know. How can we leave it up to individual teachers what and how they will teach and yet ensure that, across content areas and grades, students are learning what they should?

The concept of a *team* approach is crucial here. We are opposed to top-down mandates of "study skills" courses, modules, or units, because they cannot work given the nature of studying and studying instruction discussed so far in this chapter. Yet, we are deeply concerned about the current lack of instruction in how to study that the vast majority of America's schoolchildren receive. Instead of mandates, we encourage the faculty of each school to work together as a team to decide what ways to study they will attempt to teach their students by the time they move on to the next level of schooling. For example, each K–5 elementary school faculty should engage in a process by which they decide what they will teach in each subject at each grade in the area of studying that will prepare all of their students to be able to study successfully in sixth grade.

If you are fortunate enough to teach in a school where the faculty engages in a team approach to teaching studying, we encourage you to participate actively as a member of that team in advocating for the kind of studying instruction outlined in this chapter. However, if you teach in a school where their is no systematic or organized attempt to teach studying schoolwide through the grades, we encourage you to develop an apprenticeship model in your own classroom. Teach only those study processes, strategies, and systems you understand, believe in, and can integrate with your content teaching. You will have helped your students learn to study your subject better, whether or not anyone else in your school does likewise.

Specific Content Area Applications

● STUDYING IN THE ENGLISH/LANGUAGE ARTS CLASSROOMS

English/Language Arts curriculums, like those of most other content areas, include a broad array of outcomes. Among other things, students in English/Language Arts are expected to learn how to write essays, letters, memos, and poems; understand advertisements, plays, short stories, and novels; present themselves during interviews, public presentations, and work groups; and value, appreciate, and personally respond to literary accomplishments. Concentrating on generic study techniques that provide students access to these outcomes is one way English/Language Arts teachers manage such crowded curriculums.

Reciprocal Teaching (RT) is an approach to studying English/Language Arts that deserves consideration. RT denotes an instructional approach for teachers as well as a study system for students. It offers a set of specific learning conditions as well as a set of specific mental operations.

The RT instructional approach emphasizes teacher-student and student-student conversations, or dialogues, about understanding texts. It calls for cooperative effort and sharing. While reading short sections of a passage, for example, teachers and students think aloud. They talk about the mental processes they are using to make sense of what they are reading.

Teachers typically fade their instruction during RT. They initially take the lead in describing particular strategies they are applying, then they gradually relinquish this role as students describe their use of the strategies with other segments of text. When participating in small groups, students often write their responses on overhead transparency sheets for whole-class sharing. Teachers scaffold instruction during RT by commenting on students' efforts ("That's a good start. What do others of you think might be important to say?"), offering additional modeling ("I think the reason for selling the camel needs to be included here."), and hinting at next steps ("Now what should you do to make sense of this passage?"). Praising valid actions, providing passages at different levels of difficulty, and posting written prompts about RT strategies are additional possible scaffolds. Teachers explain why and when particular strategies are appropriate.

The original RT study system, or repertoire of mental operations, consists of four cognitive strategies: summarize, question, clarify, and predict. Teachers and students talk about how they are employing these mental actions relative to specific sections of reading materials. If the class or a small group were reading *Shabanu, Daughter of the Wind,* individuals would take turns describing their summaries, questions, clarifications, and predictions. For the episode when Shabanu's father sells Guluband, the family's prize camel, one student might briefly summarize what happened, produce a question such as "Why was Guluband sold?", clarify the way Shabanu's father went about selling the animal, and predict what will happen next. As the student talks about these things, others chime in with their thoughts. They might add to the summary, suggest additional questions, offer other items for clarification, and produce their own predictions.

The RT learning target is independence. After multiple focused conversations about passages conducted in groups, individuals are expected to conduct their own dialogues internally. Individuals are expected to become independent and think through their own summaries, questions-and-answers, clarifications, and anticipations. When emphasizing this individual action phase of RT, you might call it "talking to yourself" or "having an internal dialogue." This aspect obliges individuals to utilize inner speech—the voices within their minds—to determine text meanings. Students are expected to address possible interpretations and evaluations internally before settling on certain ones.

When using RT in English/Language Arts class with narrative passages, you might retain its approach to instruction but modify its cognitive strategies. Consider modifications such as reducing the number of strategies from four, having students select only the one or two they believe most appropriate for a particular section, or substituting strategies. You might replace the original RT strategies (summarize, clarify, question, predict) with some of the essential thinking processes described in Chapter 1 such as connect, generalize, or image if these seem more appropriate for your students and the materials they are reading. For instance, students internally might orchestrate connections among text ideas and previous experiences, think through possibilities for a passage's overall message, and construct and reconstruct images of key scenes until they are satisfied. Indeed, RT's value seems to come from its collaborative, explicit, sense-making approach to instruction more than from its specific strategies being taught. Students benefit when they exert concentrated efforts to learn and make public what they are doing.

● STUDYING IN SECOND-LANGUAGE CLASSROOMS

Helping students become independent lifelong learners is a central goal of education. In second-language classrooms, this means developing students' desires and abilities to continue their language learning after graduation. Promoting effective instructional settings and word learning strategies are two ways to approach this goal.

Second-Language Instructional Settings

As noted in Chapter 1, the overall setting of a classroom substantially affects learning. Second-language learning is no exception. Teachers play an especially crucial role in promoting meaningful settings that begin a lifetime of second-language learning.

Effective second-language teachers promote meaningfulness by stressing cultural studies along with linguistic studies. Effective teachers go beyond having students translate printed passages, memorize word meanings, and complete grammar exercises. Instead, they emphasize second languages as a means of examining and expressing the cultures from which they come. Students are immersed in the modern customs and ancient traditions of a culture, and they examine history and geography associated with the language. They experience the second cultures firsthand through field trips and guest speakers, and they experience audiovisuals of the culture's sights and sounds. Language learning is embedded in cultural learning.

Word Learning Strategies

Teachers who present only the meanings of words encountered during class shortchange students when they leave class. Second-language users with few word learning strategies are limited when they encounter unfamiliar terms and their teacher is not available to explain them. To avoid this situation, effective second-language teachers emphasize word learning strategies.

A frequently underestimated word learning strategy is determining the depth of knowledge needed for particular terms. Knowing only that *truffles* are edible and that *taupe* is a color might be sufficient for some learners but not for others. Learners need to become adept at determining the words that warrant their attention and the degree of knowledge that they require. Second-language teachers promote this adeptness by involving students in selecting words for study and determining their meanings. Teachers regularly have students identify the important words in reading materials, presentations, and audiovisuals, and they have students talk about the meanings they produce for the words. To stimulate these practices, effective teachers regularly hold discussions in response to questions such as these two:

"Which terms should be learned?"
"What needs to be known about each term?"

Second-language teachers also emphasize word learning strategies by helping students become "word detectives," sleuths who take advantage of word meaning clues. Effective second-language teachers stress context as a powerful clue to word meanings. After deciding on a passage's terms that should be emphasized, teachers help students figure out their meanings by examining the ways they are presented. They do this by regularly talking about students' reactions to a question such as this one:

"What does the passage reveal about the meaning of this term?"

Searching for cognate relationships (e.g., discerning the connections between the Spanish *naturalmente* and the English *naturally* as described in Chapter 5) is another good way to utilize word meaning clues. Teachers can accustom students to search habitually for shared meanings among words that look and sound alike by regularly asking students:

"Do you know any words that look and sound like this word?"
"Are any of these look-alike/sound-alike words related to each other?"

To see how contextual and morphemic clues combine, consider this sentence: *All rocks formed from fiery hot magma are called igneous rocks.* The context clearly implies that *igneous* means *formed from fiery hot magma.* And since the beginning of *igneous* looks and sounds something like the beginnings of *ignite* and *ignition,* a morphemic connection based on *ign* become apparent. Students can generalize the meaning of *igneous* to something like, "rocks formed by fire or volcanic action." To help students combine contextual and morphemic clues, you might ask something like:

"What are the connections between what the passage reveals about the word and its relation to look-alike words?"

If contextual and morphemic clues are insufficient, then independent learners consult references such as dictionaries, glossaries, encyclopedias, and other people. References are consulted only after determining that a term is important to understand and that the available clues do not fully reveal its meaning. Indeed, learners consult references to confirm and refine word meanings as much as to gain completely new understandings. In the preceding example, learners might seek confirmation to the meaning of *igneous,* and they might look up *magma* for initial ideas if they don't have any clue to its meaning. To help students consult references at appropriate times, you could ask:

"When understanding a word is crucial and the clues to its meaning are insufficient, what do you do?"

Finally, making and reviewing word study cards is a time-honored word learning strategy. Recording new terms on the front of study cards and supplying clarifying information on the back is a powerful tool for continually upgrading one's second-language learning. Writing the clarifying information in one's native language enlarges the the possibilities of what can be included. Learners might record definitions, explanations, sentence contexts, mnemonic devices, related words, and illustrations to clarify the unfamiliar word meanings. Reviewing the study cards, separating the words that are understood immediately from the ones that are not, and resolving difficulties are additional steps that promote word learning over time.

● STUDYING IN THE MATHEMATICS CLASSROOM

Mathematics may be the subject that most people feel inadequate about how to study. When students are doing math homework or preparing for a math test, their lack of effective study procedures can lead to frustration and poor performance. Here are some ways math teachers help students become more successful and independent in their learning of mathematics.

Study Cards

Requiring students to make a set of study cards during a math unit and then teaching them how to use that set of cards to study for a test helps students develop an important study strategy that only a few above-average students would probably figure out on their own.

After each type of problem covered in the unit has been taught and practiced, require the students to pick one problem of that type from their math book. Choosing one of moderate, rather than low or high difficulty, is generally best. Each student should write that problem on one side of a 4×6 index card. It should be written in every different way the book or you, the teacher, would write it. (See Figure 7.4 for an example of a math study card from a middle-school math class.)

On the other side of that same four-by-six index card, each student should write the page number(s) in the book where the explanation of how to work that kind of problem is to be found, followed by the steps the teacher recommends for solving that kind of problem, followed by the problem worked correctly. (See Figure 7.5.)

After each student has completed this study card, it can be handed in or checked by a partner. Once it has been checked, it is added to the student's growing deck of math study cards.

Before a test, you should demonstrate how to use the deck of math study cards for study. Shuffle your deck and then pick the top card. Work the problem on the front without looking at the back of the card. Then turn the card over to check both your answer and how you worked it. It is helpful to students if you get one or two problems right and then "miss" one. On the one you miss, show them how to use the card to check step-by-step what you did. Show them how to use the pages from the book that explain how to do that kind of problem when you can't remember exactly what one of your steps

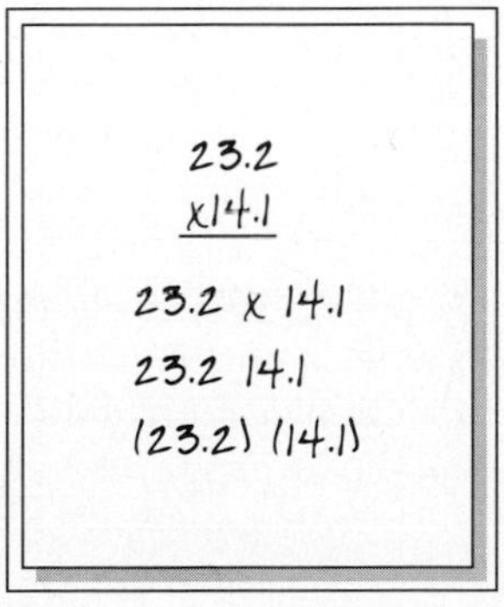

Figure 7.4 Math study card front

pages 187–189

1. Copy the problem in vertical form.
2. Check to see if the decimals line up.
3. Check to see if the numerals line up.
4. Multiply the top number by the first numeral on the right of the lower number.
5. Put a zero on the right, then multiply by the second numeral of the lower number.
6. Put two zeros on the right, then multiply the third numeral of the lower number.
7. Add the part answers together, starting on the right and keeping numerals straight.
8. The answer has the number of decimal places that the two numbers have together.

$$\begin{array}{r} 23.2 \\ \times 14.1 \\ \hline 232 \\ 9280 \\ 23200 \\ \hline 327.12 \end{array}$$

Figure 7.5 Math study card back

means or what your teacher said about it. Provide time during class for students to study some for the next test using their deck of math study cards. Encourage them to use their study cards outside of class as they prepare for the test. Students who use their deck of cards for study and feel that it helps them are more likely to begin developing their own decks of math study cards after you stop requiring all students to do so.

Self-Regulation

No component of studying is more important for mathematics than self-regulation. Consider the kinds of students who usually do well in math. They know when they "have it" and expend little effort and exhibit little anxiety afterward on that concept. On the other hand, they also know when they are having difficulty and seem able to formulate the right questions to ask to elicit the help they need. Moreover, they seem to know when a parent, a fellow student, or a teacher is the most likely person to know the answer to a particular question. At times even, they are able to keep working at one or more problems until they figure out what they need to know without help. The successful student of mathematics is almost always a self-regulated student.

The problem with some math instruction is that it seems based on the assumption that all the students are already self-regulated learners of mathematics. The teacher shows students how to work a particular kind of problem and then assigns them practice exercises. It is their responsibility to know when and what they don't know and to seek the appropriate help from the appropriate person at the appropriate time. Unfortunately, such an assumption is often inappropriate!

Successful teachers of mathematics help students become more self-regulated by requiring them to predict and self-monitor during math lessons. Instead of starting out by working a problem for the class, the teacher presents a problem to the class and asks them to predict individually whether they can solve it correctly or not (he can even require them to write down a "yes" or "no" in the margin of their notes). If a number of students are certain that they can or uncertain about whether they can or not, the teacher has the class take a minute and try to solve the problem at their seats. The correct answer is shared and students discuss any difficulties. Then, the teacher tries to help them determine how they could have anticipated where they would have trouble. If most of the students seem certain that they cannot solve the problem, the teacher has different students explain what there is about the problem that has them stymied. In either case, the teacher still teaches everything she would have otherwise taught, but only when students have been made aware that they really need to know what is being taught.

A different problem is presented to the class and, again, they are asked to predict individually whether they can solve it or not. This process takes a little longer at first until the students become more self-regulated, but it pays off in reduced math anxiety and negative attitudes toward math on the part of many students. Once students are more self-regulated during math lessons in class, they can be encouraged to be more self-regulated when studying math outside of class.

● STUDYING IN THE SCIENCE CLASSROOM

Science is an extremely important subject that many students have difficulty learning. Here are some ways science teachers help students become more successful and independent in their learning of science.

Graphic Organizers

To learn science, a student has to acquire a large number of facts, terms, and concepts. Unfortunately, teaching this basic level of science knowledge causes many students to become unable "to see the forest for the trees" and to conceive of science as "just one darn thing after another!" Graphic organizers are an extremely important tool for helping science teachers give their students the big picture and to show them relationships between that big picture and science facts, terms, and concepts. Just as importantly, students can learn to create their own graphic organizers independently so that they can assist in their own mastery of both the parts and wholes of science.

For example, some chemistry teachers make the Periodic Table of the Elements on the wall of their classrooms an integral part of their course. In the beginning, the teacher explains what a chemical element is and contrasts it with a compound. As students are taught the concept of *atomic number,* the teacher refers to the Periodic Table to show them how the elements are arranged in increasing order of atomic number from left-to-right and top-to-bottom. As students are taught that the elements can be subdivided into groups that act somewhat alike when forming compounds, and share other properties as well, the teacher refers to the Periodic Table to show them how sections of it cluster together into identifiable groups such as alkali metals or noble gases. Later, as students are taught the chemistry of these different groups of elements, they learn about the K, L, M, N, O, P, and Q electron shells. The teacher then regularly refers to the Periodic Table to show the students how the number of electron shells that an element has determines which of the seven rows or "periods" that element is in. As the teacher teaches the students that the number of electrons in the outer shell of an element determines how it forms compounds with other elements, the teacher also shows students that the number of electrons in the outer shell determines which column of the table that element is in. Once they understand how it works, students are encouraged to refer to the Periodic Table in their chemistry textbook as they study. Throughout, students are not allowed to forget that all the specific facts, terms, and concepts about chemical elements they are learning fit together into a grand scheme.

A *data chart* (labeled rows and columns with information in the cells) like the Periodic Table is only one kind of graphic organizer that a chemistry or other science teacher can use to show the relationships between the whole of a course, unit, or topic and its parts. With respect to studying, however, it is important to follow the effective use of graphic organizers by teachers with activities that have students work in small groups to represent graphically the relationships they understand among a set of facts, terms, or concepts. For example, at the end of a unit on electricity in a middle-school physical science course, the students could be put in mixed groups of four or five students each and given a list of key terms from the unit: current, conductor, induction, insulator, resistance, semiconductor, and voltage. The task would be for them to web "electricity" using those terms and others they find helpful. The groups can do these webs on transparencies or sheets of chart paper and some can be shared with the whole class. Of course, this task assumes that the teacher has previously used webs as graphic organizers while teaching the course.

As students improve in their ability to represent graphically the key terms, facts, or concepts of a science topic or unit, they can be shown how such an activity helps them prepare to answer test questions about the relationships among those terms, facts, or concepts. This will motivate some of the students to construct graphic organizers as a study strategy.

Mnemonic Devices

What are the colors of the rainbow in order? If you are like we are, you know the answer to this question because you remember the memorable nonsense word, *roygbiv*, or strange name, Roy G. Biv (red, orange, yellow, green, blue, indigo, violet). One of us still remembers eras in order he learned decades ago in historical geology by constructing the sentence, "Come over soon; don't miss pepperoni pizza" (Cambrian, Ordovician, Silurian, Devonian, Mississippian, Pennsylvanian, Permian).

No other subject is so vocabulary intensive as science. The number of terms which must be learned in any science course is often daunting for students. Teaching them a few mnemonic devices that you have found helpful will increase their ability to remember sets of terms. With respect to them learning how to study science better, it is important to have the class construct a mnemonic occasionally to help them remember a particular set of important terms. The students who find these mnemonics helpful are more likely to produce ones on their own when studying science outside of class.

STUDYING IN THE SOCIAL STUDIES CLASSROOM

Social studies courses are often marked by their breadth of content coverage and thoughtfulness of conceptual issues. If students are to take advantage of this breadth and thoughtfulness, they must learn how to study both social studies content and its conceptual implications. Here are some ways social studies teachers help students become more successful and independent in their learning of science.

Graphic Organizers

To learn social studies, a student has to acquire a large number of facts, terms, and concepts. Unfortunately, teaching this basic level of social studies knowledge causes many students to become unable "to see the forest for the trees" and to conceive of social studies as "just one darn thing after another!" Graphic organizers are an extremely important tool for helping social studies teachers give their students the big picture and to show them relationships between that big picture and social studies facts, terms, and concepts. Just as importantly, students can learn to create their own graphic organizers independently so that they can assist in their own mastery of both the parts and wholes of social studies.

For example, some American history teachers use data charts to help their students see the significance of the people, events, and dates they are learning. A *data chart* is a graphic organizer consisting of labeled rows and columns with information in the cells. Figure 7.6 is an example of a data chart that helps students see relationships among the specifics they are learning about the years leading up to the Civil War.

After having students fill the cells of this data chart with information from their textbook, class notes, and other sources, the students can easily be led to consider expansion, slavery, and the economy across the five administrations instead of only within each. Moreover, the chart facilitates students seeing

	Expansion	Slavery	The Economy
James K. Polk (1845–1849)			
Zachary Taylor (1849–1850)			
Millard Fillmore (1850–1853)			
Franklin Pierce (1853–1857)			
James Buchanan (1857–1861)			

Figure 7.6   The Five Presidential Administrations Leading Up to the Civil War

relationships among expansion, slavery, and the economy during these years. The data chart increases the likelihood that the students will think about the possible relationships across administrations and factors without the teacher having to tell students directly what those relationships are.

A data chart is only one kind of graphic organizer that an American history or other social studies teacher can use to show the relationships between the whole of a course, unit, or topic and its parts. With respect to studying, however, it is important to follow the effective use of graphic organizers with activities that have students work in small groups to represent graphically the relationships they understand among a set of facts, terms, or concepts. For example, at the end of a unit on types of government in a middle-school social studies course, the students could be put in mixed groups of four or five students each and given a list of key terms from the unit: anarchy, aristocracy, authoritarianism, autocracy, capitalism, communism, democracy, fascism, monarchy, oligarchy, republic, socialism, and totalitarianism. The task would be for them to web "government" using those terms and others they find helpful. The groups can do these webs on transparencies or sheets of chart paper and some can be shared with the whole class. Of course, this task assumes that the teacher has previously used webs as graphic organizers while teaching the course.

As students improve in their ability to represent graphically the key terms, facts, or concepts of a social studies topic or unit, they can be shown how such an activity helps them prepare to answer test questions about the relationships among those terms, facts, or concepts. This will motivate some of the students to construct graphic organizers as a study strategy.

Discussing

In social studies, conceptual understanding is crucial. That is why successful social studies teachers use as many essay questions on tests and assign students to write as many short papers as they have time to grade. Unfortunately, many students have real difficulty showing what they know in a short paper or an answer to an essay question. Perhaps the best way to prepare students to do the kind of thinking that essay questions and short papers require is to have class discussions from time to time on the kinds of questions the teacher asks and paper topics the teacher assigns.

Two-Column Notes

Two-column notes (Palmatier, 1973) is a note taking system which helps students organize information under specific topics and gives them a study system which they can use alone or with a partner. Students take notes on one side only of loose-leaf notebook paper. Before taking notes, they draw a line vertically down the paper leaving a 3-inch column on the left. They leave this left column blank making their notes based on the lecture, video, or reading only in the wider right-hand column. When they finish taking their notes, they go back through them and label each with a word or phrase which tells the topic of each section of notes. To study from these notes, they work by themselves or with a partner, folding their paper so that they can only see the left column with the topics. Trying to anticipate questions that might be asked, they answer the questions using information they remember from the folded-away right column of details. To check their recall of important facts, they fold back the paper and see if they have included all pertinent ideas. While studying, they deal with all notes that have a particular topic entry even if these are separated by other topic entries. If students who have taken notes on the same lecture, video, or text section study together, they can compare notes and add details from each other's that they omitted to enter into their own notes and then "test" each other by constructing possible questions for each topic and trying to recall the pertinent details.

Teachers use a variety of strategies to teach students how to take and study from two-column notes. Some teachers divide a transparency into two columns and, with the overhead light off, make notes in the right column while reading or viewing something with the students. The students are also taking notes simultaneously and after each section, the teacher turns the light on and helps students compare their notes with those he or she has written on the transparency. When all the notes are taken, the teacher and students work together to decide on a topical word or phrase to write in the left column. Finally, teachers demonstrate how to use the notes to study by folding the paper, coming up with possible questions related to each topic, constructing an answer, and unfolding the right-side notes to see if important details were included in the answer.

Another way of helping student learn two-column note taking is to give them a set of notes with the right column already filled in and have them decide what topical word or phrase to put in the left-hand column. They then use these notes to study as described above. Here is one page of some two-column notes taken about modern day South Africa:

South Africa Since 1994

Government	400-seat national assembly
	80-seat senate
	President Nelson Mandela
	1993 first all-race election
People	43 million people
	32 million Africans (blacks)
	6 million Afrikaners (whites)
	4 million Colored (mixed ancestry)
	1 million Asians (India)
Land	Southern tip of Africa
	Bordered by Namibia, Botswana, Zimbabwe, Mozambique, Swaziland
	mostly plateau
	mild climate

● STUDYING IN THE "ACTIVITY" CLASSROOM

Think of the studying you have done as you have learned the field you teach. While reading and writing play a significantly smaller role in your field than they do in social studies, science, or English, they have helped you at times to learn what you now know and can do. Your students may not be aware that reading and writing have *any* part to play in your course. Here are some ways teachers of activity courses use literacy to help students become more successful and independent in their learning.

Study Cards

Requiring students to make a set of study cards while they are learning a procedure in your class and then teaching them how to use that set of cards to study for a test helps students develop an important study strategy that only a few above-average students would probably figure out on their own.

As you are teaching the procedure, select an important term, step, or rule that your students in the past had trouble remembering. Each student should write that term, step, or rule on one side of a 4 × 6 index card. On the same side of that card, each student should write the page number(s) in the book, if there is one, where the explanation of that term, step, or rule is to be found.

On the other side of that same 4 × 6 index card, each student should write the question that the term, step, or rule on the other side is the answer to. If the term, step, or rule on the other side is the answer to more than one question, then more than one question should be written.

After each student has completed this study card, it can be handed in or checked by a partner. Once it has been checked, it is added to the student's growing deck of study cards for this procedure or the procedures being taught during this unit.

Before a test, you should demonstrate how to use the deck of study cards to study from. Shuffle your deck and then pick the top card. Ask the question(s) on the front aloud and then try to answer it (them) aloud without looking at the back of the card. Then turn the card over to check whether you answered with the right term, step, or rule. It is helpful to students if you get one or two terms, steps, or rules right and then "miss" one. On the one you miss, show them how to use the card to study that term, step, or rule (put it in a "missed" pile that you review after going through the deck one time). Show them how to use the pages from the book that explain that term, step, or rule when you can't remember exactly what your answer means or what was said about it. Provide time during class for students to study for the next test using their deck of study cards. Encourage them to use their study cards outside of class as they prepare for the test. Students who use their deck of cards to study with and feel that it helps them are more likely to begin developing their own decks of study cards for difficult terms, steps, or rules after you stop requiring all students to do so.

Writing Summaries of Procedures

After you explain or demonstrate how to do a particular procedure, have students write a quick summary of the steps and rules you have taught them. Then, pair the students and have them swap their summaries. Each student reads her partner's written summary to see if she understands and agrees with it. This process is faster and less threatening than if you watch each one of the students try to do the procedure, and yet it usually reveals many of the misunderstandings and gaps in what the students understand about how to do the procedure. Respond to the questions that arise.

Images and Rhymes

Mnemonic devices help us remember difficult or tricky procedures. Many people still remember how to use a screwdriver or wrench properly by recit-

Literacy in an activity class.

ing the ditty: "Righty tighty, lefty loosey." Great basketball players often practice hitting crucial, last-second free throws over and over again in their minds so that, if the situation arises, they will have an image to help them remember how it feels to make those shots when the pressure to panic is intense.

Share with your students any images or rhymes you have used to help you remember procedures at difficult or stress-filled times. Encourage and give them time to construct their own images or rhymes to help them remember the procedures you are teaching them or to prepare for tests or performance situations when they might forget under pressure.

Looking Back

Teachers can instruct students in how to study. More and better studying instruction would help all students be better prepared to learn from their current courses, future schooling, and lifelong learning opportunities. You encountered four key ideas in this chapter: (1) Studying is personal, but students benefit from experiencing a variety of ways to study each content area; (2) the ability to study includes several major components; (3) there are important principles of instruction in how to study; and (4) teaching all students how to study requires a team approach across content areas and grades.

Add to Your Journal

Record in your class journal your reactions to this chapter. What lessons or units in how to study have you experienced? What were their strengths and limitations? What were their similarities and differences? Which study strategies will you emphasize with your students? What instructional routines do you foresee for highlighting study? How do you plan on implementing studying instruction in your teaching?

REFERENCES

ALVERMANN, D. E., & MOORE, D. W. (1991). Secondary school reading. In R. Barr, M. L. Kamil, P. Mosenthal, & P. D. Pearson (Ed.), *Handbook of reading research* (Vol. 2, pp. 951–983). New York: Longman.

AMES, C., & AMES, R. (1984). Systems of student and teacher motivation: Toward a qualitative definition. *Journal of Educational Psychology, 76,* 535–556.

BARRON, R. F. (1979). Research for classroom teachers: Recent developments on the use of the structured overview as an advance organizer. In H. L. Herber & J. D. Riley (Eds.), *Research in reading in the content areas: Fourth report* (pp. 171–176). Syracuse, NY: Syracuse University Reading and Language Arts Center. (ERIC Document Reproduction Service No. ED 037 305).

BORKOWSKI, J. G., CARR, M., RELLINGER, E., & PRESSLEY, M. (1990). Self-regulated cognition: Interdependence of metacognition, attribution, and self-esteem. In B. F. Jones & L. Idol (Eds.), *Dimensions of thinking and cognitive instruction* (pp. 53–92). Hillsdale, NJ: Erlbaum.

CORNO, L. (1986). The metacognitive control components of self-regulated learning. *Contemporary Educational Psychology, 11,* 333–346.

DEVINE, T. G. (1991). Studying: Skills, strategies, and systems. In J. Flood, J. M. Jensen, D. Lapp, & J. R. Squire (Eds.), *Handbook of research on teaching the English language arts* (pp. 743–753). New York: Macmillan.

JACKSON, F. R., & CUNNINGHAM, J. W. (1994). Investigating secondary content teachers' and preservice teachers' conceptions of study strategy instruction. *Reading Research and Instruction, 34,* 111–135.

MOORE, D. W., & READENCE, J. E. (1984). A quantitative and qualitative review of graphic organizers research. *Journal of Educational Research, 78,* 11–17.

MOORE, D. W., READENCE, J. E., & RICKELMAN, R. R. (1983). An historical exploration of content area reading instruction. *Reading Research Quarterly, 18,* 419–438.

NORMAN, M. H., & NORMAN, E. S. (1968). *Successful reading.* New York: Holt, Rinehart & Winston.

PALINCSAR, A. (1994). Reciprocal teaching. In A. C. Purves (Ed.), *Encyclopedia of English studies and language arts* (pp. 1020–1021). New York: Scholastic.

PALMATIER, R. A. (1973). A note taking system for learning. *Journal of Reading, 17,* 36–39.

PARIS, S. G., & WINOGRAD, P. (1990). How metacognition can promote academic learning and instruction. In B. F. Jones & L. Idol (Eds.), *Dimensions of thinking and cognitive instruction* (pp. 16–51). Hillsdale, NJ: Erlbaum.

PEARSON, J. W., & SANTA, C. M. (1995). Students as researchers of their own learning. *Journal of Reading, 38,* 462–469.

Pressley, M., Levin, J. R., & Delaney, H. D. (1982). The mnemonic keyword method. *Review of Educational Research, 52,* 61–91.

Rosenshine, B., & Meister, C. (1992). The use of scaffolds for teaching higher-level cognitive strategies. *Educational Leadership, 50,* 26–33.

Simpson, M. (1983). *Recent research on independent learning strategies: Implications for developmental education.* (ERIC Document Reproduction Service No. ED 247 528).

Simpson, M. L., Hayes, C. G., Stahl, N., Connor, R. T., & Weaver, D. (1988). An initial validation of a study strategy system. *Journal of Reading Behavior, 20,* 149–180.

Thomas, E., & Robinson, H. A. (1972). *Improving reading in every classroom.* Boston: Allyn & Bacon.

Wade, S. E., Trathen, W., & Schraw, G. (1990). An analysis of spontaneous study strategies. *Reading Research Quarterly, 25,* 147–166.

Weisberg, R., & Balajthy, E. (1989). Transfer effects of instructing poor readers to recognize expository text structure. In S. McCormick & J. Zutell (Eds.), *Cognitive and Social Perspectives for Literacy Research and Instruction* (Thirty-eighth Yearbook of the National Reading Conference, pp. 279–286). Chicago: National Reading Conference.

ADDITIONAL READINGS

Thorough descriptions of studying and guides for instruction in how to study are found in the following:

Devine, T. G. (1987). *Teaching study skills: A guide for teachers* (2nd ed.). Boston: Allyn & Bacon.

Gall, M. D., Gall, J. P., Jacobsen, D. R., & Bullock, T. L. (1990). *Tools for learning: A guide to teaching study skills.* Alexandria, VA: Association for Supervision and Curriculum Development.

Pressley, M., Johnson, C. J., Symons, S., McGoldrick, J. A., & Kurita, J. (1989). Strategies that improve memory and comprehension of text. *Elementary School Journal, 90,* 3–32.

This book presents a scholarly description of aspects of graphic organizing:

Novak, J. D., & Gowin, D. B. (1984). *Learning how to learn.* New York: Cambridge Press.

Self-regulated learning is described fully in the following:

Corno, L. (1987). Teaching and self-regulated learning. In D. C. Berliner & B. V. Rosenshine (Eds.), *Talks to teachers* (pp. 249–266). New York: Random House.

Pintrich, P. (1995). *Understanding self-regulated learning.* San Francisco: Jossey Bass.

Many handbooks written for students about how to improve their studying are available. Here is a good one for upper-grade students:

Gall, M. D., with Gall, J. P. (1988). *Making the grade.* Rocklin, CA: Prima Publishing and Communications.

chapter **8**

Student Inquiry

Looking Ahead

Parents have learned to fear the announcement by their schoolchildren that "I have a report due Wednesday. I have to do Brazil." Students often come home with a general topic, and their parents help them limit the topic, find resources, and put a finished report together in a reasonably organized fashion. Parents typically go through much stress and strain helping their children produce such reports. Likewise, teachers often have difficulty leading each and every student through the stages of such projects, and students have even greater difficulty completing the tasks independently. This chapter addresses ways to facilitate student inquiries.

As we enter the twenty-first century, recognizing the need for information, locating good sources, gathering what is needed, and applying it to speciifc situations is becoming a critical competency. Well-formed decisions about personal and occupational issues depend on well-developed inquiry processes.

Many consider inquiry and research to be mysterious and specialized endeavors. However, these terms can be demystified by thinking of them as a state of mind. *Inquiry* and *research* refer to the process of producing convincing answers to interesting questions. People become curious about something, so they set out to learn more about it. Student researchers should generate questions that are interesting and answers that are convincing. Children who are required to simply "do Brazil" probably have little interest, few questions, and limited strategies for becoming engaged in the task, a situation that works against becoming independent lifelong learners.

This chapter accentuates inquiries that use multiple-source documents and oral interviews. These are its key ideas:

1. Inquiry is a special feature of integrated units of instruction.
2. Asking engaging researchable questions is essential to inquiry.
3. Locating sources and information within sources is essential to inquiry.
4. Organizing information is essential to inquiry.
5. Students share what they learned in a variety of ways.
6. Students become independent when teachers gradually fade their support and hand over responsibility to students.

INQUIRY IS A SPECIAL FEATURE OF INTEGRATED UNITS OF INSTRUCTION

Many models of teaching involve student inquiry. General educators (Martinello & Cook, 1994; Wiggins, 1987) and those affiliated with academic specialties such as science (Lawson, Abraham, & Renner, 1989) and language arts (Harste, 1994; Hillocks, 1986) long have promoted learner-centered investigations. Many secondary schools now have graduation requirements that call for students to exhibit the products of inquiries conducted over several months. Inquiry advocates believe that the most permanent and transferable learning occurs through personal involvement and self-controlled analyses (Brooks & Brooks, 1993). Inquiry-based educators believe that students who receive just teacher-directed instruction are at risk of learning to perform only on command.

The professional literature typically groups inquiry with educational concepts such as problem solving, research projects, experiential learning, and inductive teaching. Inquiry often is linked with information literacy, "the ability to access, evaluate, and use information from a variety of sources" (California Media and Library Educators Association, 1994). Unlike direct didactic teaching, inquiry-based approaches take a somewhat indirect, facilitative role in students' learning. Although teachers provide support in whole-class, small-group, and individual settings, students assume primary responsibility for planning, conducting, and evaluating their investigations. During inquiry activities, teachers act as a guide on the side more than as a sage on the stage.

Active participation is an important dimension of inquiry-based teaching (Boomer, et al., 1992; Short, Harste, & Burke, 1996). Teachers emphasize participation when they have students take the lead, or at least serve as partners, in their instruction. Rather than make unilateral decisions about learning outcomes and activities, teachers collaborate with students to form mutual decisions. When inquiry is emphasized during integrated units, students play a large role in selecting the focus of study and choosing procedures. They certainly might utilize library materials, but their research also would extend to interviewing people, writing for information, and conducting experiments. Students also evaluate how well they accomplish their outcomes.

Forming generalizations is another important dimension of inquiry-based teaching (Joyce & Weil, 1996). As explained in Chapter 1, students generalize when they form conclusions based on data. They synthesize information to produce a statement that ties together many facts. The distinction between teachers presenting generalizations to students and students forming their own is important. To illustrate, in Chapter 2 our integrated unit plan on smoking tobacco included generalizations about advertising techniques. The plan calls for an instructor to present advertising techniques, have students locate cigarette ads that exemplify each type, then have students produce their own ad. The teacher presents the generalization, and students produce examples of it. Instruction proceeds deductively, from the whole to its parts. But when emphasizing inquiry, the teacher ensures that students have access to numerous cigarette ads, then he or she helps students infer the commonalities. The teacher can ask open-ended questions such as: "What can you say about these advertisements?" "What do the ads have in common?" "How are the ads attempting to convince people to purchase their brands?" The teacher provides examples and stimulates thinking, and students produce the generalizations. Here instruction proceeds inductively, from the parts to a whole.

When facilitating student inquiry, help students form their own generalizations. This is done by providing students access to abundant materials related to a specific issue. Students can form valid conclusions only when they examine meaningful sets of information. They need to examine several cigarette ads to form valid generalizations. They need numerous reading materials about heroes to conclude what it takes to be one. You can also foster generalizations by ensuring that students investigate issues conducive to such thinking. Primary-grade students probably would have trouble reaching a conclusion about why air exists, but they could explain why winds occur. Finally, spur students to test and refine their initial generalizations. If students conclude that cigarette ads emphasize humor, have them support this conclusion by comparing the number of humorous ads with the number of nonhumorous ones. If students conclude that courage is what it takes to be a hero, have them support this statement with examples of people considered to be heroic.

Student inquiry readily occurs during integrated instructional units. If a unit focuses on heroes, alienation, inventions, weather, space, or careers, then students take the lead in exploring aspects of these topics in depth. They might concentrate solely on the central question of a unit (e.g., "What does it take to become a hero?") or they might address a particular favorite sport hero (e.g., "What can I learn about Michael Jordan?"). Attention to group-oriented unit objectives occurs along with attention to individual inquiry-oriented ones. Like interdisciplinarity (see Chapter 2), inquiry is a special feature of integrated units.

Once students begin conducting inquiries into selected aspects of topics, events, or novels, they take the lead—or at least share it. But even as partners in the inquiry process, you play a significant role developing learners' strategies.

Research projects motivate students to evaluate and synthesize information.

Students require support posing engaging and researchable questions, finding information, synthesizing ideas among multiple sources, and sharing what has been learned (Dreher, 1995; Roser, Strecker, & Ward, 1996; Spivey & King, 1989; Stahl, et al., 1996). You support, or scaffold, students' efforts when they conduct inquiries. The next four sections present ways to help students ask questions, locate information, organize information, and share what has been learned.

Do It Together

As a group or pair, think back to the independent research projects you completed in elementary and secondary school. Which projects were your favorites? Why? Which were your least favorite? Why? Each group or pair should briefly summarize their discussion for the rest of the class.

ASKING ENGAGING RESEARCHABLE QUESTIONS IS ESSENTIAL TO INQUIRY

Questions for individuals or small groups serve the same focusing function as central questions for a whole class during integrated units. Asking engaging and researchable questions leads to effective inquiries. Engaging questions elicit a sense of connectedness. They involve students by linking academic contents with personal concerns. Students address issues and ideas that they choose and that they perceive to be useful and interesting in the present rather than in some unforeseen future (Macrorie, 1988).

Engaging questions also command students' attention and action over time. They frame the gaps in learners' knowledge in a way that allows a range of thinking processes and efforts. Conversely, questions should be narrow enough so students achieve satisfaction and a sense of closure to their inquiries after exerting reasonable effort. Inquiring into what it takes to be considered a hero would be engaging and researchable for middle-grade students. Neither naming one hero from Greek mythology nor describing every recognized hero in the world would be engaging or researchable. Indeed, problem *finding* might be an inquiry activity that is as important as problem *solving* (Getzels & Csikszentmihalyi, 1975).

As with integrated and interdisciplinary units presented in Chapter 2, teachers introduce inquiry units by grabbing students' attention and arousing their curiousity. They kick off units with concrete sensory phenomena that stimulate thinking and questioning. Once students' interests in and backgrounds for a topic are developed, strategies that involve brainstorming are appropriate for helping students form engaging researchable questions. Poster Questions, What You Know and What You Don't Know, and Question Box are strategies that can be performed with the whole class, small groups, or individually. Although we present the following as distinct entities, you could combine aspects of them as students move through this part of the inquiry process.

Poster Questions

For Poster Questions, an organizing center is listed on a sheet of chart paper, an overhead transparency, or the chalkboard, so students can brainstorm questions with the teacher. The *wh* words, who, what, when, where, why, and how, are good entry points for inquiries. Teachers initiate the organizing center to be studied—*danger*, for example—then help students frame inquiries by attaching *wh* words to the organizing center. A central question for the whole class, one for each small group, and ones for each individual could be produced this way. Students ask questions such as, "*Who* are the most dangerous people we meet?" "*What* dangers occur inside and outside school?" "*When* do we encounter danger?" "*Where* are the most dangers encountered?" "*Why* do dangers exist?" and "*How* can we overcome dangerous situations?" Many more questions could be posed for each *wh* word.

The questions are posted for inspection. Those that are too narrow for engaging inquiry (e.g., "*Who* set the Chicago fire?") might be moved aside. Students could then seek information on selected questions. Their searches need not consist only of trying to find answers to the posted questions. Indeed, the purpose for inquiry may be to try to generate additional questions or areas of research. After reading and talking to others independently, students look again at the posted questions and compare the answers they have gathered.

Children discuss Poster Questions in order to evaluate what has been learned and generate additional areas of investigation.

They inspect the original questions, modify them, and go off again to find additional resources.

What You Know and What You Don't Know

What You Know and What You Don't Know is similar to K-W-L (Carr & Olge, 1987) (see Chapter 4, Comprehension, pages 127 to 128) because it entails calling up prior knowledge and building motivation; it differs from KWL with its emphasis on framing engaging researchable questions. As with Poster Questions, an organizing center is displayed. Students call out ideas they associate with the center. All information is put down, whether accurate or not. Students then organize the bits of conceptually related information and display them.

Once the ideas are displayed, unknown information becomes much more readily apparent. If an upper-grade science topic is the human circulatory system, students might develop a category for diseases. Anemia, leukemia, and hemophilia might be listed. Questions then can be generated about names of other blood- and heart-related diseases, as well as on the nature and treatment of each disease. Under *What We Don't Know* students might list "What other circulatory diseases are there?" "What causes each circulatory system disease?" and "What cures each circulatory system disease?" Groups of students

Students brainstorm researchable questions during inquiry units.

then take questions, searching for information that validates what is already listed, adding new information, and refining the questions.

Question Box

Question Box involves placing a box for questions where it is readily available to students at all times. The teacher encourages students to write down questions that occur to them. Students might ask questions such as, "Why is the sky blue?" "What is France like?" "Why do the number of degrees in the angles of a triangle always equal 180?" or "Why is oxygen necessary for combustion?" The questions might or might not address the organizing center of units being pursued in class.

Once or twice a week questions are taken out of the box, and the teacher models putting the question into a form that can be answered. For example, "What is France like?" could be recast as "How is the geography of France different from that of the United States?" or "What do U.S. tourists notice most frequently when they visit France?" As can be seen with this example, the teacher rewrites the pupil's personalized query into a number of focused questions that can be answered through research. When teachers demonstrate how to limit broad, unfocused questions, students become better able to formulate researchable questions themselves. As with the other strategies presented in this book, fading from teacher modeling to student independence is the goal of this technique.

Modeling researchable question asking is only a part of the Question Box teaching strategy. Once questions have been focused, the teacher and students brainstorm places where students might find the needed information. Students are encouraged to list specific types of books and magazines as well as to mention resource people whom they might contact. For the question, "Why is the sky blue?" students might list the titles of science magazines, their science book, the school principal, the encyclopedia, the almanac, and TV weather forecasters. After a list is compiled, pupils are encouraged to search for more science books to add to the list. Once this large list has been compiled, students are ready to set out to find the answer. Meanwhile, a classroom chart with the question at the top can list the answers that students predicted before beginning the search, as well as what was found during the search. This activity can be conducted as a short routine similar to discussing daily news events and reading aloud.

LOCATING SOURCES AND INFORMATION WITHIN SOURCES IS ESSENTIAL TO INQUIRY

Along with engaging researchable questions, students need access to information (American Library Association Presidential Commission on Information Literacy, 1989). Efficiently locating sources and their appropriate information is essential to inquiry. A productive way to help students in this endeavor is to emphasize key words.

Key words open storehouses of information such as libraries, the Internet, textbooks, encyclopedias, and people. Key words encompass many concepts. "If you are going to the store for milk, orange juice, root beer, and diet cola," you might say to your class, "what word could you use to refer to all those items?" Discuss students' responses, such as *beverages* and *drinks,* in order to demonstrate that a few key words lead to many, many specifics. Point out how a few different key words can be used to cover the items. Once students grasp the power of key words, show how to use them with written and oral sources.

Written Sources

As inquiries progress during units of study, school media specialists often are quite helpful in introducing students to specific sources such as library contents, computer telecommunications, and content area textbooks. The variety of content area reading materials described in Chapter 3 are candidates as inquiry project sources. Teachers follow up initial demonstrations by guiding students through group and individual inquiries using these sources. Two key word strategies that media specialists or teachers might present are Key Word Guess and Key Word Scavenger Hunt.

Key Word Guess   Begin Key Word Guess by displaying the questions selected to guide an inquiry. Then write underneath the question key words that might lead to answers. The following is a Key Word Guess that fourth-graders created:

Where did Native Americans live?

Indians	countries
teepees	states
homes	climate

Who were Native-American leaders?

chiefs	medicine men
Crazy Horse	leaders
Indians	Chief Joseph
Sitting Bull	shaman

What did Native Americans eat?

cooking	food
gatherers	basic needs
Indians	farming
hunting	survival

Not all of the key words listed above would lead to the information being sought; however, this is true of the key word guesses that adult researchers generate. Adults list the most likely candidates for key words and check them out. While checking, they alter the list of key words. In trying to locate articles about oral language use, one of us came up with the following list of key words to check in the Education Index: *oral language, oral communication,* and *talking.* While searching for articles under these phrases, the index directed us to yet another term, *conversation.* The altered list, with *talking* dropped and *conversation* added, yielded several appropriate articles. Student researchers likewise can alter their key word lists.

After students list their key word guesses, they go to a library, a search engine on the Internet, or an index in their textbooks to see what can be found. In the example above, the class learned that *Indians* would be a good key word for all of the questions.

Key Word Scavenger Hunt   Key Word Scavenger Hunt is a teaching strategy that allows students to practice locating information. It addresses information location strategies for multiple topics rather than for a student's particular inquiry. Students first are led as a whole class through introductory exercises to see how to locate information that answers various questions. Then they work in pairs or as individuals to locate information for a Key Word Scavenger Hunt list. The following are some practice items used with intermediate-grade students:

1. A word used in New England for factory is *mill.* How many kinds of mills does your textbook tell about?
2. What is adobe?
3. What is a nuclear reactor? What key words could you use to find information?

Interviews

Conducting oral interviews seamlessly blends reading, writing, listening, and speaking as student researchers gain access to information (Graves, 1989). Interviews can range from highly structured question-answer sessions between an expert and a novice, conversations among several people with varying degrees of expertise on a topic, and informal questions posed during guest presentations or field trips and other outside-of-school explorations. We recommend interviews as standard features of inquiry projects.

When involved in somewhat structured question-answer interviews, young students should begin with familiar, friendly sources. Family members, school personnel, and peers are appropriate candidates for interviews in the early grades. Secondary students can begin interviewing unfamiliar people who are expert in students' inquiry topics. Once a person has agreed to be interviewed, many teachers send the person a brief letter outlining the nature of the students' projects and a description of how the information will be used. Such a letter is especially helpful if the interview is to be tape-recorded.

Question-answer interviews work most efficiently when the researcher has specific inquiries written in a set order. If students investigate schools of the past, asking the interviewee to "Tell me about your school days" may not be very productive. Instead, the students should be prepared to ask questions about teachers, other students, lessons, tests, discipline, and so on. These key words should be jotted down at first and then developed into complete questions before interviewing a subject. Interview questions, like the ones guiding an overall inquiry, should be specific, but not so narrow that they can be answered with a "yes" or "no." Asking source people follow-up questions such as, "Can you tell me more about that?" or "What else do you remember?" is a useful way of getting more complete information.

Tape-recording the interview is a good way to maintain a record of what was said; taking notes during the interview is also recommended. After leaving the interviewee, students should write down what they learned. This summary might be shared with the interviewee in order to check for accuracy and elicit additional pertinent information.

Before sending students out to conduct interviews, teachers frequently demonstrate the procedure by interviewing a guest in the classroom. Students also may want to practice interviewing one another before going outside the classroom.

Try It Out

Form groups of about three. Conduct sessions of Poster Questions, What You Know and What You Don't Know, Key Word Guess, and oral interviews. Then talk about how you think these sessions would play out in a K–12 classroom. What would you need to do to ensure their success?

Interviewing is an important component of research.

ORGANIZING INFORMATION IS ESSENTIAL TO INQUIRY

Organizing information is an ongoing task facing student researchers (Hoffman, 1992). Young researchers who are seeking answers to "What do bears eat?" soon discover that information is available about the eating habits of different types of bears, at different times of the year, and at different ages and locations. Older students looking at how people measure time soon discover the great complexity with which scientists have addressed this issue. Students frequently gather and report all the information they find because they consider everything to be of equal importance ("If it's not important, then why was it written there?"). Helping students be selective is an essential inquiry unit scaffold.

Computer tools such as *Idea Fisher, Inspiration, Research Paper Writer,* and *Writer's Helper* help students selectively organize their data collection by providing basic report structures or writing frames. Such software enhances students' abilities to produce notes, categorize information, and, in some instances, cite information. Whether or not computer tools are available, students benefit from support in organizing information while conducting inquiries.

Producing Notes

Regular comprehension lessons as described in Chapter 4 and study strategy lessons as described in Chapter 7 help students select information that answers their questions. Producing notes about what one encounters in multiple sources is a logical extension of reading for specific purposes in a single source.

Note taking differs from note making. Taking notes implies that the reader mainly lifts information from a source, using phrases from the passage. Making notes might involve jotting down exact wordings, but it also includes personal examples, questions, and related information from other sources. The note maker is not only taking from the source but also adding to the information. When you make notes you are far more likely to learn the material than when you merely take notes because you are consciously connecting the new to the known. You are also monitoring more when you make notes because you need to be aware of how much you know in order to add personal examples or raise questions about the material.

A good way to introduce note taking and note making is to produce notes on overhead transparencies about a passage encountered during a unit. Think aloud your decision-making process while recording the notes you think most appropriate. After demonstrating and explaining your process several times, have students volunteer their ways of producing notes. Offer feedback, remembering that there are many avenues to good study strategies. Have students meet in small groups to produce notes jointly or to react to what each member produced individually. Again, display the notes through overhead transparencies so everyone can see the products.

Categorizing Information

As information accumulates during an inquiry, students need to categorize what they find. It is not efficient to write bits of information on separate file cards or sheets of paper and organize them at the end of a project. It is far better to establish categories and group facts into categories as the research progresses. In this way, students can see which categories are lacking information and whether new information corroborates or contradicts earlier findings. When categorizing information students might see the need for establishing new categories or revising old ones. Discovering these needs often occurs when students talk about the status of their inquiries in small groups. Three ways to record categories involve question cards, data charts, and webs.

Question Cards   A simple technique for maintaining category identities is to use question cards. Students list questions to be answered on note cards or on paper, one question per card or sheet. Whenever pertinent information is located, students write notes underneath the question. Later on, students group the information on each card or sheet according to its various aspects. This grouping becomes the form for answering that particular question. Figure 8.1 is an example of a student's question card for a study of Connecticut, and Figure 8.2 shows how the information about that state was organized into categories.

Data Charts   G. McKenzie (1979) describes data charts as a tool to help students categorize information. He suggests making a grid on paper, with the research questions listed across the top and the resources to be used listed along

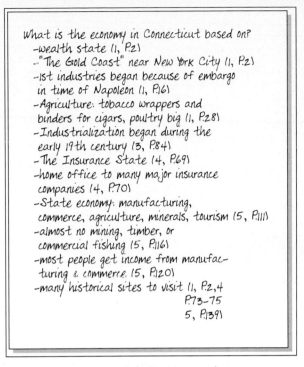

What is the economy in Connecticut based on?
  -wealth state (1, P.2)
  -"The Gold Coast" near New York City (1, P.2)
  -1st industries began because of embargo
    in time of Napoleon (1, P.16)
  -Agriculture: tobacco wrappers and
    binders for cigars, poultry big (1, P.28)
  -Industrialization began during the
    early 19th century (3, P.84)
  - The Insurance State (4, P.69)
  -home office to many major insurance
    companies (4, P.70)
  -State economy: manufacturing,
    commerce, agriculture, minerals, tourism (5, P.111)
  -almost no mining, timber, or
    commercial fishing (5, P.116)
  -most people get income from manufac-
    turing & commerce (5, P.120)
  -many historical sites to visit (1, P.2,4
                                    P.73-75
                                    5, P.139)

Figure 8.1   Unorganized Question Card

the side. Each box of the grid then contains the source's information related to the question. Sparsely worded notes are used in order to conserve space and encourage students to use their own words when writing the report. If a particular source provides no information about one of the questions, an *X* is placed in that square. Figure 8.3 shows a data chart for investigating the career of Ernest Hemingway.

When introducing data charts, we have found that it is helpful to have a large sheet of paper posted in the room or to use a transparency on an overhead projector. Show students how to record information in the proper location of the chart. Students should also be sent out to locate other sources to add to the left column.

Another type of data chart lists questions across the top of a chart and aspects of the questions down the side. For example, if the topic is wild animals, the questions across the top might be "What does the animal eat?" "Where does the animal live?" and "What dangers does the animal face?" Down the side, rather than listing sources, several different wild animals such as tiger, leopard, and lion are listed. Figure 8.4 is an example of this type of data chart.

Data charts are useful for arranging information, and they help students evaluate what they have gathered. For example, students might be directed to

What is the economy in Connecticut based on?
    General Background
        –State economy: manufacturing, commerce
            agriculture, minerals, tourism (5, P.111)
–most people get income from manufacturing &
commerce (5, P.120)
–wealthy state (1, P.12)
Historical Background
–Industrialization begun during the early
19th century (3, P.84)
–1st industries begun because of embargo
in time of Napoleon (1, P.16)
Commerce
    –"The Gold Coast" near New York City (1, P.2)
    –The Insurance State)4, P.69)
    –home office to many major insurance
        companies (4, P.70)
Tourism
    –many historical sites to visit (1, P.2,4 P73-
                            75, 5, P. 139)

Agriculture
    –Agriculture: tobacco wrappers and
        binders for cigars; poultry big
                            (1, P.28)

Figure 8.2   Organized Question Card

the wild animals chart and asked to decide which animal ate the widest variety of food, lived in the most unusual habitat, or faced the greatest dangers.

Webs   As noted in Chapter 4, webs are flexible outlines that graphically depict the relationships of the parts to the whole and to one another. Figure 8.5 is a web of the history of Connecticut produced by a middle-school student. In the middle of a web is the topic being researched, and radiating out from the center are the subtopics stated either as questions or as words and phrases. Pieces of information about the subtopics are listed around the subtopics, though not necessarily in any specific order.

A web is a good way to depict information that students produce during sessions of What You Know and What You Don't Know, and that students eventually gather. When you introduce webs to students, use the organizing center of the unit being pursued and list questions around it. Next, have students tell what they know or think they know about the topic and list that information next to the questions. Students then find more information from their sources, return to the web, and revise it in light of the new information. The initial web is a good way to introduce a unit, and the final web is a good basis for a unit culmination.

Sources	What was his life like?	What themes did he pursue?	What was his influence?
Smith & Jones			
Brown			
Linn			

Figure 8.3 Data Chart for Ernest Hemingway Report

Animals	What does the animal eat?	Where does the animal live?	What dangers does the animal face?
Tiger			
Leopard			
Lion			

Figure 8.4 Data Chart for Wild Animals Report

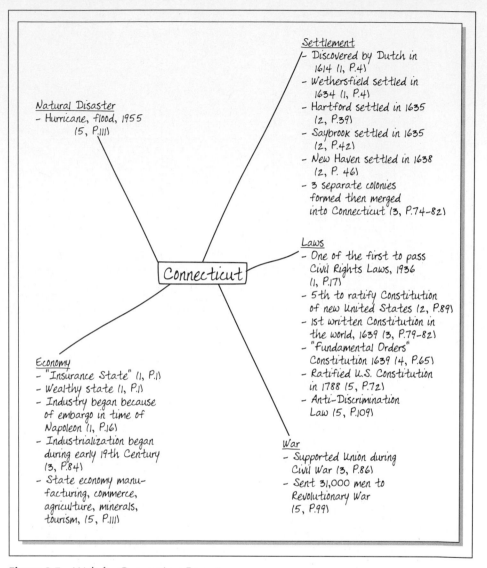

Figure 8.5 Web for Connecticut Report

Citing Information

An important point to convey to students is the need to record their sources accurately. Accurate records are necessary both for others to check the information and for the students themselves to return to, if necessary. The simplest way to record sources is to make a numbered list of all sources by title and date, including all visual, oral, and written sources. As shown in Figure 8.5, when students find something they want to use they can jot down the informa-

Webs provide a basis for writing well-organized reports.

tion, placing the appropriate identification number after the information, and including a page number if using a written source.

Maintaining the Focus of Research

A word of caution: Students who are seeking information frequently lose their focus. They often become so involved with tangential information that they are led far astray of their original question. One way to help students remain focused is to have them meet in groups regularly during the week to talk about how their projects are progressing. These conversations help students crystallize their learning and their next steps. Additionally, students often carry a folder with their question written on the front so that they can frequently refer to it. Students should be told that the only information to be put into that folder is information related to the particular question. It is a good idea, however, to give students another folder labeled "Miscellaneous" or "Other" into which they can put all of the other bits of interesting information that they accumulate. The second folder might become the basis for another inquiry.

Try It Out

This section has described a number of ways to help students organize information. Select one of the strategies you have used in the past. Think about any problems you had applying the strategy and what you might have to do to make it easier for students to use.

STUDENTS SHARE WHAT THEY LEARNED IN A VARIETY OF WAYS

The initial steps in conducting inquiries (posing engaging researchable questions, locating information, and organizing the information) differ only slightly from the planning steps for writing presented in Chapter 6. The main difference is that planning an inquiry places greater emphasis on gathering new information (i.e., getting it together). The sharing information step of the inquiry process encompasses the culminations described in Chapter 2, the report and response activities presented in Chapter 3, and the drafting and revising stages of the writing process detailed in Chapter 6. Student researchers at all levels benefit from sharing with others what has been learned. Such sharing deepens the understanding both of those who did and did not conduct the inquiry.

Student researchers generally feel compelled to share all the material that they garnered during their searches. They want credit for all the information that they worked so hard to obtain and frequently have difficulty paring down the information to that which directly answers specific questions. Such reporting results in undesirably long and convoluted pieces. Inform your students that expert researchers generally know more than they include in their reports and that students should likewise not try to include every bit of information they gather.

Reporting sometimes is done in an informal, casual manner. Students are assembled after spending time conducting their inquiries in order to share what they have learned in impromptu fashion. If the class spent time in the library investigating customs of dress, then a discussion about those customs might ensue; if students were sent home with the task of asking available adults how they came to their current occupation, then the findings can be informally shared the next day.

As we discussed in Chapter 3, students should have several options for how to react to what they read. Findings can be written up in a formal report, or they might be shared through multimedia formats that embed writing in visuals and realia, as is done in most science fair projects. Students might dramatize scenes. No matter what form is used for sharing, scoring guides that describe the criteria for self-assessment and external assessment are appropriate. The following presents three ways (written, oral, and visual) to transfer and share information according to somewhat formal sets of specifications.

Written Sharing

Students typically require support transfering information from their question cards, data charts, or webs into written report form. Question cards lend themselves most easily to long reports, as students group all the pieces of information listed under each question into even smaller categories. If you and your students do not have access to report writing technology, you might show them how to transfer each piece of information under one question onto a small strip of paper and then to arrange those strips physically into categories. Each question might include two, three, or more categories. Students might glue, staple, or tape the strips of information onto another sheet of paper with the question at the top to create a reorganized version of the original question sheet.

After this reorganization, show students how to turn each question into a topic sentence for a paragraph or section in a manner similar to that used with one-paragraph essays. For example, the question "What are the main industries in Connecticut?" might be recast into the topic sentence "Connecticut has five main industries." The bits of information beneath the question on the question card then become the supporting details for the topic sentence.

Reporting the information gathered onto a data chart can be quite straightforward. For example, the data chart in Figure 8.3 can be the basis for a traditional five-paragraph essay. The first paragraph is the introduction, which prepares people for the upcoming questions (e.g., "Three aspects of Hemingway's life seem to have been very important"). It may also tell why the topic is important (e.g., "Ernest Hemingway was one of the most influential and well-known American authors of the twentieth century"). The second through fourth paragraphs address the three questions, turned into topic sentences, along the top of the data chart (e.g., "Hemingway had a vigorous lifestyle," "Hemingway focused on five primary themes in his writing," and "Hemingway influenced a generation of writers"). The fifth paragraph is a summary of important findings. A data chart works especially well for short reports.

Turning a web into a written report follows a similar pattern. Show students how to arrange the details for each subtopic according to the desired order of presentation. Subtopic headings become topic sentences, and the bits of information become the supporting details. Be prepared to demonstrate this method of organization more than once, providing sufficient guidance when students practice it.

Once information has been organized, students draft and revise their written reports following the guidelines presented in Chapter 6. Reports can be improved by having students go through the revising step of the writing process. Peer response groups work especially well; since each student has been trying to write a similar type of paper, he or she brings to the group the same knowledge of the paper's form.

At the beginning of the year in elementary school, where teachers have inexperienced students, a structured approach to sharing reports is frequently useful. For a unit on domestic animals, for example, the class would generate a series of basic questions. Questions might include these: "How does this animal help us?" "Where does it live?" "What does it eat?" and "What does it look like?" Each child selects a different domestic animal from a group students have previously called up and writes a web about the animal. When it is time to produce the written report, the children decide how many paragraphs each report should have, as well as the order of each paragraph. They might also talk about what the introductory and concluding paragraphs should include. Each student then goes off to write a short report on his or her domestic animal, using illustrations if possible. These individual reports are revised through writing conferences with the teacher and peer editing groups, and the revised reports are bound into a classroom book on domestic animals.

Students frequently prepare constructions or artistic presentations for a report, such as scale models of the Parthenon, the Globe Theater, or the solar system. Consider leaving the objects on display around the room for a few weeks, letting written explanations serve as the means of sharing.

In secondary school, be sure to balance the reports that are due in each class. If you teach two class sections of the same course, require a batch of reports to be done at staggered times during the semester, rather than assigning everything for the final week of the term. Maintaining such a balance allows you to spend more time helping students prepare their reports and gives you more time to react thoughtfully to the final products.

Oral Sharing

Transferring information for oral reports is slightly different from the procedures for written reports. Students giving oral reports must rely on note cards or some other type of reminder to help keep the order of presentation straight. Key words and apt phrases should be recorded so that students can glance at them to maintain their flow of speech. For instance, a student reporting on Connecticut might have made the following list: "Industries . . . manufacturing . . . defense products . . . ship building at Groton . . . transportation equipment . . . electrical machinery." Such telegraphic writing clearly differs from the form of a written report.

A good aid for students giving oral reports is to support their talks with visuals and realia. Props allow speakers to maintain focus by discussing the aspects illustrated by each prop. Oral reports allow immediate questioning, prompting researchers to give additional information about what they have learned. Thus, teachers should allow time for questions after an oral report.

One possibility to save class time during oral reports is for only some students actually to report to the whole class. The others can tape-record their presentations and place them with explanatory material in the classroom or school library for others to hear on their own time. One advantage of this technique is that no matter how well done the reports are, listening to 30 oral reports in a few days is bound to be boring, whereas listening to ten over several days can still be interesting.

Another time-saving device is putting students into teams to prepare a panel presentation. Each panel member could be responsible for researching an aspect of the topic. Some teachers station students with reports to give at separate locations throughout the classroom, and then have various groups of listeners rotate among the presenters. This strategy forces the presenters to repeat themselves, but repetition can be beneficial and the class routine has been varied a bit.

Visual Displays

Chapter 3 enumerates a wide range of book projects: visuals, concrete objects, models, and dramatizations. Students enjoy creating illustrations, time lines, murals, maps, collages, homemade transparencies, and models. They enjoy, too, being able to collect objects and arrange them for others. These can all be used as the basis for visual displays to share information learned. To help these projects meet the communication expectations teachers have for research reports, you could follow some of the guidelines given for science fair projects.

Projects need to be highly visual, self-descriptive, focused, and succinct. Communicating this to students means explaining that the display ought to be appealing, eye-catching, neat, and interesting. The question being investigated and shared ought to be clear to anyone looking at the display. The entire project ought to be contained within a relatively small space (since no classroom is ever large enough). The research topic being shared should be an interesting one to investigate and of a scope that is neither too large nor too picayune for the students' research capabilities.

Visual displays could be incorporated as part of an oral or a written sharing, too. For evaluation purposes, students should decide, however, which of the three types of sharing is carrying the bulk of the information. Visual displays should have a minimum of oral or written information.

Listen/Look and Learn

Briefly describe to a teacher each of the three ways to share information: written reports, oral reports, and visual displays. Ask the teacher which ones he or she has used and why. Ask the teacher to describe strengths and limitations of each of the sharing formats used. Would the teacher try any of the others you have described? Which one(s) and why?

STUDENTS BECOME INDEPENDENT WHEN TEACHERS GRADUALLY FADE THEIR SUPPORT AND HAND OVER RESPONSIBILITY TO STUDENTS

Students become independent when they receive support accomplishing meaningful tasks and then the support fades away as students become proficient. This process applies to inquiry, also. When students are engaged in inquiry, teachers help them identify questions, locate information, organize information, and report information. Students as a whole class can observe how to accomplish certain strategies, then they can perform the strategies in small groups and individually as teachers gradually release their guidance. Such fading occurs throughout the school year.

In the elementary grades, teachers might walk the whole class through an inquiry unit. Teachers show students how to investigate and report a subject, with the teacher and students jointly producing a finished product. Later in the year, when a different unit is studied, teachers can remind students of the processes they used before. For the second unit to be researched, students might work in small groups rather than with the whole class. As students develop research skills, they are able to carry out the research task more and more independently. At the secondary level, teachers refine students' research skills. If students are already adept at locating information through an index, teachers might show them how to use an Internet search engine. Practically all upper-grade students benefit from attention to their note making skills. Secondary teachers also remind students of the skills they learned in earlier grades.

Most students who copy reports from another source do so out of ignorance and desperation. They are unaware of any other system for generating a written report. Several techniques can help prevent copying in your classroom. Taking students through the steps described in this chapter will model the research process for them. You might want to require checkpoints to monitor progress. These checks should not be presented as punitive; rather, make it clear that all students need feedback about how successfully they are dealing with the various stages of a report. Thus, if a student is organizing information on a data chart, check whether key words are being used, whether a variety of sources has been located, and whether sources are being identified with page numbers. This checking can be done by the inquiring student, by peers, by parents or paraprofessionals, and by teachers. Such checking, by the way, helps prevent student procrastination.

Making all initial reports oral or visual, with students not permitted to read reports but only to use notes, stresses original work. Most students are unable to memorize a long selection from the encyclopedia, so they use their own words. When you enhance their ability to speak from notes, you raise their confidence in their ability to write their own reports and present themselves to others.

Many capable students have been rewarded through the years for plagiarism by receiving good grades from teachers. As long as more emphasis is placed on the product of the research, rather than on learning the process well, copying will continue to be a problem. Typically, we can assume that a good grasp of the process will result in a good product. However, we have all known students who were very good at finding information, but whose verbal skills prevented them from sharing it in a clear manner. By the same token, many good students admit to moving effortlessly through school, doing little work, but presenting their material so well that they get good grades.

In your classroom, you might monitor students at each step of the research process. Thus, students produce questions, locate sources, and produce and organize ideas before drafting and revising a report. Remember that the main concern is teaching the process of finding and sharing information on a topic; the final product, the report, reflects students' proficiencies with the process.

Assessing student reports is never easy. Figure 8.6 contains a scoring guide for middle-school written reports on Traditions, a social studies unit on long-

---

REPORT ON TRADITIONS
SCORING CRITERIA

Student:

Content					
At least three traditions are described fully.	10	8	6	4	2
Unfamiliar traditions are compared with familiar ones.	10	8	6	4	2
Contexts of the traditions are complete.	10	8	6	4	2
Values of the traditions are complete.	10	8	6	4	2
Mechanics					
Organization There are a clear beginning, middle, and end. Major and minor points are distinguishable.	10	8	6	4	2
Creativity Vivid language is used in imaginative, effective ways. The paper grabs the reader's attention.	10	8	6	4	2
Sentence structure Sentences are consistently well formed. Run-on sentences and sentence fragments do not appear.	5	4	3	2	1
Punctuation, spelling, and capitalization All ending punctuation is correct. Internal punctuation (especially commas) is appropriate. All words are spelled correctly. Appropriate words are capitalized.	5	4	3	2	1
Neatness Writing is legible. Margins are appropriate. Paper is clean. Any illustrations are clear.	5	4	3	2	1
Location of Information					
Sufficient number	10	8	6	4	2
Varied	5	4	3	2	1
Credible	5	4	3	2	1
Focus on the topic	5	4	3	2	1

Figure 8.6 Research Report Scoring Criteria

standing customs and practices related to events such as holidays, meals, and courtship. The guide contains three sections—content, mechanics, and location of information; some items are worth a maximum of ten points and some a maximum of five. Giving students a copy of the guide allows them to see how you weigh the different criteria, and it offers explicit guidelines for self-assessment and self-reflection. Learners can assess their own work when they know the criteria for assessment. Allow room on the list for comments for each evaluation area. Be specific with your comments. If you write nothing or only innocuous comments, such as "good job," evaluations are largely ignored, whereas more specific comments receive attention.

Distribute inquiry guides such as in Figure 8.6 when your students begin their reports. This practice promotes concentration on desired outcomes, even though the outcomes can be stated in general terms (e.g., "Describe the traditions fully"). Students typically appreciate knowing their teachers' expectations and knowing that the expectations leave room for student decision making. Furthermore, producing such guides beforehand takes time during the planning stage of instruction, but it saves time when helping students with their projects and when evaluating final products. The number and type of scoring criteria, their values, and the format of the guide depends on your expectations and your students' sophistication.

Looking Back

Learning the research process is more important than producing a polished report; otherwise, teachers could be satisfied with students who submitted reports purchased from commercial services. Therefore, help your students develop the excitement and eagerness to answer questions that will carry them through the more mundane aspects of this process; in this way research becomes something they look forward to rather than dread. We have described six key ideas in this chapter to help you better teach the research process: (1) Inquiry is a special feature of integrated units of instruction; (2) asking engaging researchable questions is essential to inquiry; (3) locating sources and information within sources is essential to inquiry; (4) organizing information is essential to inquiry; (5) students share what they learned in a variety of ways; and (6) students become independent when teachers gradually fade their support and hand over responsibility to students.

Add to Your Journal

When involved in inquiry projects, were you introduced to strategies similar to the ones presented here? Compare the way you generated research questions in elementary and secondary school with the procedures described here. Do you consider yourself an independent researcher? Why? What can you apply from your own background to your future classroom? What kinds of research experiences will you give your students? Why? How often will your students be engaged in research activities? Why?

REFERENCES

AMERICAN LIBRARY ASSOCIATION PRESIDENTIAL COMMISSION ON INFORMATION LITERACY (1989). *Final Report.* Chicago: American Library Association.

BOOMER, G., LESTER, N., ONORE, C., & COOK, J. (Eds.) (1992). *Negotiating the curriculum: Educating for the 21st century.* London: Falmer.

BROOKS, J., & BROOKS, M. (1993). *The case for constructivist classrooms.* Alexandria, VA: Association for Curriculum and Supervision Development.

CALIFORNIA MEDIA AND LIBRARY EDUCATORS ASSOCIATION (1994). *From library skills to information literacy: A handbook for the 21st century.* Castle Rock, CO: Hi Willow Research and Publishing.

CARR, E., & OGLE, D. (1987). KWL Plus: A strategy for comprehension and summarization. *Journal of Reading, 30,* 626–631.

DREHER, M. J. (1995). *Sixth grade researchers: Posing questions, finding information, and writing a report* (Research Report No. 40). Athens, GA: National Reading Research Center, Universities of Georgia and Maryland College Park.

GETZELS, J. W., & CSIKSZENTMIHALYI, M. (1975). From problem solving to problem finding. In I. A. Taylor & J. W. Getzels (Eds.), *Perspectives in creativity.* Chicago: Aldine.

GRAVES, D. (1989). *Investigate nonfiction.* Portsmouth, NH: Heinemann.

HARSTE, J. C. (1994). Literacy as curricular conversations about knowledge, inquiry, and morality. In R. B. Ruddell, M. R. Ruddell, & H. Singer (Eds.), *Theoretical models and processes of reading* (4th ed.) (pp. 1220–1242). Newark, DE: International Reading Association.

HILLOCKS, G. (1986). *Research on written composition: New directions for teaching.* Urbana, IL: Educational Resources Information Clearinghouse and National Council for Research in English.

HOFFMAN, J. V. (1992). Critical reading/thinking across the curriculum: Using I-charts to support learning. *Language Arts, 62,* 121–127.

JOYCE, B., & WEIL, M. (1996). *Models of teaching* (5th ed.). Boston: Allyn and Bacon.

LAWSON, A. E., ABRAHAM, M. R., & RENNER, J. W. (1989). *A theory of instruction: Using the learning cycle to teach science concepts and thinking skills.* Monographs of the National Association for Research in Science Teaching (No. 1). Cinncinnati, OH: National Association for Research in Science Teaching.

MCKENZIE, G. (1979). Data charts: A crutch for helping students organize reports. *Language Arts, 56,* 784–788.

MACRORIE, K. (1988). *The I-search paper.* Portsmouth, NH: Boynton/Cook.

MARTINELLO, M. L., & COOK, G. (1994). *Interdisciplinary inquiry in teaching and learning.* New York: Merrill.

ROSER, N. L., STRECKER, S. K., & WARD, T. J. (1996). "What I wanna know is why Sam Houston's mom named him after a city": Moving (slowly) toward inquiry in fourth grade. In D. J. Leu, C. K. Kinzer, & K. A. Hinchman (Eds.), *Literacies for the 21st century: Research and practice.* Forty-fifth Yearbook of the National Reading Conference (pp. 134–145). Chicago: National Reading Conference.

SHORT, K., HARSTE, J., & BURKE, C. (1996). *Creating classrooms for authors and inquirers* (2nd ed.). Porstmouth, NH: Heinemann.

SPIVEY, N. N., & KING, J. (1989). Readers as writers composing from sources. *Reading Research Quarterly, 24,* 7–26.

STAHL, S. A., HYND, C. R., BRITTON, B. R., McNISH, M. M., & BOSQUET, D. (1996). What happens when students read multiple source documents in history? *Reading Research Quarterly, 31,* 430–456.

WIGGINS, G. (1987). Creating a thought-provoking curriculum: Lessons from whodunits and others. *American Educator, 11*(4), 10–18.

Computer Software

IDEA FISHER. IDEAFISHER SYSTEMS, INC., 2222 MARTIN #110, IRVINE, CA 92715.

INSPIRATION. INSPIRATION SOFTWARE, 2920 S. W. DOLPH CT., PORTLAND, OR 92719.

RESEARCH PAPER WRITER. TOM SNYDER PRODUCTIONS, 90 COOLIDGE HILL RD., WATERTOWN, MA 02172.

WRITER'S HELPER. CONDUIT, UNIVERSITY OF IOWA, 100 OAKDALE CAMPUS M306OH, IOWA CITY, IA 52242.

ADDITIONAL READINGS

The following sources provide especially useful information about helping students inquire into their worlds; the first set addresses elementary students, but many of the techniques apply to secondary students as well:

BEACH, J. D. (1983). Teaching students to write informational reports. *The Elementary School Journal, 84,* 213–220.

COPENHAVER, J. (1993). Instances of inquiry. *Primary Voices, 1,* 6–12.

CUDD, E. T. (1989). Research and report writing in the elementary grades. *The Reading Teacher, 43,* 268–269.

CUDD, E. T., & ROBERTS, L. (1989). Using writing to enhance content area learning in the primary grades. *The Reading Teacher, 42,* 392–404.

HENNINGS, D. G. (1982). A writing approach to reading comprehension: Schema theory in action. *Language Arts, 59,* 8–17.

MONSON, R. J., & MONSON, M. P. (Eds.) (1994). Literacy in the content areas: New definitions and decisions for the 21st centruy [Special issue]. *The Reading Teacher, 47*(7).

The information in the following sources focuses on secondary students, but many of the techniques also apply to elementary students:

LARSON, R., HECKER, B., & NOREM, J. (1985). Student experience with research projects: Pains, enjoyment and success. *High School Journal, 69,* 61–69.

SCHUMM, J. S., & RADENICH, M. C. (1984). Readers'/writers' workshop: An antidote for term paper terror. *Journal of Reading, 28,* 13–19.

These sources accentuate student-centered personal approaches to inquiry with various age groups:

MACRORIE, K. (1988). *The I-search paper.* Portsmouth, NH: Boynton/Cook.

MANNING, M., MANNING, G., & LONG, R. (1994). *Theme immersion: Inquiry-based curriculum in elementary and middle schools.* Portsmouth, NH: Heinemann.

The role of collaborative learning during inquiry is described in these two articles:

DAVEY, B. (1987). Team for success: Guided practice in study skills through cooperative research reports. *Journal of Reading, 30,* 701–705.

WYATT, F. (1988). Rethinking the research project through cooperative learning. *Middle School Journal, 20*(1), 6–7.

The following describes inquiry projects in various subjects:

English

KASZYCA, M., & KRUEGER, A. M. (1994). Collaborative voices: Reflections on the I-search project. *English Journal, 83*(1), 62–65.

PERRIN, R. (1987). Myths about research. *English Journal, 76*(7), 50–53.

WILLIAMS, C. (1993). Social action begins at school: The research paper revisited. *English Journal, 83*(3), 44–49.

Mathematics

KINNEAVY, K. (1996). The pond: Doing research together. *Mathematics Teaching in the Middle School, 1*(9), 696–702.

Science

ARMSTRONG, K., & WEBER, K. (1991). Genetic engineering: A lesson on bioethics for the classroom. *The American Biology Teacher, 53*(5), 294–297.

BREGER, D. C. (1995). The inquiry paper. *Science Scope, 19*(2), 27–32.

SHORT, K. G., & ARMSTRONG, J. (1993). Moving toward inquiry: Integrating literature into science curriculum. *The New Advocate, 6,* 183–199.

TRISLER, C. E. (1996). Whose water is it? *Science Activities, 32*(4), 16–21.

Social Studies

Brown, C. S. (1988). *Like it was: A complete guide to writing oral history.* New York: Teachers and Writers Collaborative.

Dimmitt, J. P., & Van Cleaf, D. W. (1992). Integrating writing and social studies: Alternatives to the formal research paper. *Social Education, 56,* 382–384.

Reissman, R. (1995). In search of ordinary heroes. *Educational Leadership, 52*(8), 28–31.

Weinberg, S. K. (1996). Unforgettable memories: Oral history in the middle school classroom. *Voices from the Middle, 3,* 18–24.

Looking back at suggestions for inquiry-based instruction provides perspective on current recommendations. Three substantial writings from the early 1900s on this topic are as follows:

Good, C. V. (1927). *The supplementary reading assignment.* Baltimore, MD: Warwick & York.

Kilpatrick, W. H. (1919). *The project method.* New York: Teachers College Press.

Whipple, G. M. (Ed.). (1920). *New materials of instruction* (Nineteenth Yearbook of the National Society for the Study of Education, Part I). Bloomington, IL: Public School Pub. Co.

PART

II

. . . In the Content Areas: K–12

*P*art II of this book illustrates how the principles and methods of instruction described in Part I can actually be implemented in the classroom. The information is presented in the form of a chronological narrative through fictional teachers' journals. This part of the book demonstrates how teachers might integrate the many aspects of reading and writing in the content areas throughout an entire school year. Part I compartmentalized information according to topics, but life in classrooms is not so orderly. Teachers must balance instruction in comprehension, vocabulary, literature, writing, study skills, and research within each day and across 180 days of school. Part II provides perspective on how teachers make this balance work.

In the next chapters you will meet four fictional teachers. Belle Lance teaches primary grade students. She is entrusted with the crucial task of getting youngsters off to a good start. Belle's students have only rudimentary content reading and writing skills, and she must launch them on the way to independence. Along the way, she must develop students' understanding of such subject matter as transportation, measurement of time, the five senses, and human wants versus needs. Connie Tent is a fifth-grade teacher. Her students are more sophisticated than Belle's, but they still have much to learn. Connie directs her students to information in the content areas and likewise furthers the development of her students' independence. Hugh Mann teaches the humanities in middle school; he is assigned three sections of American history and two sections of eighth-grade English. Hugh is a second-year teacher who takes a little longer than Belle or Connie to teach as well as he would like. Do not be alarmed by how traditional and uninspired he is at the beginning of the year. We think it is important to show that a relatively inexperienced and conservative teacher can make real progress toward more balanced and effective content instruction. Finally, Annie Mull teaches high-school biology and consumer math. She must both deliver information and teach students to acquire information independently. In addition, she balances a process approach with a textbook approach to biology and must teach students to solve word problems in math.

You may want to read only one of the fictional accounts that follow if you are primarily interested in only one grade level. However, reading all the chapters will provide you with insight into how teachers develop students' thinking processes and literacy skills across the grades. Knowing what students have encountered earlier in school and what they will encounter in the future provides perspective on their present needs. Furthermore, instructional strategies for one grade level frequently are applicable at other grade levels.

As you read what follows, we hope you will learn how teachers engage students in meaningful instruction. We hope you will see how instruction builds and changes in one grade level and across grade levels. Perhaps most important, we hope you will evaluate the information presented here and apply what seems most sensible when you teach in your own classroom.

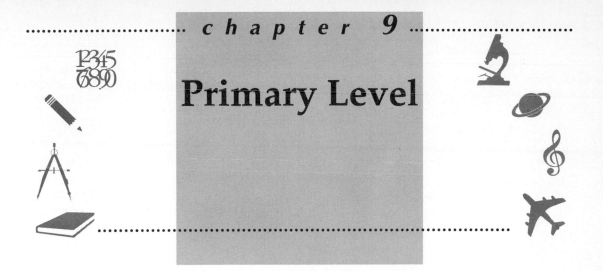

chapter 9

Primary Level

AUGUST

Every August I experience the same excitement that I did 33 years ago, when I first began school at age 5. Paul, my husband, laughs at me, saying, "Belle, you're as bad as the kids about wanting to get back to school!" I guess I am, but that is a much nicer feeling than the reluctance I see from some other teachers in our school district. I have heard about "teacher burnout," but my own theory is that burnout generally occurs when you are frustrated with your job and no longer feel you are accomplishing anything. Fortunately, I do feel successful, and I am grateful that I can work at something I truly love! Nevertheless, when I come back to school each August to ready my room for September, I have a mixture of feelings: apprehension about who I will be "living with" for the next nine months and excitement about teaching yet another group of youngsters to read and write easily, successfully, and joyfully. These feelings are complicated this year by a new classroom structure. Because our district has had a population surge, some of us have been asked to have combination-grade classes. I will "loop up" with half of last year's first-graders' to second grade; the other half of my class will be incoming first-graders.

And added to all that, I am even more charged up than usual since I just completed my master's degree a couple of weeks ago! I signed up to be one of our school's representatives for the school district's writing project, too. My thesis addressed the effects of using content area subjects to help improve children's reading skills. As a result of my findings, I am convinced that I need to integrate more reading and writing with the content of social studies, math, and science in my classroom. I will work with the district committee to get more of that information out to all teachers.

I've been sitting here for the past week, trying out one schedule after another, and it's not as easy as I had anticipated. I think I need to start this year as usual, with set times for science, math, and social studies instruction every day, using textbooks as part of the reading material. I may come up with another plan for later in the year. I have sat here for a week surrounded by pieces of paper with lists of important elements to include in my classroom this year, and the problem has been trying to come up with a workable plan that will include them all in the limited time I find myself with, especially with both first- and second-grade curriculum to deal with. Fortunately, with our spiral curriculum, the same topics are taught each primary-grade year, just with more depth.

Thinking Processes

First of all, there are nine thinking processes that I must systematically and frequently include in my lessons: call up, predict, organize, connect, image, monitor, generalize, evaluate, and apply. By incorporating each of the nine thinking processes on a regular basis, I will be teaching the content areas and developing skills that students can use in life as well as school.

Independence

Most importantly, I am going to emphasize student independence in learning. It really frosts my cookies to have someone I meet for the first time comment that they couldn't tolerate my profession because they wouldn't want to wipe noses and tie shoes all day. What an idea people must have of primary-grade students! Admittedly, these students cannot do what fifth-graders can, but we teachers can, and must, expect that they be responsible for their learning to an ever-increasing degree. In fact, teachers who do not foster independence in learning are condemning their students to a "learning welfare" system that children will find hard to break out of later on. My battle cry for the year will be, "Get those kids off welfare!" As I think about it, having half the class as second-graders should make that goal easier. They'll be able to model a lot for the first-graders.

But, I ask myself, how can I meet these glorious goals of mine this year? I suppose the answer will unfold as the year progresses. What follows is my daily schedule, but I reserve the right to alter it should I find it necessary or appealing to do so!

Schedule

8:15–8:45	Attendance, news sharing, plan the day
8:45–10:00	Reading meetings
	Learning centers
	Writing projects
10:00–10:15	Morning recess
10:15–10:30	Read to class or do storytelling
10:30–11:15	Math groups
	Learning centers
	Writing projects

11:15–11:45	Lunch
11:45–12:00	Read to students
12:00–12:30	Science lessons—Monday, Wednesday
	Social studies lessons—Tuesday, Thursday
	Writing projects and conferences—Friday
12:30–1:00	Art—Monday
	P.E.—Tuesday, Thursday
	Writing projects and conferences—Wednesday
	Music—Friday
1:00–1:30	Language arts focus lessons
	SSR
1:30–2:15	Learning centers
	Independent work time
2:15–2:40	Read to/Write to lesson
	Review the day
	Prepare to leave
2:45	Dismissal

Learning Centers

I have designed many independent learning activities for the learning centers, where I will use tapes, picture directions, and color codes to help students who are not yet fluent readers. Students can turn on the tape recorder where I have recorded directions for certain activities, which frees me from having to explain everything in person. I also make use of rebus pictures, using pictures of scissors where they are to cut, and so forth. Each center is color-coded so that students can tell where to go for the different assignments given in their daily work folder. The math, science, and social studies centers contain materials that will help students learn more about the units of study we'll do this year. The eight centers I have placed around the perimeter of the room are a library corner, a language arts center, a math center, a tape and TV center, a computer center, an art center, a social studies center, and a science center. Occasionally I will create an extra center, such as one with cooking utensils for when we have classroom cooking.

In the morning, students will rotate among teacher-directed group work, learning centers, writing activities, and practice activities. In the afternoon, since I won't have reading or math groups then, I can circulate among those in the centers and those doing seatwork in order to do some over-the-shoulder teaching as children need questions answered. Each child's practice activities will include assignments to let everyone practice the skills already taught in reading group, as well as the concepts introduced in science and social studies units.

Reading Materials

Additionally, I plan to read to the children at least once every day, and I will give them a daily opportunity to read materials of their own choice. The reading and listening materials will be drawn from the finest of children's story books as well as from informational books. Such models of clear and interesting writing will demonstrate to my students how to organize their own writing. Storytelling and oral reports are two other regular features that I will use frequently to model oral composition techniques. By beginning the day with sharing of current events topics, they can develop better skills in content area reporting. In addition, they have a reason to pay attention to what is happening in the world around them.

I'm so pleased I got the tables that I asked for, rather than individual desks. All of my students' work materials will be kept in individual, brightly colored cardboard boxes stored around the edge of the room, but the tables will allow a lot more flexibility in grouping students for different activities. Tables encourage them to talk with one another and let's them cooperate easily on tasks.

This journal will focus on how I plan to incorporate reading and writing in the content areas. It certainly cannot represent everything that goes on each day in a classroom. Well, only a couple of more items to put up on the bulletin board in the back of the room and then I can call it quits until the children arrive. Oh! I am getting so excited!

SEPTEMBER

And so September is over. Getting the children used to the routines took up an enormous amount of time; schooling is not innately understood. A good part of the month was spent just in helping them learn the appropriate behaviors to use in learning centers and at their seats. We have only one rule in our classroom: Respect yourself and others. We spent a lot of time talking about what that looks like in and out of the classroom. What are the behaviors associated with respecting yourself? respecting others? It ties very well into the social studies unit for the month as well.

Integrated
Unit

Our first social studies unit was entitled "Me and My World." The primary grades, K–3, all have this same unit, but the concepts for each vary dependent upon the grade level. I will have the three concepts for first posted along with the five for second. I will plan some joint projects, but they will also have individual projects to do dependent on grade level. I will have to model a lot of projects. Before going into the specifics of the unit, however, I want to record some of what I learned about them during the unit as well as from their school records.

Every year I think I have gotten the most unusual group ever, and this year is no exception. (Can this condition continue forever?) I have two sets of twins. Michael and Michelle are both supportive and independent, rather unusual for twins. I had them last year, so they should have no difficulty being in the same classroom. But I fear that Steven and Stephanie are another story: Stephanie functions at a much lower level than Steven does, and he constantly picks on her for missing questions, turning in sloppy or late work, and not reading as well as he does. I suggested to their parents that they need to be separated, for both their sakes, and the parents would not hear of it! They think that Stephanie needs Steven to challenge her. None of my arguments could convince them otherwise, though they did agree to help try to tone down Steven. Other students who will be a challenge are Kazu and Mariane. Kazu has just come to the United States from Japan and speaks no English. Mariane is somewhat better off since her family came to this country from Brazil last year, though at home they spoke mainly Portuguese until she started first grade. I speak some Spanish, and since Portuguese and Spanish are very similar, we manage to communicate. For Kazu, however, I checked a Japanese dictionary out of the public library. I've also met with his parents, who speak some English, to learn from them some common phrases I will need such as, "Do you understand?" "How do you say _____ in Japanese?" and courtesy phrases such as "Please" and "Thank you." Carlos is another student who is not proficient in using English, though he understands much of what is said to him.

Dave and Jim, neighbors and friends from birth, are two students who did not have an easy first-grade year. They seem not too interested in school except for P.E., recess, and lunch. They have enlisted a couple of first-graders, Ray and Ken, in their escapades. At the other extreme are those who came to first- and second-grade reading already or reading very well. David, Pat, Sharon, Bjorn, and Brianna seem to enjoy everything we do, probably because they understand what is going on and why. Good classroom instruction should challenge all students to higher levels of functioning and thinking. That is certainly my goal. My other eight students seem "average" and are moving along well. It's not easy trying to plan lessons for so many levels of students. Even the "average" ones are so diverse that they certainly cannot all be treated alike.

Integrated
Unit

The "Me and My World" unit took all of September since we worked on it only on Tuesdays and Thursdays. The primary grades' unit builds from the individual to families to neighborhoods to the community at large to our state, nation, and world. The focus in our unit is on the uniqueness of each person as well as the many things all of us have in common. Children learned about these two ideas in myriad ways. Many literature books, both old favorites and newer ones, address both concepts. For the whole month we have been reading

Trade books

books like *There's a Nightmare in My Closet; Leo the Late Bloomer; Frog and Toad Together; It's Me, Hippo!; Frederick; I Have a Sister—My Sister Is Deaf;* and *The Triplets.* In addition, I brought in such concept books as *A Snake Is Totally Tail; Is It Hard? Is It Easy?; Sugaring Time; Handtalk: An ABC of Finger Spelling and Sign Language;* and *People.* I used those books both for this unit and for our first science unit on the five senses and the human body—a nice compatible set of units to work on simultaneously. These books point out the similarities among people as well as provide information about those who, due to certain handicaps, must deal with life differently. The children had all expressed curiosity about Sharon's thick glasses, asking how she could see through them since they were unable to. Jakeitha's wheelchair also was a subject of study as students learned how many things she could do as well as they could without the use of her legs.

Thinking
Processes

The "Me and My World" unit was introduced by talking about alike and different. To start things off, students were asked to call up the names of types of transportation. Though the content seemed way off the topic, I wanted to use items that could be easily classified by children in a variety of ways. The

Meaning
Vocabulary

various types—boats, cars, trucks, trains, planes, and so on—were listed on a chart. We talked about how all of the things on the chart were alike, with me listing, as students dictated, how the things were alike. Then students were assigned to groups and told to look for pictures or models of the different forms of transportation listed or of new ones that they discovered. In this scavenger hunt activity, I planned the groups so that each consisted both of very capable students and of those who needed more guidance. Students were able to use independent seatwork time for this activity on both Tuesday and Wednesday, as well as checking at home for pictures and models on Tuesday and Wednesday nights.

Groups

On Thursday, each group brought its pictures and models to school. I used the big bulletin board on the side of the classroom to pin up all the transportation pictures, with the models on a table underneath. I had cut apart all the names of the types of transportation from the chart, and we placed them by the appropriate pictures or models. Then I asked if they could organize or regroup them in any other way. Total silence met this question. But I waited it out. After ten seconds, Pat asked, "Do you mean by how many wheels they have?" We had quite a discussion about wheels and had to turn to several reference sources to settle the debates that arose. I find this a good way to model using references to answer questions that we have. That broke the dam, and the students realized that there were many possible ways to group the transportation pictures they had found. Next they grouped all the red pictures and models together, all the green ones, and so on, regardless of the number of wheels. Then they grouped all the forms of transportation by how many people they could carry—one, a few, or many. A fourth grouping consisted of sorting types by where they traveled—air, land, or water.

So that they would apply their new understanding of grouping to our unit of study, I gave a list of each person's name in our class, including mine, to each group and asked them to think of at least two ways of organizing that could show how people are alike and at least two ways to show how they are different. On the following Tuesday they sorted us all into diverse groups by gender, hair color, and so on. They also put Jakeitha, Sharon, Michael, Michelle, and me into a group they labeled "black people." This activity helped them to organize their world, one of the essential thinking processes.

Writing

Along with organizing, we worked on writing activities. They each compiled a book of facts about themselves, as part of my content language experience lessons. I read a number of biographies and autobiographies to them. After reading several during the Read to/Write to lessons, explicitly pointing out features as I read autobiographies and wrote my own for them, I explained that they were going to write autobiographies. They had to draw pictures of their family, home, pets, friends, favorite things to do, and so on. Under each picture, they had to tell about the picture.

After each person had completed his or her book, they all had to number each page and write in the numeral on the labeled table of contents page I had given them. They worked on this activity on the Wednesday and Thursday afternoons that I had set aside for writing conferences and groups. Within their small groups, they helped one another to copy over their sentences correctly and make sure that page numbers were in order and matched the table of contents page.

Interviewing

I also gave the children five questions to go home and ask their parents about, one at a time, over a three-week period. I have found that if you give children several questions at once, they frequently forget both the questions and the answers. However, if I give only one question on each day that we have social studies, students can generally remember to ask the questions. These five questions became the basis for the single paragraphs about each student, which they dictated and were then placed on the bulletin board along with their pictures. The five questions were as follows: When were you born? What was your parents' favorite thing about you when you were a baby? What did you like to do best when you were little? What was the funniest thing you did when you were little? What is the best thing about you now? Each question was turned into a statement using sentence stems again, such as "I was born . . ." and "When I was a baby. . . ." The compiled statements were then written right after one another to make the autobiographical paragraph. Not all

Writing

the children could read their completed paragraphs, but they surely tried! And they loved having the paragraphs read to them. I used these paragraphs frequently during reading group time throughout the month since the paragraphs were planned to use much of the same vocabulary I was trying to teach and since they were intrinsically interesting.

The number of mathematics tie-ins I could do was amazing! We had graphs all over that room—who was native to the state and who had moved from somewhere else, as well as such family facts as siblings, pets, number of family members, favorite family foods, and at-home chores. A few Venn diagrams allowed children to see how they could be part of several groupings or attributions simultaneously.

There are so many children representing various cultural groups that I have also been reading to them daily from folktales. For most of the children, I have had no problem finding folktales for their culture groups, and when I did find it difficult, I contacted parents for help. Two different parents came in to the class and told stories that had been told to them as children. It made those stories especially interesting to the class. One of the things we have noted as we discuss the stories is how themes are used over and over and how the characters experience the same feelings as we do. Children are learning to value differences as well as our shared humanity.

Integrated Unit

Thinking Processes

The science unit on the five senses was also interesting and fun. So many activities can help develop the nine thinking processes! We made charts as the children called up things they could hear. I wrote their responses on chart paper, allowing enough room for them to add illustrations. Another chart was used when I told them that I would be writing down words and they had to find the organization I was using and predict which label would be placed on it. For this activity, I wrote a word and asked them to predict another word to fit the category I was thinking of. If they guessed correctly, I wrote that word; if not, I said, "That is not an example." No one was to say the name of the category yet; I wanted to get many examples of each category so that nearly all the children would be in a frenzy claiming to know the category. The first thing I wrote was ice cream. The first discarded guess was candy. The second guess, ice cube, was added to the list. After several more guesses, both examples and nonexamples, we came up with a list that they all agreed could be labeled "Things That Feel Cold," including ice cream, ice cube, snow, my dog's nose, fan, and a glass of milk.

Writing   They also made books for this unit: a feeling book of textures, a seeing book of colors, and a hearing book of sounds. For each of these they had to call up possibilities and organize them (for example, putting all loud sounds together). The second graders wrote these books as well, but at a more sophisticated level. Children were constantly connecting what they already knew to new information they were gathering. They then applied that knowledge by creating books. As before, they took some of the group writing time to work on their books and to help one another evaluate how well they had accomplished

Reading   the assignment. At the end of the month, I used the various books they had
Materials   made for the science unit as reading material during reading group time.

OCTOBER

Word Wall   Many of the children who come to first grade are able to count to ten or more in a rote fashion. But asking them to connect that knowledge to sentences with numbers in them is quite a leap for many students. Thus, I have made a Word Wall above the chalkboard just for math terms. Two other walls contain the list of commonly used and high-interest words that we use for writing. On the number Word Wall, I have the numerals 1 through 10 right beside the words and pictures of the corresponding number of objects for my first-graders as well as my non- or limited-English speaking children. Other math words, such as geometry terms, will be added as needed. I have also placed $+$, $-$, $>$, $<$, $\times$, and $=$ up there with the corresponding definitions of each symbol. They love playing "be a mind reader," in which I try to get them to guess the math word or symbol I am thinking of. Following is an excerpted version of one such exercise:

Me: It's on the Word Wall. Write your guess on the first line.

Ray wrote $<$.

Me: It's a numeral.

Ray wrote 6.

Me: It's more than one.

Ray wrote 6 again.

Me: It's less than six.

Ray wrote 5.

Me: You get this when you add two and three.

Ray excitedly wrote 5 again, waving his hand frantically in the air. He was among a group of three who had correctly read my mind before the final clue! He was proud.

Word Problems Since the first-grade math groups are doing addition, I decided to try yet another way to get them to understand symbols and number words better, as well as to use more writing. I had them convert the number sentences in their math series into small word problems. The first ones were very simple. Using sentence stems, I gave them a formula for writing number sentences as word problems. For adding, I gave them the following sentences to fill in with numerals of their choice:

I have _____ books. I got _____ more.

Now I have _____ books.

For subtraction, they have this one:

I had _____ toys. I gave _____ away.

Now I have _____ toys.

The second-grade-level sentence stems got a bit more complicated by adding in irrelevant information for them to learn to ignore. When doing the modeling, however, Dave and Jim wanted me to exchange the nouns in the two problems; they would rather give away books than toys!

The children were told to make up their own word problems as the final step. They enjoy coming up with unusual items to add and subtract, challenging one another to further heights of ridiculousness, especially in this month of ghoulish happenings! Here is one of Steven's that made the rounds to great appreciation, temporary spellings and all:

I have three vanshing vampiers. I got three more.

Now I have six vanshing vampiers. But how can I have six if they keep vanshing?

Thinking Processes Twice a week, all the children bring to their math group a word problem that they have created. These are exchanged, and as a part of their independent work, the children must write each word problem as a number sentence and draw an illustration to demonstrate the word problem using sets. They may go to the person who did the original problem in order to discover what certain words mean. This is especially important for the children who cannot yet read more than a few words. They are allowed to use pictures in place of the words in their problems. Kazu, who understood Steven's word problem, was fascinated with the notion of vampires, even though Steven himself has only a fuzzy idea of what vampires are. I feel good about how much children are monitoring, evaluating, and applying when they do these exercises.

We also had great fun with an activity I found in *Books You Can Count On: Linking Mathematics and Literature.* As the authors of that book directed, I read the poem "Mice" by Rose Fyleman and had children work together on the worksheet shown (Figure 9.1). Reading their explanations of how they solved the problem gave me lots of interesting insights. One group started drawing mouse bodies and adding body parts while crossing them off the worksheet. Another group figured out that with four legs and two eyes to a mouse, they could group legs and eyes to see how many mice were possible. A third group started cutting up the worksheet and glued mouse parts to bodies they drew. I was very impressed with how they went about solving this problem and then explaining their solution. This was a wonderful problem for the first- and second-graders to complete together.

Integrated Unit

In order to help the children better understand their role in their world, our social studies unit pursued several different activities this month. First we had to discuss the definition of a family. Since there are so many families which do not fit the traditional two-parent structure, we defined family as a group of related or unrelated people who live together because they care about one

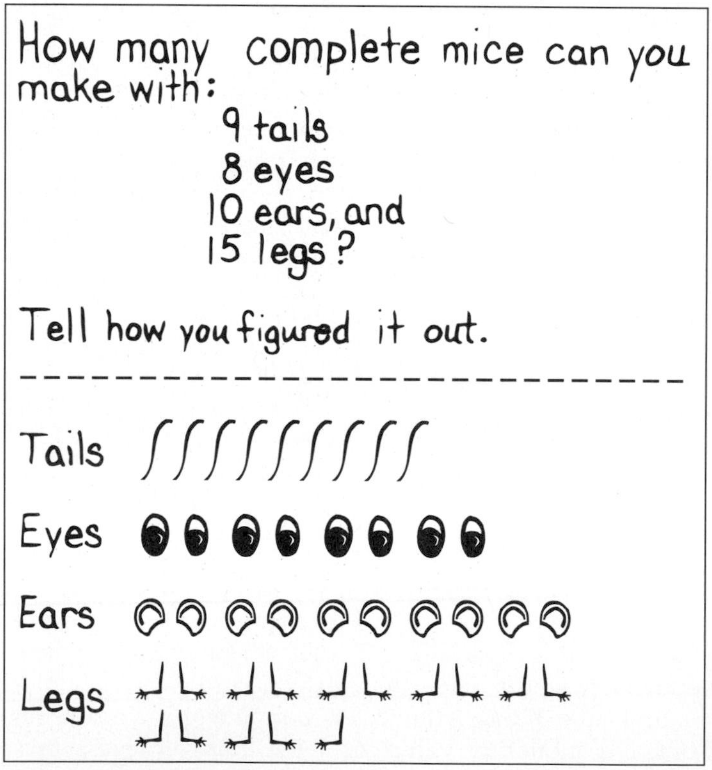

Figure 9.1 Mice math sheet

another and who try to help one another in a variety of ways. Families could consist of any number of adults and children. Each child then drew a picture of his or her family and wrote a few sentences telling how the members showed their care for one another and the responsibilities each filled in the family.

Organizing Information

We took the information from last month's graphs (how many people in the family, chores, adults' jobs, and so on) and put them into a data chart with questions along the top and children's names down the left side.

Writing

Using the data chart entries, children wrote paragraphs about themselves and their families. No names were written on the paragraphs, and I read them aloud to the whole class during social studies time as we sat in front of the data chart, trying to predict with each new sentence who the person could be. They loved the puzzle aspect of this listening comprehension lesson, which allowed them to review the questions asked and connect the answers with a name. Here is Dave's edited paragraph:

> Me and my dad, we live together. Dad, he drives a bus for the city. I have lots of stuff to do at home like take out the garbage and wash the dishes sometimes and dust the tables and stuff and help my dad wash clothes at the laundromat. I have always lived in this apartment even before my mom died. The most interesting thing about me and my dad is that we are going to win the lottery and go to Hawaii on a vacation for two weeks!

The information was also taken into the second-grade content of the roles people play in the communities they live and work in. It was interesting to hear them categorizing jobs as helping or service jobs, for example.

Integrated Unit

This month's science unit dealt with the time and the calendar: How many hours in a day, days in a week, weeks in a month, days in a month, months in a year, and days in a year? Talk about some tough concepts! We do our daily calendar during the opening exercises each day. You know, the "Today is Monday. It is sunny" type of activity. A child, with help where needed, names the month, the day, and the year. Whenever a new month begins, together we

Meaning Vocabulary

count how many days there are in it and count other items like how many Mondays there are or how many birthdays there are in the month. Nevertheless, the concept of "what is a week" is still tough to communicate to first-graders. Even some second-graders are still struggling with it. To many of them, a week is five days; weekends don't count since there is no school! I've saved all the calendars for the current year from my husband Paul's bakery business, plus the ones the banks give away, and others I came across—it doesn't matter one whit that most of the months have been gone for some time now. The children dismantled the calendars and then organized the pages by putting all the Januarys together and so on. After the pages were all grouped

Groups

by the twelve months, I assigned two children per month and told them to figure out how all the Januarys, Februarys, et cetera, were the same. They discovered to their delight that regardless of the picture on the calendar, all the Januarys had 31 days listed.

Thinking
Processes—
Organize

The months were then grouped by cold ones and hot ones, fitting some, like October and April, in between. We also spent some time talking about events during the past year, birthdays, Christmas and Hanukkah, Thanksgiving, Fourth of July, and so on. What kind of weather were we having then? Did the event happen long ago or not so long ago? The relativity of some of these terms only added to their confusion. When they said Christmas happened during a cold time, we went to the cold months group and found December. They always had trouble with the idea that all months don't have the same number of days. They'll begin to understand that concept a little better when they learn to divide 365 by 12! Their other concern was why all months don't start on Sunday (or Monday, if they still think of five-day weeks), but they are slowly beginning to understand. We made a continuous calendar for the bulletin board that shows the first day of each new month right beside the last day of the old one. So they are beginning to realize that each month is connected to the one before it. The second-graders especially enjoyed information on how other cultures used to track time.

Content
Journals

To help them understand days in the week better, I had them all keep journals for the month. During the school week, they wrote in their journals here, but each child took two pages home to write in over the weekend. I had xeroxed off the journal pages, so that each one had the date already on it; all they had to do was fill in the day of the week and then write at least one sentence about something that happened to them, or that they saw, or about the weather. Naturally, Dave, Jim, and Ray consistently forgot their journals over the weekend and also forgot to bring back the sheets of paper on Mondays! I gave them extra sheets I had made, so that they could make up something for Saturday and Sunday during their Monday work time. At the end of the month, we stapled all the sheets together with a cover for each identifying it as the October journal. I know that many parents will prize these short anecdotes in years to come. And I do believe they are gaining some sense of what a week is compared to a month. Journal writing has been highly touted in this writing workshop I've been attending and does seem to work for kids. They talked about dialogue journals there, too, but I am not sure how I could do that with 24 students. Maybe I should ask how I should start.

NOVEMBER

Independence

Despite the onslaught of the holiday season, which really begins right after Halloween, it has been a great month. The children are fairly well set in our routines now, so that they know what they are to do and when and, more important, why. I make it a point to explain how the learning center materials will help them to learn. I have found it is worth it to take that little bit of extra time to help children understand why they are doing something.

SSR

On my schedule of sustained silent reading (SSR) and read-aloud time, I am now taking ten minutes for reading aloud, with the children having up to five minutes of reading or examining books quietly on their own. I have found that since some of them are not actually reading during this time, they may need two books to "read" during SSR. They spend their time looking at the pictures and even matching some words they know with ones found in the books. "Sustained silent reading" is probably a misnomer with most of these second-graders, since there is a low roar of "mumble reading" going on. Young children find it nearly impossible to read silently, as do immature older readers and readers of materials too difficult for them. That's all right; at least everyone is engaged with books, even Jim and Dave! I do allow students like Pat and Jakeitha to read beyond the 10 minutes—and they do!

Integrated Unit

Holidays are big events to children, associated as they are with changes in routines, presents, special happenings, and clothing. Therefore, as an ongoing primary unit in social studies this year, we are studying the various holidays associated with each month. Some months are chock-full of holidays, while others are sparse. I have had to do some digging to come up with interesting holidays to study. However, October, November, and December are all full months. As part of our study of Thanksgiving, I brought in cookbooks like *The Taming of the C.A.N.D.Y Monster*, *Kids Are Natural Cooks*, and *Kids in the Kitchen*.

Trade Books

From these we adapted recipes to an easier form for children to follow, putting each recipe on a big sheet of chart paper back in the cooking center, so that we could do some classroom cooking for the dinner we shared with the kindergarten class. Even Kazu and Mariane were thrilled, although Thanksgiving wasn't a holiday they had heard of before. Six groups each prepared a different food for the feast: cranberry relish, pumpkin muffins, turkey soup, popcorn, salad, and a fruit juice punch.

Groups

Using the cookbooks provided a real reading experience. To help them connect even more, we looked up information about all the foods in a variety of reference books, so that while we ate, each group told where its food came from and how it was prepared. I met with each group during social studies time to read them a little more about their foods, and they compiled a data chart of the information. The popcorn group told us about the Indians introducing the Pilgrims to popcorn and how kernels of corn were thrown around the edge of the fire rather than being cooked in a pot as we do now. They even told how people have gotten salt by collecting it from the sea or from natural salt deposits.

Inquiry

It made sense, therefore, to tie in the measurement unit from the math series with all the cooking activities. What better way to learn what a cup or a liter is than by having to measure out a cup of something for a recipe? That's really developing meaning vocabulary with "the real thing." I had the kids do a "water run-through" of their recipe before they tried it with the real ingredients. If a cup of flour was called for, they had to measure out and add 1 cup of water to the bowl. Cleanup was pretty easy, and the children got some idea of

Meaning Vocabulary

Groups

how much they could expect to have in their bowls when working with the real thing. Each cooking group had children from each of the three math groups so that I knew I had some very capable people in each group on whom I could count. Each group practiced its recipe three times with water run-throughs, so the days of the actual cooking went smoothly. My friends are always amazed at what children can create with an electric skillet and a crock-pot! As for the thinking processes, the children certainly had ample opportu-

Thinking
Processes

nity to evaluate and apply their knowledge. There was a fair amount of predicting going on with some of those recipes, too!

Integrated
Unit

Before beginning the social studies unit on local and global neighborhoods, I had the children call up their experiences with people, buildings, and activities in their neighborhoods. I then had them predict what they thought we would be learning about in our unit. We made a big chart with their predictions of the most important people, buildings, and activities they thought would be included. They also predicted concepts we might learn, such as, "People help one another," which were likewise put on another chart. As the month went on, they found that they needed to add additional words and concepts to the charts. The information about how neighborhoods are alike around the world was an interesting piece that the second-graders presented to the first-graders.

Inquiry

The sources of information we used included interviews with community helpers for first-graders, films, speakers, and field trips, all liberally supplemented with books that I read to them which they located on their own. For homework, they were encouraged to check out a book from our classroom collection—pulled together just for this unit—and take it home for someone to read to them. We put together feature matrices of the people, buildings, and neighborhood activities about which they were learning. Based on those feature matrices, they wrote paragraphs that formed the basis for the review materials at the end of the unit. Some children are already quite good at monitoring what else needs to be located. Pat looked at the feature matrix of neighborhood buildings and noticed that we had left out houses! See Figure 9.2 for the feature matrix done on people in the neighborhood and some edited paragraphs written from it.

The neighborhood unit has been quite a busy one, but I think the children now have a much clearer idea about who provides services and goods for them. And, of course, by writing so frequently about the different aspects of

Content
Journals

the unit, their composition abilities have been improving. In their journals this month I had them each choose several community helpers, services, and buildings (local or global) to draw pictures of and write about. I could even make out some of the words in Ray's temporary spellings this time:

firfitres are god becus they hlep pepl ho is brn up i lick to liv with tem and go down tat bug po

(Firefighters are good because they help people who is burned up. I like to live with them and go down that big pole.)

	Wears uniform	Works with people	Works for people	Have to have
Police officer	X	X		X
Firefighter	X	X		X
Grocer			X	X
Mailcarrier	X		X	
Medical helpers	X	X		X
Utility workers			X	X
Gas attendant			X	

People in Our Neighborhood

There are many people who help us in our neighborhood. Some do jobs we couldn't do by ourselves. We need police officers and firefighters and medical helpers because they do jobs that we don't know how to do. We need grocers and utility workers because they bring us stuff we couldn't get if they didn't help us. We could get our own mail or pump gas into the car if we had to.

Some helpers wear uniforms like police officers, firefighters, mailcarriers, and medical helpers. That way you can tell real easy who they are when you need help. Some people just wear their own clothes to their jobs.

Police officers, firefighters, and medical helpers help save people. But some helpers just do jobs for us, like grocers, mailcarriers, utility workers, and gas attendants.

We need all of our community helpers because each one does a special job. That makes everybody's life easier because we don't all have to do everything.

Figure 9.2 Feature matrix

DECEMBER

I, for one, am glad to have this break time. Not only do I plan to use my time on holiday and family obligations (my poor little girl, Vera, has hardly seen me this month), but I also find this an excellent time to regroup and plan for the next part of the year. I know that not even half the school year is over, but it seems that more than half the year has been covered by the time January rolls around. The children have come so far since September, reading and writing so many different things now.

Computer Technology The children have been doing some very elementary kinds of word processing on the microcomputer. We have a school computer and printer in our room. Up until now the first-graders have mostly just worked on keyboarding skills with cardboard templates and the computer keyboard and have played with some of the software designed to teach beginning programming skills.

Writing The second-graders are already composing on the computer (when they can get to it!). The first-graders are mightily impressed that the second-graders can do so much. I just introduced using the computer for revising writing. What a hit! Even Jim and Dave wrote more than they usually do and begged to write more! Children love to see their revised copy emerge tidily from the printer with very little effort. I'll bet I have trouble getting them to go back to revising on paper after this.

Integrated Unit

The continuing unit on holidays was very big with the children, of course, especially as they learned about how Christmas is celebrated around the world. They found it fascinating, if a bit disconcerting, that La Befana the witch (Italy) and little elves (Norway) deliver holiday presents in other countries. We also looked at Hanukkah and celebrations associated with the winter solstice.

Comprehension Lesson

One strategy I have used somewhat successfully with this unit is Take Two. For each of the countries for which we studied the Christmas customs, I pulled four true statements from the passage I was going to read to the children. Here are the ones I selected from the passage on Italy:

1. Italian children have gifts brought by the witch La Befana.
2. Italian people eat eels for their Christmas feast.
3. La Befana was a witch who was too busy cleaning her house to go see the baby Jesus with the Three Wise Men.
4. Italian children open their gifts on January 6, the Feast of the Epiphany.

Two were main ideas from the passage and two were details. I read the four statements to the children in advance, pointing to the words of each numbered statement on the chart I had prepared earlier. I told them that all the statements were true, and that they were to listen as I read to determine which two were most important. After I read the passage, I asked each student to write down the numerals of the two true statements that contained the most important information. They love the secrecy of revealing their answers this way. All guesses were collected, and a group composed of Ray, Mariane, Sharon, and Dave compiled a tally for each of the statements.

Not surprisingly, the first time I tried Take Two, each of the four true statements got nearly equal votes. It was very clear to me that children who are only used to telling true and false are not able to detect what is the most important information. Luckily, the two main idea statements did receive a couple more votes than did the detail statements, so I built on that and helped students who had chosen the two main idea statements to explain why those two were most important. They are not very good at articulating reasons yet, so I can understand why some of my colleagues don't want to try higher-order thinking activities with young children. I still believe it's worthwhile, however. I tried to help children see that details occur just once in the text, whereas most important ideas are mentioned more than once. Also, details help give more information about important ideas. I used a web to show how we might organize information in the section read to them. Slowly, as the month went on and as we worked through the countries' holiday celebrations, most of the children began to see what was meant by "most important" information. They were getting so good that by the seventh country I introduced a twist on take two. After I read the four true statements to them, they predicted which two would be the most important. They listened to confirm or alter their guesses. I took a show of hands for the first guess and wrote the numeral beside each statement. The second guess was done in writing as before.

Integrated
Unit

Meaning
Vocabulary

The science unit we worked on was about solids, liquids, and gases. I began the unit by starting a big content web on the back bulletin board. In the center of the web were the words *Forms of Things.* Radiating out from the center were the terms *solids, liquids,* and *gases.* We met back by the bulletin board, and they started calling up "things." I wrote each of their contributions on separate cards to use later in a closed Word Sort, similar to what we had done with transportation earlier in the year. Of course, they at first named objects that were solids. I then started probing to get them to name liquids, asking what were some things they could drink, where they played in summer, and how they cleaned themselves. Then we used a Word Sort to separate all the items into like groups. As I showed them how to separate the cards into groups, I asked them to think how all the objects under each label were alike so that we could start to develop tentative definitions for solids, liquids, and gases. Not a single gas had been offered, so only liquids and solids had listings. With all the examples in front of them, we came up with some tentative definitions for solids and liquids. First they said you could feel both, so I wrote that on a card beside each label. Then they told me that solids stayed in a certain shape and liquids were the shape of the container they were in. Those two definitions were written on the board. Good start! After listening to books and watching films with information about solids, liquids, and gases, they should have even more to add to the chart.

It became immediately apparent that gases had no items listed under it. Jim suggested that we write *gas* on a card and place it underneath the term *gases.* Others said we couldn't do that because gas is a liquid. I must say, I ended the lesson with all of the children in a state of cognitive confusion! I gave them some homework to do. They were to talk with their parents, siblings,

Inquiry

friends, bus driver, or anyone else to see if they could come to school with the name of at least one gas to add to the bulletin board.

Several children remembered to do this and came in with the name of a gas. Other children looked in science books for help. The problem with this unit is that the gaseous state children are most familiar with, air, is composed of several gases. I wrote the names of several gases, such as hydrogen, oxygen, and helium, on the web. We talked about ways gases were used in everyday life, such as in oxygen masks and balloons filled with helium. Even though the children will not be expected to know the names of these gases, they are fascinated by having such big words in their room!

I decided to focus on causes and effects to help them see some relationships among the three forms of matter. For example, I asked them to listen as I read a section of a book to find out, "Why does a balloon have a shape if air (a gas) has no shape of its own?" and "What happens when an ice cube is left in a glass on the windowsill?" Then they were ready to try some experiments on their own.

Writing

As we talked about each experiment, I made a content language experience chart for each, labeled with the number of the experiment we were performing. For the first experiment, I brought balloons to school. Here is what the chart looked like:

Air Is Something—Experiment One

Mrs. Lance gave us balloons. (Dave)
Nothing was in the balloons at first because we checked and they were flat. (Pat)
Mrs. Lance let us each blow up our balloon. (Steven)
It didn't look like anything was in our balloons, but they got big so something must have been inside and it was air! (David)
Mrs. Lance chewed an onion and then blew up a balloon. (Michelle)
She make balloon go boom. (Mariane)
We smelled what came out of the balloon and it smelled like onions. Yuk! (Jim)

Other experiments and charts were made to demonstrate changing solids to liquids (by melting hard candy in the electric skillet) and turning liquids into solids by freezing or cooking. Evaporation was shown by putting ice cubes into the skillet and boiling them into nonexistence. Cause and effect statements were easily generated with all these experiments. For example, "Why did the solid suckers become liquid?" and "What happens when ice cubes are boiled?"

Content
Journals

Students wrote steadily in their content journals about experiment results, hypotheses to explain results, and possible experiments to try. All the children are fascinated by the experiments, and the amount and quality of their writings confirm that.

It's been quite a month! I, for one, am ready for R&R.

JANUARY

Content
Journals

I have always enjoyed January so much because the children and I are both glad to be back to school and into a routine again. January is one of our more exciting months because I do try to provide many types of interesting activities. By the end of this month, I found it hard to believe that children were writing so much or so well in their journals. I guess it makes sense that if they regularly write and get reactions to their writing, their composition skills will improve. I look at two to three journals a day so I can react to all of them over two weeks. The children have been writing twice a week about the science unit on animals, which will continue through February. Here are excerpts from several journals:

We lerned that there are many kinds of animals. Some animals have hare and some have faethers. Some have scales. Sometimes babys are born from there mommys and sometimes they hach from eggs. (Pat)

All stuf is liveing or non-liveing. And anmals is part of the liveing ones. Anmals are liveing becuas they ned food and watre and air and they have babys. (Steven)

amnls have baby amnls they ned eet and dwink wotr. (Dave)

Revising Clearly, the children have been learning many new ideas while they are writing in their journals. Journals are a chance to get their ideas down. We can always work on editing the sentences when they turn entries from their journals into oral or written reports. So when I write a note by a journal entry, I react only to how accurate the information is, and I raise points that help elaborate their information: "Name some animals who are like this." "Why do animals need to eat and drink?" and "I would like to know more about _____." Such queries cause them to think more about their entries. Occasionally I encourage them to rewrite entries to incorporate the points I suggested. The longer entries that result are usually more accurate!

Assessment I used to have children make booklets to go along with the units we were studying. But to do the booklets, I either wrote sentences on the board for them to copy or asked them to tell me some things to write about and then again had each child copy what I had written. I am happier with the journals since each child is challenged to write independently. Some write a whole page! I can see clearly how well each is able to apply what they have been learning rather than how well they can copy my ideas. Content journals require students to call up, organize, connect, form an image, monitor, generalize, evaluate, and apply. Not too bad for one little old strategy!

Groups I also put the students into heterogeneous groups every week or so and have them share what they have written in their journals with one another. I find that they all go away from those writing groups with more ideas to write about and with ideas, too, of ways to make their own entries better. As in all peer response groups, group members ask each other questions to elicit more information that will clarify the ideas stated. Some of the children have started keeping a journal for social studies, too. As you might guess, these are the children for whom writing is easier and more satisfying: Pat, David, Sharon, and John. Kazu and Mariane are also keeping their own journal for social studies so that they can improve their English language skills. Periodically they show me what they are writing, and I react to it just as I do to the science journals. I wonder if I should ask all of the students to write about social studies, too. I need to think about that one for a little while.

Each time the students form themselves into groups, it gets a little bit easier; they are really beginning to know what to do and how to do it. I am well on the way to my goal of independence with this kind of organization for writing.

Independence I introduced the one-paragraph report to the kids this month, too. Each report begins with a topic sentence, explained to the children as the one sentence that tells the most important information, followed by supporting details. After all our experiences before the holiday break with Take Two, the children finally understand what I mean by "most important." We once constructed reports after viewing a film for our social studies unit, "Needs and Wants." I set the purpose, instructing the students to watch and listen to remember everything. After the film, children went to their heterogeneous groups (organized so that each group would have students who could model good thinking and language) and listed all they could remember. Then they sorted the statements into main ideas and supporting details. That way, they could select one main idea as their topic sentence for the one-paragraph essay and pick out several supporting details as well.

Groups

All groups then watched the film again to check the accuracy of their information. They made changes in their reports in their peer group sessions. Each group came out with a written report done on chart paper that was hung in the room, each group member's name listed on the paper. Children feel such pride in being part of a successful effort! Even though at this point Jim, Dave, and Ray would be unable to produce such a report independently, they can each be part of their various groups to complete the task.

Integrated Unit

To introduce the unit on wants and needs, I listed the two terms on separate pieces of chart paper and asked the students to talk about things they wanted and things they needed. We came up with an enormous number of frivolous and necessary items! For them, it seems that wanting and needing are the same thing. We talked about the difference between the two terms through a Remember When activity in which I recalled things I needed as a child, how they were obtained, and why they were necessary. I then did a Remember When with wants I had had as a child. After I was done (and did they listen attentively—children love to learn more about their teacher's personal life!), I asked them to tell me the difference between want and need. Then they word-gathered wants and needs to put on the two charts. Sometimes we had to talk through where a word or phrase belonged because a child would insist it was both a want and a need. For example, Ray said pizza was both a want and a need. After discussion, it was decided that pizza belonged to the general category "food." So we made a heading that included many kinds of food for the need list. Chocolate cake went on the want list, since you could get along without that kind of nourishment (couldn't you?). Toys all went over to the want list. It took a couple of sessions to get everything down they wanted to list, but with my gentle guidance, we had examples of needs in each of the categories: food, clothing, shelter, air, and water, tying science and social studies together.

Meaning Vocabulary

I have been feeling so tired lately that I am having a hard time keeping up with all that's going on here! I must need to up my vitamin intake.

FEBRUARY

Integrated Unit

The wants and needs unit continued in social studies, as animals continued in science. I made one new addition: All the students now keep content journals for social studies, too. I have continued the holidays unit, which really picked up this month of presidents' birthdays and Valentine's Day.

Web   At the end of the month, the children constructed a web for animals that we placed on the back bulletin board. It was a great way to call up, organize, connect, form an image, and review information. I've put a sketch of it in my book so I'll remember it for future years (see Figure 9.3).

To apply what they had learned about animals in an art activity, each student was to take one of the seven groups we had studied and create a new animal with the characteristics of that group. Dr. Seuss has definitely had an influence on these kids; they were undaunted by either the creation or the naming

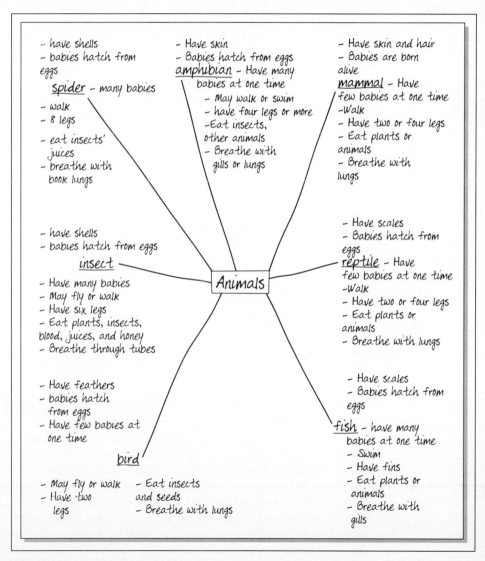

- have shells
- babies hatch from eggs
  <u>spider</u> - many babies
- walk
- 8 legs
- eat insects' juices
- breathe with book lungs

- Have skin
- Babies hatch from eggs
  <u>amphibian</u> - Have many babies at one time
  - May walk or swim
  - have four legs or more
  - Eat insects, other animals
  - Breathe with gills or lungs

- Have skin and hair
- Babies are born alive
  <u>mammal</u> - Have few babies at one time
  - Walk
  - Have two or four legs
  - Eat plants or animals
  - Breathe with lungs

- have shells
- babies hatch from eggs
  <u>insect</u>
- Have many babies
- May fly or walk
- Have six legs
- Eat plants, insects, blood, juices, and honey
- Breathe through tubes

- Have scales
- Babies hatch from eggs
  <u>reptile</u> - Have few babies at one time
  - Walk
  - Have two or four legs
  - Eat plants or animals
  - Breathe with lungs

Animals

- Have feathers
- babies hatch from eggs
- Have few babies at one time
  <u>bird</u>
- May fly or walk
- Have two legs
- Eat insects and seeds
- Breathe with lungs

- Have scales
- Babies hatch from eggs
  <u>fish</u> - have many babies at one time
  - Swim
  - Have fins
  - Eat plants or animals
  - Breathe with gills

Figure 9.3   Animal Web

of their critters. They all had to write short descriptions of what their animal looked like (hair, scales, feathers, and so on), how its young were born, and what it ate. They used the data charts we had made for each of the seven animal groups as their source of information. All animals were put on display in the form of pictures, clay models, papier mâché, and so on, with cards that each child had written describing the animal. We invited the principal, our upper-grade student helpers, and the parents in for a tour of this unusual zoo.

Word Wall Our major review activity for wants and needs consisted of review sentences that students constructed from the key words I had listed on the Word Wall throughout the unit. Since I now put reading, science, math, and social studies words on the same Word Wall, I find that it helps to use color coding. All the green words are for science, yellow is math, red is reading, and blue ones for social studies. To write review sentences for social studies, students first had to locate all the blue cards on the Word Wall. For some, that was a task in itself.

Groups In small groups the children listed each word on small pieces of paper. With all the words in front of them, they were told to think of two sentences about what we had been learning, using at least two of the words in each sentence. After each group had had a chance to give one of their sentences, I asked if any other sentences had been developed that were not already listed. As they were given to me, I wrote the sentences and then circled the two words from the Word Wall. In this way, they could see which words had not yet been used and constructed additional sentences using quite a few of the leftover words! Here is their final review sentences chart on needs:

What We Need

We need and want many things. (Stephanie)

We need clean air and water or we would get sick and die. (David)

We need food so we don't starve. (Jim)

We need clothing, shelter, and warmth so we don't get too cold and die. (Jakeitha)

We need love and safety because people need more than just stuff to keep from dying because we need to not get hurt and to feel good about ourselves. (Pat)

Needs take care of how you live and how you feel about yourself. (Michael)

Word Problems The children are studying money in math, so the yellow cards on the Word Wall are the names of the coins and the symbols of dollars and cents. The second-graders' money unit includes currency of other countries as well. The children have been writing some pretty hard word problems for one another with these new words, asking for some addition, subtraction, multiplication, and division beyond their required level in the math series. What astounds me is that children who seemingly cannot add or subtract above ten can in fact make change and therefore can do difficult addition and subtraction when money is involved. Children today seem to have more money and to have handled it earlier than my generation did! I helped Jim to see that what he was able to do with making change from a quarter was harder than what he was having trouble with in math. He couldn't believe it! All those numerals were related to money? He has really gained confidence in his math ability as a result of this little insight. He now makes all of his addition and subtraction problems deal with money and then it seems to make sense to him.

Well, I had my own little insight at the beginning of this month about the reasons for my increasing fatigue, and the doctor confirmed it. 'Long about July, Vera is going to have a new little brother or sister! Just wait until I tell the children!

MARCH

Near the end of the month, Kazu asked me if I was getting fatter! I thought it was a good time to break the news to the children, since I will get only "fatter and fatter" and I would rather they know why. They immediately wanted to pull out the webs and data charts we had put together for animals so that they could see where I fit. They had apparently forgotten that people are mammals, et cetera, et cetera. I pulled the charts out, and we all gathered around them on the floor to see if I met the characteristics. The children were fascinated. What did it really mean that the baby would be born alive? Was the baby alive now? They seemed to be in more of a mood for the animal unit now than when we originally did it.

In response to their questions, I sent a note home to parents explaining my condition and the children's questions. Would they mind if I tastefully presented some basic information about how babies are created and develop? Some parents did object, of course, as is their right, and I arranged for those children to engage in an art activity out of the room while I shared *How Babies Are Made* and *How You Were Born*, dealing with beginning sex education concepts. The children were fascinated and wanted to know if the same held true for other animals. Therefore, this month has included a review of the growth and development of baby animals in each of the seven categories. All of the children in the class found the information, presented in greater depth due to their increased questions, to be much more interesting the second time around. It's amazing what motivation does for learning. And I thought I had done a good job with motivation earlier. Just goes to show you!

I am glad that I took the additional time to go back to the animal unit. I think we teachers are probably afraid to do that, since we feel the pressure to continue marching through all the assigned units. But in this case I saw clearly that our review was really time well spent for the students. A bit serendipitous, but isn't that what it's all about—seizing the teachable moment?

Nevertheless, we did finally begin the science unit on plants. The children's first questions were about how baby plants were made! So that is where

Trade Books (margin note)

Integrated Unit (margin note)

we began our data chart. But the children quickly lost interest when they discovered that plant reproduction was not nearly as interesting (to them) as was animal reproduction. The rest of the unit then continued pretty much as I had planned it. We took field trips to the local plant nursery and the grocery store so they could see the real thing. Many of the parents who had begun seedlings for their home gardens were willing to contribute seeds for our experiments. Using the outline shown in Figure 9.4, which I had first used when introducing animals, I was able to show the children how plants fit into the world around them. This outline is a little different because it shows one big idea broken down into successively smaller parts. The web we did on animals took that one section of the outline and developed it more; the same thing will be done with plants.

Inquiry   If plants are living things, I asked, what do plants need (to use a word from social studies!)? Children called up what they knew of plants and hypothesized about plant needs. We then constructed a series of experiments as we had done with solids, liquids, and gases. Each experiment concerned one of the plant's needs—air, light, water, or food. I had children predict what they thought might happen and listed the predictions on a content language experience chart. Here is the chart for one of the experiments:

Experiment #3: Plants Need Water

Guesses: Both plants will grow if they have air and light.
　　　　One plant will not grow if it doesn't have water.
We put two pots in the window and they both had seeds and dirt and we
　　didn't cover them up. (Ray)
I got to be in charge of one pot and I had to give it one tablespoon of water
　　every day. (Jim)

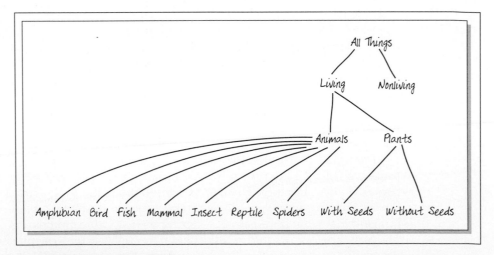

Figure 9.4　Living Things Web

I was in charge of one pot and I wasn't allowed to give it any water at all. (Michelle)

For long time it did not look like anything going to grow. (Kazu)

But, presto bingo! One day we saw something green in Ray's pot and a plant grew and nothing grew in Michelle's pot. (Sharon)

This must mean plants need water but how much is a very good question. (Steven)

A good question indeed, so we got some seedlings and experimented with the amount of water and discovered that too much water will kill plants as easily as too little. A good lesson for me with my house plants!

Integrated Unit Fractions was the math unit of the month. I am glad that I have pulled out the units on measurement, time, money, and fractions for students to work on all at once. Even if some children cannot add or subtract very well, they may understand fractions, especially with all the cooking activities we have continued to do. "Interrupting the regularly scheduled program to bring them this important unit" is not only motivating but also a great pick-me-up, since math can seem to be only number-crunching for students at this level. They love doing the real thing with objects we cut into fractional parts and playing "be a mind reader" with the fraction symbols and words on the word wall.

March has ended and I am feeling a tad more energetic these days. Thank goodness the school year will end before the tiredness returns! It's hard to believe we are on the countdown months!

APRIL

Inquiry April has always been one of my favorite months. The world becomes colorful again, and the warmth is so welcome. We took some of our plants outside to see what might happen to healthy plants if they weren't kept warm enough. The black leaves on the tomato plants gave some indication, but students were puzzled about how the spinach had survived the same temperatures. That led into some research about when plants can be started outdoors and why. This has been a very interesting unit for the children, calling upon many research and writing skills.

Content Journals The children wrote twice a week in their science journals about the various experiments we were doing. Some children even proposed additional experiments, which would have impressed the National Science Foundation with their complexity! The emphasis this month has been not so much on plant **Meaning Vocabulary** needs for survival as on the different kinds of plants and such terms as *root*, *stem*, and *leaves*. We looked at the functions of these plant parts and at food plants, sorting them by whether we ate their roots, stems, leaves, or several parts. Children were astounded to discover that we ate the part of the potato that grows underground. I used an old book that still has great information **Trade Books** (how much can carrots change, after all?), *What's Inside of Plants*. I also used a book on different food plants, *In My Garden*.

Reading Materials

At the beginning of the school year I always wonder how I am going to fill up all the wall and bulletin board space in my classroom. By this point in the year I am wishing for more. It seems that every available space is covered with content language experience charts, illustrations, webs, and Word Sorts. There are also displays of books and magazines for our current units in the appropriate learning centers. Every week during the scheduled library time (though of course children may go to the library at other times as well), we find another piece of information to bring back to the displays. During these weekly trips, I have been modeling how to search for a key word to locate information in the card catalog. The children have also gotten to know the names of some authors fairly well, too. "Oh, here's another book by Dr. Branley," someone may say as they locate another science book. Some of these authors are becoming as familiar to them as are storybook authors Sendak, Lobel, Van Allsburg, Kellogg, Seuss, Steig, Mayer, and Marshall.

Thinking Processes

We have been taking data charts to the library for a couple of months now, so that when we find out something new, we immediately add it to the chart along with the source. Filling in the data chart at the library has really helped children learn to organize, connect, monitor, and generalize. As we fill out the charts, they monitor where we have little or no information so that we can search for more.

Inquiry

The children have discovered that some questions on the data chart are not as important as others. Thus we strike off some questions and write in substitutes. Students have also discovered that you cannot ask questions that are too specific ("Why is it colder at Aunt Ruth's house than it is here?") or too general ("What happens in January?"), as we have spent considerable time at the card catalog unable to find anything out about such questions. Then we talk about broadening or narrowing questions to make them more useful. For instance, we talked about where Aunt Ruth lives, posing such questions as, "Is the weather different in different places?" "What causes the weather to be different in other parts of the country?" "Which parts of the country usually have warm weather and which have a lot of cold weather?" I feel good about their developing research skills.

Integrated Unit

The social studies unit this month was easy to do. It was about rules and why they are necessary. Since I started the year with our one rule, we have spent a lot of time since discussing the reasons for rules and the impact on their behavior. At the beginning of the year, children really had little idea why they should not talk too loudly in the room. Now they understand much better. We talked about rules for different places, which are really sets of expected behaviors that allow all to do what they are supposed to with little interference from others.

To show them the alternative, I bravely (foolishly?) abolished rules for one morning in the room, having warned our principal, Mr. Head, what was coming! Children crowded into the most popular centers and didn't go near others; children talked very loudly and missed being called to math group time; children didn't finish their work; children interrupted one another or got up and left groups before they normally would have been allowed to. Dave and Jim thought that this day was wonderful; most of the others, however, did not like being uncertain of what was expected of them and did not like the rudeness of some of the other children. We had a discussion during the next social studies period on the reasons for our rules and on what makes a good rule. We broadened this, of course, to playground and bus rules, home rules, and community rules.

I explained that long ago, before schools were available to all, most people could not read. People learned the rules for living together in the newly forming cities and towns of medieval Europe by listening to the tales told by storytellers. These storytellers would travel around from place to place telling tales that made the rules very clear to those listening. I reminded them of some familiar folktales, and we talked about how the characters behaved. We identified appropriate and inappropriate behaviors based on the story events and whether characters were rewarded in the end. I read a bunch of familiar and new folktales to the children, and we continued our analysis into societal rules and how they evolved. All the children came out of this experience with a greater appreciation for why societal rules developed. These discussions and brainstorming sessions were a prelude to each child making an oral report about a rule. They had to state the rule and explain the reason for it. I find that they can plan such short oral reports by making a few notes on cards so that they are not just reading a written report.

Another busy month ends, and I find myself concerned about the nearness of the end of the school year with tons more left to accomplish! I have this same feeling every year—when will it end?

MAY

Parent conferences early this month took up an enormous amount of my time, both for preparation and for the actual conferences. However, the parents and I gained a lot from the exchange of information. I always prepare the children for the conferences by telling them what I am going to tell their parents. Then I ask them to write down something they would like me to tell their parents that they are doing well. That's yet another way for them to monitor their learning, review what they know, and organize their thoughts.

Thinking
Processes

Integrated
Unit

In math the children were learning to tell time and in science they were studying what caused time to change, so we worked on the two units together. Time is such an abstraction. When you try to explain the passage of time, how the earth rotates around the sun while simultaneously turning on its axis, you are into heavy stuff. We showed how the earth moves (even though we can't feel it) by putting a stick outside and measuring the position and length of the shadow cast over time. This was a great way to apply their previous work with linear measurement to their new study of time. They began to predict what would happen as the day went on, predictions that I wrote on a chart so that they could test their hypotheses. Using the strategy "A picture is worth a thousand words," I chose films as the best way to help them grasp this unit. I also **Trade Books** used such books as *What Makes a Shadow?* and *The Day We Saw the Sun Come Up.* We did a lot of one-paragraph essays to break the information into smaller bits for better understanding. Here is Kazu's first-draft paragraph on days:

> A day is 24 hour long. Each day earth go around pretty fast so we have day and night. In 24 hour we have dark and light. Seven day make one week, and 365 day make a year. That mean earth turn around and around many time and make many day and night time.

Integrated A combined social studies and science unit dealt with machines and how
Unit they make work easier. Children first met as a whole class to talk briefly about the reason for having machines (to make work easier through pushing, pulling, and lifting) and then to hear about six types of simple machines (complex machines were for later). I had them call up jobs they had seen their parents doing or they had done themselves. Then I put them into small groups and **Groups** asked them to go on a scavenger hunt to locate the machines used for each job or pictures of the machines. When students brought their findings in, we examined each one as best we could to see how simple machines were used to make more complex ones. For some this was easy to see. A crowbar was a lever, a wheelbarrow used wheels, and a pulley was the simple machine on which an elevator was based. However, dishwashers were tough. We asked Steven and Stephanie's father, an appliance repairer, to come in and talk to us about how some machines work. That helped some, but I'm afraid I didn't prepare him well enough about how basic he needed to be. The only thing they really understood was that gears were used. Good enough, I guess.

Web We constructed a web on one bulletin board to list the simple machines we were studying: gear, lever, ramp, wheel, pulley, and screw, also showing examples of the tools that used them. We made a picture of each simple machine and outlined where the machine fit into pictures of tools. We also made a feature matrix listing each simple machine on the left and characteristics along the top. As we examined various simple machines, we filled in the feature matrix.

Content Children wrote in their journals about the simple machines they saw used
Journals around them and how they made the work easier. All in all, I think the children are beginning to understand the need for tools and how people's lives have been made easier with the development of tools. I showed a film about Native Americans who had lived in our state long before Europeans came to America. One part of the film dealt with the tools that Native Americans had used. Children were very surprised to find that the Native Americans had not discovered the wheel, since it is such an important part of many tools. They saw how Native Americans' transportation development was limited by this lack. I had them brainstorm what we would not be able to do if the wheel had not been invented. We then did the same for the pulley and the lever. Finally, children wrote descriptions in their journals of life without these machines.

Inquiry

During independent work time, the students had to create a new tool using one or more simple machines. During art, they made a model of this tool from clay or wood. Then they wrote a card describing their tool, listing its name, what it would be used for, and which simple machines it used. Those descriptions were refined during their peer group sessions and we were finally ready to invite guests to examine the products of our learning. Then we moved onto complex machines and went through the same process.

A tough month with such hard concepts to work on. We are now only days away from the end of this school year and I can hardly believe that the time is over.

JUNE

As I looked back at my first entries about what I had intended to do this year, I was pleasantly surprised at how well I did. I discovered, for one thing, that I had been promoting many of the essential thinking processes with the units I had always taught and the methods I had always used. But I found myself getting rid of some activities that I realized were not helpful for developing thinking processes nor student independence and substituting in others that were. I guess that setting goals at the beginning of the year alerted me to be aware at all times of the value of each activity I used with the children. Certainly I can see great growth in both their content reading and writing abilities. Requiring them to write about the content areas from the beginning was a new idea for me, and it really worked. I gave up using my language arts textbook about January because the children were so far ahead of the skills we were expected to cover at each of their grade levels. Just through regular writing activity and responses from me and their peers, children's writing was more organized and better developed than I had ever seen for young children. Part of this is due, I'm sure, to the fact that they have learned about topic sentences and the need for supporting details. Additionally, the children this year wrote more total words; more different and varied words; and longer, more complex sentences than have my students in previous years.

Independence

The children are far more independent in their learning strategies than any group I have ever had. I guess all the modeling with gradual fading to student independence paid off, not to mention the modeling of the second-graders for the first-graders. Not only did I "cover the content," but also I think that, for the first time, the majority of students learned it, too. There is no doubt in my mind that next year I will include even more strategies to help children learn to think as well as learn facts.

Thinking
Processes—
Organizes

Helping the children organize information was a big part of my lessons, since children at this level need to bring some order to all the random facts they are acquiring. I used many webs, data charts, and one-paragraph essays, and did a lot of modeling followed by guided practice, allowing them to extend their learning with personalized inquiry. What a great year!

And now, off for the summer, which, with July looming, is going to be a pretty busy one for me. Maybe I can work on some more strategy development while I'm in the hospital!

REFERENCES

ANDRY, A. C., & SCHEPP, S. (1968). *How babies are made.* New York: Time-Life Books.

BARRETT, J. (1983). *A snake is totally tail.* New York: Atheneum.

BULLA, C. R. (1962). *What makes a shadow?* New York: Crowell.

CHARLIP, R., & MILLER, M. B. (1974). *Handtalk: An ABC of finger spelling and sign language.* New York: Four Winds.

COLE, J. (1984). *How you were born?* New York: Morrow.

EDGE, N. (1975). *Kids in the kitchen.* Port Angeles, WA: Peninsula Publishing Co.

GOUDEY, A. E. (1961). *The day we saw the sun come up.* New York: Scribner.

GREEN, M. M. (1960). *Is it hard? Is it easy?* New York: Young Scott Books.

GRIFFITHS, R., & CLYNE, M. (1991). *Books you can count on! Linking mathematics and literature.* Portsmouth, NH: Heinemann.

KRAUS, R. (1971). *Leo the late bloomer.* New York: Windmill Books.

LANSKY, V. (1978). *The taming of the C.A.N.D.Y. monster.* Wayzata, MN: Meadowbrook Press.

LASKY, K. (1983). *Sugaring time.* New York: Macmillan.

LIONNI, L. (1967). *Frederick.* New York: Pantheon.

LOBEL, A. (1972). *Frog and toad together.* New York: Harper & Row.

MAYER, M. (1968). *There's a nightmare in my closet.* New York: Dial.

OESCHLI, H. (1985). *In my garden.* New York: Macmillan.

PARENTS' NURSERY SCHOOL. (1972). *Kids are natural cooks.* Boston: Houghton Mifflin.

PETERSON, J. W. (1977). *I have a sister—my sister is deaf.* New York: Harper & Row.

SEULING, B. (1980). *The triplets.* Boston: Houghton Mifflin.

SHRIBERG, L. K., & NICHOLAS, C. (1980). *Kids in the kitchen.* New York: Wanderer Books.

SPIER, P. (1979). *People.* New York: Doubleday.

THALER, M. (1983). *It's me, Hippo!* New York: Harper & Row.

ZIM, H. (1952). *What's inside of plants?* New York: William Morrow.

chapter 10

Intermediate Level

AUGUST

Next week the students will arrive, and as always I am not ready and anticipate the year with my usual feelings of fear and excitement. Finding out last week that I would be teaching fifth grade rather than fourth was a shock and a disappointment at first. After two years in fourth grade, I was finally getting a good handle on what needed to be taught and had developed some good units. But when Ruby died so unexpectedly, Mr. Head asked me to move to fifth grade. "Connie," he explained, "Miss Stone was the Rock of Gibraltar and we need that kind of experience and stability in fifth grade. I know you are just starting your third year of teaching, but you are so stable and creative. I know you can fill the void left by Miss Stone's tragic death." I am not at all sure Connie Tent can even begin to replace Ruby Stone, but I am glad Mr. Head has such confidence in me! I will just have to learn some new content and develop some new units. Fifth-grade science content is interesting, and I know the kids and I will enjoy learning all about our country, Canada, and Latin America. I have traveled in most of the United States and some of Canada, so I should be able to help make that study real for them. Teaching health will be a problem. There is no curriculum guide to work from, and the textbook looks very hard. I will have to figure out how to make that material understandable and exciting when the time comes.

Schedule   I have a schedule and an overall plan for the year that I hope will result in a less choppy day, week, and curriculum. I was bothered both years I taught by the lack of time to study anything in depth and by the fact that we teach the skills of reading, writing, and computing but never relate these skills to learning about the world. It is so difficult to integrate reading, spelling, language, and math with the other subjects when each uses a separate textbook and an unrelated set of skills. I'm not comfortable just making up a whole curriculum and chucking all the texts (although that is tempting!). So, being a typical Libra, I have worked out a schedule that seems a good compromise. Monday through Thursday, I will divide the mornings up between the various skills subjects. We will begin with a 45-minute math period and then take the next two hours for reading and language arts.

We will go to physical education just before lunch. After lunch, the students will have 15 minutes for SSR-sustained silent reading—in anything they choose to read. Last year the students really came to look forward to this quiet interlude in our day, once they got used to it.

After our 15 minutes of silent reading, I will read to them for ten or 15 minutes. I have read to students my previous two years and my fourth-graders loved it. I hope my fifth-graders will, too. I am going to try to read books that are in a series or whose author has written several other books, because I know that will motivate students to read the other books. I am also going to read some of the good fiction, biographies, and informational books that complement our science, social studies, and health units.

We will then spend 80 to 85 minutes on a science, social studies, or health unit. I have decided to work on one unit at a time for several weeks, using large blocks of time to really focus on what we are learning. Nothing was more disorienting to me and my students last year than trying to do 30 minutes of science, 30 minutes of social studies, and then fit some health in. Just when we were getting into something, I had to say, "We will get back to that science question tomorrow but now it is time for social studies!" I think this short time and these quick transitions were the main reasons the students and I did not get as interested in what we were studying as we could have. Still, I have tried to follow state guidelines about how much time to spend on each subject area. During each nine-week grading period, we will do two two-week science units, one one-week health unit, and one four-week social studies unit. Health is not really getting as much time as it needs, but several of the health units can be combined with our science unit on the human body. Then we can spend all day Friday learning about our current unit. Friday will be my integration day!

On Friday, we will not use any textbooks. Rather, we will spend the whole day reading, listening, writing, speaking, and computing problems relating to our unit. We will also do art and whenever possible will relate music and P.E. to what we are studying in science, social studies, or health. I am very excited about this plan. I hope that by taking all day Friday to do content area work, we will be more excited about our units, learn more, and better apply the strategies we learn the other four days.

In addition to my new schedule, I have established some new goals for myself and my students this year. At the top of my list is to help students develop their thinking skills. Of course we will focus on these as we learn the

Thinking Processes

scientific processes of observing, predicting, experimenting, controlling variables, and so forth. But I also want to help students use their thinking processes as they read and write. To this end, I will try to assure that they are practicing nine thinking processes: call up, predict, organize, connect, image, monitor, generalize, evaluate, and apply. I have therefore developed a checklist to use each time I teach a comprehension or writing lesson (see Figure 10.1).

Meaning Vocabulary Another major goal is to emphasize meaning vocabulary. It is clear to me that the major reason students cannot read, write, or learn in their content subjects is that they lack appropriate meanings to link with the new words they must learn. I am going to have a Word Wall for each unit and will try to provide real and visual experience from which they can build new meanings. I will also help them connect their experiences to new concepts, using many analogies as I help them develop their own analogies. Finally, I will help them become "word detectives," noticing how words like *nation* and *international* are alike so that they can figure out many new big words when reading on their own.

Inquiry Helping students to become good writers and researchers is my third major goal. One of the major reasons for devoting Friday to integration is so that we have time to go to the library, locate resources, learn information, and organize and report on the data. You simply can't do this in 30 minutes, and I know I was never taught these important skills. I just had to figure them out as I went along. My students will get a better education than that.

Independence Finally, I am going to work toward making my students independent learners. This will be hard: I tend to want to spoonfeed them information to be

Date	Call Up	Predict	Organize	Connect	Image	Self-Monitor	Generalize	Evaluate	Apply

Key: C = comprehension lesson; W = writing lesson

Figure 10.1 Thinking Processes Checklist

sure they all get it. But I know that they won't always have me there to do that. I shudder to think of how much those middle-school teachers will expect them to do and feel an obligation to do everything I can to prepare my students. This goal of independence is one I will work on all year, but I have dedicated March, April, and May specifically to this purpose. I even wrote it in big red letters on these months in my calendar.

Well, as always I have high hopes. I know I won't accomplish everything I want, but I will accomplish more with this schedule and with my four goals of developing thinking skills, meaning vocabulary, writing and researching skills, and independence clearly established. I just wish someone had shown me how to do this before I started to teach. I could have done so much better my first two years. Could it be that someone did try to teach me and I just wasn't ready to learn it?

SEPTEMBER

I survived September! To anyone who hasn't taught, that may sound like an overstatement, but to teachers, September is the hardest month. You have to set up all the classroom routines and expectations and get to know a whole new group of students. This year, I also had to learn about fifth grade, get my new schedule working, and begin work on all my ambitious goals. Too ambitious, perhaps.

My new schedule does seem to be working. On Monday through Thursday, I like getting the math and language arts essentials accomplished first thing. Concentrating on just one of the content area subjects each afternoon really helps us focus. But Friday is clearly everyone's favorite day. I started off the year calling this Integration Day, but the children call it the Special Day, so I have started calling it that, too.

SSR   SSR is now running smoothly. It took a few weeks for the students to realize what sustained silent reading meant. I had to be quite firm in making sure they all had a book—two if they thought they would need two for 15 minutes—and that they sat right down to read. I then sat down too and set my timer for fifteen minutes. The first two weeks it took almost ten minutes to get everyone actually sitting down with a book. That meant I had less time to read aloud to them and our unit work started a little late. But now they walk in from lunch, pick up their book from our classroom library if they don't have one in their desk (which most do), and immediately begin reading. It just goes to show you what determination and routines will accomplish.

I did have a problem with Dave and Jim not reading the first day. We had all settled down with our books, and the next thing I knew they were laughing and talking with each other. I let them see how shocked I was. I walked right over to them, looked them straight in the eye, and delivered my lecture. "Perhaps you didn't understand," I began. "This is sustained silent reading time. It is the special 15 minutes we take out of a busy schedule each day just to enjoy a good book. You have just interrupted me and everyone else. I don't expect to be interrupted again. You have your books. Open them and read them." I then returned to my seat facing the class and resumed reading. They were shocked enough to be quiet for the rest of the 15 minutes. But the next day, they tried it again. This time I went one step further. I moved two chairs on either side of my chair and put Jim and Dave with their books into them. Dave was scarlet with embarrassment. Jim tried to look unconcerned, but I could tell he was embarrassed, too. The next day, without saying a word, I moved two chairs on either side of mine before we began SSR. I think Dave and Jim got the hint because they did not disturb us and the chairs remained vacant. I don't think Dave and Jim actually read during SSR. They are very poor readers, and I think they try to defy me by just sitting with their books open and not reading. But I ignore them as long as they are quiet. They have not interrupted us since (and neither has anyone else), and I noticed them actually turning pages recently. You may not be able to make a horse drink, but if you lead him to water regularly and don't allow him anything else to drink, the chances are pretty good that sooner or later, he will drink! So, SSR is now established, and I don't expect any more problems as long as I do it each day and read as the students read.

This is a most unusual group of kids. Bo says I say that every year. But, this year it is verifiable. I have not one but two sets of twins. Michelle and Michael are both delightful. They don't seem to compete with each other; indeed, they're quite supportive. Steven and Stephanie, on the other hand, should have been separated. Belle tells me that she wanted them separated way back in second grade, but the parents wouldn't hear of it. They want them together so that Steven can help Stephanie. "Help" is not the word I would use to describe what Steven does to Stephanie. Poor Stephanie is just a slow student, and Steven always picks on her when she does not catch on right away. I try to stop it but it is difficult since this appears to be a long-established pattern. I have already requested a conference with their parents. Then, there are Kazu and Che, both Korean. Kazu is a top student. Che came to our country only recently. He will be another top student once he learns English, but he is currently struggling. At least Kazu can help him. Hernando also knows very little English, and no one here speaks Spanish. I am learning a little and I have some Spanish books for him. I never realized when I was in school how many children I would teach who knew little English and how necessary it is to make adjustments for them.

I worry about Ray because he is so quiet. I can never get him to talk. He has little confidence and is always sure he will be wrong. Unfortunately, I think his perception is usually true! I am looking for some strength I can capitalize on but haven't found one yet. He is very uncoordinated, and the kids never want him on their sports teams. He appears to have no talent for art or music, either. Surely there must be something he does well!

The rest of the children seem quite average, although David, John, Sharon, and Pat seem to be unusually intelligent. As always, I have a class full of the complete range of intelligence, motivation, and talent, and it will be a real challenge to see that all—both the brightest and the slowest—make some progress.

Integrated Units

We did a social studies unit on the geography of the United States, Canada, and Latin America this month. We made a word wall, which was hard to limit to only 40 words since there are so many terms they need to understand. I had to decide on the basis of which words educated adults knew and so included words like *latitude, longitude, continent,* and *equator.* I used many videos to provide visual experiences from which to build meaning. Of course, we became experts at maps and globes, constructing a variety of maps during the course of the unit.

Comprehension Lesson

We did a listening comprehension lesson in which I set the purpose by using a problem/solution format. The magazine article I read to them talked about problems that people living in North America must work together to solve. Before I began, I had them write down three major problems on one side of their notebook; as they listened, they filled in the proposed solutions on the other side. After I finished reading the article, they told me their proposed solutions. Then there were several disagreements, and I had to reread parts of the text. It appears that they can understand well if facts are stated explicitly but have difficulty when a concept requires them to make an inference. As I reread the parts of the text, I tried to explain how relating the text to prior knowledge allows you to make certain inferences, but I know not everyone understood. I will have to work on this.

Writing

We have done some writing, and the results are not good. Many of my students don't like to write and don't write well, so my goal of making them good writers and researchers may be a little ambitious. But I am not going to give up trying to improve their writing. We probably just won't get as far as I had hoped. I plan to teach them to write paragraphs next month, since it appears that no one but Sharon and Pat has that skill. These students may indent from time to time, but where they "push it in" bears little relationship to where new ideas begin.

Thinking Processes

This month I am proudest of the progress I have made toward improving their thinking skills. My checklist for the nine thinking processes has many entries. I have found that it is quite natural to have students call up their past experience and make predictions based on it if you only remember to do so. It also seems to generate more interest to start from what they know and think. We have classified our Word Wall words and outlined several topics as a way of organizing information. I am also getting better at helping students connect the new things they are learning to what they already know. "Remember what we learned last Friday . . ." is becoming a normal part of my repertoire. Having students image is also fairly normal, once they start to do it. "Now, close your eyes and picture yourselves on that mountain in western Canada. It is 6000 feet up and covered with snow . . . ." I find that the students like to form images of things both before and after they have learned about them from listening, reading, or viewing. Self-monitoring happens most frequently when students have had a breakdown in comprehension, and we must reread part of the text to clarify a point.

Generalizing also tends to occur quite naturally as I take the last few minutes of each lesson to try to bring closure on what we have learned. At the end of each lesson, I take a few minutes to ask them what they think are the most important things we have learned so far. If I have time, I have them each write down the three most important things they have learned and then share some of their responses. Sometimes they give me specific facts, but often their responses are generalizations or conclusions based on many facts. At the conclusion of our unit this month, Pat said that the most important thing she had learned was that all people couldn't live in exactly the same way because the places they lived were so different!—a truly high-level generalization about the relationship between geography and sociology!

Evaluate and apply are harder processes to teach, although I do try to remember to ask such evaluative questions as, "Do you think this is a good solution?" and "Would you like to live in this part of the continent? Why? Why not?" We did apply our knowledge when we made maps, and when we described various geographic features of different countries and had imaginary space invaders decide what they should pack if they were going to settle in that region. I must continue to think of ways to incorporate these two thinking skills on a daily basis. My checklist shows we are not practicing them nearly as often as we are the other seven.

Now that we are off and running, I expect to make great progress toward meeting my goals in October.

OCTOBER

Integrated Units

Energy and our solar system were the topics of the two science units we did this month. The students loved the energy unit because we learned many of the basic concepts during P.E. We played soccer and related the energy source and energy receiver to the players. Transfer of energy was easy to understand once the students grasped that the food they ate gave them energy, which they then transferred to the ball when they kicked it.

The solar system was also fun to study. We led into it from our energy unit by beginning with the idea that all energy in our solar system originates from our sun. The most important concepts that I wanted them to learn were the following: how our planets orbit our sun, the various size and distance relationships in our solar system, and some of the distinguishing characteristics of each planet.

Trade Books

Before reading about planets in our science book, the students created two models of our solar system. We used reference books (*The Planets in Our Solar System, How Did We Find Out About the Universe?*) to find out each planet's size and distance from the sun. One model showed the relative size of each planet, using assorted round objects to represent size. The students were amazed to see Mercury represented by a tiny marble and Jupiter by an enormous beachball. Another model showed the distance of each planet from the sun. We had to use the hall to represent how far away Neptune and Pluto were. These two models helped the children image the size and distance represented by those huge and abstract numbers. It also helped generate interest in learning about the planets.

Comprehension Lesson   When looking at the science chapter in our text, I realized that the way the various planets were described fit very well into a semantic feature matrix graphic organizer. I listed the planets down one side and their major features across the top and had everyone copy this pattern into his or her science notebook. See Figure 10.2 for the feature matrix they copied.

Based on what they already knew, I told the children to put a + or × to indicate whether a planet had a particular feature. If a child was unsure about a particular feature, the space was to be left blank. "If your mind is blank, leave the space blank," I explained. See Figure 10.3 for the feature matrix that Ray filled out before reading the text. As you can see, his mind was blank on many facts. I was particularly amazed to see that he was unsure whether Jupiter, Neptune, Pluto, Saturn, and Uranus orbit the sun!

Next, the children read the science text section on planets. The children were clear about their purpose for reading: to confirm or change the pluses and minuses on their feature matrix and to fill in blank spaces. As the children read, erasers were used liberally and quiet cheers and groans indicated that the children were actively comprehending rather than passively getting through the pages. When the children had finished, we performed a group task: to correctly fill out our class feature matrix. For every space, I had the

	Closer to sun than Earth	Larger than Earth	Has moon	Has rings	Orbits the sun	Inner planet	Smallest	Largest	Has life as we know it
Earth									
Jupiter									
Mars									
Mercury									
Neptune									
Pluto									
Saturn									
Uranus									
Venus									

Figure 10.2 Planets in Our Solar System

	Closer to sun than Earth	Larger than Earth	Has moon	Has rings	Orbits the sun	Inner planet	Smallest	Largest	Has life as we know it
Earth	−	−	+	−	+	+	−	−	+
Jupiter	−	+	+	−		−			−
Mars	+	−	+	−	+	+		−	−
Mercury	+	−		−	+	+			−
Neptune	−	+		−		−	−		−
Pluto	−	+		−					−
Saturn	−	+		+		−			−
Uranus	−			−		−	−		−
Venus	+	−	+	−	+			−	

Figure 10.3   Ray's Feature Matrix: Planets in Our Solar System

children signal thumbs up if they had a plus and thumbs down if they had a minus. If I got a close-to-unanimous reply (a few are always too lazy to raise or lower their thumbs!), I put the plus or minus in the appropriate space. No response meant that we still did not know the answer, even after reading. For some spaces, there was still disagreement, so I had the children return to the text to argue their points and I again discovered the problem they have making inferences. Many children believed that the text did not say whether Pluto was larger or smaller than Earth, so I had David read the sentence stating that "Pluto is probably the size of Mercury." David explained that since we know that Mercury is smaller than Earth, we can figure out that Pluto is, too. While the text did not directly state that there is no life as we know it on Jupiter, the text does state this: "There is no water on Jupiter." I had to explain to the children that since life as we know it requires water, and since there is no water on Jupiter, there cannot be life as we know it on Jupiter. This "since . . . therefore" reasoning is always required for comprehension, but for many of my students, if the text doesn't say something explicitly, they don't get it! At least with this lesson and task afterward, I could see where they were not making inferences and so could lead them back to the book and explain the reasoning.

Figure 10.4 shows the feature matrix as we finally completed it. As you can see, several spaces are still blank, even after reading. Pluto is so far away that we don't know if it has a moon or rings or if it might have life as we know it. We are also not sure about life on Uranus and Neptune. Jim was disturbed by

	Closer to sun than Earth	Larger than Earth	Has moon	Has rings	Orbits the sun	Inner planet	Smallest	Largest	Has life as we know it
Earth	−	−	+	−	+	+	−	−	+
Jupiter	−	+	+	−	+	−	−	+	−
Mars	−	−	+	−	+	+	−	−	−
Mercury	+	−	−	−	+	+	+	−	−
Neptune	−	+	+	−	+	−	−	−	−
Pluto	−	−			+	−			
Saturn	−	+	+	+	+	−	−	−	−
Uranus	−	+	+	+	+	−	−	−	−
Venus	+	−	−	−	+	+	−	−	−

Figure 10.4   Planets in Our Solar System

these blanks and wanted to vote on what to put there. I don't know if he was serious or just putting me on, but I tried to explaih that you can't make truth by voting on it!

Inquiry   On Friday, we went to the library to do some more research on planets. I chose Venus and showed the students how I used the card catalog and other resources to find more information about Venus. I then divided them into groups for the other eight planets and helped them as they found information. **Groups** Each group decided on three facts besides those we had read about in our text, and one person in each group wrote these three facts on a chart to display in our room. Of course, I had showed them how I selected three facts about Venus and wrote these on my chart. They were very proud of their charts and of their burgeoning research skills—as was I!

Writing Lesson   Finally, I used their interest in planets to do a writing lesson on how to write a paragraph. Of course, I began by modeling for them as I wrote a paragraph on Venus. First, I reviewed what I knew about Venus from our feature matrix. Then I read the three additional facts from my chart. I told them that there were many different ways to construct paragraphs but that today we were going to write paragraphs with a topic sentence, three detail sentences, and a concluding sentence. I pointed to the title of our feature matrix, "Planets in Our Solar System," and explained that their paragraphs' topic sentences should get the planet into its topic—which in a feature matrix is the title. The next three sentences should describe some details about the planet from the feature matrix or chart. The final sentence could do many things; often it gave a fascinating fact or an opinion. As the children watched, I talked through my construction of topic sentence and my selection and construction of detail and concluding sentences and wrote the following paragraph on the board:

> Venus is one of the planets in our solar system. Venus and Earth are about the same size. Venus is hotter than Earth because it is closer to the sun. Because there is no water on Venus, it can't maintain life as we know it. Venus is called the evening star and is the favorite planet of many people because it can often be seen on a clear night.

Having modeled how to write a paragraph, I had each child choose his or her favorite planet and write a paragraph about it. I reminded them to have their first sentence tell how their planet related to the larger topic of the feature matrix. Three sentences should then give specific information about their planet, based on the feature matrix, the charts, or any other information they knew. A final sentence should end the paragraph in an interesting way. "Remember, you can't include everything you know in just one paragraph. Just include what you believe is most important and interesting," I reminded them.

As the children wrote their paragraphs, the model paragraph, the feature matrix, and the charts were all available to them. When the paragraphs were written, I let several children read theirs to the class. I was amazed when Ray volunteered. His paragraph on Mars was a lot like mine in form, but it was all correct, and most important, he had volunteered to read! This was a most successful writing experience. The children actually seemed to enjoy it. I guess when you know the information, have the correctly spelled words in front of you, and have seen the form modeled, writing is not so arduous. In fact, I overheard Kazu comment, "The paragraph just wrote itself!"

Trade books I encouraged the students to read science fiction related to outer space this month. Among the most popular books were *Planet Out of the Past; The Deadly Hoax; The Doors of the Universe;* and *Another Heaven, Another Earth.*

NOVEMBER

Integrated Unit Our first health unit was a success. The topic was "Your Emotions," the major idea being that we all experience a range of feelings, some happy and some not. In looking at the text, I thought the information was fairly trite and was unprepared for the response of my students. Many of them clearly thought that fear, anger, and inadequacy were emotions unique to them. They were amazed to read that we all feel these emotions—children and adults alike—and there are healthy and unhealthy ways to deal with them. We did many skits and a lot of **Groups** talking. I put them into small groups, gave them a description of some events in a child's life, and had them decide which emotions that child would probably feel and how best to deal with them. They worked well in their groups, better than I had expected. I think their concentration and the strength of their discussion stemmed from the immediacy of the topic to their own lives. I had a time limit for the groups and had each group prepare a summary of their discussion. I think this structure also helped to keep them on task.

Trade Books   In the weeks before our unit, I had read them *Bridge to Terabithia* and *Ramona Forever.* I was able to refer to these characters and their emotions as we worked in our unit. Finally, I assigned each student to find a book in which the character experiences some strong emotions and to prepare a short report listing the emotions, the reasons for them, and the way they were handled. They all did a good job with these reports—even Dave read *The Flunking of Joshua T. Bates* and reported on it. I know the unit was a success because I have heard the children use the terminology in talking among themselves. I think they now have more empathy with each other when they are experiencing strong emotions. They also seem to have a better idea of how to handle emotions. I heard Jim say to Bob, "I'm angry at myself right now, so you and me will both be better off if you just stay clear for a while." I think before our unit, Jim might have just hauled off and hit Bob. Next year, I think I will start the year with this health unit.

Scavenger Hunt   Our social studies unit took most of the month. We learned about the European settlement and expansion of the United States and did our first scavenger hunt. To prepare for the scavenger hunt, I read through the materials I wanted the students to read or listen to and wrote down all the interesting things that students might find either an object or a picture for. Here is the list:

prairie	wagon train
canal	textile
pioneer	trains
totem pole	lantern
basin	broad ax
Rocky Mountains	gold
mission	immigrant
cotton gin	Indians
sod house	spinning wheel
grub hoe	iron skillet

We did the scavenger hunt during the week that we worked on our health unit. I had hoped that by the time we actually started the settlement and expansion unit, the students would have been motivated by the search. Before I started the children on the scavenger hunt, I asked them to call up their experiences with scavenger hunts. Many had been on them and explained how you had a limited time to find a bunch of things. I helped them to see that no group usually found everything but that the group that found the most was the winner. I then divided the class into six groups of four and gave each group the list. I appointed a leader and recorder for each group. We read over the 20 items on the list and discussed what they were. If the group was unsure about something, I suggested they would have to find out for sure if they were to find the correct object or picture. To my question "Where can you find out more about what these words mean?" they responded, "Dictionaries, encyclo-

Groups

pedias, and other library books." "Right," I said, "and I will let each group go to the media center for 15 minutes this afternoon to look up the things you are unsure about." I then explained that real objects or models counted two points, while pictures—photographs, magazine pictures, tracings, or drawings—counted one point. I warned the students that I would not count any "thrown-together" drawings or models. They would have one week to find and make what they could. I also asked them not to bring anything to class that they could not hide in their desks until the appointed day—next Friday. "You don't want the other groups to see what you have," I chided. Finally, I told them that just as in real scavenger hunts, I was sure that no group would be able to find an object or even a picture for each word. The knowing glances that passed from Sharon to Pat and from Dave to Jim let me know that my challenge was going to be met.

I let the groups meet several times for just a few minutes during the next week. I emphasized whispering and secrecy, and the children soon got into the mood of the hunt. I gave them tracing and drawing paper as needed and granted their requests to go to the media center alone. I knew my effort to get them interested in our unit was working when I ran into my old friend, Lib Booker, a librarian at our public library. She remarked on how many fifth-graders suddenly wanted books on our country's discovery and expansion!

On Friday morning, there was much excitement. I let each group display what they had scavenged and then had each group tally their score—two points for each object, one for each picture. Most of the groups had pictures of almost everything and objects for common things, such as gold and the lantern. After the groups had done their own tallies, I double-checked the points of the winning group: Sharon, Michelle, Bob, and Ray. They had made a papier-mâché model of the Rocky Mountains, a small wooden totem pole, and a sod house out of mud. They also had a miniature wagon train. The others were amazed. I can tell that there will be a lot of models constructed for the next scavenger hunt.

As their prize, I let Sharon, Michelle, Bob, and Ray have the rest of the morning off to put up their bulletin board. Sharon very neatly lettered cards for each word, and they all arranged and stapled the pictures collage style. They put the labeled objects on a table that they pushed under the bulletin board. A title and credits, "The Settlement and Expansion of the United States by the Scavenger Hunt Winners—Sharon, Michelle, Bob, and Ray," completed the display that would serve as a springboard for our study. This first scavenger hunt was a success, but I believe the next one will be even better now that the children understand what to do. I already heard some groans and comments like, "We could have made those things, too."

Inquiry We finished this unit with a research day. During our unit, we had developed a list of explorers. I added a few names to this list and then assigned each child a partner. The partners picked one explorer that they wanted to learn more about. Then we made a list of WH questions to which we might seek answers. Here are the questions the students came up with:

What did the explorer explore?
When did the explorer explore?
Where did the explorer explore?
How did the explorer get here?
Why did the explorer come here?
Who was in the explorer's family?
Who did the explorer find while exploring?
How were the explorers treated by the people they found?
How did the explorers get the money to explore?

Partners

To model for them how to locate and organize information, I picked an explorer that no one else had picked and showed students both how to locate sources and how to find information within those sources. I read aloud from the information I had found, with the students stopping me when I read the information that answered one of our questions. I recorded each answer next to its question. When we found some fascinating information that didn't answer any of our questions, David had the idea of adding P.S. at the bottom for miscellaneous facts. The children then worked in pairs under my direction. I had paired the better and the weaker students so there was a lot of one-to-one teaching going on. I have decided that only one teacher cannot possibly teach 24 individuals, so I must maximize partner and group work for my students to teach one another. I no longer feel guilty about these pairings since Belle told me that research shows that the child tutor often learns more than does the tutee!

DECEMBER

Meaning Vocabulary

To me, December, not February, is the shortest month of the year! Between doing holiday things with the children here and preparing for the holidays myself, I find it very hard to accomplish any of my normal academic tasks. I did unexpectedly add another Word Wall to our room. Of course we have one on the side bulletin board that changes as our unit changes. But when I discovered recently that many of my students did not really understand many of the words in their math books or its symbols and abbreviations, I turned the space above the front chalkboard into another Word Wall for math items. Since I began it so late, I added five terms each day this month until I got them all up. We spent a good part of our math period learning these symbols and attaching appropriate meanings to them. From now on, I will add new terms gradually as we begin a new chapter in math. I select the terms from the fifth-grade textbook, but there is much overlap for my group working in the fourth-grade book, and I know it will help them next year to have learned the essential fifth-grade math vocabulary. Here is the math wall as it currently looks. As you can see, I have translated the symbols and abbreviations.

hundreds   remainder
billions   less than (<)

right angle	percent (%)
sum	ray
kilometer (km)	tens
round off	prime number
difference	digit
product	estimate
quotient	centimeter (cm)
divisor	factors
dollar ($)	common divisor
cent (¢)	greater than (>)
angle	degree (°)
thousands	millions
average	acute angle
obtuse angle	addends
regroup	meter (m)
ones	multiples
even numbers	odd numbers

Each day at the beginning of our math time, I have the students number a sheet of paper from 1 to 5 as I call out the definition of five terms or write something on the board to express them. The students write the word for each term and then we check. Here are some meaning cues I gave them, followed by the answers in parentheses:

1. 2, 4, 6, 10, and 106 are examples of this. 1, 3, 5, 107, and 409 are not (even numbers)
2. The symbol for less than (<)
3. The abbreviation for kilometer (km)
4. When I do this problem ($64 \times 35 = 2240$), the numbers 64 and 35 (multiples)
5. For the same problem, the number 2240 (product)

Be a Mind Reader

I also use a game called "Be a Mind Reader" that students particularly enjoy and that helps us review the meanings for these terms. Again, students number their paper from 1 to 5, but this time I think of only one term and give five clues for it. The first clue is always the same, "It is one of the words, symbols, or abbreviations on our math wall." The children always moan, but I tell them to try to read my mind and guess what I am thinking of. They write their guess on the first line. The remaining four clues narrow down the problem until by the fifth clue, only one answer is possible. As I give successive clues, the children continue to write the same one unless my clue tells them that theirs can't be right. Here is one set of clues I used:

1. It's one of the words, symbols, or abbreviations on the math wall.
2. It is a symbol.
3. It is not "<" or ">."

4. This symbol refers to money.

5. This symbol means dollar.

Jim guessed this one on the first clue! He was so proud! "How did you do that?" everyone asked. "He read my mind," I responded. Jim beamed and I was delighted he was getting some positive attention. Some children need a little luck to shine, and Be a Mind Reader allows the chance for that lucky guess.

I wish I had started the year with work on these math terms, but it just didn't occur to me until recently that not understanding what the book said was a part of my students' problem with math. It is clear from their improved work that this vocabulary work is helping. Next year, I'll start a math wall the first week of school!

Integrated Units

We did manage to complete a science unit on the ocean this month. Many children had not been to the ocean, and it is a hard concept to explain to someone who has never experienced it. I relied a great deal on visuals. I got from the state department media center two good videos that helped the children to see the ocean's enormous size and to build concepts for terms like low tide and high tide. I did a prediction activity to set the purpose for a viewing lesson on a video that showed the various parts of the ocean bottom. I gave the students the following list and asked them to guess which things we would find on the ocean bottom:

Comprehension Lesson

mountains	slope
shelf	fences
roads	cracks
floor	oceanographers
treasure boxes	plains
ridges	continents

Of course, many of the students didn't know the ocean bottom is called the floor or that there is a continental shelf there. They accused me of tricking them, and I protested, "You know I would never do such a thing!" We talked about the different meanings of floor and shelf. I also had to allow that although our video hadn't shown a treasure box, you might indeed find one on the ocean's floor.

Thinking Processes

Prediction has been quite a successful way to help the children have clear purposes. Sometimes I use prediction in an open-ended way. I might have said, for example, "Name some things that you think our video will show at the bottom of the ocean." Other times, I give them a list of things or of true or false statements; have them make guesses about them; and then they read, listen, or view to confirm their predictions. It is amazing how much more actively they read after making that small investment of guessing or predicting. They attend very carefully when they want to find out how they did! I guess this is a normal part of human nature, and I am glad I can capitalize on it to help them become more active learners.

I suppose the high point of the whole unit was when Bo brought in his scuba diving equipment and some things he has collected in and near the ocean. The children seemed to hang on his every word. Bo has never had much experience with children and had been a little nervous about coming. He really got into it and even expressed regret that we couldn't take the whole crew with us when we go to the shore for the holidays. I must admit that I am attached to my children—but not that attached!

JANUARY

Integrated Unit

We spent this entire month on a combined health and science unit on the human body. The four chapters of the health book and the one in the science book covered much of the same information. I borrowed some bones and a lot of models from Annie Mull, who teaches at the high school. I had an X-ray technician and a pediatrician come in and talk to us. We have become more health-conscious since we began our study. We kept charts of the food we ate and the exercise we've had, and we evaluated how well we were nourishing and exercising our bones and muscles. (The children were amazed to learn that I go to a health club several times a week. I brought my sweat suit and my tape one day and taught them a few aerobics routines. They loved it!)

Word Problems

Math has once again been the focus of much of my creativity. The math wall vocabulary activities have definitely helped, but I noticed the children are still having a great deal of difficulty with word problems. I know that computation is not their main problem because I set up the computations for some word problems that many of them had missed and the children breezed right through them. Their difficulty seems rather to be a lack of understanding of what they are trying to find out and an inability to figure out which operations to perform. I have been taking them through a set of steps that I hope will improve their ability to think through word problems. I have listed these steps on a chart, and each morning we work through several problems following these steps:

1. Decide what question the problem asks you to answer.
2. Decide what facts are given.
3. Estimate your answer.
4. Decide which operations to do in which order.
5. Do these operations to get your answer.
6. Compare your answer to your estimate.

Coming up with the steps and writing them on the chart was the easy part. The hard part is teaching the students to follow the steps! As with everything, I began by modeling what to do. I made up a word problem related to members of the class. (They are always more motivated and attend better when the problems are about them.)

Sharon, Pat, and Sarah all want to make cheerleading outfits. It will take 3 yards of cloth for each, and the cloth costs $4.99 per yard. How much money do they need to buy enough cloth for all three outfits?

Modeling   I wrote this problem on the board as I read it to the class. I then modeled how to go through the five steps. (*Modeling* is just a fancy term for thinking aloud as you do something, so the kids can figure out what you're doing and why you're doing it.) "Well," I began, "I have to figure out what the question is and it is a little tricky. The question is not how much cloth they need, although I will have to figure that out, too. The question is how much money they need in all." I then wrote, "How much money in all?" next to step one. Next to step two, facts, I wrote, "3 yards for each outfit; 3 outfits; $4.99 per yard."

"Estimating is important," I mused aloud, "so that I can tell if my answer makes sense or if I misplaced a decimal point or did something else dumb like that." (The children tittered at the idea of their teacher making dumb mistakes.) "If the material costs $4.99 per yard, that is close to $5.00. There are three of them, so if it only took one yard each, that would be $15.00, but it takes 3 yards each. Three times $15.00 is $45.00. The answer will be a little more than $45.00." I then wrote "$45.00" next to step three.

For step four, I reasoned that since I knew how much one yard cost and wanted to know how much 3 yards cost, I would have to multiply. I would then know how much it would cost for one girl, and since there were three girls, I would have to multiply again. I wrote, "Multiply $4.99 × 3 1/2; multiply that times 3" next to step four. Finally, I did the calculation, compared $52.40 to $45.00, and decided my answer was indeed "in the ballpark."

After modeling the whole procedure for the students, I took them through several other problems and let them help me decide what to write and why. Then I had them turn to a set of word problems in their books (those working in fourth-grade math used their book) and had each student write down only the question he or she was trying to answer. I went around and gave help as they worked. It became very clear that deciding on the question was not easy or automatic for many of them.

On the following day, we worked together on just that step—deciding the question. I gave them many problems that used their names and we decided what questions were being asked. I then assigned them a page of word problems they had already worked on (not very successfully) and had them write the question for each one. We continued to work on determining the question for a few days and then went on to step two, determining the facts. This was easier for them. Step three, however, estimating the answer, continues to be a problem. Many of them still can't come up with a reasonable estimate. This worries me, because the people who are good in math always have an estimate to provide them feedback. I hope that if we continue to work on this skill all year, they will get better at estimating.

Step four, deciding which computations to do in which order, is also difficult, but we are continuing to work on it. The last step, when we finally get to it, will be easy. If computation were all there was to word problems, my students would be home free! At least the children and I now have a systematic way of attacking these problems and I understand how much complex thinking goes into them. Bo has heard me talk all month about word problems, and he says the steps I am teaching—determining the problem, gathering facts, considering a reasonable solution, deciding what to do in what order, and then actually solving the problem and seeing if your solution works—is how we solve not just word problems, but life problems. Perhaps the process I am teaching my students has a wider application than I realized!

I am also emphasizing using these steps to solve the word problems I give them on Friday. All year, I have integrated some real-world math applications with our study of whatever topic we were exploring. We have done lots of measuring and graphing. Now, I am going to make sure that I give them some written word problems to solve about each topic. Next month, we will be taking an imaginary voyage to Canada, and I have some great word problems ready for them to think about and solve. Each morning I plan to put on the board two problems that will require them to use their research and math skills. I will give them until lunch to find the needed information and correctly solve the problem. They will get a bonus point on their math grade for each one they correctly solve. I think this will really motivate some of my brightest students. Here are the two I plan to give them for the first day:

Inquiry

How much larger (in square miles) is Canada than the United States?

How much higher (or lower) is Canada's highest mountain peak than our highest mountain peak?

FEBRUARY

Integrated Units

Canada was our social studies adventure this month. We pretended all month that we were actually there to explore this vast and diverse land. Several of the children had been to Canada, and they became our guides. Pat's grandmother had emigrated from Canada, and Pat shared the stories she had heard. We learned a little French and a lot more geography. We also used our new Internet hookup to do some of our Canada research.

Content Journals

This was also a month to do a lot of writing. Developing good writers has been one of my goals all year, but I have not given it as much time as I think it deserves. For this unit, I decided we would write every day. One way I accomplished this was to have the students keep journals. This fit in with our idea that we were not just learning about Canada but actually imagining ourselves there. We kept journals—my boys would object to their being called diaries—of the major things we had seen and what we had learned. Each day, at the end of our social studies time, we had five minutes to write in our journals. Just as for SSR, I stuck firmly to the idea that this five minutes is sustained time for silent writing and I wrote, too. At first, the children were unsure about what to write, but I assured them that they were recording personal remembrances, impressions, and questions, with no particular form or content that they needed to include. They were their own audience, and the only restriction was to relate their writing to our study of Canada. As the month went on, the children became used to this time and, as with SSR, they seemed to enjoy it. I did not grade what they wrote, but I did check to see that there was an entry for each day and that the entry related to Canada. The daily points they got for recording their thoughts accounted for a small portion of their grade.

Grading their work has been a problem all year. In skills subjects like math, spelling, language, and reading, it is fairly easy to give a grade. The children are working on their own levels. Once I have modeled and provided guided practice with the skills, I feel comfortable testing their ability to perform them independently.

Grading their work on the units, however, is much more difficult. I believe that a grading system should motivate all students to work hard. This is easy to say and not nearly so easy to do. Many of my students—Dave, Jim, Hernando, Che, and Ray, most particularly—have very limited prior knowledge of the subjects we are studying. They are also limited by lower reading ability and, for Hernando and Che, limited command of English. If I simply taught the fifth-grade content and then gave them a comprehensive test, they would fail. Some teachers think they should fail if they can't do "fifth-grade" work, but I know that children come with different abilities. Just because they are all in fifth grade does not mean they all have fifth-grade ability.

Then, there are those on the other end of the spectrum, specifically Sharon, Pat, David, John, and Kazu. These children bring huge stores of prior knowledge, motivation, and intelligence to our units. They probably already know most of what we are supposed to learn in fifth grade. My grading system must motivate them, too. I can't let them think that they don't have to study but can just slide by on what they are fortunate enough to know.

The problem is complex, and I am not totally happy with the solution I have worked out. For each unit, I set up several parts that count toward total grade points. I give points for daily assignments, such as the journals and homework, which I never grade but simply check to see that "a good effort was made." Of course, a good effort from Hernando is not of the quality I expect from David, but I can determine this fairly easily. By now, all the kids know what it means to see, "You just threw this together—no way!" on their assignments. Knowing that life is not perfect and that no one can complete all assignments every day, I always have more assignments than can be counted for points. For the Canada unit, for example, I had 35 assignments, short daily and homework activities including the daily journal entries. The children could get up to 30 points out of the 35. Thus anyone who was there every day with the first 30 assignments did not have to do the last five! The children loved this and tried to get all the first ones done so they could "lay back" later. I had already planned to make the last five assignments less crucial than the others because I knew that many of the children would not need to complete them.

The second part of the grade comes from the unit tests. We had three tests on Canada that were all worth ten points, plus two bonus points. The ten points part of the test was taken by everyone and included the most important information, which we had learned in class and reviewed. The other two points was based on any other information intended to challenge my really top students. Only children who chose to took the bonus part of the test.

Projects   Finally, I gave my students credit for up to three projects. These projects ranged from research projects to reading additional books on Canada (*Canada's Kids* and *Take a Trip to Canada,* among others) to creating models, maps, visuals, or realia. For the most part, students did these projects out of school, although we did have some time to work on them on Fridays. These projects were each worth ten points if they were done well. Again, "well" differed for different children, but all children knew I didn't accept sloppy work.

Thus for the Canada unit you could get 30 points for daily assignments, and anyone who was making a good effort should have gotten these. The test on the most important concepts accounted for another 30 points, which again everyone should have gotten. The bonus tests and projects were there to motivate my top students, although most children did at least one project per unit. For Canada, two of the slower students—Che and Bob—did three good projects.

For the most part, I am happy with this grading system because it does seem to motivate my slow students to work with me and learn the most important information, and my top students to do projects and bonus test points. Of course, not everyone is happy with this system. John's mother complained about her son's C in social studies. I had to show her that he just hadn't put out much effort. He had not attempted any bonus test points and had done only one project. "He must learn that he must earn his As," I explained. She agreed to see to it that he made a greater effort during our next unit.

Writing   In addition to our journals, we did other writing activities this month. I have been saving the free postcards I get at motels, and the children learned the postcard form, which they enjoyed. We also used our computer mail program to become "key-pals" with a fifth-grade class in Canada. I had met Kay Beck at a meeting I attended last May and when I realized I would be teaching fifth-graders about Canada, I wrote to set up a pen pal arrangement with her. By the time we were to begin our pen pal friendships, we discovered we had both just been connected to the net and decided that the kids would all enjoy being "key-pals!" The children love having real friends in another country, and we will continue our e-mailing for the rest of the year. Who knows? Some of them may remain key pals for the rest of their lives!

MARCH

Independence   It's a good thing I wrote the word Independence in big red letters on my March, April, and May calendar months way back in August, or the year might have ended before I realized that I needed to move my children (I must stop thinking of them as children—they will be big middle-schoolers in five **Meaning** months!) toward becoming more independent learners. This month, I have **Vocabulary** tried to show them how they can independently learn new word meanings.

Instead of me previewing the unit on plants and selecting the key words, I had the students look through the science chapters and write down words that seemed important to them of whose meanings they were not totally sure. I gave them about five minutes for this, then I made a list of all their words. I chose those I considered most important and least known, and we pronounced them and talked about what they might mean. Of course, some students knew some words. But no one could tell me the meanings of words such as monocot, dicot, and photosynthesis. I told students that as we studied plants, I would help them see how they could use their texts, our dictionaries and other reference books, and their own common sense to learn meanings without my telling them or showing them. Some of my students looked a little skeptical and so was I, but I knew that I must attempt to move them toward independence since they were sure to meet some "sink or swim" teachers in the coming years.

Fortunately, most of the words that the students had identified were also the words that I had deemed most important for them to learn. I added two words—vascular and nonvascular—and left the rest of the list as they had written it. That meant we had more words than I usually allot, 20 for a two-week unit. But they had chosen some words that I thought most of them knew and others that were so obscure I didn't intend to focus on them much. So I left their list intact. That night, I divided their list into words for which I thought they had no meaning and words for which they had experienced the concept but did not know the technical term. Fortunately, there were only four words for which I thought they might have little or no experience—chlorophyll, photosynthesis, carbon dioxide, and stomata. All the other words, though unfamiliar to the children, represented something they had experienced. They had all seen ferns, but did not know the leaves were called fronds. They had all seen vascular plants—trees, tulips, and carrots—as well as nonvascular plants— mosses. Likewise, they knew some plants lived only one year—annuals—and others lived a long, long time—perennials.

I then looked through the chapters in their science book to find pictures from which students could build or call up their experience and to see what context clues were provided by the words. Finally, I looked at the list to see what morphemic clues the new words contained. For all the words for which the students had meaning, I found that the pictures, words, and morphemes would help the students call up their experience and connect it to the new words. The problem came, of course, with the process of photosynthesis and its related words, chlorophyll, carbon dioxide, and stomata. I knew that the text explanation of this process would make no sense; even though the children could read the words, they would not understand what was actually meant by them. I decided to follow the suggestion in the teacher's guide providing for direct experience through an experiment: we would deprive some plants of light, others of water, and others of air, by smearing petroleum jelly on both sides of the leaves. Still other plants would be given light and water and not smeared. Over the two weeks of our science unit, we watched the deprived plants grow. I helped them connect this experience with photosynthesis by

Direct
Experience

explaining that light, water, and air, from which plants get carbon dioxide, are all required for plants to make their own food. I further explained that all green plants got their green coloring from a chemical called chlorophyll and that the air enters the leaf through stomata, the tiny openings that we had clogged when we smeared petroleum jelly on the leaves. The plants that died had chlorophyll, as we knew from their green color, but because we had deprived them of light, water, or carbon dioxide, they could not make food and died. This process of making food, I explained, can be done by all green plants, and it is called a big word—photosynthesis.

The experience I provided for the children allowed them to build meaning to associate with photosynthesis and the related words. I used pictures, context, and morphemic clues to help them call up and link their experience with the unfamiliar words. I have been using these clues all year, but this month I focused more on the pictures and context in the textbook and tried to get the children to discover the morphemic clues themselves.

Context   To begin my lesson, I circled the words *vascular, nonvascular, botanist, biennials, conifers, monocots, dicots,* and *life cycle* on the chart of words the students and I had selected to learn. I then had each child write a definition for three words of his or her choice. By now, the children know that they can write whatever they think, even a silly definition or something the word sounds like, and that we then compare these guesses made without context to our more probable guesses made from context. I let the children share a few of these guesses, and the class hams always have a good time. Dave said that vascular was what you had left after the vase had shattered. Jim suggested that a botanist was a scientist who studied bottles. Sharon said that life cycle was a new kind of bike you didn't have to pedal. The children enjoy their silly guesses, but the guessing serves a serious function, too. When we read a word in context or see a picture, sometimes we think we knew all along what the word meant. The guessing focuses the children's attention on the words and lets them see that they don't really know what they mean. After guessing, they are curious to find out the real meanings and see clearly how much the context and pictures help.

I directed the children's attention to certain sentences and pictures in their books and asked them to explain the words' meanings based on what they read and saw. In previous units, I had written context sentences on the board or provided pictures from magazines, books, or filmstrips. But now I wanted them to utilize the resource in which they were most apt to encounter unfamiliar words—their textbook. As the children explained their meanings based on the text, I probed to get them to explain their reasoning, since often the book doesn't come right out and say, "This means that." I also helped the children to connect their own experiences to the words. "Can you name some vascular plants you see on the way to school?" I asked. "Some nonvascular plants?" I let a few children look up some of the words in our encyclopedia to give us other examples of the meaning. Finally, I had each child write the words on a page in their science notebook along with our class definition, an example, and, if they liked, an illustration.

Morphemic Clues

To help children use morphemic clues, I directed their attention to the word *conifer* and asked them if there was anything about the word that would help them remember that conifers are plants that produce seeds in cones. With my help, they noticed the cone-conifer relationship. I then asked them what word we could use to describe someone with courage. To describe something associated with danger. I wrote their responses on the board next to the root word (courage, courageous; danger, dangerous). I then wrote *conifer* and *coniferous,* and the children saw that coniferous was a word used to describe conifers. In a similar way, I helped them to see that bicycles have two wheels, to bisect is to cut in two parts, and biennials are plants that live two years. I also pointed out that many words that start with bi- have nothing to do with two, reminding them about biographies. Morphemic clues are helpful, but in English, they can mislead you. I try to remind my students to check morphemic clues against the other information in context and pictures.

Inquiry

We did many other activities in our unit on plants. We created a class horticultural guide to which each child contributed by researching and writing a one-page illustrated report on a selected plant. The books *Being a Plant* and *Plants Up Close* were most helpful. We took on a beautification project, planting some lovely shrubs donated by Hernando's dad and some pachysandra and ajuga that we dug up at my house.

Writing Lesson

We even wrote some poetry: plant cinquains. Cinquains are poems for nonpoets. There are many different ways to create these five-line poems. In this unit we brainstormed ideas for each line as a group. Then each child selected from the brainstormed list or came up with more ideas of his or her own. We wrote cinquains about monocots, dicots, conifers, annuals, and perennials as a way to review their important characteristics. The first and last line of the cinquain were the same for everyone—the topic of our cinquain. For the second line, we brainstormed a list of *-ing* words that described the topic. For the third line, we brainstormed examples of the topic. For the fourth line, we brainstormed four-word phrases and sentences that summed up the topic. Each child then chose or made up two *-ing* words, three examples, one four-word phrase or sentence, and created his or her own unique cinquains. Here is Ray's cinquain for dicots. I am so proud of him!

Dicots
Blooming, growing
Pines, roses, beans
Two seed leaves each
Dicots

APRIL

Well, April was Latin America month! I feel like I have been on one of those "see six countries in four days" tours. I am sure that we could have studied Latin America all year and still had more we wanted to learn. There is just never enough time! At least, I think we accomplished the major goal of the unit: to give our youngsters some understanding of the similarities and differences between us and our southern neighbors.

Comprehension
Lesson

I have tried to use more graphic organizers in my comprehension lessons this month in my continuing crusade to move my students toward independence. In earlier units, they completed many partial outlines, feature matrices, webs, and time lines that I set up for them. This month, I had them make outlines, webs, feature matrices, or time lines from their reading assignments, but I did not give them the headings or categories or tell them how many boxes or slots to fill in. This was hard for all of them, and Hernando, Dave, Jim, and Stephanie did not write much down after reading. We had to spend far more time following up the reading and constructing the outline, feature matrix, web, or time line. But most students did get better by the end of the month and if I can

Note-taking

teach them to preview text and decide on a note-taking structure—which is really what outlines, features matrices, webs, and time lines are—they will be able to determine and note the most important information by themselves.

Inquiry

We have also continued to work toward becoming independent writers and researchers. This month, we created a travel book, and I had each child type the final copy as a way of getting them to use the word processing skills they have been learning during our weekly computer lab time. My artistic children did some wonderful illustrations, and we duplicated the book so that everyone could take a copy home and take his or her family on an imaginary journey to Latin America. I must admit that the children worked as hard as I did, and they were very proud of their creation, as was I. I have tried all year to give them real audiences and purposes to write for, but this was my most successful attempt. Creating a real book to share knowledge about Latin America with their families was indeed a real purpose for a real audience.

We spent the first week with maps, globes, and other resources studying the geographic, cultural, and political boundaries of Latin America. The children were amazed that there are more than 30 countries to the south of us, ranging from tiny Trinidad to huge Brazil. During the next week, we did an in-depth study of Mexico, which I used to model the research and writing process we would use to create our book. First, I had them generate questions about Mexico. Then we tried to organize them. We decided that there were questions about people (How many people live in Mexico? Why do people from Mexico come to the United States? Where did the people in Mexico come from?), customs (What do they like to eat? Do they go to school in summer? Do they have Christmas too?), government (Who is their president? Do they have a good government?), and the economy (Where do people work? Why are so many people poor?). We put two questions into our all-important miscellaneous category.

I put each category of questions on a transparency, and we trooped off to the library to locate sources likely to contain the answers. Using the card catalog, *The Readers' Guide to Periodical Literature*, and indices of reference books, we collected quite a few. We found seven books devoted entirely to Mexico! How could we find our answers without reading everything? Of course, we brainstormed some key words to find the information more efficiently. For some questions, it was easy to come up with a useful key word. Food helped us find information about what people eat. For other questions, it was more difficult. To answer the question about why people come to the United States, I had to suggest that we look under emigration and economy.

As we were finding our answers, we also found other information, so we added some categories. Our question about where people came from led us to information about Mexico's early history, creating an early history category. We also decided that since we were writing a travel book, we needed information about recreation and good places to visit—another category. Eventually, we had transparencies with information about the people; early history; the government; the economy; customs; things to do and places to visit; and, of course, miscellaneous. The children wanted to write down everything they had found, but I tried to show them that in our one travel book we could not duplicate the information in many books devoted solely to Mexico, especially since we wanted to cover all of Latin America. I modeled for them how I decided what seemed most important, but when they got started on their own work, it was clear that setting priorities and limiting notes is a skill they won't master this year!

During the third week, the students researched their chosen country. Previously, I have had them do this research in small groups or pairs but, keeping my independence goal in mind, I decided they should try it on their own. I did assign smaller countries, which have much less information to plow through, to my slower children. I don't think anyone noticed this, and it made the task more manageable for everyone. Each child had one sheet of paper for each category, with some questions and key words. With the help of our librarian, we located sources for everyone and helped students to find the information within. Of course, Dave, Jim, Hernando, Stephanie, and Ray required the most help, but even they put out a good effort and found some information. Much of what they found was very hard for them to read, so I read a little to them and helped them write down the important facts. It is at times like this that I wish the pupil-teacher ratio were about five to one! Fortunately, some of my students finished their research and helped the ones who needed help to make workable notes.

Writing Lesson   Finally, we got ready to write the reports. We decided to use a standard form with one paragraph for each subtopic. I pulled out my transparencies on Mexico and showed the children how to combine the information into paragraphs on the people, early history, and so forth. By now, most of the children have a good idea about how to construct a good paragraph. The fact that the notes were organized on separate sheets of paper around subtopics helped them keep their paragraphs on track. We used miscellaneous information in our concluding paragraph if appropriate. We had to make some return trips to the library for missing information or to check contradictory facts. I had shown the children how to write the source for the information in the margin in case they needed to find that information again, but I think most of them forgot this little detail! In some cases, we simply could not find the source so we found another one or deleted the information.

Revising/ Editing   Once the first drafts of the reports were written, I paired the children to read theirs to each other. They were to listen for information only at this point, to help the writer make the piece clearer or more interesting. I myself sat down with Dave, Jim, Hernando, Che, and Ray and helped them finish sentences and clarify what they meant as much as I could. Once the children had revised for content, we began the editing process. Again, I had them work with their partners first. This time I had the partner read the piece aloud as the writer looked on. I have been having them edit like this all year and it is most helpful to the writer. Writers cannot generally proof their own writing since they read what they meant to write, not what they actually wrote. Bob wrote, "Were did the erly peoples of trinidad come from." When Kazu read this, he noticed the misspelling of where, the unnecessary s on peoples, and the need for a capital T on Trinidad. Once Kazu pointed these out, Bob saw them too and fixed them. They both missed the fact that *early* was misspelled and that the sentence should have ended with a question mark, but three out of five is better than none.

Once the partners had worked together to edit the papers, I did a final editing and then each child typed his or her paper. It took awhile but they helped each other and they were so proud of the professional look of their travel books.

MAY

This month, we finished our final two science units: matter and animals. The children already had a tremendous amount of prior knowledge about animals; from what I can tell, it is part of the science curriculum at every grade level. I know I taught an animals unit in fourth grade and Belle teaches one in second. Matter, on the other hand, was another matter! Jim even showed his language prowess when I got frustrated with their inability to keep mass and weight distinctions straight: He asked, "But Miss Tent, what does it really matter?"

Meaning Vocabulary   We continued our push for independence and they are actually acting more like middle-schoolers. Once again I let them preview their textbook for vocabulary words and tried to focus their attention on picture, context, and morphemic clues as well as show them how our dictionaries and reference books could help them develop meanings for unknown words. As I mentioned, we had a great deal of difficulty making the mass/weight distinction. Of course, children think of weight as how many pounds they are, which is in fact their mass. Weight, or the amount of pull between objects, is a concept many of them never did understand. It helped to have them view films of astronauts and to realize that the astronauts still had the same mass but were weightless because of lack of gravity. We used a balance scale to measure mass and made a simple pulley scale to measure weight. I do believe my more able students understood the difference by the time we finished.

Inquiry

The conceptual difficulty of the unit on matter was balanced by the ease with which my students approached the unit on animals. Even my struggling students knew most of the information in our textbook, so we read it quickly to remind ourselves of what we knew and reestablish the terminology. Then we spent our time researching various animals and their habits. I divided the class into five groups, each to become experts about one class of animals. One group learned about invertebrates. Another group studied both amphibians and fish, because there are so few amphibians. The other three groups studied reptiles, birds, and mammals. We decided that each group would create an "encyclopedia" for their class of animals and that we would donate these to our school library as this fifth grade's graduation present to the school. The encyclopedia would include a general introduction giving characteristics of the animal class and illustrated pages for as many different animals as we had time to do.

Of course, we brainstormed a list of questions about each animal, classified the questions, and decided on key words to help us locate information. We then set up a data chart with the questions along the top and room to list the various animals down the side. I also had the children keep a list of sources, each of which they numbered as they added it to their list. They then put the number and page number next to the various pieces of information they found. This was not perfect but they did note more source information than they had last month.

Groups

In addition to everyone's main function of finding and recording specific information, I gave each child an official duty. In each group, one child was the leader, keeping all the group's information and making sure everything got done. I tried to put good organizers in every group and appoint them leaders. Another child in each group was appointed reference librarian, taking primary responsibility for locating sources and keeping information accurate. I appointed an art director for each group, although all the children could do art, and I provided tracing paper for the less artistic. The art director was to oversee the production of the art, however. I also had an editor, who looked at each article before it came to the editor-in-chief (me!). Finally, each group had a production manager whose job it was to put the finished pieces into the book and see to pagination, binding, cover design, index, and so forth.

It is hard for me to believe even now how hard all my children worked. They took their individual responsibilities very seriously and were determined that their group's encyclopedia would be the best. Parents told me stories of weekend trips to the public library and of hours their children spent reading, drawing, checking off what was there and what was needed, designing covers, and editing. We did not type the books this time but let the children write the pages in their neatest handwriting. I had no idea some of them could write so well.

The idea of giving every child some special responsibility worked out much better than I had anticipated. It used the strengths of all and made each child feel that his or her contribution was critical. The groups—which contained bright and slow, industrious and lazy, impulsive and reflective children—all worked well and developed a strong sense of cohesion. Next year I shall have to find more ways to assign groups in which each has a special responsibility.

JUNE

Why is it you think the year will never end and then it ends before you are ready? This year's students are grown-up middle-schoolers now, and I am looking forward to a super fifth grade year next year, knowing so much more than I did when I began this year.

We did our final health unit in the final week of school. This was a required unit on drug abuse. I still contend that fifth-graders are too young to be considering this sophisticated topic. I was surprised, however, at how much some of them knew. Jim suggested we have a scavenger hunt, but I demurred.

Thinking Processes

In looking back over the year, particularly at my ambitious goals, I am "cautiously optimistic"! My checklist demonstrates that, for the first time in my illustrious teaching career, I paid more than lip service to helping students learn the thinking skills that seem to be the foundation for all other learning. The two I always found hardest were, of course, the highest-level ones, evaluating and applying. But as the year went on I did learn how to phrase questions so that students would have to evaluate and apply what they were learning to new situations. And I finally got in the habit of saying, "This question requires a lot of brain power. You will have to think and decide what your answer will be. I don't want to see any hands until I have counted slowly to five." This five seconds of wait time was crucial to the students' ability to develop thoughtful answers and, as research suggests, improved the quality of their answers dramatically. I also tried to assign projects that required evaluation and application.

Meaning Vocabulary

Meaning vocabulary was probably the area in which I felt most satisfied with the progress we made toward our goals. I was particularly excited to see that students could select their own words to learn, and could independently apply the strategies I taught them to learn the appropriate meanings.

Research/ Writing

My students made tremendous progress in writing and researching, but they are still a long way from where I would like to have had them when they went off to middle school. I guess these are such complex processes that they take a very long time to develop. Some children, Sharon and Pat particularly, are indeed independent writers and researchers. My strugglers made some progress and seemed to learn a lot of content as they engaged in writing and researching, but their skills are still very rudimentary. Many of my average children also made progress in learning how to write and do research, but they continue to need a lot of guidance. I always wonder how much real teaching they get once they leave elementary school. My friends who are high-school teachers are always ribbing me about my "misguided" beliefs that the only real instruction goes on at elementary school. I hope in this case that they are right because, even with good elementary instruction, these kids still have much content to learn as well as independent learning strategies.

Next year I plan to use the same schedule as this year, with one exception. I am going to use both Monday and Friday for integration. By the end of the year, I found all kinds of opportunities to integrate math, reading, and writing into the units. I also found that there are always art, music, and drama possibilities. I even found some ways to integrate physical education activities and games into what we were studying. There just wasn't enough time to do all the integration I wanted to on just one day. In addition, I could tell that the children were much more motivated and involved on our integrated days. Their excitement convinced me that one day a week is just not enough. I chose Monday and Friday so that we can have a big kickoff and then a grand finale. I think it will also help all of us to get over the "Monday blahs" to know that Monday is going to be a "Special Day."

Mr. Head, who was skeptical about my Friday integration at the beginning of the year, was actually very pleased with what he saw on Fridays and sent other teachers to observe. He even suggested I might want to consider two days of integration. I didn't tell him I had already decided to do so!

All in all, a quite successful year! Now, if I can just stay at the fifth-grade level another year or two, I think I could get quite good at this. This summer, I plan to become proficient in Italian and French as Bo and I and some other friends take our railpasses through Europe!

REFERENCES

ASIMOV, I. (1983). *How did we find out about the universe?* New York: Walker & Co.

BRANLEY, F. M. (1981). *The planets in our solar system.* New York: Crowell.

CLEARY, B. (1984). *Ramona forever.* New York: Morrow.

COLLIER, J. (1983). *Planet out of the past.* New York: Macmillan.

CORBETT, S. (1981). *The deadly hoax.* New York: Dutton.

ENGDAHL, S. L. (1981). *The doors of the universe.* New York: Atheneum.

HOLBROOK, S. (1983). *Canada's kids.* New York: Atheneum.

HOOVER, H. M. (1981). *Another heaven, another earth.* New York: Viking.

LYLE, K. (1983). *Take a trip to Canada.* New York: Franklin Watts.

PATERSON, K. (1977). *Bridge to Terabithia.* New York: Crowell.

PRINGLE, L. (1983). *Being a plant.* New York: Crowell.

RAHN, J. E. (1981). *Plants up close.* Boston: Houghton Mifflin.

SHREVE, S. (1984). *The flunking of Joshua T. Bates.* New York: Knopf.

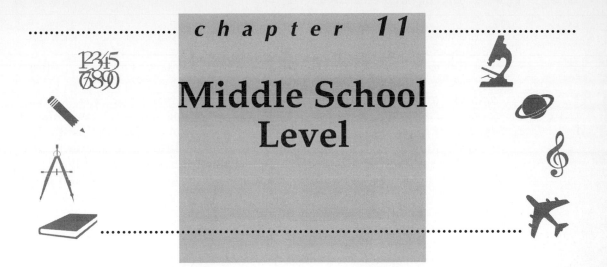

chapter 11

Middle School Level

AUGUST

My name is Hugh Mann, and this is my second year of teaching. Last year I taught American government at one of our district high schools, but this year I will be teaching American history and English/language arts at a middle school. The philosophy of middle-school education appealed to me—I have always appreciated the benefits of working as part of a team and being serious about adolescents' developmental needs—so I sought and got this job.

My teaching assignment is somewhat unusual. Due to much shuffling among district personnel, I will teach three sections of eighth-grade American history and two sections of eighth-grade English. I will be part of the Falcon core, which consists of four teachers and about 130 students. The students circulate from class to class among four teachers for their history, English, science, and math basic courses, as well as among other teachers for journalism, second language, music, and other exploratory courses. Organizing teachers and students in cores (other terms I've heard for this organizational scheme include *teams, pods,* and *families*) allows us to support students' academic and social development in a somewhat coherent and consistent manner. This is the first year for us Falcon core teachers to work together, so I imagine we will become more proficient working as a team as we move through the year.

I must confess that my student teaching and my first year of teaching were largely matters of staying alive. The students and I got along well, and they seemed to be learning, but I frequently was at a loss while planning lessons.

There were so many things to plan for, and I often seemed to fall back on the traditional teaching practices that I experienced as a student.

This year presents several challenges. Working in a middle-school core for the first time, working with a student clientele that every year includes more minority group members, and capitalizing on the technology my new school offers are a few of the things I wonder about. My reaction to the curriculum guides for my courses still is near panic: "How can I ever cover all this stuff?"

And a big issue is my desire to create effective instructional settings for my classes. I believe in the power of classroom settings so strongly that I've recorded in my planbook five characteristics of effective ones (literacy engagement, meaningfulness, active participation, academic challenge and support, and social support) to constantly remind me to promote them as much as possible.

So now you know something of my teaching situation and my background. One more item you might find interesting is that books have always been a part of my life. I even read for fun in high school when most of my friends barely touched a book—unless it had especially interesting pictures. I am commited to developing the reading and writing abilities of my students. I believe that a big part of my job is helping adolescents use literacy to become independent lifelong learners. I know that I can provide my students many valuable ideas and facts about history and English, but I also realize that my students need to hear from others besides myself, especially when they graduate and I'm no longer around. Stay tuned, and as I report my teaching adventures each month in this journal, we'll find out how I do.

SEPTEMBER

Study Strategies

After orienting students to all the policies, procedures, and rules of eighth-grade life in general and the Falcon core in particular, one of my first American history activities was to take my classes through a "tour" of the textbook. I pointed out its table of contents, glossary, and index. Within each chapter I directed attention to the introductions, conclusions, boldfaced print, footnotes, illustrations, maps, graphs, and review sections. I wanted to accustom the students to the text so they could efficiently predict, organize, and review while moving through it. I told them we would rely on many printed resources for learning American history, but the text would be a good basic reference.

When I recommended reading the end-of-chapter questions before reading the chapter, several students spoke up. One student, Ken, thought my recommendation sounded like cheating; Judy informed me that she did it all the time because her parents had suggested it; and Lonnie sullenly announced that if they had to answer the questions, then it only made sense to go to them first, find the answers, and be done with it. I responded that the special features of a textbook were intended to help people learn and that I did not plan to have students merely copy down answers to sets of questions. "I want to develop your abilities to think, not to regurgitate," I declared rather pompously. "Use the special features of the book in order to learn what is presented. We'll spend most of our class time discussing what you've read."

We Falcon core teachers had met before school opened and planned the year. One decision was that we would have identical class rules, address identical life-management skills (like drug awareness, career exploration, and personal decision making), and teach the identical study strategy (as it applies to each discipline), but we also decided that each of us would begin the year with his or her own unit of content.

The first unit in the American history text was entitled "Early Years in America"; the text covered this in about a hundred pages with chapters on Native-American culture before Columbus's arrival, the European age of discovery, and England and Spain in the New World. Well, my students and I discussed our way through these chapters, and, frankly, the discussions weren't very productive. Our treatment of the first chapter typifies how the others went.

Discussion

The students came in on Monday, having been told to read the chapter on early Native Americans over the weekend. I was ready to go. "What did you think of the chapter?" I asked. When nobody responded right away, I called on Ken. "There sure were a lot of tribes," he answered. Nobody else had anything to say. I could see some of the students in the back begin to put their heads down for a nap or whisper to each other, so I immediately asked another question, "What did you learn about the tribes?" Judy piped up that they played different ball games. "Mr. Mann, the Eskimos played some kind of kickball, and I think the book said the Algonquins invented lacrosse." Rod, who appeared athletic, wanted to know how lacrosse was played. I told what I knew, and the discussion picked up as comparisons were made between lacrosse and the various other sports the students knew. I chimed in to explain in some detail how catching and throwing a ball with a lacrosse stick differed from catching a baseball and either hitting it with a bat or throwing it. Before I knew, the hour was over and our discussion of the chapter had ended. I felt uneasy about all our meanderings that had passed as a discussion, but the next class came in and I didn't have time to sort out my discontent.

Meaning Vocabulary

In order to help develop vocabulary, I reproduced word puzzles from the teacher's resource book. The puzzles consisted of words with their spelling scrambled accompanied by definitions. For instance, UTRIPSAN was next to "Fundamental religious group that established a colony under the auspices of the Massachusetts Bay Company." When I passed out the first set of scrambled words, Judy completed it in about ten minutes and asked if she could make up her own for the class to do. At the other extreme, Victor never turned his in. I asked him about it, and he reported that English was not his first language, so he never had been very good with English word puzzles. He said he had enough difficulty with English when it came at him straight. In general, the classes worked busily completing the worksheets; however, I began wondering if the assignments were just busywork or if they were eliciting new insights into the words and their meanings.

Language arts probably should be called "language skills" because it covers topics such as parts of speech, sentence construction, and report writing. There is very little about the artistic, creative side of language in the text. I decided to cover language skills Monday through Wednesday and literature on Thursday and Friday. Language skill work mostly consisted of me explaining various rules and definitions ("Proper nouns name particular persons, places, or things") followed by exercises in locating the item that had just been defined ("Underline the proper nouns in the following sentences").

Reciprocal Teaching

As I mentioned earlier, at a beginning-of-the-year planning session, Falcon core teachers decided to teach our students one study system. We decided on reciprocal teaching (RT) because many researchers and practitioners have attested to its power and because it seemed flexible enough to fit all our disciplines. In English class I introduced RT during the first unit in the literature anthology, which addressed "Moments of Truth." After silently reading and talking about what the first story had to say about moments of truth, I told the class about RT. Hoping that they were convinced that giving it a try might be worthwhile, I showed them how I employed RT with the story we just had read. Relying on three specific strategies, I talked through my summary, images, and questions regarding a short section of the story. Next, the whole class looked over the next section I specified, and students volunteered their summaries, images, and questions. Classmates contributed to each others' comments, and I praised their efforts at comprehension and their especially apt statements. We did this a few more times the first day, then the class formed teams of two to continue with RT other days.

When the class formed into pairs, I noticed Victor and Theresa, two students with limited English proficiency, joining forces. When I asked whether or not their pairing up was by their choice, they said yes. Victor told me, "This way, if we get stuck trying to explain ourselves, we can switch to Spanish." "Okay," I said, "first talk about the RT strategies as much as you can—and help each other—in English, but use Spanish to get through any rough spots."

All in all, I think my classes were uneven this past month. I was satisfied with the textbook tour I conducted in American history and the RT introduction in English because I think the group will be able to apply these strategies toward becoming independent lifelong learners. But the discussions we're having seem unproductive, and the students seem like automatons when completing the vocabulary and language skills exercises. They don't seem to be thinking very deeply. In checking my list of effective settings, I seem high on academic challenge and support as well as social support, I'm okay with literacy engagement and active participation, but I'm going to have to do something about meaningfulness.

OCTOBER

Discussion

Our discussions in American history moved this month from very loose to very structured. I was getting concerned about our talk going off on tangents, so I resolved to hold the class closer to the text. This month's unit was on the

American Revolution, and one day we were talking about the early events in Boston. After dealing with the Stamp Act, the Quartering Act, and the Boston Massacre, we got to the Boston Tea Party. Lonnie wanted to know why it was called a "party." After I stated that some words have several different meanings, Rod interjected that the Boston Garden, home of the Celtics basketball team, really wasn't a vegetable or flower garden. "Who are the Celtics?" Victor wanted to know. Well, Ken eagerly began explaining the overall won-lost record of this team and the past triumphs of Larry Bird, Bill Russell, and Bob Cousy when I interrupted forcefully, "No more talk about words with multiple meanings! What did Lord North and King George do after the tea was dumped into the harbor?" As soon as I got the answer that I wanted ("passed the Intolerable Acts"), I asked, "What did the Intolerable Acts consist of?" After Judy finally supplied the correct answer, I continued with questions such as, "When did the First Continental Congress meet?" "What actions did it take?" "Why did General Gage order a march on Concord?" and "Where did the Second Continental Congress meet?" Answering these questions kept all my students on their toes, and we moved efficiently through the textbook chapters, although I must confess that I began feeling like a prosecuting attorney. I also began to wonder about the meaningfulness of this exercise, thinking I might be promoting only rote memory in my students.

Periodicals   A high point this past month was the arrival of the first edition of the weekly magazine we'll be receiving during the year. Our Falcon core had a small budget for instructional supplies, and I urged spending much of it on extra reading materials. I'm glad I did because the magazine is quite appealing! It has many visuals, lots of color, timely articles, and features that the students really like. I pass the magazines out each Friday, the students read them on their own, then as a whole class we talk about whatever they want. I connect the magazine contents with ongoing unit contents as much as possible.

Multi-cultural Literature   An interesting event occurred with one issue of the weekly magazine. The issue devoted its entire contents to Halloween, presenting historical background on this celebration and explaining some current controversies about observing it. Victor then commented on the traditional Mexican observation of Days of the Dead, which the magazine ignored. He explained how Mexican people honor their ancestors during this celebration, making offerings and clearing grave sites. I truly was fascinated with what he had to say, and the class seemed to respect his comments, too. I was glad Victor was comfortable enough to share part of his heritage with the class, and I was equally glad the class received it in the spirit in which it was intended. "I've got to promote more of these intercultural exchanges," I thought.

Meaning Vocabulary   The scrambled word puzzles began losing their appeal by the end of September, so I began setting aside about thirty minutes a week for vocabulary work using the dictionary or the textbook. I wrote a list of important words on the board, and the students copied the words and looked up their definitions. This started off about as well as the puzzles because everybody kept busy and almost everybody turned in completed papers. The students worked with such abstract terms as *sovereignty, loyalist, representation, inalienable right, and confederation;* the list also included names such as Lafayette, Greene, Adams, Hamilton, and Jefferson.

Groups   In English I implemented a rather successful grouping system to help with our study of the parts of speech. I introduced the grouping system by explaining the value of collaboration. I read some excerpts from business leaders' reports calling for today's students to learn how to work in groups and described the changes in the workforce that called for group interaction. Next, I explained that each student would be responsible for his or her own learning as well as that of their teammates. "Individual and group scores will be maintained," I pronounced. Other guidelines were that I would assign group membership, productive group interaction would be emphasized as much as academic learning, the groups would last for one month before forming new ones, and they would always meet in the same spot during group work time.

Before turning the students loose, a group of five came up and demonstrated particular roles individuals played (mayor, scribe, timekeeper) and a few important interactions (praising others, summarizing, taking turns talking). This simulation was to identify key features of group work for the students to emphasize when they were in their groups.

Then I explained the day's assignment, which was conducive to group work. Following the contents of the language arts text on pronouns, I presented specific elements, such as personal, relative, and demonstrative pronouns, then distributed handouts calling for appropriate pronouns to be inserted in sentences ("Those who hurt others hurt _____."). I established a time limit, so that groups who didn't finish in class had to do so on their own. When time was up, I collected the papers and then went over them with the class. To be sure, analyzing the types of pronouns was a bit of a drag—I wonder what effect knowing which pronoun is which has on anything?—but I must say that the group work stirred the class to participate actively in a rather positive way. Even Lonnie got involved with his two friends and actually turned something in. I'm going to have to look for ways to merge active participation with meaningful learning activities.

Reciprocal Teaching   RT is moving along in our literature study. The paired individuals seem to be helping each other, although I rearranged a few teams when I saw how unproductive they were becoming. (In fact, I checked with my Falcon core colleagues about their experiences with a few disruptive students, and we now have a consistent corewide plan for helping them learn to control their behaviors.) On several occasions I had RT team members write their summaries on an overhead transparency, then the class talked about what they liked about each one and asked questions about unclear ideas. On other occasions I had the pairs sketch a scene that they associated with what we just had read. Theresa produced a stunning illustration that was especially rich with meanings. Again, the class praised features of the sketches, then they questioned the "artists" about other features. The teams seemed to be having trouble with the questioning portion of RT; they were asking low-level questions like "What was the boy's brother's name?" So I intervened and said that all questions should begin with "I wonder. . . ." I offered several of my wonderings in regard to a few sections, and the teams then took control again.

As I look back on October, American history still doesn't seem to be engaging my students' thinking the way I want it to. As in September, we're moving through the material, but the students don't seem to be connecting anything they're learning with their present lives. The discussions have become recitations, and the vocabulary work still is drill work. I'm still having difficulty with meaningfulness. I'm glad for the history-related magazines, but I wonder how they fit the curriculum. Something else is going to have to happen!

The group work in English is allowing some very active participation among the students as they deal with the mechanics of language and the RT procedure in literature. The RT instruction in my class and others of the Falcon team seems to be paying off; the students actually seem to be acquiring a learning strategy!

NOVEMBER

Our study of "The New Nation" in American history this month leveled off at a new plateau. My procedure of assigning certain pages and then discussing them just wasn't succeeding. The discussions either ranged far from the topic, or I ended up conducting an interrogation that emphasized isolated facts. This month I got tired of discussions and spent most of the time lecturing and showing movies. I began the lectures and movies when we came to the section of the text about the Bill of Rights. We had slogged our way through federalism and checks and balances, and I was getting no response to my questions about the first ten amendments to the Constitution. As a result, I just began talking. There were few interruptions, so I continued. Occasionally someone wanted to know, "Is this going to be on the test?" to which I answered, "Maybe." The next day I showed a surprisingly interesting movie that detailed the contents and implications of the Bill of Rights. Basic liberties such as freedom of speech, protection from unreasonable search and seizure, and due process of law were made somewhat real by the situations enacted in the film. Most of the class actually watched the movie, there were no discipline problems, and my preparation time was practically zero. I'll probably continue with this lecture-and-film procedure a little longer.

Meaning
Vocabulary   Vocabulary instruction took an upswing this month. The word puzzles and searches for definitions had kept everybody well occupied, but little learning seemed to go on. The students rarely remembered the definitions and were at a total loss to explain the terms in their own words. So one day I decided to address vocabulary head on. First, I listed terms for the unit on a bulletin board and said we were going to develop deep understandings of these few specific terms. I then explained each term by forming analogies, that is, by connecting new concepts and terms to something I thought the students had

already experienced. For example, strict construction and loose construction were two high-sounding terms with somewhat vague meanings that came up during our study of the Constitution. "Let's say that you get grounded at home for doing something against the rules," I explained, "and a school club or team that you belong to is going somewhere after school the next day. Would you be able to go?" Judy volunteered the fact that she had never been grounded, but, if she were, her parents probably would make her come home right after classes. On the other hand, Allison contemptuously reported, "They wouldn't dare try to keep me in the house every afternoon and evening." Ken reported that it probably would depend on the mood his parents were in each day, and Rod was sure that he could practice with his team but would then need to be home soon afterward. I pointed out that some families seemed to interpret the "grounding" punishment strictly while others saw it loosely. Thus distinguishing strict and loose constructions of grounding, I explained how Jefferson and Hamilton's debate over a federal bank was based on the conflict between strict and loose constructions of the Constitution. This explanation seemed to take hold and I made a mental note to connect more terms with students' lives in that way.

Two words, *party* (as in Federalist party) and *cabinet*, came up in this unit and deserved special attention. These multiple-meaning words can be really confusing for some students—I thought of Victor and Theresa especially—so I explained their meanings in American history as clearly as possible, pointing out how those meanings differed from general uses of the terms. I reminded the class about the Boston Tea Party and compared that use of the term with its uses in Federalist party, being a party to a crime, and weekend party. As I explained each term, the students took notes. This way of developing vocabulary definitely makes the students depend on me for information, but there is a lot to learn and sometimes my explanations are the best way to get that information across. In fact, my lectures seem to be getting the students' attention, but I wonder if this is the best way to teach.

The group work during language skills exercises in English continued nicely this month. Allison brought in some soft rock albums from home, so we play background music during this time. Terry, perhaps the hardest-working student in school, really gets involved with these worksheets; whereas Allison more than once questioned the value of knowing the difference between an action verb and an auxiliary verb. "Mr. Mann," she would say, "sometimes I just get tired of answering your paper questions."

Seeing how my concentration on a few vocabulary terms in history paid off, I tried something similar during English literature. I incorporated "The Most Important Word" into the RT conversations we were having. To introduce this strategy, I read aloud a brief poem by Shel Silverstein and explained which word from it was the most important. I targeted *helpful,* saying that it best expressed the poet's message about the main character. Lonnie disagreed, saying that *shrewd* was better, but he couldn't support his argument when I pressed him. "What part of the poem supports the fact that he was shrewd?" I

Comprehension Lesson

asked. Allison stepped in and gave quite a convincing argument for shrewd that would never have occurred to me. I accepted her argument, noted her logic, and complimented her on her insight into the poem.

The next day we had a lively discussion about whether *witty* or *muscle* was the most important word in a particular section. Students who argued for either term came up with some logical reasons for their choices. Finally, Victor spoke up. "What's the answer, Mr. Mann?" I knew I was in a dilemma. Giving my answer would limit future discussions because students simply would be trying to anticipate what I would say; on the other hand, not giving an answer seemed unfair because students like to have closure on a problem. Additionally, I must admit that I was becoming used to playing the role of the all-knowing teacher, so not giving the "correct" **Quick** answer was difficult. My solution was to have students write their choices **Writes** and justify them on notebook paper. This allowed students to get some closure in their minds, and it allowed me to evaluate their rationales rather than their actual choices.

As soon as I had the class write about their most important word, I knew I **Reciprocal** should continue this practice. Connecting writing with RT just made sense. **Teaching** From then on, we modified the RT procedures so that sometimes students thought through their responses before the whole class or in small groups or pairs, and sometimes they thought through them individually and wrote them down. We began keeping RT journals, special notebooks for each student to record his or her reponses. Sometimes the students wrote their RT responses before sharing them with others.

The attention to vocabulary and the writing additions to RT made good sense. Additionally, the RT discussions continued to stay on track without me asking a thousand picky questions. Whenever a student would offer a summary, choose a word, share an image, or express a question, either I or his or her partner would ask something like, "What makes you think that?" or "What leads you to that?" The class was involved in a collaborative, explicit, sensemaking approach to what they read.

Reading RT also allowed me to vary students' reading materials. After everyone **Materials** seemed proficient with the RT routine, I brought in several stories written at different levels of difficulty and had each team choose one. The stories all related to dreams, the anthology's unit topic. Including materials of different levels provided appropriate challenges for my good as well as poor readers. The task was to write RT responses for each section I had designated. I went from group to group and had them explain their responses to me. Both Victor and Theresa offered good comments, although in both cases I thought they had more to say than actually was expressed. Time was too short for me to get to all the teams, so I collected all the papers and reacted to those I had not addressed.

Assessment Individual competencies with RT formally was assessed two ways during the end of the month. I read aloud a short passage while the class followed along. The students then recorded their RT responses on a separate page. Next, they evaluated themselves by rating their responses. In a few words they explained how well they thought they had summarized, formed an image, identified the most important word, and questioned (i.e., wondered about) the passage. Then I collected the papers and evaluated how well they thought they had summarized, formed an image, identified the most important word, and questioned (i.e., wondered about) the passage. The success of most students indicated that they were catching on to this system of learning; I hoped they would continue it when I wasn't reminding them to do so.

In English our discussions were productive, group members interacted well and completed their tasks, and all my—and my core's—attention to RT seemed to be paying off. Vocabulary study in American history also picked up this month, thanks to highlighting a few key words and forming analogies. But I'm still looking for a way to engage students with what they read in this class.

DECEMBER

Integrated Unit

A major change begun in English this month involved integration of instruction. Integration had been a big topic at several of our Falcon core meetings, so I thought I would jump in and see what happened. Of course, two of our members wanted to integrate instruction across the disciplines—to be interdisciplinary—but I wanted to be sure I could be integrated within my own classes before reaching across to others. As a result, my science and math colleagues produced an interdisciplinary unit just between themselves.

In English I had felt uncomfortable with the fragmentation of doing worksheets on superlative degree in the grammar book, for instance, and reading about personal codes of conduct in the literature anthology. This fragmented way of doing things was relatively easy to manage, but it lacked the meaningfulness that I thought an English class should have. Science fiction was an upcoming unit in our anthology, so I decided to center my instruction about that topic.

With science fiction as my organizing center, I thought about a central question that would provide an overarching purpose to the unit and position the students as problem solvers. I selected "What is the value of science fiction?" thinking that this was a worthwhile and provocative issue with which students could relate. The culminating activity could be one of three: (a) give a speech, (b) produce a poster, or (c) write a movie review.

I kicked off the unit by showing brief movie clips and some action figures from *Star Wars* and *Star Trek*. The class immediately began voicing their beliefs, experiences, likes, and dislikes of these media blockbusters. After forging these links, I posed the central question, "What is the value of science fiction?" Lonnie exclaimed that making money was the obvious answer, but he became reflective when I asked for his evidence and whether or not his was the only possible answer. We brainstormed other possiblities about the value of science fiction before I explained the procedures we would be following.

The next day I read a short story written by Ray Bradbury to the class. I don't think too many male secondary-school teachers had read to these students. The story I chose was punchy and reasonably short; I reviewed it the night before I presented it, and I read it with as much force as possible. I told myself that I was at a speech contest, the students were the judges, and I intended to impress them. Well, the group attended to every word. It was a great experience! I think they were amazed at how much fun it was to form their own images while listening rather than have a filmmaker form the images for them. Again, we brainstormed possible values of such stories.

Extending my read-aloud activity to students' book projects inside and outside of class was not too difficult. I met with the school librarian to learn what science-fiction books were available. We turned up individual copies of numerous books and found a class set of *Flowers for Algernon*. I then announced to my eighth-graders that during inside-of-class book study groups they were to continue the reciprocal teaching responses they had been doing, and that they were to follow the response format I had begun on the value of science-fiction novels. Judy reacted to my news in a surprisingly negative way, "Science fiction, yucch! Why do we have to read that stuff?" I again explained the topic and informed the class that tying novels in with the short stories we would be reading made all kinds of sense—at least in terms of deepening

Trade Books insights into a topic. "Besides," I said, "there are some great science-fiction books. *The Postman, Moonwind,* and *Singularity* are fantastic new books, and *The Martian Chronicles, 20,000 Leagues under the Sea,* and *2001: A Space Odyssey* are classics. You'll love them! Trust me."

Book Projects The students had choices of ways to respond to the novels outside of class. I divided the assignment among the "big four" literary elements—plot, setting, character, and theme—and provided alternatives for considering those elements. For instance, students could consider setting by diagramming a stage for a scene to be dramatized or by drawing a map depicting locations in the story. Students analyzed characterization by completing an adjective checklist or by justifying their choices of popular actors and actresses to portray the main characters. Once I got to thinking about it, I saw many options for eliciting responses to stories. Some examples that emerged included the following: select a piece of representative dialogue, choose the book's most important word, describe a change that occurred in a character, explain how a situation you've been in is similar to one in the book, convince a movie producer that your book should be made into a movie, and write the book's epilogue. I tried to provide a mix between strongly academic options ("What was the theme of the story?") and more artistic ones ("Create a mobile that represents the story.").

Thinking Processes The students seemed to appreciate this new freedom, and more thinking processes seemed to be in evidence with the new system. Some of the images produced when students dealt with setting and character were outstanding; the connections students drew between their lives and the characters' were sharply drawn; and the hypothetical sales pitches to movie producers were organized well. Moreover, students seemed to like the combination of clear expectations plus some freedom of choice.

Extending the language skills work to science fiction took more planning on my part, but it seems to have paid off. Writing informal letters and business letters was a unit objective in our language arts text, so I tied letter writing into science fiction by having students compose letters that were related to situations in the stories. For instance, as a group we read another great Ray Bradbury story about a hunter who went back in time to shoot dinosaurs. "Okay, group," I said, "We're going to write a letter to a close friend describing the trip." After detailing the topic, audience, role, and form of the assignment a bit more, I projected an overhead transparency of a model letter. I pointed out aspects such as where the date went, how to address the letter, how to sign off, and how to develop the composition. My model letter was brief, but it did have an introduction, a chronological description of the trip (which I pointed out as only one way to go), and a summarizing statement at the end. The students then went to their groups for ten minutes to brainstorm and organize what they intended to say. Finally, 20 minutes of class time was devoted to individuals writing their letters. Rather than grade the letters themselves, I gave one point to each letter written according to the form I'd presented. Students who didn't follow the form were given another chance.

The same basic procedure was followed with business letters. I assigned a business letter to a government agency requesting a permit to take hunters back in time. Possible governmental objections posed by the story were to be countered in the letter. Again I explained the task, modeled the writing of a business letter, allowed the students to generate and organize information before writing, and then let them write. As with the lesson on informal letters, I took the skill from our language text and applied it to our current topic. I still assigned one or two of the skill book exercises as practice in letter writing, but the skill had already been tied into the content of our study. I don't know why I didn't do this earlier.

Our study of science fiction culminated with student write-ups and reports. Those who presented speeches did a great job. A few even dressed up as Han Solo, Captain Picard, Captain Nemo, and others when explaining the value of reading about them. Some good inisights were shared; we heard of advances predicted by science-fiction writers and of the potentials for good and bad that awaited us.

And finally, thank goodness for the holiday season! Teaching is hard work, and I was ready for a break. My social life took a dip during the past four months, so I've been trying to revive it during this time. Some college friends came into town, so we had some catching up to do. I invited my core colleagues as well as Diane Sek, a first-year science teacher at school, to one of our parties, and Diane handled herself well with my rowdy friends. She and I talked shop for a few hours, but that's what we had most in common. I told her how I integrated what I taught in English, how the group assignments and book projects worked, and how frustrated I was with American history. She said she had some problems with her classes, but that basically she was getting along fine. It was fun comparing observations about teaching with her.

JANUARY

Well, I made some major changes in American history this month. At the beginning of the month, students were coming late to my class and some were even skipping. This upset me because I had thought at least I had kept things moving. I spent a good amount of time preparing my lectures, I always included some humor, and I was familiar with the quirks of every VCR in the school because I showed so many tapes. Allison was the one who helped me see the light. She came into class one day muttering about another session of brain death. "Allison, what are you talking about?" I asked. She looked me straight in the eye and replied, "When do we get to do something in here? All we do is listen to you or some electronic voice." I didn't confront her, but I did think about what she said. Maybe she was right. Perhaps I overreacted to the unsatisfying discussions we had at the beginning of the year. I thought about what was working so well in my English classes, and I decided to try some similar practices in American history.

Reading
Materials

A small change I instituted involved the weekly magazine we received. The classes still seemed to enjoy them, which I think was a positive outcome, but my whole-class discussions about what they had read weren't getting too far. And to my chagrin, I realized I hadn't been conducting reciprocal teaching with my history classes. Consequently, I began selecting one of the short articles from each issue and leading my classes through RT sessions. Since the students had been performing RT in their other classes, they easily picked up on the procedure with the magazines. Lonnie declared that he and the others should select whatever strategy they wanted to use and talk about, and, after giving it some thought, I decided that would fit the spirit of my magazine use. So now RT is occuring in my history classes, too. The circle of study strategy instruction in the Falcon core now is complete.

Comprehension
Lesson

In the American history textbook, we were finishing the Civil War and Reconstruction when I first attempted to guide comprehension of part of the text. My planning consisted of several steps. First, I decided what portion of the book my students would read. In September I had everybody read every page of the text. That was unreasonable because the text simply contained too much information; after all, I, too, was learning new material. Thus, I decided to show a film about the major Civil War battles and to have students concentrate their reading on the aftermath of the war. Once I decided to have students read only about Reconstruction, I further pared down the points I wanted them to understand. The text provided more than enough information, so I decided that it would be good for my students to read in order to find out why Reconstruction had ended. I asked, "Why would a seemingly good thing stop?" Asking this question was like asking the central question during the science fiction unit, to provide an overarching purpose.

Then I had to figure out what my eigth-graders needed to know in order to learn even more. I decided to spend some time explaining the reasons for Reconstruction as well as the terms *carpetbagger, freedman, sharecropper, scalawag,* and *Ku Klux Klan.* The first three terms could be presented by calling attention to look-alike terms. For instance, *free* and *man* gave awfully good clues about the meaning of that word; the students just needed to develop them a bit. In order to explain the reason for Reconstruction, I decided to present another analogy. The comparison this time was between reconstructing the South and making up after a family fight. I intended to point out how the winner actually comes out even further ahead if the loser is welcomed back and the wounds are healed. This analogy was meant to develop students' background knowledge and motivate them to read. All of this planning took about an hour. One hour seemed like a lot of time at first, but it occurred to me that if it worked, my life in the classroom would be much more productive.

I began the lesson at center stage once again. I informed the class that they needed to know important concepts in order to understand Reconstruction. I then went through my analogy of a family fight and pointed out the parts of the compound words. Next, I had them open their books to the pages on Reconstruction in order to survey the information for one minute. Then I presented the central question for the reading: "Why did Reconstruction end? If healing the wounds of a family fight is so important, then why did the healing process stop?" This purpose for reading seemed especially useful because the students couldn't just scan the pages to find a specific fact, nor could they answer my question based on what they knew already. They needed to read the whole passage, and they needed to read between the lines. Reading materials other than the text was a distinct possibility, too.

As the students were reading, I sat at my desk and read also. This was to model the actions I wanted them to follow, and it allowed me one more opportunity to brush up on the information. After almost everybody had finished reading, I repeated my original question, "Why did Reconstruction end?" The discussion that followed was amazingly productive. Rod didn't interject any comments related to sports, and Ken didn't go off on any tangents. Even Terry, who rarely spoke up in class, contributed some thoughts. After a while, I imposed some organization by saying, "Okay, let's see if we can list the major reasons on the board." We then listed four major reasons: corruption, incompetence, economics, and changes in leadership. Next I said, "Take another few minutes, reread the text, see if we've listed all the major reasons, and see if these four are correct." Nobody came up with any substantial changes, so the list was left for the class to copy into their notes.

This strategy for guiding students through a section of text had many similarities with the integrated unit activities I had been conducting in English. Perhaps the biggest similarity was that students knew in general what they were looking for when they were reading. Before, even Judy had seemed to have difficulty separating important from trivial information. That's not surprising when you look carefully at textbooks; they seem to consist of just one darn fact after another. It's also not surprising when you consider the questions I had asked after reading; students needed to memorize the whole passage because they never knew what I might ask about. Setting overarching provocative purposes (i.e., central questions) before reading seemed to help considerably.

My comprehension lesson on the Reconstruction worked well, but I was concerned that my students might come to depend on me totally for direction. What would happen when I wasn't around to tell them what to learn? I liked providing clear, specific direction, but I wanted my students to provide some direction on their own. Because of this concern, I implemented my third change of the month. After guiding comprehension, I began fading my instruction.

Independence

Fading myself out of center stage and my students into center stage will take place over a long period of time (as I learned when presenting RT to my English classes), but this was the month I began to bring my students in on the act of setting purposes for reading comprehension. After a few weeks of me setting the purposes, I began by having the students set their own. "Okay, group, what is the first thing you should do when getting ready to read in order to learn?" I asked. Judy responded that looking over the material in order to gain an impression of what was coming should be done first. Allison spoke up, "Once you know generally what to expect, you should establish some goals about what you intend to learn." When I was reasonably sure that the group knew the strategies for approaching a text, I had them apply those strategies to what we were reading in American history. Rod spoke up, saying he thought they simply should read in order to determine what new information they could discover. The group agreed that was a good enough reason for reading, so they got into their books. After reading, I said, "You know that you should follow up to see if you got the information that you set out to get, so let's do it." Students reviewed the new information they gathered by listing the new facts and ideas they had gained.

My supporting comprehension of assigned readings in history, as well as my fading of that support, made a big difference in the general tone of the class. Students seemed more involved in the content, and I felt as though I were providing some skills that students could take with them across the curriculum and to high school and beyond.

FEBRUARY

Interdisciplinary
Unit

This month the Falcon core decided we needed to link our course contents better that we had been doing. We were relatively satisfied with our reciprocal teaching program, with our parental communications, with our student team-building exercises conducted over the months, with our life-management skills program, and with our concerted plans for our problem children, but we never integrated our course contents the way some wanted, through interdisciplinary units. Looking at Valentine's Day on the calendar led us to settle on relationships as our organizing center. I finally felt ready to enter this new way of teaching.

Trade Books

Relationships easily fit the coursework I was pursuing in English. Some fine novels deal with relationships among family members and racial groups, so I had students in the book study groups look into older books such as *Black Boy, Roots, I Know Why the Caged Bird Sings*, and *Cry, the Beloved Country*, as well as such newer books as *The Moves Make the Man* and *Going Home*. Again I learned that some assignments really stimulate some students, while leaving others cold. Requiring outside-of-class book projects seems to have worked well for Theresa, my student who rarely spoke. Theresa read *Roll of Thunder, Hear My Cry* and astounded me with a series of pen-and-ink sketches of scenes from the book. She showed fine technical skill producing the sketches, and her selection of scenes depicting Cassie's encounters with prejudice was just incredible. I showed the drawings to Di, over in science, who informed me that Theresa always did superior, creative work in her class. You never know exactly how things are going to work.

Writing Lesson

I also connected the language arts skill of interpreting advertising techniques with the organizing center of relationships. First, I had my student assistants find examples of magazine and newspaper ads that emphasized the interpersonal relationships their products promised to stimulate. Within a few minutes they found beer, cigarette, automobile, and mouthwash ads that subtly associated the product with personal relationships. I passed around such examples in my classes so the students could experience them directly. Then I gave the following assignment: "We're going to collect advertisements and display them in brochures for a fifth-grade class at our elementary school. Locate at least two ads that imply that their product is associated with close interpersonal relationships. Write a brief description of what the ad subtly promises and mount it for display." We devoted three days to completing the brochures, and I delivered the acceptable ones to Connie Tent, a very nice fifth-grade teacher in our district whom I had met at a party.

The next step in my lesson progressed from locating what others had produced to having students produce their own. "Take one short story or novel you've read that deals with relationships and create an advertisement for it. Be sure to stress the relationships theme in your ad. Your audience consists of other eighth-grade students." Having studied similar ads already, the students seemed to have a fairly good idea about how to start.

After everyone had produced an ad, I had the students prepare to work in groups to revise their first efforts. Since they had worked together so much during reciprocal teaching, I figured these revision groups would go well. "As you know, no composition is ever perfect after the first attempt, but with a little help from your friends, you might approach perfection on the next attempt or two." I demonstrated how I wanted the group members to work as peer response teams in order to polish each other's work. I displayed an ad for *Cry, the Beloved Country* that I had created for this demonstration and made the following comments: "The most effective aspect of this ad, I think, is its layout. The pictures and lettering are well-balanced. The ad is eye-catching. The one thing I would like to know more about is the general topic of the book. The terms *riveting* and *sensational* don't provide much insight into the relationships described in the story. I would like to know more about the connections this story depicts." After commenting this way, I paused and then explained what I had done. My students were aware that I had first praised the positive features, then asked questions about the negative ones. I made it clear that my comments about the negative features were couched as requests for information ("I would like to know more about . . .") rather than as direct criticisms ("The weakest part of this writing is . . .").

Following this demonstration, I presented a few more ads and had students comment on what they liked and what they wanted to know more about. I then gave the final assignment: "All right, now please get into your groups and do to each other's ads what we just did to mine. However, instead of saying your comments aloud, please write them on a separate sheet of paper. When you get everybody's comments, then redo your ads as you see fit. You are to turn in to me your first drafts, the comments, and your second drafts."

Most of the groups functioned well with this somewhat dangerous assignment. I was afraid that the comments would either be so snide and hurtful or so gushy and congratulatory that they wouldn't be useful. Lonnie and Allison started insulting each other's work—in a good-natured way, I think—but they stopped when I reminded them that their comments were to be written.

Once the ads were finished, I posted some, with the authors' names concealed, on the bulletin board. I hid the authors' names because peer pressure is intense with this age group and displaying work might leave someone open to hurtful comments. On the other hand, I wanted to display some ads in order to model exemplary ones, increase interest in the topic, provide a focus for what we were doing, and just plain dress up the room. Some of the middle-school classrooms I've been in look more like waiting rooms to contain people for an hour than like places to stimulate learning.

Interdisciplinary Unit

The organizing center of relationships also fit well in American history. Setting a clear purpose for learning—in this case, establishing a central question to a unit—proved to be a great stabilizer for keeping us on track while allowing us to go beyond the book. This month we were into the westward movement, so the central question that I set was "How did relationships shape—and become shaped by—the westward movement?" This question opened doors to much exploration. We identified possible relationships within and among families, ethnic groups, and economic classes as people moved west. To gather information, we went to the computer lab where students logged onto the Internet. They moved through the *Oregon Trail* and *Gold Rush* simulations. We went to the library where we found books on the Comstock Lode, the transcontinental railroad, the pony express, the Plains Indians, and so on. Whether we ventured outside or stayed inside class and encountered particular facts and ideas, I frequently asked, "How does this help us understand how relationships shaped—and were shaped by—the westward movement?"

Asking this central question in American history helped turned the details we were encountering into facts-in-action, and it provided clear guidance for writing. For instance, twice a week I began class by having the students produce a quick write on the relationship theme. One writing prompt was "What is the connection between personal relationships and the pony express?" The responses I sampled went beyond predictable references to maintaining family ties to maintaining business and governmental ties to maintaining the image of the lone messenger galloping across the plains.

MARCH

As the name of this month suggests, in history we marched through the Great Depression, the New Deal, and World War II. At the beginning of the year I was concerned about getting through everything, but my decision to focus on central questions was a lifesaver. We might be focusing on less, but the students seem to be learning more. Our Falcon core decided that the relationships unit worked well, but we needed to continue on our own this month.

Book Project   Now I am using the textbook selectively; I am no longer a slave to it. In fact, I'm expecting book projects now and am providing class time for students to work on them. The history classes could choose either a literary or an expository book. Topical books, biographies, and fiction were fair game for this assignment. I figured that students could learn as much, if not more, from a biography of General Custer as from some factual treatise on Plains Indian warfare. The only stipulation I set was that I had to approve the book before students began reading it. I granted these approvals before and after class as students brought their books to me for a quick check.

The book projects first called for the learners to summarize their books' contents. I showed them examples of summaries, so I felt reasonably confident that they were familiar with what I expected. Additionally, students were to produce a "creative" response to their book. I passed out a list of possible responses, including visuals, realia, dramatizations, and written or oral compositions. Students might produce a time line or a collage; they might bring in representative artifacts; they might stage a brief play; or they might write a special dictionary for their book.

The American history book projects are meant to deepen students' understanding of specific aspects of history while allowing me to press on through the different eras. The projects allow both good and poor readers to tackle materials that present appropriate challenges. The projects also allow attention to historical themes rather than just a particular era. For instance, World War II was one of our topics this month, so I promoted *Hiroshima* along with other eras' war-related books, such as *The Red Badge of Courage, All Quiet on the Western Front,* and *Warday.* Students who reported on these books invariably commented on the power of their themes.

Inquiry   To make history more relevant, I began oral history projects. While studying the New Deal legislation, I asked if any student's relatives had worked in a CCC or WPA project. Terry volunteered his grandfather, and I conducted an interview with him. Mr. Donahue related some fascinating stories about why he joined the CCC in the 1930s, what the camps were like, and how some of the jobs were completed. Each class member then was responsible for completing a brief oral history project. They prepared questions, recorded interviewees' responses, and wrote up reports.

Meaning Vocabulary

Vocabulary still is being emphasized in history. I present new words and their meanings throughout each unit, and I spend time asking students to present the new vocabulary they are recording in their journals. Analogies and pictures are used most often when presenting the meanings for the words, and we've put on a few skits to help develop concepts. Rod and Judy presented a well-received skit this past month related to deficit spending. They played a newlywed couple with limited finances wanting to buy a state-of-the-art stereo system. After much debate, they resorted to using a department store credit account and then having to come up with the money later. Rod and Judy then stopped the skit and explained how a married couple using a credit card to buy a stereo is similar to a government agency using deficit spending to pay for items such as freeways and defense hardware.

Class time also was spent with the "alphabet soup" of New Deal innovations so that students would become more aware of abbreviations and acronyms. CCC, WPA, NRA, TVA, and AAA were some of the abbreviations that I presented. Students also came up with contemporary abbreviations such as FBI and CIA as well as acronyms such as SCUBA (self-contained underwater breathing apparatus) and MADD (Mothers Against Drunk Driving).

Another vocabulary tactic I used was to highlight common parts of derived words. Many social studies terms contain morphemes that are helpful in figuring out the meanings of new words as well as retrieving the meanings of old ones. During one week with the New Deal, *conservative, unconstitutional, intrastate,* and *progressive* were the key vocabulary terms containing morphemes. I knew I should point out the root word in *conservative* because it is related to several words: *conserve, conservation, conservationist,* and *conservatory.* I listed the five words in a column, aligning the shared part, and asked what the words had in common. It was obvious that all five words contained *conserv,* so the discussion then was directed to its meaning. "Keep the same," "preserve," and "traditional" were associated with conserve. I also indicated that I was sure these terms had counterparts in Spanish, Victor translated all four for us, and we again noted the Latin derivation of many words. I closed this five-minute lesson by drawing attention to the fact that looking for morphemes in words was helpful but occasionally misleading: "Remember, folks, *undone* means 'not done,' but *uncle* does not mean 'not cle.'"

Writing

In English we continued the study of relationships even though the other teachers had moved on. I must say, most of the students are becoming quite independent with their writing. They are well aware that every composition has a topic, audience, role, and form, and they now seem to determine those aspects automatically before writing. They also generate and organize information on their own before writing. Their revising is becoming automatic, although I do occasionally need to remind them about it.

As part of the unit on relationships, we read *West Side Story* in class and I showed a movie of *Romeo and Juliet*. "Hey, Mr. Mann," Ken called out, "why don't you let us write our own play?" "Why not?" I said. "I'll be here to help, but now you all know what you need to do in order to compose a play, so go to it." This was an extremely loose assignment, but I wanted to see just how independent this class was.

To my great satisfaction, the plays turned out quite well! I gave some class time to play production, but some time also was spent outside of school. Some students worked in groups, and others worked individually. Some wrote for young children, some for a teenage audience, and some for adults. They all used the same basic form, with stage directions and characters' lines presented as in *West Side Story*. Each group who wanted to present their play to the class practiced it in a conference room in the library, which turned out to be a great stimulus for revision. I didn't pressure all the groups to present their plays because time simply wouldn't allow it. Having some plays presented orally and some only in written form worked out fine. As with other group assignments, points were awarded for acceptable work, although in this case a play was worth five points.

APRIL

Inquiry Unit   The major emphasis this month in history was on an inquiry unit. My Falcon team members and I realized we had addressed integration (perhaps talking about it more than accomplishing it!) but we had done little about inquiry. The other three team members encouraged me to devote a substantial part of April to an inquiry project, saying that they would help where they could. In fact, Al Iteration, my English teaching counterpart, said he would join forces with me.

In history we had done brief projects throughout the year, looking up information about famous people and places and sharing it orally in class, but April became the month for large-scale researching and reporting. I figured students would be reasonably interested in studying the American history unit "A Decade of Change: 1960–1969," so I launched research projects on that era. One of my first steps was to help students ask researchable questions. First, I told the students about the general nature of the research they would be conducting, then I had them skim the chapter of the text that dealt with the 1960s. I wrote 1960–1970 at the top of the chalkboard and the words *Cuba, equal rights, Berlin, space exploration, John F. Kennedy,* and *Great Society* at the heads of columns. "What do you know about these topics?" I asked the class. As information was presented, I placed key words under the headings. *Ted Kennedy; Martin Luther King, Jr.; Bay of Pigs; Cuban Missile Crisis; Peace Corps;* and *Lee Harvey Oswald* were some of the terms that were listed. When Theresa spoke up to contribute Cesar Chavez's name, I gladly recorded it. I then took one of the words and asked, "What do you know and what don't you know about this term?" I again listed the information and questions that were presented. Following this class brainstorming, students brainstormed in groups. The lists they made of what they didn't know pointed out the need for research.

The next day I spent more time helping students formulate researchable questions. I reminded the eighth-graders that questions typically began with a *wh* word (who, what, when, where, and why) and that while *why* could give the most trouble, it could also lead to the most interesting research. Following this brief introduction, I moved into a question-asking exercise. "Meet with one other person about one of the topics you are interested in researching," I directed. "Write down all WH questions about the topic that you can think of. For instance, if you took Peace Corps, you might ask, 'Where do Peace Corps volunteers work?' 'When did the Peace Corps begin?' 'Why was it begun?' and so on." The two-person teams were given exactly five minutes for brainstorming questions about one topic before I directed them to move to the other person's topic for five minutes. Following this exercise, many of the students had the beginnings of an inquiry project.

Locating information in order to answer questions and generate new questions was the next step. I assumed that everybody had been introduced to aids such as indexes, encyclopedias, and the library catalog, so I designed a scavenger hunt as a quick and dirty refresher. I came up with questions such as, "What page of our history textbook contains information about the *Lusitania?*" and "How many books does the library hold on the topic of nuclear energy?" We spent two days scrounging around the library and the computer lab to locate the appropriate information. I reviewed students' answers in class and probed to see whether everyone was comfortable locating information in the traditional sources.

Computer Technology   Thinking that some of the better Internet search engines might be new to my eighth-graders, I asked our librarian to present it to my classes. As for all aids for locating information, the role of key words in using it well became apparent. The students saw that a few key terms were essential for research. For instance, Lonnie wanted to investigate "flower power," which he had heard was a mass movement of the 1960s. He was having trouble getting started, so I suggested looking under "youth movement," "counterculture," "protest," and "hippie."

Along with printed materials, each student was to interview at least one person. I had already demonstrated interviews when Terry's grandfather came to class for the oral history project. The students had seen how I covered the questions I had prepared beforehand, how at certain times I simply said, "Can you tell me more?", and how I explained the presence of my tape recorder. I told my students they could interview the other Falcon core teachers about the 1960s—even though I knew most of them had not even been born then.

Thinking Process: Organize   As students began locating information about their topics and refining their questions, the hardest part began—organizing the information. I had been teaching how to take notes from text, so my classes had a bit of a head start on this aspect of organization. One of my more frequent generic purposes for comprehending (which I had borrowed from English) had been, "Read in order to choose the three most important words from this section." After reading, students would explain why the three words they selected were most important; then I would explain my choices. At first Allison, Judy, and Ken were the only ones to volunteer their most important words, but more students began to open up as they became comfortable with the lesson. In fact, the students and I eventually began producing the same three words for the same reasons, indicating that we were beginning to organize text information in the same way.

Taking good notes from a passage is only the first step in organizing information; putting the notes into a logical framework is the other step. Constructing webs was my answer to organizing the mass of notes that students acquired. When I first introduced webs in class as part of my comprehension minilessons, I got the "Aha, I understand" response from several of my low-achieving students. It seemed that for the first time they understood the logic of organizing information on paper. Because we had constructed several webs in class, my suggestion that individuals construct their own webs was readily accepted. Terry created a web that I used as a model. He had taken a large sheet of drafting paper and neatly written his topic, "Beginning the Vietnam War," in the middle, surrounded by his subtopics, "French withdrawal," "Ho Chi Minh," "Ngo Dinh Diem," and "Gulf of Tonkin Resolution." He had then written key terms underneath each subtopic. Terry's paper demonstrated how to impose order on the mass of facts and ideas that researchers invariably uncover. He admitted that he probably would need to change his organization as he continued locating information, perhaps adding Viet Cong, but he was proud of the initial framework he had produced.

As we moved through the steps of asking questions, locating information, and organizing information, I had the students show me their work so I could help monitor their progress. Staying in touch systematically during these beginning steps seemed valuable as I was able to defuse many potential problems. For instance, Rod had decided to investigate the Soviet Union during the 1960s. "What do you want to know about the Soviet Union?" I asked. He replied that he would figure that out after doing some reading. A few days later I had the students turn in statements of their topic and research questions, and Rod still was unsure of what he wanted to do. I met with him briefly the next day, and together we decided that a study of U.S.-Soviet relations on nuclear testing would be interesting and feasible. Helping out during the research process was far more helpful than simply reacting to the finished product.

I also checked on students' webs before giving them the go-ahead to begin writing, a time-consuming but worthwhile procedure. Each student turned in a web that showed the order of presentation of the subtopics, along with the primary information associated with each subtopic. The webs were difficult to interpret because they were only outlines, but I could form impressions about

Webs

who had a sense of direction and who was floundering. I wrote specific suggestions when I could, and set up brief meetings with those who required more complete overhauls.

Writing   Once the webs were approved, students went to work on their written reports. I presented models of reports that the Falcon core had on file so that the class had an idea of what their reports should look like. I required both a first and a second draft. And this was when I called on my English teaching counterpart on the core, Al Iteration. "Al," I said, "let's get you involved now. I've helped the kids ask questions, locate information, organize what they are going to say, and produce a first draft. Why don't you work with them on revising what they have and producing a second draft?"

Revising/   Al set it up so that a student of the author's choice and he both reacted to
Editing   the first draft. The two questions that were to guide the first-draft readers were, "What was the most interesting aspect of this paper?" and "What do I want to know more about?" The students had experience reacting to others' work, so things went smoothly. After responding to the comments about their first drafts, students wrote second drafts and again submitted their papers to another student for a check on the mechanics of spelling, punctuation, and capitalization. This version then was turned in to Al for his ratings on the mechanics of the paper. I received the papers next and rated the contents. One thing I learned for next year was to stagger the times that the reports were due. I had three classes working on reports, and the paperwork I faced when all the papers came in at once was staggering.

MAY

Good old May, my favorite month! Spring was here in full force, and so was baseball season. The baseball practices and games after school added to my responsibilities and decreased my time for lesson planning. It's a good thing my students had become quite independent.

Independence   We moved away from the text more and more throughout the school year. The students increasingly relied on library books, brochures, web sites, and articles for their reading material. I would describe the available materials, and the students, working in their collaborative groups, would select the one or two titles they wanted to pursue. For instance, we were studying U.S. immigration during the 1980s, so many of Gary Soto's books were reading choices. One group selected *Living Up the Street*. Individuals took the role of various characters, and they presented selected portions through readers theater. The group members—not I—decided how they would respond to the book.

Portions of the history text still were required reading, but I didn't preteach as many concepts or set purposes as much as I used to. The students did that for themselves. When I established the fact that the portion of the text on President Reagan's terms of office was to be read, I asked the class, "What do you need to do?" Terry answered, "Look it over, think about what we already know about the topic, and decide what we should read carefully for," which indeed captured the essence of reading for a purpose. "Then go to it," was my directive. After a while, we decided that a time line was called for, so after reading, one was created on the board, separating the trivial from the noteworthy information.

Meaning Vocabulary

Vocabulary was handled much the same way as comprehension. Students identified the key terms and proposed ways to handle them. They pointed out the acronym in *laser* (light amplification by stimulated emission of radiation); identified the root word in *miniaturization;* and connected the changes in lifestyles begun by the computer age with the changes that had occurred at the beginning of the industrial age. My role was simply to keep the class on track as I continually asked, "What terms do you need to know? What can you do to understand and remember each term?" I was comfortable posing such a question because throughout the year I had demonstrated ways to learn vocabulary. Of course, my help still was needed. *Reaganomics* was a term that the students easily separated into *Reagan* and *economics,* but that didn't do much to explain the underlying concept. I had to step in and explain the plan of cutting personal taxes as well as federal spending in order to reduce inflation. The morphemes and the passage context simply didn't provide enough for gaining insight into that term.

Content Journals

A practice that I began hesitantly in April but pursued much more confidently in May was journal writing. Most of the writing I had students do consisted of quick writes or taking notes. The research projects involved a good deal of writing, but they occurred too infrequently. The idea of having students informally record their impressions of historical topics really appealed to me. Once journals were started, I occasionally made a specific assignment, such as, "The average life expectancy has increased from about 47 in 1900 to 74 at present. Write a letter to our mayor informing him what the city needs to do in order to handle the increasing numbers of elderly people."

Grading

Grading the journals was bound to be a problem, especially with students like Lonnie who rarely do anything if it's not for a grade, so I modified the point system I had used for group work. A certain number of pages needed to be filled with some evidence of independent thought in order to deserve one point. At the end of a month, 20 points were possible, so students with 18, 19, or 20 points (that is, those with 90 percent or more of the possible points) earned an A; those with 80 to 89 percent of the possible points earned a B, and so on. Most students produced the required amounts of writing and got a good grade for their journals. But more importantly, journal writing allowed students the opportunity to think through topics presented in class. It also seems to have promoted independent writing abilities; the most notable difference between the first entries and the later ones was the amount of writing that was produced.

Book Projects

A good deal of writing was being produced independently in my English classes. In fact, this month's book projects consisted of some exceptional pieces of writing. This month's topic in literature was sports, so books such as *The Amateurs* and *Jackie Robinson* were candidates for book projects. Rod read about George Plimpton, the writer who assumed the role of different professional athletes; he then wrote a poem about Plimpton that paralleled "Casey at the

Bat." Allison read a biography of Ingrid Kristiansen, a distance runner, talked informally with some of her athletic friends, and produced several insights into why individuals might devote themselves to competitive distance running.

JUNE

School is out, baseball season is over (we had a winning season), and the students have gone to their various summer adventures. As I think back over the year, I realize that class sessions definitely picked up once I provided better direction and when I allowed students more choices in their learning activities. Next year, especially in history, I need to provide meaningful instruction in September. It took me too long to get the good stuff going in those classes

In history and English, the students seemed to appreciate being prepared for the passage and knowing what to look for when they read. As I began fading my instruction, it was heartwarming to see the class take responsibility for their learning. I also feel good about some of the creative and insightful responses some of the students produced when they decided on their own learning.

Once I integrated skill work with literature topics in English, I felt much better about my writing instruction. Working on sentence structure in the context of meaningful passages, rather than with worksheets, made a lot more sense to me as well as to the students. I seem to have faded my instruction pretty well in writing and reading. The students could all independently plan, draft, and revise a composition rather well, or at least they all knew the steps to follow! And I got off to a good start with reciprocal teaching, so they seemed independent there, too.

Developing the students' vocabularies seemed to progress well. Rather than simply have the class copy dictionary definitions, I made every effort to present new terms in meaningful, memorable ways. Analogies, pictures, skits, webs, and morphemes seemed to help. I plan to spend more time next year helping students develop their vocabularies independently. For instance, once I show the class how to form analogies, I will gradually shift that thinking process over to the students.

The book projects, group work, and research projects all went smoothly enough and students seemed to benefit from them. These projects involved both good and poor readers and writers in activities at appropriate levels of difficulty. I'm convinced that one of middle-school teachers' biggest challenges is accommodating the wide range of individual differences that each class presents. The projects seemed to go far toward meeting those differences.

This last journal entry summarizes the parts of my teaching that I intend to keep and the parts I intend to change. I've decided that middle school is for me. We Falcon core teachers need to plan more interdisciplinary work, but I think we did a good job integrating study skills instruction among the four of us. The students were great. They were an active and often unpredictable group, but that's what I liked about them. They need me here.

In August I'm going to reread this whole journal, paying special attention to these closing comments. Developing independent lifelong learners still is my goal. I fully intend to keep refining my instruction. At the end of ten years,

I want to be able to say that I had ten years of experience—not one year of experience ten times.

REFERENCES

ADAMS, R. (1975). *Watership down.* Riverside, NJ: Macmillan.

ALLEN, M. (1987). *Jackie Robinson.* New York: Watts.

ANGELOU, M. (1970). *I know why the caged bird sings.* New York: Random House.

ASHER, S. (1987). *Everything is not enough.* New York: Delacorte.

BRADBURY, R. (1970). *The Martian chronicles.* Garden City, NY: Doubleday.

BRIN, D. (1985). *The postman.* New York: Bantam.

BROOKS, B. (1986). *The moves make the man.* New York: Harper.

CALLAHAN, S. (1986). *Adrift: Seventy-six days lost at sea.* Boston: Houghton Mifflin.

CLARKE, A. C. (1968). *2001: A space odyssey.* New York: New American Library.

CRANE, S. (1944). *The red badge of courage.* New York: Heritage.

HALBERSTAM, D. (1985). *The amateurs.* New York: Morrow.

HALEY, A. (1976). *Roots.* Garden City, NY: Doubleday.

HERSEY, J. (1946). *Hiroshima.* New York: Knopf.

HEYERDAHL, T. (1950). *Kon-Tiki: Across the Pacific by raft.* Chicago: Rand McNally.

KEYES, D. (1966). *Flowers for Algernon.* New York: Harcourt, Brace & World.

KINSELLA, W. P. (1982). *Shoeless Joe.* New York: Ballantine.

LAURENTS, A. (1958). *West side story.* New York: Random House.

LAWRENCE, L. (1986). *Moonwind.* New York: Harper.

MOHR, N. (1986). *Going home.* New York: Dial.

PATON, A. (1948). *Cry, the beloved country.* New York: Scribner's.

REMARQUE, E. M. (1938). *All quiet on the Western front.* New York: Buccaneer.

SLEATOR, W. (1985). *Singularity.* New York: Dutton.

STRIEBER, W., & KUNETKA, J. (1984). *Warday.* New York: Warner Books.

TAYLOR, M. (1978). *Roll of thunder, hear my cry.* New York: Bantam.

TRUMBO, D. (1939). *Johnny got his gun.* New York: Lippincott.

VERNE, J. (1925). *20,000 leagues under the sea.* New York: Scribner's.

WOLFE, T. (1987). *The bonfire of the vanities.* New York: Farrar, Straus & Giroux.

WRIGHT, R. (1945). *Black boy.* New York: Harper & Row.

ZINDEL, P. (1968). *The pigman.* New York: Harper & Row.

chapter 12

High School Level

AUGUST

I feel a little strange keeping a journal. I used to keep a diary when I was a girl. I wonder if I am regressing. Dr. Knowles, who taught the content area reading and writing course I took in my senior year, suggested that keeping journals allows teachers to do something they seldom have time for—to pause and reflect. He also said that a journal allows you to look back across the year and be reminded of the little triumphs that are frequently overshadowed by the daily problems teachers face. I have decided to keep this journal on just two of my classes this year, one of my regular biology classes and my consumer math class. When Dr. Knowles talked about keeping journals, he suggested we focus on our most challenging classes. From the look of the names on my preliminary rolls, the two classes I've picked should certainly be that!

In the six years I've been teaching, I have vacillated between a textbook approach and a process approach to teaching biology. When I first started, I was strongly influenced by the methods used by my supervising teacher during student teaching. I made a great deal of use of the textbook, supplemented with lectures. Of course we had our lab periods, but these tended to be isolated from the content we were learning. This approach kept the students busy and was obviously what they expected. Soon, however, I found that most students were not learning very much. My below-average students seemed bewildered much of the time. My average and above-average students did satisfactory or even excellent work, but when I referred to something we had studied only a few weeks before, almost all looked blank. Nor were the students very interested in biology. One student said to me that very first year, "Miss Mull, this stuff is as dry as a bone!" Can you imagine how I responded to him? I am ashamed to admit that, out of my frustration, I said sharply, "Well then, why don't you moisten it with a little sweat from your brow!"

It became obvious that, to almost all my students, "Mull's bio class" was either a boring frustration or a dull obstacle course. My hopes of making biology, the study of life, an inspiring and edifying experience seemed no more than a naive dream. I sought advice from the principal, assistant principal, science supervisor, chair of the science department, and other teachers, all of whom generally agreed that I was "too idealistic" and should realize that there is a limited amount that can be accomplished with "today's kids." So I continued teaching biology the same way for the next three years until I had become quite adept at assigning the textbook, lecturing, directing occasional labs, and giving tests. I never became any more satisfied with this way of teaching, however. The summer after my third year of teaching, I had a crisis. I finally made up my mind that I could no longer stand what I was doing. A radical change was in order, and I made it. I swung to the pure process approach that my undergraduate science methods courses had so strongly advocated. Everything we did was hands-on. I brought living things into the classroom, and we dissected numerous plants and animals. We used the microscopes and interactive biology CD-ROMs regularly. The students did become more interested, but I soon discovered that while they remembered the hands-on experiences, most could not organize their thinking along more global and abstract general principles. In other words, they could not relate the hands-on experiences to a "big picture."

As you can imagine, I gradually began to get frustrated and even cynical. During this time, there was increased pressure in my school system to raise test scores, making me feel that I had to cover everything in the biology curriculum whether my students had time to learn it or not. Trying to cover a lot of curricular ground using demonstrations, experiments, computer simulations, and field trips can really strain a teacher's system!

This year, when I first walked into my classroom, I found that I had burned out. I couldn't face teaching again. Biology was my major in college and I had always liked it. However, biology is the most often failed high-school subject in my state, and it is also the most failed subject in the high school where I teach. Students often dread it before they take it, hate it while they take it, and criticize it as they look back on it.

The beginning of school this year was a time of real introspection for me. The more I thought, the more I realized that I had been lying to myself, kidding myself along for at least the previous year. Now I could fool myself no longer. I wanted to do anything but teach. I wanted to be anywhere but walking down those halls into that laboratory-classroom. I carefully considered my options. I was not tied down with a husband or children. I was only 27 years old. I had a little money saved and my car was relatively new. I was free to resign my job to go wherever I wanted to, change careers completely if I wanted to. I thought of going to work for a biological supply company near where my parents live. On the other hand, I thought that I might like to begin a career in retail sales, selling women's clothes or shoes.

But another force within me pulled strongly in the other direction. I really believe in education as a positive factor in influencing young people. I looked back fondly on the teachers across my school years who seemed to enjoy teaching and who had taken an interest in me and taught me things that I needed to know. How had they avoided burnout? Or had they? Perhaps they had just hidden it from us. Finally, one night that first week of school, I called one of my teachers whom I remembered particularly fondly and who lives only 25 miles away. She had been my life science teacher in seventh grade. She graciously invited me to her home although I had not seen her in more than ten years.

The next evening I arrived at Mrs. Plante's house a little after five o'clock, and she welcomed me in. It was so good to see her. Though she was noticeably older than I had remembered, her face brought back so many sweet memories to me. We hugged each other and began to catch up on news about my old classmates and my other middle and high-school teachers. Time passed quickly. Before I knew it, it was time for me to go and I had not even broached the subject I had really come to talk about.

"Oh, Mrs. Plante," I blurted out, "I'm miserable in my job. That's why I really needed to talk with you. How have you stood it all these years?"

"So that's it, Annie," she sighed into her coffee. "Has it been this bad for— how many years have you taught?"

"Five, not counting this one. No, I was pretty happy my first year because I thought I would get better. And I did, but so many students aren't learning very much and they don't particularly like biology or think it's worth much. I just don't think I can stand to do this any more."

"Annie," she asked, "why do you think you became a biology teacher?"

"I always loved the sciences, and biology in particular. I also love kids, especially teenagers. I thought teaching high-school biology would be the perfect marriage of those two loves."

"You don't think you're good at teaching, do you?"

"Mrs. Plante, it's strange that you should ask that. I get good evaluations, and everyone seems reasonably pleased with what I'm doing. But I still feel like a failure almost all the time."

Professionalism   "People who see themselves as professionals are always interested in finding out what needs doing so they can do it. Other people's evaluations aren't good enough for a professional."

"Up to a point, you're right, Mrs. Plante. I'm not satisfied with what I'm accomplishing in my classes even if everyone else is. If this is the best it gets, I want out. Let somebody else mind the mental morgue!"

"Do you think that is the best it gets, Annie?"

"I suppose I'm beginning to think so. Actually, I'm pretty arrogant down inside. I used the traditional method and got pretty good at it. Then I used the vanguard method and got pretty good at that, too. But neither method pro- duced a high-level understanding or appreciation of biology except in a few students who already knew a lot and were interested when they started."

Suddenly, Mrs. Plante looked very old. "I don't know what to tell you, Annie. Maybe you are too idealistic. Maybe it is too much to expect most stu- dents to grasp the big picture of biology and to like it as well."

"That means I have to resign and do something else. Thanks, Mrs. Plante, for helping me see what I must do."

We talked longer, but nothing else substantive was said. I had made up my mind and Mrs. Plante seemed to agree with me. I drove home, sat down at the computer and typed my letter of resignation, then went to bed.

That night, I had a dream that was to change my life. In the dream, I was led kicking and screaming to a post and tied there. Then a firing squad of two soldiers came and took aim at me. Just as they were about to fire, I realized that one was Dr. Bass, the professor who had taught my science methods class in college, and the other was Mr. DeBoer, my supervising teacher during student teaching. I called out that I had done my best, but they continued to point their rifles at me, frowning. Suddenly, Dr. Knowles, the professor of my content-area reading and writing course, appeared from nowhere and untied me. I grabbed a pistol from somewhere to shoot my two executioners, but Dr. Knowles took the gun from me and said, "No, you'll need them both." He walked over to dis- arm them as well, forcing them to shake hands with each other in spite of their resistance. As their hands finally clasped, he turned to me and asked, "Do you see?" All I could say was, "See what? Tell me what I'm supposed to see!" I said that over and over to no avail until I woke up in a sweat.

My first reaction was to try to forget my dream, but I couldn't get it out of my mind. During breakfast and in the shower, it vividly came back to me, and each time it did, my mind seemed almost ready to understand what Dr. Knowles had meant.

As I drove to school, I suddenly remembered something I had once read or heard, "If two intelligent people totally disagree about something, you can be reasonably sure that they are both partly right and partly wrong." In an instant, I saw everything clearly. Textbooks and lectures aren't wrong if prop- erly used, but they can't provide concrete experiences; demonstrations, experi- ments, computer simulations, and field trips aren't wrong if properly used, but they can't ensure high-level thinking. What I needed was a way to integrate the two, to use the strengths of each to compensate for the weaknesses of the other. Dr. Knowles had taught us how to use direct experiences to build the basis for understanding abstract concepts. He had also taught us that you can't just assign a textbook; you have to be sure that students know their purposes for reading. Writing can also be used to help students organize and integrate information. I remembered with regret how I had yawned through his class, resenting instruction in reading and writing when I wanted to teach biology. I drove right home and dug out my notebook and the textbook from his course.

Then I tore up my letter of resignation. I'll give it a year, I said to myself with determination. If it works, fine. If not, well, I gave it every chance.

SEPTEMBER

Web

Dr. Knowles taught us that main ideas and generalizations are important aids to learning. First, these key concepts are themselves the most important content to be learned. Second, knowing the main ideas helps us to learn the less important ideas that support them. As a result, I decided to start out this year by giving my students a firm grasp of the overall structure of biology. Neither the textbook nor the lab manual provided students such a structure, so I had to construct the structure for myself out of both of these sources, my own knowledge, and various other references.

After spending a couple of classes introducing the students to the laboratory, the textbook, and the lab manual, I placed the diagram shown in Figure 12.1 on the bulletin board.

To introduce my students to the structure of biology, I only had to teach them to understand the diagram. First, we discussed the term *biology* itself. What would we study in biology class and what was not included in that discipline? I allowed the students to name all the things they could think of that we would and would not study, and I told them whether they were right or not. Some things they named were not even in the domain of science, though most were. Many of their items fell under other branches of science, such as astronomy, geology, chemistry, or physics. In only one class did they have a good sense of the meaning of biology. Second, we spent some time on the terms *zoology* and *botany*. Again, I allowed the students to name a large number of examples and nonexamples of each, on which I commented.

Direct
Experience

At this point, as always, I taught my students the proper handling and use of a microscope. It takes time, but an ounce of prevention saves the school money! I then brought out the microscopes. The students took turns at their

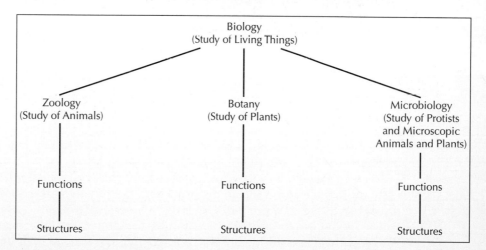

Figure 12.1   Biology web

tables viewing some prepared slides of common organic and inorganic sub-
stances such as hair and dust. When I was sure they understood the term *microscopic,* I introduced them to what I thought would be a new domain of life for
them: protists. At this point, I defined *protists* only as "all living things that are
neither plants nor animals." Most of them had trouble believing that there
could be life that was neither plant nor animal, but I was able to get them to
suspend judgment. Based on these understandings, I then led them through a
discussion of microbiology and what we would cover under that heading on
the course diagram. Finally, they understood that virtually all life that can be
seen with the naked eye is either plant or animal, but that microscopic life
includes plants, animals, and protists.

I knew that they might have some difficulty understanding what was
meant by *functions* and *structures* on the diagram and I moved to the chalkboard for those lessons. I wrote "Functions" at the top of the board, underlined
it, and wrote "Structures" at the top of the board on the other side, underlining
it as well. Under Functions I wrote, "walking," "talking," and "smelling";
under the word Structures I wrote, "legs," "mouth," and "nose." I then asked
for volunteers to explain the difference between functions and structures. In
each case, I told them where they were correct and where they still lacked some
insight. After a while, everyone appeared to have a good grasp of the difference, so I wrote "tasting" in the middle of the board. I required each student to
take a piece of notebook paper and tear it in half. On one half they were to
write a large dark *f* and on the other, an *s.* They were given a few seconds to
examine the examples still listed on the board; then I had them classify "tasting" by raising the appropriate piece of paper. I did not allow students to show
their papers before or after I gave them a signal, but only at that one moment.
Then we discussed the correct classification and the reasons for it. I continued
to put words in the middle of the board for them to classify until they became
automatic at getting them right. Eventually, they were able to classify correctly
terms like *heart, stem, imagine,* and *transpire.*

We then returned to the course diagram on the bulletin board. I asked
them to predict what we would study this year in biology. After some discussion, they came to understand that we were going to study the three kinds of
living things, animals and plants (both microscopic and not), and protists, and
that we would study them by learning the functions that they perform and the
structures that enable them to perform those functions. I fielded questions
about specific issues, using the diagram whenever possible to show where
their question fit into the overall structure of biology. I left the bulletin board
up so that students could see at a glance "the big picture" of our year of studying
biology.

This process took a lot of time. At first, it was difficult for me not to be impatient, for I remembered that in the past I had spent no more than a few minutes
on each of the six terms in the diagram. I had merely defined them, the students
had written down these definitions, and we had gone on to other things.

Now that I had decided to teach each of these terms and their interrelation-
ships until the students understood them clearly and could apply them, I was

shocked at how long it took. Why, no wonder no one has learned very much biology in my other classes—I've thrown out major concepts as if they were minor facts that needed only to be memorized!

Once the students had a grasp of the diagram, the class was assigned to read the portions of the text that pertained to the overall structure of biology, and to how that structure has gradually developed as biology has grown as a science. It's not enough to expose students to a concept; I must continue to work with them on that concept until I am sure that they truly understand it.

Oops! I have been so intent on carrying out my new approach to teaching biology that I have just let my consumer math class ride. Well, they're about to ride me out of town on a rail! I must do something different from what I am doing there, too. The course is supposed to be a practical study of consumer arithmetic for students who are not outstanding in mathematics. So why is the first chapter of the textbook filled with discussions of "interpolating and extrapolating data," and exercises with nothing but confusing word problems to solve? Help!

OCTOBER

Word Problems

I began the month in my consumer math class by trying to help my students with word problems. I never realized how much of consumer math consisted of word problems! Word problems present a major difficulty to almost all groups of math students. Fortunately, I came across some research by H. Ballew and J. Cunningham that showed me how to diagnose my students, determining what areas of word problem solving were holding them back. Because we had not yet begun Chapter 2 in our math textbook, I picked out the word problems from that chapter and randomly assigned them to one of three testing conditions as Ballew and Cunningham had done. For test A, I set the word problems up in pure computational form, "the computation test." For test B, I simply wrote down all the numbers from each problem in the order they appeared in the problem. I called this "the problem interpretation test." For test C, I presented the problems exactly as they were in the book (oh, the miracle of copying machines!). Each test had 14 items.

On successive days, I gave the three tests to the class. Test A was merely handed out and taken up after a reasonable time, and I simply graded each problem for the correct answer. When I gave test B, I handed out the pages with the numbers on them and read aloud each problem to the students as they followed along, looking at the numbers. I gave them time to work each problem before reading them the next one. By this method I eliminated the need for them to be able to read the problem in order to interpret it. I graded each problem on Test B, not for correct answers per se, but for whether the problem was correctly set up or not—that is, whether they would have gotten the right answer if they had done the computation properly. When I graded test C, I gave the students two scores, one based on how many problems they had set up correctly (the reading and problem interpretation score) and one based on the number of correct answers (word problem solving score). I came up with the following averages for my class on the four scores generated from the three tests of fourteen problems each:

Computation Average Score	Problem Interpretation Average Score	Reading and Problem Interpretation Average Score	Word Problem Solving Average Score
11.7	11.5	9.2	7.4

I was shocked that my students averaged only 7.4 out of 14 word problems correct when they had to do everything independently. Yet, their average score on the computation test shows that they can generally do the arithmetic that the word problems require; their average score on the problem interpretation test shows that they can generally figure out what computations to do and in what order. Their major difficulty seems to be reading! They did far worse on problem interpretation when they had to read the problems than when I read the problems to them. They also seem to have difficulty with what Ballew and Cunningham call "integration"—the ability to read, interpret the problem, and compute simultaneously—as indicated by the fact that their word problem solving average score was lower than any of the other three. For this class, then, I must design activities to improve ability to read word problems and to integrate skills in solving word problems or give up trying to teach them to apply the arithmetic they know to consumer situations.

I wonder how a similar process of math diagnosis—determining what areas of word problem solving are holding students back—would have turned out last year when I was teaching a section of algebra II or the year before last when I was teaching a section of geometry. As I look back, I think that both classes had relatively less difficulty with reading, but relatively more difficulty with problem interpretation and integration than this year's consumer math students are having. Of course, I wouldn't know for sure without constructing and administering the three tests.

Comprehension Lesson   Meanwhile, I have also been doing a unit on reading and understanding advertisements in consumer math. My students are so gullible! I have had the hardest time getting them to see past the hype to consider the facts. Finally I decided to require them to rewrite a number of newspaper, magazine, and radio ads, eliminating everything that is not factual information. Then, we talked about making purchasing decisions solely on the factual version of the ad. Most of the time, they realized that they were no longer interested in making the purchase. But some seem to resent their new understanding. Ken and Allison both said that it was more fun to be convinced to buy something than to be so analytical! Maybe when they're earning their own money, they'll feel differently.

Our first major biology unit has been "The Cell." When the students came into the room on the first day of that unit, they found the seven lab tables prepared for groups of students. At each table was a scalpel, some forceps, an onion, several glass slides, two eyedroppers, some toothpicks, staining solution, and a microscope. The students followed the directions I had passed out **Direct** to them, a xeroxed sheet that told them to look at a layer of onion tissue and **Experience** some scrapings from the inside of their cheeks under the microscope. In each case, they looked at the materials both before and after staining them. I explained to them that they were seeing cells—the basic unit of all living things except viruses. Their lab manual contained a drawing of a cheek cell and an onion cell and they were required to find the various parts of these drawn and labeled cells in the real cells they were viewing. I then distributed a set of questions that led them to compare the cells in the onion layer with those from inside their cheeks.

In the follow-up lesson, I used the interactive CD-ROM that allows students to examine cells from a large number of different plants and animals, rotating them and increasing or decreasing the magnification. With these labs, I focused their attention on the major commonalties and differences between plant and animal cells.

Students were then assigned to read the part of the textbook outside of class that described the development of cell theory by various scientists. Their **Writing** purpose for reading was to write a one-paragraph summary of the major contribution of each scientist. The next day, I selected students at random and had them read paragraphs they had written about various scientists.

At this point, I reminded them of the difference between functions and structures and explained that the chapter they were going to read next described the functions and structures of the cell. I showed them the graphic organizer in Figure 12.2.

Their purpose for reading the next chapter was to fill in the graphic organizer on paper while they read. The text described functions and structures in a clear and literal fashion, but to understand the links between particular functions and structures required careful reading. I was convinced that this assignment would help students to process more deeply the concepts I considered most important than just telling them to read the chapter would do.

The next day, the students came in and I took up their completed diagrams. With their books closed, they then suggested how to fill in the diagram I had on the board. I did not correct any of their suggestions, just kept them on task and facilitated consensus when they got bogged down. When they had achieved consensus on a completed diagram, we opened our books and made corrections together. Finally, we ended up with a correct diagram.

For the remainder of this unit, I will use a combination of lectures, experiments, computer simulations, and demonstrations, as well as content comprehension lessons using graphic organizers like the one in Figure 12.2, to teach

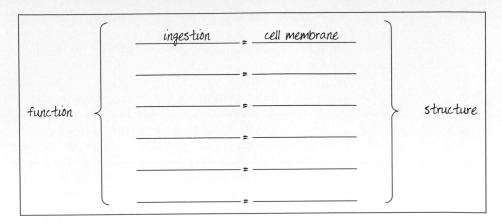

Figure 12.2   Graphic Organizer

the students about various types of cells. We are making extensive use of the microscopes with both preprepared slides and slides that we prepare ourselves. We are also making a detailed study of the structures and subfunctions that permit each function of the cell. And we are examining the similarities and differences among plant cells, animal cells, and protists.

NOVEMBER

In biology, we finished our unit on the cell during the first part of the month. By the end of the unit, most students could label the various structures in a drawing of a cell and could write a brief explanation of the function of that structure in various types of cells. The difference between the most and the least successful students was in their understanding of the cell's more complex structures and functions. The range between my top and bottom students is as great as it has been in the past, but the amount learned by the bottom students is far ahead of any year I've ever taught. These methods seem to be working

Web well. My emphasis on main ideas seems to facilitate the learning of facts and details. The quality of student questions is higher than ever before and they appear much more interested in biology, perhaps because they can always relate what they're learning to the basic structure of the discipline.

Graphic   Following the unit on the cell, I created a new bulletin board with a new
Organizer diagram (see Figure 12.3). I explained to the students that they were now ready to study the structures and functions of the various kinds of plants, animals, and protists. I showed them the diagram and told them the order in which we would investigate these various forms of life during the rest of the year. We began by using the microscopes and CD-ROMs to study the structures of protists and their functions. From there, we began the study of plants by learning about the structures of algae and their functions.

Animals	Plants	Protists
Invertebrates		
Sponges	Algae	Diatoms
Coelenterates	Fungi	Protozoans
Worms	Mosses and liverworts	Bacteria
Echinoderms	Ferns	Viruses
Mollusks	Cone-bearing plants	
Crustaceans	Flowering plants	
Arachnids		
Myriapods		
Insects		
Vertebrates		
Fish		
Amphibians		
Reptiles		
Birds		
Mammals		
Nonhumans		
Humans		

Figure 12.3   Living Things

Inquiry   I have also decided this month that I want my students to be able to do library research in biology—a basic skill that all biologists certainly need. Moreover, anyone with questions needs to know how to find accurate answers to them efficiently. Consequently, I developed an approach that requires library research and does not allow mere copying from sources. I gave students a mimeographed copy of the following list:

Fields Related to Biology

Anatomy	Eugenics	Microbiology
Bacteriology	Exobiology	Molecular biology
Biochemistry	Genetics	Morphology
Biophysics	Gnotobiotics	Paleontology
Botany	Heredity	Pathology
Crybiology	Histology	Phenology
Cytology	Limnology	Physiology
Ecology	Marine biology	Taxidermy
Embryology	Medicine	Zoology

Writing Lesson   I then wrote the words *compare* and *contrast* on the board and asked them about those words. They generally manifested a good understanding of the two terms. I told them that we as a class were going to write a short composition on the board, "comparing and contrasting botany and zoology." They were given three minutes to try to write the first sentence and to list any details they thought should be included individually. When this brief planning time ended, I took the chalk and stood at the board. "Who has a particularly good first sentence for our composition?"

Allison volunteered that first sentence and I wrote it down as it was dictated to me: "Botany and zoology are both fields of biology."

I then led them to give me sentences comparing what they knew about botany and zoology with what we had already learned. Thus we gradually completed our group composition. My role was only to require consensus and to remind them of the task as often as necessary. Through creating a group composition, every student came to understand what a compare-and-contrast paper is. I reminded them of the list I had given them and told them to select two fields on which to write a compare-and-contrast composition based on library research. One week later, after some preliminary library research, they submitted their pairs of fields to me for my approval. The compare-and-contrast papers themselves were due one week after that.

Word Problems

In consumer math this month, I have really worked hard on helping my students with word problems. I have consistently used two approaches to improve students' ability to read the problems. First, I have tried to get them to transfer their ability to interpret word problems that they hear to their own reading, as I alternate between having them hear a problem and having them read one. I read the first problem to them and give them time to solve it. All pencils are put down and then a student who I see has it right goes to the board and works that problem. We briefly discuss why it was worked that way. Then students read the next problem to themselves and work it. Again I choose a student to work it correctly on the board. We discuss why that problem was worked that way. The method seems simple, but students do better on the third or fourth independent problem than they did on the first. I believe they will continue to improve.

I also use an overhead projector so that I can uncover a word problem one clause at a time as we try to solve it as a group. The goal is to solve the problem by seeing as little of the problem as possible. Everyone has to explain any suggestion he or she makes. The students are getting good at reading carefully and using all the information in each word in the problem.

The major factor in integrating skills to solve word problems seems to be lots of successful practice. Unfortunately, that means that only those students for whom word problem solving is already easy can learn to do it well (the rich get richer!). So I have employed two means for providing students with successful practice. First, I have procured math textbooks and workbooks from grades four through eight and have selected consumer-oriented word problems from them. I duplicated these problems to give out to my students, without

Homework

telling the students where I got them. They make perfect homework assignments because the students can work them successfully and are therefore less likely to "practice their ignorance." I made the mistake of telling Mr. Burr that I was going to do this. (He teaches the other sections of consumer math.) He told me that the students wouldn't do their homework unless it was challenging for them. Rather than arguing with him, I just tried my idea. The proportion of students doing their homework has actually increased since I initiated this practice. I do not understand why we think our top students should perform tasks that they can do well while our bottom students must be given tasks that are nearly impossible for them. If challenge rather than success motivated students, our least capable students would be the most motivated!

Word Problems

The second thing I did to improve integration of word problem solving skills was periodically to assign students to work five problems in class that they have previously solved. This time, however, I place them under a tight time limit. They must both get the answer right and show all their work to get credit for a problem. I determine a daily grade based on the time they take:

Daily Grade		Time
A	=	2 minutes
B	=	3 minutes
C	=	4 minutes

Missing even one problem because of a careless mistake results in a daily grade of D, regardless of time spent. At the end of each amount of time, students who are finished put down their pencils and turn their papers over. I spend the next minute walking around and writing the number of minutes on the back of each turned-over paper.

This system has really cut down on carelessness, a major problem these students have with word problems. And I am seeing an overall improvement in both their success and their attitude toward word problems. At least now when they miss a word problem, it is usually because of their computation or problem interpretation rather than their reading or integration.

DECEMBER

Concept Development

Since I recently read C. Santa and D. Alvermann's *Science Learning: Processes and Applications,* I have become more aware of several problems with my students' reading of our biology textbook. This book stresses the difficulty of getting students to read (or listen) for conceptual change in science. Apparently, most students in science are just trying to get the assignment completed satisfactorily rather than really trying to learn what is being taught. This leads to the persistence of misconceptions even after reading or hearing information that should have cleared them up!

Chapter 6 in this book, by K. Roth, used the illustration of how students' misconceptions of photosynthesis continued even after their study of that process was completed. Since we were studying photosynthesis this month anyway, I decided to see if my students were like the ones Roth had examined. Boy, were they!

When I asked my students on the test to write an essay on how plants get their food, almost all of them mentioned from the soil or the air or both, even though the book stated clearly that plants manufacture their own food through the process of photosynthesis. This was so, even for most of the students who otherwise correctly defined terms and completed short-answer questions. It became obvious to me that the students were often just memorizing information rather than using that information to revise their knowledge and understanding. They had come to the study of biology with their own theory of how plants get food, and they seemed destined to leave biology with some additional terms and facts but the same incorrect theory intact.

Comprehension Lesson

I developed a simple and straightforward approach to helping students realize that their preconceived notions may be incorrect. I asked them the same questions in advance of reading that I wanted them to be able to answer after reading. They answered them individually in writing both times. I then led them through the book-based answers to the questions by showing them in the book exactly how the answers were presented. I then had them compare their postreading answers with both their prereading answers and the book-based answers. It was a revelation to many of them. "Why, I just answered the questions the same way both times!" admitted Sarah. "I thought that was what the book was saying, too, but it wasn't."

Thinking Processes— Evaluate

Ambrose angrily asked me if I was trying to brainwash them! His insolent but important question helped me realize that critical reading is also required when reading or listening for conceptual change. We certainly don't want to disregard everything we think just because a book contradicts it. I explained to Ambrose and the class that I would require them to know what the book was saying, not that they agree with it.

Comprehension Lesson

This process of comparing their own ideas before reading with the ideas of the text in an objective fashion has really helped my students' comprehension of the text. Only a few students still persist in reading their own notions into the text, and they are making some progress.

Biology is supposed to be the study of life. This month, I also thought it was the study of words! My efforts this year to combine the process and traditional approaches have been largely successful, but I have still been concerned about how little some students were learning. Students like Lonnie, Theresa, and Ambrose failed the first nine weeks in spite of all my efforts.

Professional Growth

Right after Thanksgiving, I went to an all-day content area reading workshop sponsored by the regional education center. These things are usually a waste of time but I had heard that Dr. Wurdz, the presenter, was quite practical, so I decided to give it a whirl. Am I glad I did! He spent all day convincing

Meaning Vocabulary

us that it is the onslaught of new vocabulary that hurts most students in content areas and he targeted the sciences as being particularly at fault. He gave us several passages to read from high-level statistics and management textbooks, and none of us could understand a thing we read. It became perfectly clear to me that if you don't have immediate access to the meanings of important words, comprehension of a passage is downright impossible!

Dr. Wurdz also showed us that there are two kinds of vocabulary words: the easy ones to teach and the toughies. The easy words are those for which kids already know the meaning but not the word that represents the meaning. His example was the word *obstreperous*. Many students don't know what the word means, but every one of them can practice the concept! The toughies are words for which students lack both the word and the meaning. Of course, of all the disciplines, science is the most plagued by terms with which students have absolutely no experience.

During the workshop, we had to look at a chapter in our textbooks we had brought to divide the new words into those for which students probably lacked only the word and those for which they probably lacked both word and meaning. The list for one chapter in my text had 32 words—of which 24 were the tough kind! Then he told us that research showed you can effectively teach only ten tough words per week! Ten! Most of my chapters have 25 to 35 words, and I certainly can't spend three or four weeks on every chapter. Fortunately, he gave us some rules for getting our list down to the sacred number ten. First, he said, eliminate words for which students already have enough meaning. I didn't think the book would list vocabulary to be taught if most students would know it, but I found that my book had many such words. What tenth-grader doesn't know what a blade or a leaflet is? (I wonder who decides on these vocabulary lists? Have they ever seen a tenth-grader?) Next, he said, eliminate very technical terms that most educated adults don't know and that even teachers have to review before the lesson. (How did he know I sometimes had to do that?) These technical terms are defined enough in context for students who can read well to understand them for the moment, and in any case they are not words that anyone remembers. That made sense, although it is hard not to feel guilty about not teaching all these terms. Finally, he said that we needed to read the chapter again to see if any important words had been left off the text's vocabulary list. Once again, he was right. My textbook's list had left out the terms *broad-leafed*, *narrow-leafed*, and *needle-leafed*. Understanding these words was what the chapter was all about!

By following these new guidelines, I am now able to get my list of vocabulary words down to about ten per week. I still don't feel quite right about this, but if my students really learn 360 new biology words in one year, words that they really know and can use, I guess that is not a bad accomplishment. And I realize that my students must have a good command of these words if they are to understand what they read and what I present to them.

Following is the vocabulary list from our textbook's most recent chapter with the additions and deletions I have made based on these new guidelines. Words marked with an X I have totally eliminated from consideration: We won't discuss it, there won't be activities that use it, and it won't be mentioned on any test I give. Bracketed words are those I added to the list. For example, I eliminated *fibrovascular bundle* while adding its more common name, *vein*. Then

I marked with an asterisk each word that I planned to emphasize in both teaching and testing, leaving the other words to be learned by students on their own. A common word, *leaf*, remained on the list because of the precision of its definition in the chapter.

*	abscission		leaf
	sheath		palisade mesophyll
	cuticle		pinnate leaf
x	fibrovascular bundle	x	spine
x	insectivorous plant		stoma
*	mesophyll	x	transpiration
	petiole	*	[compound leaf]
	fiber	*	[simple leaf]
	sessile leaf	x	bundle
	mesophyll	*	epidermis
	stipule	x	guttation
x	tendril		leaflet
*	[broad-leafed plant]		palmate leaf
*	[narrow-leafed plant]	x	sclerenchyma
*	[needle-leafed plant]		spongy
	blade	x	succulent leaf
	epidermal hair	*	venation
	guard cell	*	[vein]

Direct Experience

Once I have selected the words I am going to teach, I must be sure to focus on those words. Students have no concept for many of these words. Fortunately, the laboratory part of our course provides them with the real thing on a regular basis. I see now that one reason my dual-emphasis program is effective is that the laboratory part provides the direct experiences for many new terms. If I don't have the resources or time to develop a concept adequately through direct laboratory experience, I make sure to provide some visual experience for it. This is not difficult since we have some good videos, film loops, slides, and CD-ROMs in our media center, with more available from our regional education center. Also, our library is connected to the Internet and I subscribe to a direct Internet service provider at home. When I find a particularly good visual for a term on the net, I just print it out on a color printer. Then I can make a transparency from it or just pass it around for the students to look at.

I have also been using the visuals in our biology and math textbooks more systematically. Dr. Wurdz suggested that many students simply ignore all photographs, charts, and diagrams in their textbooks. He challenged us to assign some in-class reading and watch what the students did with their eyes as they came to the visuals. Sure enough, many of my weakest students read the text, glanced at a wonderful half-page diagram and continued reading. I could not stand the thought that the students who most needed to build the concepts provided by the visuals in the text were largely ignoring these visuals. I now do a quick, five-minute, visuals-only introduction to each chapter.

One way I do that is to give the students exactly five minutes to look at the visuals and any captions under them and to write down everything they can learn from the visuals only. At the end of the five minutes, we go around the room and each person gives me one thing to write on the board until all the information is exhausted. I then direct their attention to each piece of information on the board that I consider crucial and ask, "Where in the text did you get this piece of information?" We all look at that visual and discuss it. It is amazing to me how naive my students are in understanding diagrams and charts. After all these years in school, I just assumed they had picked up this skill, but many just don't know how to learn from a visual. They will by the time they leave my class!

Meaning
Vocabulary

Having become so attuned to vocabulary problems in biology, I couldn't help but notice that my consumer math class's comprehension is especially hampered by a lack of technical vocabulary. We are studying taxes (yuk!), and I discovered that students were not clear about the meaning of words like *exemptions* and *withholding*. Some students didn't get back money due to them because they couldn't figure out all that gobblydegook on the tax form. I have made a list of crucial tax words and we are working through some realistic student-job tax situations so that they understand what these terms mean. Imagine letting the government keep your money because you couldn't understand the silly form!

Meaning
Vocabulary
Word Book

I have had the students in my biology classes and my consumer math class begin a vocabulary notebook. This is a bit old-fashioned, but I wanted to be sure to focus my attention as well as the students' on the vocabulary, and with so much to do, I was afraid I might lose track of this component. Whenever I begin a new chapter, I put the ten or so selected words on the small bulletin board in the corner and have the students write them in a notebook reserved for vocabulary. The notebook is divided with five pages for each letter of the alphabet and the words are usually entered four words to each page. We enter only the words on the first day of each unit, then fill in the meanings as we do the activities that build meaning for the words. Eventually, for every word, we have written a personal example and a sentence that defines the word. I do not allow them to copy dictionary definitions but sometimes we look up the word to help us formulate our own examples and sentences. We may add whatever we need to make the word clear and easy to remember. If the word is hard to pronounce, we put a phonetic pronunciation next to it. If the word can be illustrated or diagrammed, we do so. If the word has a common morpheme, we highlight it and note its meaning. So far, we have been doing these vocabulary entries together, but once the students learn what I expect, I plan to assign the actual writing as homework after I have provided the in-class experience to build meaning. Here are some entries for a few of our words from the biology unit I've been teaching:

abscission (ab si shun)—*Example:* When a leaf falls off a tree in the fall.

Sentence: Abscission occurs when any leaf falls off of any plant at any time of the year for any reason.

venation—*Example:* The hard little tubes you can feel with your fingers when you hold a leaf.

Sentence: Venation is the arrangement of veins in leaves and is used to identify from which plant a leaf has come.

Root word: Vein

I give a weekly vocabulary test in all my classes, making the test cumulative across all words entered in each class' notebook so far. I give the test on a different day in each class to lighten my test-grading load. This test is tough on some of the students, but we often do some quick review activities during the last few minutes of each period. Students are finding that if they study, they can do very well on these tests, which helps their grade since the average vocabulary grade equals one big test grade each quarter. Even Ambrose did well on my last vocabulary test in biology.

JANUARY

Well, we are halfway through the year, and while far from satisfied with everything, I am more content than I have ever been with my teaching. Semester grades were better, too. My biology students have learned a lot about cells, protists, and plants, and I believe they are learning even more about invertebrates.

Grading   I have a new grading system that gives students points for effort on their in-class and homework assignments, which I don't grade but simply initial if they appear to demonstrate a good effort. Students must also fix anything that was not right after we go over the work in class, and I require them to turn in their notebook with these initialed and self-corrected assignments. I take a quick glance to see that everything was fixed and again give points toward the final grade. Students also get points for good effort on their laboratory work.

Of course, I have grades from our weekly vocabulary tests—which have gotten better each week—as well as chapter and unit test grades. About 80 percent of these test questions are concerned with the most important information, which we have gone over in class and everyone should have learned. The other 20 percent comes from reading assignments, which are not completely covered in class.

I had no Fs and only three Ds in this biology section and only one D in consumer math! I believe that all my students are making more of an effort because they see that their effort pays off. This coming semester, I am going to assign some projects whereby students can extend their knowledge

Inquiry   beyond what we are learning in class. It worries me that while students seem less frustrated and a little more motivated, they are not exactly turned on to my subject. I realize that I used to read a lot of books and magazines about biology and famous biologists and I think that is how I became so engrossed in this topic. So I plan to have my students research famous biologists next month and then we will find some way (entertaining, I hope) of sharing what they learn.

Comprehension
Lesson

I am continuing to stress meaning vocabulary and to teach comprehension lessons on textbook material. This month I did several comprehension lessons using a feature matrix to guide student reading. This seems to work particularly well in biology, where so much material is a description of different members of a classification and the features that make each distinct. The students enjoy predicting, before they read, where the pluses and minuses will go and their comprehension seems to be much better when they have something specific to look for. Usually, I have them copy the feature matrix from my transparency and fill in their guesses in class; then they read the chapter to fill in and correct their matrix for homework. When they come to class, they take out their matrix and I quickly initial those that show a good effort. Then together we fill in my matrix on the transparency, as they show thumbs up for a plus and thumbs down for a minus. As long as there is consensus, we move right through it. When some thumbs are up and some are down, I know that comprehension has broken down and leave that space blank. We then reread the part of the textbook that discusses the point and resolve our disagreement. The students keep the corrected feature matrices in their notebooks and even claim to study them before my tests! This is a very efficient way of organizing a lot of information and helps students who are not good notetakers to keep their information in an organized fashion. See Figure 12.4 for one of the feature matrices I used this month in biology.

Quick Write

I have used a Quick Write review strategy this month that works quite well. It is called "three to a customer." You ask the students to write down three things they remember about a particular topic, limiting them to two minutes. Then you call on students one at a time to tell just one thing each that no one else has mentioned yet, so they have to listen to what others are saying. The goal is to see how many different things the class as a whole can remember. We keep score on a little chart and the competition seems to appeal to them. The first time we did it, they remembered a total of 18 items, which I recorded. The next time, they remembered 25. This Monday I said, "Let's make sure your brains have not totally atrophied over the weekend. Take out a sheet of paper. You have two minutes to write three things you remember about arthropods." And I heard Rod say, "Twenty-five is the number to beat!" Sure enough, they had a total of 27 different things written down. Now they try hard to remember something unusual or trivial in order to accumulate a large total. A little friendly competition with themselves seems to add to their motivation!

Thinking
Processes—
Apply

We have had fun in consumer math this month. I am a *Consumer Reports* devotee and as I was looking through their ratings of microwave ovens I realized this was a perfect periodical for my math kids. I found the annual car issue (April) and after leading my kids in a general discussion of which cars they loved and wanted to own (a very hot topic for tenth-graders), I pulled out *Consumer Reports*. I asked them to write down their dream car, how much they thought it would cost, how much they would have to pay for it each month if they borrowed 90 percent at 12 percent interest for four years, and what its mile-per-gallon rating, repair record, and crash test ratings were. Then I paired

Feature Matrix

Features/ Examples	Crustaceans	Myriapods	Arachnids	Insects
Jointed Legs	+	+	+	+
Segmented Bodies	+	+	+	+
Hard Exoskeleton	+	+	+	+
Gills	+	–	–	–
Three pairs of legs	–	–	–	+
Four pairs of legs	–	–	+	–
Antennae	+	+	–	+
Trachae	–	+	+	+
Crabs	+	–	–	–
Centipedes	–	+	–	–
Spiders	–	–	+	+
Termites	–	–	–	+
Shrimp	+	–	–	–
Grasshoppers	–	–	–	+
Millipedes	–	+	–	–
Ticks	–	–	+	–

Figure 12.4   Arthopods

them up with copies of the article and had them work out the real figures! Such a bunch of shocked, disheartened kids you have never seen. Even Ken was momentarily taken aback, until finally he said, "Well, I'll just have to make my first million faster!"

Only Allison was unconcerned. "My father is buying me a Jaguar on my next birthday," she smirked.

FEBRUARY

In addition to finishing up the study of invertebrates and beginning the study of vertebrates, February was famous biologist month! When I was a teenager, I loved biology, and it has always bothered me that "love" is hardly the correct verb to describe my teens' reactions to the subject. As I was considering how I came to love biology, I remembered that I got a junior science set for my tenth birthday and that I was always collecting plant and insect specimens and per-

Periodicals   forming various experiments on them. We subscribed to *National Geographic*

and *Smithsonian* magazines at home, and they often had fascinating articles with great pictures on various plant and animal life forms. Mr. Lively, who lived three doors down from us, was a biomedical engineer, and while I wasn't quite sure what a biomedical engineer did, it sure sounded fascinating. In addition, I became interested in biographies, particularly biographies of famous scientists. I read every one I could get my hands on and discovered that these scientists had led very interesting lives. In addition to their important discoveries, many of them were adventurous, courageous people with compassion for humans and animals. After reflecting on the development of my love affair with biology, I realized that it had much to do with real things and real people and little to do with biology textbooks and lab reports! I decided to try three ways to develop in my students the fascination I felt when I was their age. The first was the study of famous biologists that we did this month. In the coming months, I have planned to have them design and carry out a real experiment of their own, and to deal with some of the career options available to people with training in biology.

Inquiry   I decided that each student would research a famous biologist. I came up with a list of 30 and wrote their names on index cards. Each student would draw a card for his or her assignment. I knew the kids would rather pick their own, but with the exception of Charles Darwin, Louis Pasteur, and Rachel Carson, most students would not have heard of any of these scientists. I did tell the students they could try to get someone to swap with them.

Deciding how to have the students share what they learned was a difficult task. I remembered the term papers I had to write, and the oral reports I had to stand up and give with my knees knocking and my voice breaking. Somehow I knew that these traditional methods of reporting did little to promote attitudes of excitement! I worried for several days and then found the answer in the letter announcing my tenth-year high-school reunion. "At least I won't get any prizes," I chuckled, as I remembered the awards for "parent of the most kids" and "traveled farthest" that are usual at these affairs. Then I realized that I might just have found the gimmick to get my kids excited about their biologists.

After I explained to their skeptical looks that each person was to become an expert on one biologist, I told them that we would give prizes for these biologists' various accomplishments. I asked them to help me think of some awards we could give and suggested that we include demographic data, such as who had lived the longest, as well as more subjective data, such as who had made the biological discovery of greatest importance. I wrote these two things on the board and asked them to brainstorm other possible awards. They were slow to start but once they got going, you couldn't stop them. Here is the list we finally made from the students' brainstorming:

Most Ancient (one born longest ago)
Most Recent
Oldest
Youngest

Most Married (Most husbands or wives!) [Lonnie suggested this one]
Most Blessed with Children [Ken was serious; I tried not to laugh]
Tallest
Shortest
Heaviest
Richest
Most Degrees Earned
Most Important Biological Discovery
Most Adventurous Life
Most Interesting Life
Most Tragic Life
Best Biologist (Lifelong contribution)

Once the list was made, I turned the awards into questions. I put these on dittos and left room for the students to write their answers. For the subjective awards, the questions were worded as follows: "What did your scientist do that qualifies him or her for the Most Adventurous Life award?" Students were asked to write answers to all demographic questions, plus a sentence or two for any nominations they wanted to make. Ambrose asked if that meant they didn't have to write anything if they didn't want to nominate their scientist for any of the subjective awards. "You must nominate for at least one," was my exasperated response. I asked them to use three or more sources of research, to list and number these sources, and to attach this list to the dittoed sheets. Then they only needed to write down the number of the source next to each question they answered. If the information was found in more than one source, they only needed to list one source but could include more.

Students had two weeks to complete their library research. I asked them to keep secret what they found out so that the awards would be a surprise for everyone. They were not very enthusiastic to begin with, but as awards day grew closer, I heard people saying things like, "I've got the Most Adventurous Life sewed up!"

For the demographic awards, we went down the list and each student who thought his or her scientist was in contention gave the data required. These awards were granted automatically. For the more subjective awards, students had one minute to nominate their candidate and to argue that he or she deserved the award. All the students then voted. In some cases, I believe they were voting for the popularity of the student researcher rather than for the merit of the biologist but, all in all, they enjoyed it. Most importantly, they learned that biologists are real people, many of whom lead fascinating lives. Mission accomplished.

Studying   In consumer math, I have been using an idea that I gained from M. Birken. I have students use 3 by 5–inch index cards to develop a deck of review cards for a math test. For each different type of homework problem, the student generates one card. On the front of the card is a sample problem. On the back, the student writes the name of that type of problem and a step-by-step procedure for solving it. I require them to add to the deck each day by having them hold up the new cards until I see them all. At test time, the deck can be used as flash cards for studying. I required my students to use them in an in-class study session we had to get them in the habit. It has been very successful for several of the students who were having trouble remembering algorithms. I have also had particular students develop cards for types of problems they should already know how to work from previous years in school but don't.

I shared this strategy with some of my fellow math teachers. Hiram Hath, who teaches algebra II, told me he has insisted that his students who are struggling use it and it is helping them.

MARCH

Independence   My two greatest accomplishments this month were both in the cause of independence. I am pleased with how much better my students are learning and with their improved motivation, but I do feel that I am spoon-feeding them a bit too much. I decided to try to equip them with some strategies they could use to become more independent learners. I told them that they would not always have good old Miss Mull to identify vocabulary and help them summarize and review their work. (I didn't tell my biology students that if they took chemistry next year, they would have good old Mrs. "Some got it and some don't" Hardy!)

Meaning   For vocabulary, I first showed each class how I select the ten words per
Vocabulary   week that I have been teaching. (Don't tell Dr. Wurdz, but sometimes I just have to have 11 or 12. This is compensated for by the one time I had only nine!) We took the most recent list in each class and I showed them how I first eliminate those words they already know. (In biology where we continued to study the structures of vertebrates and their functions, Judy made a disparaging remark about the people who made that vocabulary list not knowing anything about how much tenth-graders knew. I ignored it but thought, "Smart kid!") Then I showed them how I eliminated very technical terms. This was hard for my students because all the words looked technical to them, but we decided that if a term only occurred once or twice, was defined by the context, and was a very picky detail, it could be eliminated. Getting them to see that there were some words they needed to add was harder. "Aren't there enough already?" Ambrose asked during one of these lessons. I had them read the introduction and summary for each chapter, however, to find the chapter's key words. Most saw that these words had to be added to the list. Once we did this, we still often had more than ten or 12, so we eliminated a few more picky terms—those used in only one small part of the chapter—and got the final list.

I had shown them all this for one week's vocabulary list and the chapter it came from. When we began a new chapter, I paired students up and had them go through it all again for this week's list. I gave them ten minutes to work and then put the words suggested by the pairs on the board. There was usually general agreement on most words (Thank goodness!) and of course some overlap on the close calls. All in all, I thought they did a good job of deciding what the important vocabulary was. Actually, the consumer math students seemed to have an easier time agreeing than the biology students did. I then had them write these words on the appropriate vocabulary note-book pages as we have done since December, and I led them to complete these entries with personal examples, sentence definitions, roots, and what-ever else was helpful.

After three weeks of having students pick the words, I decided it was time for them to decide on their own vocabulary entries. After the words were picked, I assigned each pair of students one word (two pairs overlapped) and had them decide what to write for that vocabulary entry. I encouraged them to use their textbook and classroom reference books. I instructed them to provide their own personal examples to serve as models for everyone else, and a defin-itional sentence that gave the crucial information. I reminded them that we included phonetic spelling when the word had a tricky pronunciation, illustra-tions or diagrams when possible, and morphemic information when helpful. I then gave each pair a transparency on which to write the notebook entry they thought everyone should use. They did a very good job, and I intend to con-tinue this paired working during April. In May, I will have the students come up with notebook entries on their own.

Writing   The other strategy for promoting independence is five-minute summary writing. At the end of class, in both biology and consumer math, a couple of times a week, I reserve five minutes for them to summarize in their notebooks the major things they learned that day. We did a few of these as group sum-maries so that they would get the idea, then I turned them loose. At the begin-ning of the next class, I picked two students to read their summaries as a review of what we have learned. The students are not exactly wild about this writing, but they are getting better at it. I intend to suggest that they take five minutes to write summaries at the end of other classes even when it is not assigned so that they will have something to review. There is usually some dead time at the end of most classes—but not mine! I wonder how many will write summaries if not forced to. Oh well, if only two or three learn to use this strategy, that is two or three more than would have if I hadn't taught them! Like "three to a customer," this strategy provides needed repetition on what I am teaching, yet because the review is different from the teaching, it is not boring.

APRIL

Content Journals   I have benefited so much from keeping this journal! It occurred to me that my students might also benefit from keeping one. I knew it was risky, so I decided to do it with just one class for the rest of this year to see how it goes. My con-sumer math students were elected. They have been keeping their content jour-nals now for only a month, but it seems to be catching on. All I require is for them to write a minimum amount each day about what they think of what we are studying and how well they think they are understanding it. At first, they groaned, and I had to discipline them into cooperating. Now the groaning has almost completely subsided. I get more and better questions from them. Reading the questions has helped me plan better activities and assignments also. I take six or seven home every night and read them without a pen in my hand. It's like reading that many letters. I just write a personal response of two or three sentences at the end of each one after I finish it. I'm finding out where confusion remains and where I should move on because they have it and are getting bored. I'm going to start reading them less often and see if they will continue to write as much.

While my students continued to learn new content in biology this month (we finished our study of nonhuman mammals and began studying structures and their functions in human biology), I also emphasized application of the content they had already learned. In April I tried to move them into seeing themselves as potential biological scientists. Most of our experiments and demonstrations have been more or less prescribed. While the hands-on biology we did certainly improved learning and attitudes, the students have rarely participated in actually designing experiments to investigate hypotheses that interest them. They had been studying biology without learning how to be biologists!

Thinking Processes—Apply

Inquiry

Knowing how difficult this assignment would be, I began April by telling the students to conduct and report on an original experiment investigating a particular hypothesis. Then I began the process of teaching them how to do the assignment.

First, they needed to understand what a hypothesis is and where one comes from. After a brief discussion, I saw why scientists like Edison have always emphasized "perspiration" over "inspiration" when explaining their achievements. My students certainly attributed much to scientific inspiration. Most seemed to think that ideas just "popped into biologists' heads." I told them that scientists are no different than other curious and observant people. Imagine, I explained, that a person was watering some house plants some years ago and a child asked why plants have to be watered. The adult could simply have said, "Because they will die if they are not watered."

Children being persistent, however, the child might have asked, "Why will they die without water?"

Then the adult might have explained to the child why he or she needs water and that plants need water for similar reasons. So far the adult is answering the child's questions based on the adult's general knowledge. But what if the child than asked, "After I drink water, it goes out when I use the bathroom. What do plants do with the water after they drink it?"

The adult, after thinking a moment, might have said, "I don't know. That is a very good question. Let's find out."

Imagine, then, that the adult looked in various books to find the answer and discovered that the answer was not available. Let's say that the adult thought and thought about what might happen to the water and finally guessed that the water might be given off into the air from the leaves, like a person sweating. Then let's say that the adult designed an experiment to see if leaves give off water into the air and found out that they do.

After this explanation, I asked them to help me to use it as an illustration. Any curious and observant person, even a child, has questions about living things and how they function, I explained. Then I tried to convince them that all scientific investigation begins with a question about something.

Furthermore, I explained that, when it comes to science, adults are different from children only because, by going to school, they have learned the answers to certain common questions that curious and observant people have. They do not have to be constantly confused by the world in which they live, but instead can look around them and realize that they have a certain degree of understanding of their environment. This, I said, is the major reason that everyone is required to study science in school.

At this point, I explained why it is important that people learn how to use libraries and other sources of information so that they can learn answers to questions that they do not remember or never learned. So far, so good.

But, I asked them, what happens when you ask a question whose answer you cannot find? You must try to develop your own answer by thinking about what you know. The answer you come up with is called a *hypothesis.*

At this point, I wrote on the board:

hypothesis—a possible answer to a previously unanswered question

I gave the students the opportunity to come up with hypotheses that some scientist had once developed about the same material we had studied in biology up to that point. We discussed each one, focusing the question and finding the precise wording for a possible answer. Each of these possible answers we labeled as having once been a hypothesis.

Ambrose raised an important question during these discussions, "How do you know which questions have already been answered?"

I referred him back to our previous discussion of the adult and child and showed him that there are only two ways: either, know an area of biology so well that you know what is known and what is not; or, go to the library and do research until you are convinced that you are now aware of what is and isn't known.

"So that's why biologists have to go to graduate school!" remarked Terry. I strongly supported that comment.

"But we haven't been to graduate school yet!" said Ambrose in his I'm-just-about-to-give-up voice.

"No," I agreed, "but actually that will make it easier for you. You see, we really won't be able to answer questions that haven't yet been answered about biology. You don't and even I don't have the knowledge or equipment necessary to do new research in biology. You do have a lot of questions, however, that you don't have answers to. You've been asking me such questions all year! It is those questions for which you will develop first hypotheses, then experiments. Besides, even famous scientists replicate experiments in order to check results."

Inquiry
I had gone through the units we had studied and chosen those that could be investigated by the students. I reminded them of a unit and asked them to think of important questions they still had. We listed these on the board. Through a process of brainstorming and selection, we developed quite a list of questions across the several units I had chosen. Each student then picked a question for which he or she had to think of a possible answer (hypothesis) that could be investigated by a simple experiment.

We then went back to the story of the adult and child. As a group, we planned an experiment to determine whether plant leaves give off the water that the plant has taken in. I insisted that they design the experiment themselves. I kept them on task by making them vote on decisions instead of endlessly arguing about them. They had to see any weaknesses themselves and try to repair them. Once they had the basic design of the experiment, I then gave my suggestions for improvements. I am very proud of them. They were able to figure out that they had to have some way to water the plant without getting water into the air at the same time. They had also determined that the air around the plant would have to be contained so that water could not get in from any other source. Finally, they figured out that they had to have a *control*, a space just like that occupied by the plant, but without a plant in it.

Direct
Experience
So we obtained large plastic containers, put water in two of them, and covered them with wax paper. Then we cut a hole in one of the pieces of wax paper and inserted a small plant so that the roots went in the water in the container and the top stuck out above the wax paper. We used petroleum jelly to seal around the base of the plant so that no water could get out of the bottom of container. We covered the two bottom containers with two top containers, turned them upside down, and sealed around where they joined with more petroleum jelly. Naturally, it wasn't long before the inside of the top container with the plant in it began to fog up with moisture, but the container without the plant remained dry just as the hypothesis would lead one to predict.

Writing
Lesson
Once we had completed our class investigation, I modeled how to write up the report on a sheet I had made up for this purpose. I also had several students find books that described similar investigations, including results against which we could check our own.

They then started on their individual investigations. I required them to get an approval from me at each of three points. I had to approve of the question each chose in order to prevent unnecessary duplication and to make sure that it was not too broad. Then I had to approve of the hypothesis that each one developed. I wanted to make sure it was their own hypothesis and not one they had copied from somewhere. And I wanted the hypothesis to be one they could design an experiment to investigate. Whether it was the correct answer to their question or not made no difference to me. Finally, I had to approve the design of their experiments. Here was where I did most of my teaching this month. Reasoning with them and holding conferences about their experiments took a lot of time, but I believe they learned a lot from designing them. They met in small groups to get feedback from one another while I met with individuals. After I approved the design of an experiment, I assigned a day for that student to set up the experiment in the lab. After everything was completed, I required them to report the results of their investigations on a sheet with the following entries:

> Question:
> Hypothesis:
> Experiment:
> Data:
> Interpretation:

These reports were shared with their lab partners first and revised based on those comments. I read them to make comments, and they revised them again. Finally, we published these research reports in a class book called *Our Biology Experiments,* which we shared with everyone who was interested and some who were not. Our librarian even put a copy in the science section of our library! We ended the month with quite a sense of accomplishment and admiration for biological scientists.

MAY

Inquiry

May is probably the best month for teaching biology, not just because it is almost the end of the year, but because new life is everywhere and it is impossible not to be excited about life and its science this month. We have had many things to do in studying human biology this month, so I didn't begin anything new except for their research on careers in biology. This was part of my plan to get them excited about biology. Since the famous biologists' awards had worked so well, I decided to use the same format. I wrote various careers biologists could pursue (nutritionist, teacher, animal husbandry specialist, and microbiologist) on index cards and let each student pick one. We then brainstormed a list of questions in the form of awards. The list again included objective features (highest paid, most job mobility) as well as subjective features (most prestigious, most dangerous). When we had the brainstormed list completed on the board, someone suggested that we have "booby prizes," too. We ended up deciding to try to find out about both the high and the low end for each of the career features.

The students researched the career they had picked (or "gotten stuck with," as Lonnie put it), filling in the information on a dittoed sheet. They noted sources as they had done for the famous biologists project. They had more trouble finding information this time and Paige Turner, the librarian, and I had to help them. We also made some calls to our state employment office and interviewed some people in biological careers.

When the data was compiled, we gave awards and booby prizes in each category. What category of career do you think came up with the lowest pay and was voted to have the lowest prestige? Teacher won these two booby prizes hands down, naturally! I was not surprised that teaching was at the bottom, but I was reminded of the enormous salaries many biologists make. It's a good thing that I didn't do this last year when I was at such a low point in my job satisfaction! Rod was very worried about my low salary and prestige, but Allison told him not to worry because I had "chosen" to do this and had my summers completely free!

Writing

After the awards were given, I had each student write a one-paragraph essay indicating which career they would choose if they were to pursue work in biology. They had to state the career choice and at least three reasons why. We made a tally of the various careers chosen and there was a great deal of diversity. Several students told me that they had no idea there were so many interesting and well-paying jobs for biologists and were seriously considering pursuing the career they had selected!

Meaning Vocabulary

This month, I had students in biology and consumer math select independently the vocabulary words they thought we needed to learn and write those entries in their notebooks. Most did quite well but I wonder if they will make the effort to do this next year when they are not required to. Students in both subjects have also gotten very good at writing a five-minute summary of the important information learned; I think many of them will continue to do this because they

Studying

see how useful it is when it comes time to study for a test. They even tell me that writing the summary helps them to sort out what is important and to organize the information. I have certainly found that writing this journal this year has helped me to organize my own thoughts and to reflect upon what is most important.

Meaning Vocabulary

I have continued to teach vocabulary directly to my consumer math class. I am constantly amazed at how little they understand such common terms as *interest, dividends,* and *balance.* I think next year if I teach a section of consumer math, I will start a vocabulary notebook with them at the beginning of the year. I will also use *Consumer Reports* earlier and more frequently. Their interest always piques when I use real-life newspapers and magazines to let them see how crucial is their ability to compute what things cost and where money comes from and goes.

Direct Experience

I did do one new thing in consumer math over the past two months. I had each student study stocks and then select some stock to buy with an imaginary $500. We checked stock prices regularly and charted the growth or decline of our stocks. The students got very excited, almost as if they were actually making or losing that money. Although their money investment wasn't real, the investment of time and energy in choosing and following the stock was, and their motivation to learn about the world of money grew. I just wish I had had five hundred real dollars and had invested them in Rod's stock. The boy is uncannily lucky. His stock split, and soon he had almost doubled his money. My stock, on the other hand, is now behind $46.40!

JUNE

Well, as Allison said, "She gets the whole summer off!" And thank goodness for that! Even with a good year like this one, I am ready for the change of pace in June. This summer will be a real change of pace. I am once again playing the role of student by complaining about "meaningless assignments" and "boring textbooks."

Professional Growth

I had been toying all spring with the idea of going back to school to pursue graduate work in science education. Once I knew that I do find teaching fulfilling and that you can teach even below-average students to understand and appreciate biology, I began to wonder why everyone who teaches biology doesn't feel this way. I concluded that we ourselves often weren't taught science well, and haven't been taught how to teach science well. Suddenly I wanted to run out and gather up science teachers and teachers-to-be and teach them everything that was such a struggle for me to learn. I might never have gotten past the mulling-it-over stage had I not run into Dr. Knowles at a political rally. I was so shocked to see him there—he looked just like he did when I had him for content area reading and writing in my senior year! He even remembered my name and seemed pleased to see someone he knew since he had just moved into town. "I got tired of living in such a small university community," he explained. "I have always liked this little town and have decided that a 30-minute commute is worth it to live where real people live."

We talked for almost an hour after the meeting. I told him my life history, or at least my teaching history. He was fascinated with how I had realized that I had to provide the students real experiences with science while simultaneously providing activities in reading, listening, and helping them think the material through. I almost told him about the dream in which he forced me to deal with the two components, but I wasn't quite sure enough of him to share that. I did tell him that I had started keeping a journal as he had suggested and how much it had helped me to reflect upon what I was doing.

After standing and talking on the steps for almost an hour, he began to look impatient. I realized I had been babbling on and that he had probably just been polite. I apologized but he only laughed and said, "I'm not bored—just famished. I came straight from the university to this meeting." We went to my favorite Italian restaurant and I told him even more. (Well, he is such an enthusiastic listener and asked question after question!) Finally, I told him about my frustrations with how teachers were taught. He said, "I know just how you feel and there is only one thing to do about that!" So now I am enrolled in a graduate program—though if I only take courses in summers or in the evenings, I will be old and decrepit before I finish! Some days I commute in with Jer (that's Dr. Knowles's nickname, short for Jerry, and he insists he can't spend an hour in the car with someone who calls him "Dr."!) and that is usually the hour in which I learn the most. He has so many good ideas—I don't remember him being so fascinating when I was in his class. Next year, he is going to come and watch me teach. Horrors! He is even talking about designing an experiment to see if students are learning more content and—as important to both of us—if their attitudes toward biology are improving. It is going to be such a super summer and next year should be even better than last. I must call Mrs. Plante and catch her up on my life. She would love Jer. I think I will invite her and Jer for dinner.

REFERENCES

Ballew, H., & Cunningham, J. W. (1982). Diagnosing strengths and weaknesses of sixth-grade students in solving word problems. *Journal for Research in Mathematics Education, 13,* 202–210.

Birken, M. (1986). Teaching students how to study mathematics. *Mathematics Teacher, 79,* 410–413.

Santa, C. M., & Alvermann, D. E. (Eds.). (1991). *Science learning: Processes and applications.* Newark, DE: International Reading Association.

Index